Taken for Granted

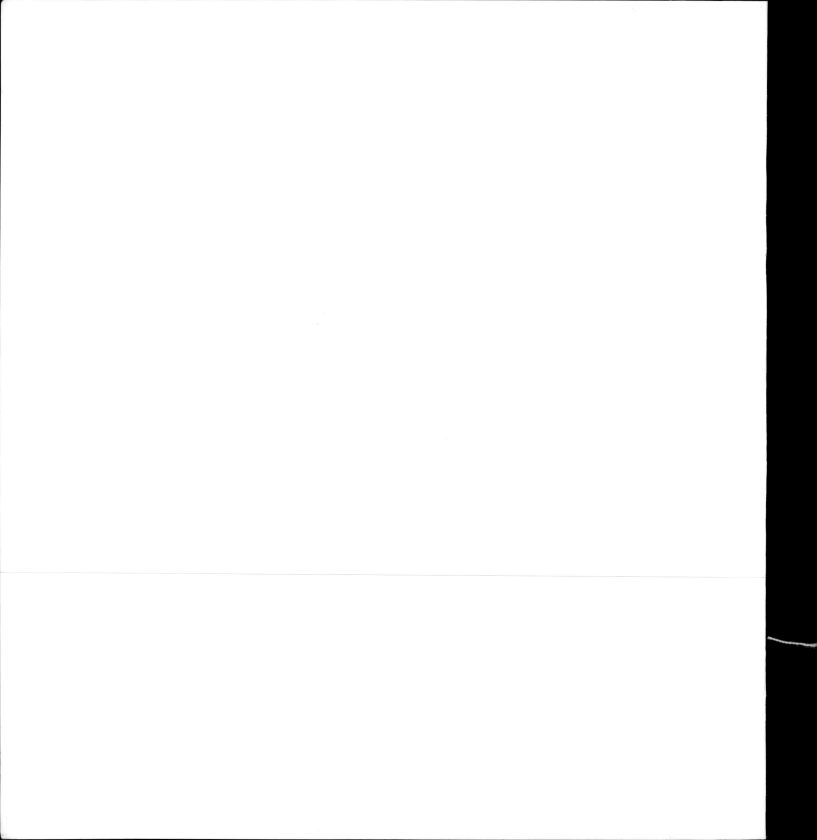

Taken for Granted

A celebration of 10 years of
Historic Buildings Conservation

Compiled and written by

Richard Pierce
Alastair Coey

Including

The Repair and Maintenance of Historic Buildings:
A Brief Guide for Owners, Architects and Agents

Written by

Richard Oram

Published by

The Royal Society of Ulster Architects
and
The Historic Buildings Council

With the support of the Northern Bank Ltd. and
the Department of the Environment for Northern
Ireland.

Photography by:
Christopher Hill
and
Anderson McMeekin Photography Ltd.

Designed by:
Rodney Miller Associates.

Printed by:
W. & G. Baird Ltd.

Contents

Foreword 1

Charles Kinahan
Chairman,
Historic Buildings Council

Northern Ireland did not have an Historic Buildings Council until February 1974. I had the honour of being appointed the first Chairman, a position I still hold. Of the original 15 members, four others are still in membership – Hugh Bass, Robert McKinstry, Harry Patten and Joe Tracey.

The English Historic Buildings Council was set up in 1953 the Scottish in 1953 and the Welsh in 1954. The long delay in setting up the Northern Ireland Council was undoubtedly a serious omission on the part of our legislators. Many buildings of importance were certainly lost in the years of inaction in an area which was much less well endowed in the first place. Northern Ireland does not have the great wealth of superb country villages, beautiful historic mansions, fine country churches going back to Norman times and before, and great world famous cathedrals. With the resources available to us it has still not been possible to list the whole province so unfortunately buildings of quality may still be lost.

The gap was to some extent filled by the dedicated work of the Ulster Architectural Heritage Society. Although their lists had no legal standing, the listings which they carried out have proved most valuable source materials and have been of great assistance to our Council's listers. By their work they helped to alert the public to the importance of legal protection for what remained of our built heritage. I feel that the whole community are much in their debt.

In the ten years since we were appointed the Department of the Environment (Northern Ireland) has listed some 6,500 buildings with the assistance of local councils. Twenty-two Conservation Areas have also been designated. We estimate that by the time that all District Council areas have been examined the total may rise to some 8,000 buildings and 30 Conservation Areas; there are 5,500 Conservation Areas in England alone. Even allowing for our much smaller size the comparison emphasises the great riches of the built heritage in England and the comparative paucity of our own.

It is undoubtedly true that in Northern Ireland we have listed buildings and designated Conservation Areas which would not have been so classified elsewhere in the United Kingdom. I suspect too that in Wales and Scotland buildings have been listed which would not have qualified in England. That there should be four separate and distinct councils in the United Kingdom was, I am sure, wise policy. Listing for conservation is not an exact science but we in the Northern

Ireland Historic Buildings Council have made it our policy to recommend for listing not only fine country mansions, handsome civic buildings and elegant Georgian terraces, but also to seek to preserve for posterity the more humble Ulster vernacular dwellings which say so much about the character and history of our people over the generations.

Ours is a 'growth industry'. The more buildings that are listed, and the more Conservation Areas that are designated, the more grant applications and the more planning referrals the staff are called on to handle. Pressures from central government for reductions in public expenditure have meant that with the best will in the world, the staff have not always been able to process matters as quickly as the public have a right to expect.

I am most grateful to all the staff of the Department who have worked with us since we were set up ten years ago and to the 24 individuals who have served on the council during that time. Government and the public have benefitted immensely from the advice (virtually free of charge), of leading individuals in their professions who have made their services available without reward and often at considerable personal sacrifice. The community has good reason to be grateful to them all and I have been greatly privileged to be their Chairman over the whole period.

Foreword 2

Denis Haslam
President,
Royal Society of Ulster Architects

It is indeed a pleasure to have been asked to write a few words of introduction to this splendid book. This is especially so, as its publication coincides so fortunately with the Festival of Architecture which is being held nationwide throughout 1984 – to mark the 150th Anniversary of the Royal Institute of British Architects, and to celebrate architecture as a social art which enriches our lives and enhances our environment.

We in the Royal Society of Ulster Architects are delighted to be a part of this celebration, and in this particular instance our contribution has been to work in conjunction with our colleagues on the Historic Building Council in order to present this detailed record of the first ten years of the Council's work. They can be justly proud that their time spent since 1974 in listing, grant aiding and conserving so many of our historic buildings, has been amply rewarded in the physical evidence of their endeavours, so well documented and illustrated in this publication. It is true to say that without the Historic Building Council's care and concern many of our architectural riches would by now have fallen into irreversible decay or else have vanished for ever from the scene.

Ironical though it may seem, one of the happier aspects of the various incursions and settlements that have occurred over the past several thousand years in this troubled isle has been the variety of architectural styles and modes of expression that each successive wave of invaders has left upon the landscape.

Down the long ages since Mesolithic man, invaders such as the Celts, the Vikings, the Normans, the Tudors and the Scots, have all left their signatures in stone throughout this island and nowhere more so than in Ulster. The discerning visitor (or indeed the native for that matter) has only to wander across the face of the province to discover for himself the wealth of our archaeological and architectural heritage. It is worth remembering that it is a representative heritage which can be shared by all who are interested in the realities of the past, rather than its diverse mythologies.

Civilized man must believe that he belongs somewhere in place and time before he can plan his own future or that of his environment with any sense of purpose and our ancient monuments and historic buildings – be they cottage or castle – mud hut or manor house – fulfil that need for identity; and for that reason alone they deserve to be maintained. These buildings are our strongest link with the past,

making history a tactile affair; through them we can feel a personal sense of that mana which often pervades such places, and at the same time pause to admire the rich diversity of style and architectural expression in the habitations of our predecessors.

In wishing this book every success it would be remiss of me to end without thanking the officials of the Historic Monuments and Buildings Branch of the D.O.E. and also the members of the Historic Building Council for their enthusiasm in promoting the inception of this publication, and to the Northern Bank for providing the funds for publication. I would like also to express a particular word of praise to Richard Pierce, Alastair Coey and Dick Oram, all members of the Royal Society of Ulster Architects whose research, editing and compilation has made it all possible.

The 'Festival of Architecture' will come and go but it is to be hoped that this book will remain in circulation for many years to come as a guide and encouragement to all who are interested in the conservation of our built heritage.

Foreword 3

Noel Simpson
Chief Accountant,
Northern Bank Ltd.

In 1824, when the Northern Banking Company began its career as Ireland's first joint stock bank, there was little indication that it would make a significant contribution to the local architectural scene. Its first premises in Donegall Place, Belfast were fairly modest ones, while its representation in country districts was at first by means of part-time agents who combined banking with other business and operated from their private houses or from the offices where they carried on their main occupation.

This unassuming start was in accordance with the prudent nature of the Bank's founders – indeed if it had spent substantial sums of money on imposing buildings during those early years its depositors would have been highly critical. But attitudes changed as the Northern Bank gained in importance and influence, and in the years to come it both commissioned from leading local architects, and acquired by purchase, some of Ulster's finest buildings. By 1970, after its merger with the Belfast Bank, the Northern Bank owned about 30 listed historic buildings in Northern Ireland. A few of these, such as Belfast (Waring Street), Bangor (Main Street) and Moneymore, are in fact even older than the Bank itself.

The needs of banking are changing more rapidly at present than at any time in the past, with computerisation and other technological developments making new and unexpected demands on staff and premises alike. Despite this the Northern Bank is determined to maintain its share of the historic and important buildings in the province to the standard which they deserve, and the Bank is proud and happy to be associated with the activities of the Royal Society of Ulster Architects and the Historic Buildings Council in preserving and recording the best of Ulster's architectural heritage.

Acknowledgements

Thanks

The co-authors wish to thank the staff of the Department of the Environment for Northern Ireland, Historic Monuments and Buildings Branch for all their help during the time that this book was being researched and written. The staff were already overworked during that period, yet the extra work involved in explaining the system of filing and in helping to identify and interpret over 6,000 files (many containing literally hundreds of pages) and over 10,000 slides was at all times carried out with courtesy, patience and kindness.

The authors also wish to thank the owners of all the properties visited for their kindness and co-operation.

Acknowledgements

Almost all of the information used in compiling this book has been extracted from the files of the Department of the Environment for Northern Ireland, Historic Monuments and Buildings Branch.

In writing the descriptions of some individual properties, the authors have been greatly assisted by the Ulster Architectural Heritage Society's well-known and invaluable lists of buildings of architectural or historic interest round the province and by Alistair Rowan's excellent publication 'The Buildings of Ireland: North-West Ulster', published by Penguin Books Ltd., in 1979.

Notes

Every effort has been made to ensure that all information contained within this book is factual. Inaccuracies may come to light after publication and for these the authors and publishers apologise.

Grant-aid to listed buildings is an on-going process. In order to avoid having to up-date information during the period taken to compile this book, a cut-off date of 30 September 1983 was chosen. Only those projects where such work was complete and grant-aid paid before that date are included.

Although a few listed buildings, notably those owned by the National Trust are open to the public at specified times, the vast majority are private properties and should be respected as such.

Introduction

Since 1968 the conservation of Northern Ireland's traditional built environment has faced unique difficulties.

The bombings, the most violent manifestation of the troubles, have destroyed many fine important buildings and monuments and countless modest vernacular buildings which are the mainstay of the visual integrity of our streetscapes.

The underlying problems from which the troubles spring add to the difficulties. Because Northern Ireland, as a political entity, is only 62 years old, with a divided image of the past and a divided hope for the future, it is difficult to establish a generally accepted image of our architectural heritage and its preservation.

If we add to this the fact that most Ulster people are only one or two generations removed from the land and are still, to some extent, keen to shake off the small farm image and to create in the towns and villages where we now live and work the brave new world of bungalows with low-pitched roofs and picture windows and, in the older houses in the streets, new glass, aluminium and plastic shopfronts which defy not only the visual integrity of the streetscape and the principles of good taste but also the laws of gravity, then we begin to appreciate the tremendous struggle which conservationists have had.

The idea of architectural conservation is not new. After all, the Northern Ireland Committee of the National Trust was set up in 1937 and, during the fifties and sixties, when the bravura of the Modern Movement was in full swing, it was generally accepted that great houses like Castlecoole and Castleward were worth preserving for posterity. But most of us also managed to allow ourselves to be carried along by the prevailing fashion of the times; the replacement of the old, the quaint and the charming by, for the most part, rather desolate, slick structures caught somewhere in style between Le Corbusier and the builder's supplier's yard.

Those who were sensitive to the values architectural, historical, social and cultural of the individual buildings and groups of buildings which were disappearing were few and far between. However, in the late sixties a small group of committed conservationists got together to form a pressure group which would draw attention to the great loss to the general standard of amenity by the replacement of the traditional built environment by new ones which did not acknowledge the existing visual harmony.

Thus, in November 1967 the Ulster Architectural Heritage Society was formed. It quickly became involved in influencing public opinion and the Northern Ireland Government of the day by publishing well-argued broadsheets, holding public meetings and sending deputations to meet Government ministers.

On 17th December 1968 a deputation from the Ulster Architectural Heritage Society was received at Stormont by W. K. Fitzsimmons, M.P. Minister of Development for Northern Ireland, Mr. C. E. B. Brett, at that meeting, summarized the governmental action sought by the society, based on legislation already enacted in Great Britain.

1. Speed up Ancient Monuments survey.
2. Urgent listing of buildings: cf. Town and Country Planning Act 1944.
3. Strengthen preservation machinery: cf. Ancient Monuments and Historic Buildings Act 1953.
4. Set up Historic Buildings Council and a system of grant-aid: cf. 1953 Act.
5. Grants for lesser buildings: cf. Local Authorities (Historic Buildings) Act 1962.
6. Grants for ecclesiastical buildings: partial powers under Planning Act 1962.
7. Define areas and groups of historic value: cf. Civil Amenities Act 1967.
8. Set up Pilot Conservation Schemes in Armagh, Londonderry and Downpatrick.
9. Introduce effective tree preservation legislation: cf. Town and Country Planning Act 1968 and Civic Amenities Act 1967.
10. Preservation and creation of footpaths: National Parks Act 1959 and Countryside Act 1968.
11. Control dumping of cars and rubbish: cf. Civic Amenities Act 1967.
12. Statutory duty on Ministers, Government departments and public bodies to have regard to amenity: cf. comparable duty under s.9 Countryside Act 1968.

This meeting marked the beginning of the U.A.H.S. lobby for the introduction of effective legislation to protect our architectural heritage.

Government was not always as receptive as at that first deputation. Regarding a very lengthy letter sent in August 1970, by the

U.A.H.S. to the Rt. Hon. Brian Faulkner M.P. at the Ministry of Development, mainly on the subject of urgent interim conservation legislation, one government official sent a memo to a colleague asking – 'Regarding Mr. C. E. B. Brett's latest effusion, would you consider the possibility of assuaging him and the U.A.H.S. by doing something on the following lines? . . .'

However, the U.A.H.S. Chairman was able to report, at the annual meeting of the Society on the 30th January 1974 that the new Historic Buildings Council would hold its first meeting two days later. That was ten years ago.

The Historic Buildings Council, which is made up of 15 people from various walks of life from all parts of the province, appointed by the Minister responsible for the Environment, ensures that as wide a vision as possible is brought to bear on the work of the Department of the Environment through its Historic Monuments and Buildings Branch.

This work includes statutory listing. To list a building is to declare it to be of such architectural or historic value as to be protected by law, for posterity, against alteration or demolition. The Department also has the power to direct government funds to be spent, in the form of grant-aid, on the repair or renovation of such buildings. It further can declare whole areas of cities, towns or villages, having consulted the local District Council, to be statutory Conservation Areas, if these areas are outstanding examples of traditional streetscape, where insensitive alteration or destruction of one building would spoil the integrity of the whole. In these areas work which affects the visual appearance of the exterior can be grant-aided.

Birthdays in themselves are of little importance. Nothing in particular happens on the actual day or in the year that an anniversary occurs, but round figures act as milestones from which the achievements of the past can be observed and measured.

This book celebrates a double milestone. 1984 is the 150th anniversary of the founding of the Royal Institute of British Architects (to which the Royal Society of Ulster Architects is affiliated) and, to mark the event, the whole year has been designated a Festival of Architecture. It also marks the end of the Historic Buildings Council's first decade. As part of the celebration of these two events the R.S.U.A. and the Historic Buildings Council have decided to publish, jointly, this book, which is virtually a catalogue of the huge amount of grant-aided work which has been carried out to individual listed buildings and to buildings in Conservation Areas since 1974.

The Department of the Environment has borne the costs of researching and writing the book, whilst the Northern Bank has underwritten the costs of graphic design and printing.

At the outset it must be made clear that the book will not attempt to comment on the architectural or historic significance of the buildings presented; merely to describe the quantity, quality and practical significance of the grant-aided work carried out in them.

The sheer numbers of buildings which have been grant-aided by the Department of the Environment is amazing. Everyone knows the obvious interesting buildings around the province like Florence Court in Fermanagh, the Guildhall in Londonderry or the City Hall in Belfast and most will be aware of the importance and attractiveness of, say, The Mall in Armagh but there are literally thousands of other buildings, ranging over a wide variety of styles, types, uses and date of construction, which are scarcely known, even in their own localities. The number of listed buildings in this relatively small province has reached a staggering 6,418 and of these almost 1,000 have been grant-aided for repairs or restoration. The number of Conservation Areas stands at 22.

The first ten years of the Historic Buildings Council's life have coincided with a time when we have all been preoccupied with the political events in Northern Ireland, but all the time the civilized, diligent work of listing, advising, processing grant applications and supervising work to buildings of architectural and historic interest has carried on, regardless of the political complexion of the building's use. Orange halls, Republican clubs, mansions, cottages, convents, banks and public houses to name but a few, all receive impartial treatment.

In many countries throughout the western world the statutory protection of fine buildings and streets is almost rendered unnecessary by the support and appreciation of the general public. We are not yet at that stage in Northern Ireland.

It may well be many more years before the work of the Department of the Environment, Historic Monuments and Buildings Branch, is fully appreciated but there can be no doubt that future generations, whatever the future holds politically, will be very grateful for the superb work that has been carried out during the last ten years.

Taken for Granted

Grant aid to listed buildings

In 1969, in advance of the legislation which now forms part of The Planning (Northern Ireland) Order 1972, two architects were appointed by the then Ministry of Development to draw up a list of all buildings of architectural or historic interest in the province. It was anticipated at that time that the two 'listers' would have the task completed in three years.

When it is remembered that in order to ensure that the list would be whole and complete, every building in the province would have to be visited in a systematic fashion (at a guess there are approximately one to two million buildings in Northern Ireland), the magnitude of the task begins to be appreciated.

At the time the two 'listers', Colin Hatrick and Charles Munro (who has since been succeeded by Richard Oram) divided the province between them and set out to draw up the lists, using Electoral Wards within counties (subsequently within District Council areas) as the basic survey units.

Three years proved to be a rather optimistic time scale for the work and, after the introduction of grant aid to historic buildings, with the same two architects advising, drawing up schedules of repair and inspecting building work, the process slowed down considerably and, in fact, remains incomplete.

The actual listing of an individual building is fairly straightforward. When, in the process of covering an Electoral Ward, a building of some significance is discovered it is recorded; slides are taken, a written description made and the location noted. There are guidelines issued by the Department for help in assessing whether or not a building should be recorded. These include the following 14 points:

Style
System of proportion
System of ornamentation
Plan form
Spatial organization
Structural system
Innovative qualities
Historical associations
Present aesthetic quality
Present value (architectural and social)
Local interest

National interest

Condition

Alterations

All the buildings recorded in that ward are then assessed by the Department of the Environment, through its Historic Monuments and Buildings Branch, having sought and obtained the advice of the Historic Buildings Council and consulted the appropriate District Council.

There are now over 6,000 listed buildings in the province.

Grant-aiding of listed buildings began ten years ago. Essentially, it is a matter of government 'putting its money where its mouth (or pen) is'. Financial assistance is provided by government to keep in good order those properties which it has already statutorily declared to be worthy of preservation; that is, to be protected by law against demolition or alteration, even by its owner, without first having applied for and received 'listed building consent'.

To apply for grant aid for work to a listed building, its owner simply fills in an application form which allows him to describe the work which he proposes to carry out. The property is then inspected by one of the two architects employed by the Department and a schedule of grant aidable repairs is drawn up. The architect subsequently inspects the work while it is in progress.

Since the repair and preservation of listed buildings is a highly specialised task, and the standards of design and construction generally fairly crude throughout the province, the Department's architects have, over the years painstakingly advised and, to put it bluntly, educated owners, designers and contractors, sometimes in the face of resentment, stubborness and indignation. It has been a case of perserverance with patience, persistence and humour which has won the respect of the literally thousands of people with whom there have been dealings.

Naturally, grant-aid is only forthcoming on those items which formed part of the original fabric of the building; for example, no grant is given for electrical wiring, central heating or any other modern convenience. Essentially the grant covers the repair or replacement, in the original style and material, of the basic elements of the original building: foundations, walls, floors, roofs, chimneys, windows, doors, external and internal plaster, boundary walls, railings, gates, and so on.

Grant-aid normally amounts to one third of the repair cost, with a higher percentage of aid given to those who can prove that the essential work to be carried out is absolutely beyond their financial means.

Almost 1,000 listed buildings have been grant-aided in the last ten years. These, and the 100 or so conservation area schemes which will be described later in this book constitute the main reason for its publication. All of these buildings, categorised by building use and by county are set out below. It would have been ideal to have accompanied each entry with a photograph, but this would have been prohibitively expensive in terms of time, money and space. Instead, approximately 120 buildings have been chosen as being fairly representative of all the building uses, with a fair geographical spread across the province, and are featured with an appropriate photograph.

There is, as one might expect, a tremendous variety of all different aspects of these buildings; a variety of size, age, architectural style and importance. There is also a great variety of grant-aided work carried out to them; sometimes tiny properties have had major restorations, while large buildings have had only small repairs, and vice versa.

Sometimes the building has a different use now from when it was built, and the properties could have been catalogued in many different ways but the most convenient has been found to be under its present use. Within each chapter the Belfast schemes are recorded first, followed by those in each county, alphabetically.

Public Buildings

The Palm House, Botanic Gardens, Belfast.

The Palm House, designed by Charles Lanyon and built by the famous Dublin ironmaster, Richard Turner, is one of the finest and earliest surviving examples of curvi-linear glass and cast-iron work in Europe. The wings built in 1839 and 1840 lean against a parapeted brick wall and the central dome added in 1852 rises majestically from the centre of the composition. The entire structure has been superbly restored, greatly to the credit of the City Council.

Recipient of grant: Belfast City Council.

PHASE ONE — CENTRAL DOME.

Grant assistance of £203,500 given towards: Restoration of dome. Professional fees.

Approximate cost of work: £407,185. Carried out from 1976 to 1980.

Structural Engineers: Gillen & Pryce, Holywood.

Mechanical and Electrical Engineers: McAuslan & Partners, Belfast.

Contractor: H. & J. Martin Ltd., Belfast.

Structural ironwork by: R. J. McKinney Ltd., Newtownabbey.

Cleaning and protection of ironwork by: Corrosion Control Ltd., Belfast.

Glazing by: R. McClure & Sons Ltd., Ballyclare.

PHASE TWO — WINGS

Grant assistance of £167,750 given towards: Restoration of east and west wings. Professional fees.

Approximate cost of work: £335,577. Carried out in 1980 and 1981.

Structural Engineers: Gillen & Pryce, Holywood.

Contractor: H. & J. Martin Ltd., Belfast.

Structural ironwork by: A. W. Hamilton & Sons Ltd., Ballyclare.

Painting by: John Hamilton Ltd., Newtownabbey.

City Hall, Donegall Square, Belfast.

The City Hall, completed in 1906 to a competition winning design by Brumwell Thomas, is an impressive Portland stone building gathered around a central courtyard with a large, copper clad, central dome and subsidiary domes at each corner. The highly decorative two-storey north front has a rhythm of coupled Ionic columns on a rusticated ground floor base, a central pedimented portico and an ungainly porte-cochère. The other elevations are of three storeys and, while less elaborate, are possibly more satisfying.

Recipient of grant: Belfast City Council.

Grant assistance of £8,000 given towards: Replacement of defective window heads on south and east elevations. Repairs to first floor balconies on north and east elevations.

Approximate cost of work: £24,557. Carried out in 1979 and 1980.

Stone repair by: Peter Cox Ltd., Mitcham, Surrey and A. Robinson & Sons, Annalong.

Linen Hall Library, 17 Donegall Square North, Belfast.

A five-bay, three-storey, corner building, formerly a linen warehouse built in 1864 to designs by Lanyon, Lynn and Lanyon in an uneasy compromise between Georgian proportions and Victorian detailing.

The Palm House, Botanic Gardens, Belfast.

5

Public Buildings

The roof is hipped and slated, walls are of yellowish grey brick with moulded rendered details and windows have plain sashes. Now the home of the Linen Hall Library the building has now been restored after many years of neglect.

Recipient of grant: Board of Governors, Belfast Library and Society for Promoting Knowledge.

Grant assistance of £9,000 given towards: Re-slating using natural slate. Repairs to rainwater goods. Professional fees.

Approximate cost of work: £51,408. Carried out in 1982 and 1983.

Architect: Young & Mackenzie, Belfast.

Contractor: McLaughlin & Harvey, Newtownabbey.

Albert Memorial Clock, Victoria Street, Belfast.

The Albert Memorial is a square sandstone pinnacled tower with four clock faces, completed in 1867 in the newly introduced German-Gothic style to a competition winning design by W. J. Barre. The robed statue of the Prince Consort emerging from a niche is by S. F. Lynn.

Recipient of grant: Belfast City Council.

Grant assistance of £7,000 given towards: Cleaning of stonework. Re-pointing of stonework. Repair of decayed stonework. External redecoration.

Approximate cost of work: £29,300. Carried out in 1979 and 1980.

Contractor: J. Rainey & Co. Ltd., Belfast.

Belfast Castle, Antrim Road, Belfast.

A splendidly sited, Scottish Baronial style building completed in 1870 to designs by Lanyon, Lynn and Lanyon. The castle is mainly of three-storeys with attics, with a great six-storey square tower rising from the south west corner. The entrance front to the west has a porch with Doric columns and the garden front has a wonderful baroque staircase snaking up from the lawn to the piano nobile. The slated roof has crow-stepped gables and conical turrets. Walls are of sandstone with corbelled bow windows and square headed window openings containing plain sashes. The castle was given to the City Council in 1934 by the ninth Lord Shaftesbury and after a period of disuse is now being successfully restored.

Baroque Staircase, Belfast Castle.

Recipient of grant: Belfast City Council.

PHASE ONE

Grant assistance of £57,800 given towards: Repairs to roof structure. Re-slating using natural slate. Replacement leadwork. Replacement sash windows in original style. Treatment of extensive dry rot. Repairs to internal plasterwork. Repairs to decorative plasterwork. Repairs to timber floors. Professional fees.

Approximate cost of work: £211,462. Carried out in 1979 and 1980.

Architects: Anthony F. Lucy & Co., Belfast.

Quantity Surveyors: Dalzell & Campbell, Portrush.

Structural Engineers: Taylor & Boyd, Belfast.

Contractor: R. J. Stothers & Sons Ltd., Belfast.

Timber treatment by: Radication Ltd., Dunmurry, Belfast.

PHASE TWO

Grant assistance of £30,000 given towards: Sandblasting of stonework. Repairs to stonework. Re-pointing of stonework. External redecoration. Professional fees.

Approximate cost of work: £77,842. Carried out from 1980 to 1982.

Architects: Anthony F. Lucy & Co., Belfast.

Structural Engineers: Taylor & Boyd, Belfast.

Contractor: Alexander Greer Ltd., Lurgan.

Town Clock and Tower, High Street, Ballymoney.

The clocktower stands at the east of the Masonic Hall which was formerly a market-house built by the Earl of Antrim in 1775. The whole building has been much altered and an additional storey, in the form of an open-arched Italianate campanile, was added to the tower in 1852. The tower is rendered, as is the remainder of the building. Below the campanile there is a clock face on each of the three outward faces and below each clock is a tall lancet window. The entrance is awkwardly offset at the base of the tower.

Recipient of grant: Ballymoney Borough Council.

Grant assistance of £1,855 given towards: Replacement leadwork to roof. Repairs to external render. Repairs to defective timberwork. Redecoration of remedial items. Professional fees.

Approximate cost of work: £5,589. Carried out in 1975.

Architect: R. Robinson & Sons, Ballymoney.

Contractor: Hugh Taggart & Sons Ltd., Ballymoney.

Town Hall, High Street, Ballymoney.

Built to 1866 to designs by William Gray in a Ruskinian Romanesque style of red and yellow brick. Much of the character was destroyed in 1933 when it was rendered and extensively remodelled.

Recipient of grant: Ballymoney Borough Council.

Grant assistance of £5,500 given towards: Repair of louvred roof ventilators. Repairs to balustrading and coping. Repairs to external render. Redecoration of remedial items.

Approximate cost of work: £19,000. Carried out in 1979.

Contractor: Hugh Taggart & Sons Ltd., Ballymoney.

Sir Thomas Dixon Buildings, Harbour Road, Carnlough.

The five-bay, two-storey former town hall together with a four-storey square tower and the bridge, which carried the limestone quarry railway, form an interesting group. They are all constructed in limestone although the main walls of the town hall and tower are rendered. The town hall and tower have been restored and have found a new use as a public library after having been threatened with demolition following a fire.

Recipient of grant: Larne Borough Council.

Grant assistance of £6,000 given towards: Repairs to chimneys. Re-roofing using natural slate. Replacement metal rainwater goods. Replacement sash windows in original style. External re-rendering. Re-pointing of stone dressings. Replacement external doors in original style. Internal re-plastering. Installation of damp-proof solid floors. External redecoration.

Approximate cost of work: £91,611. Carried out in 1983.

Architect: J. McKeown & Co., Belfast.

Quantity Surveyor: Alex. G. Meban, Larne.

Contractor: Murray & Partners, Glenariff.

Town Hall, Antrim Street, Carrickfergus.

A wide, low, seven-bay, single-storey building built in 1779 as a courthouse possibly to designs by Richard Drew an architect who is otherwise unknown. The roof, surmounted by a little pointed bronze ventilator, is hipped and slated behind a parapet with knops and a central clock. The walls, the central three bays of which project slightly, are smooth rendered with moulded quoins. The windows have Georgian-glazed sashes with moulded architraves and pediments. The doorcase is a rather clumsy pedimented affair with bulging Doric columns. The building was converted to a new use as the town hall in 1934.

Recipient of grant: Carrickfergus Borough Council.

Grant assistance of £17,000 given towards: Roof repairs. External re-rendering including repairs to mouldings.

Approximate cost of work: £63,988. Carried out in 1980 and 1981.

Contractor: J. P. O'Neill, Lurgan. Roof work by direct labour.

Fairview House and Mill House, Tannaghmore, Lurgan.

A two-storey rendered Georgian farmhouse with outbuilding and fine Victorian garden. The property forms the nucleus of a public park and has been extensively refurbished.

Recipient of grant: Craigavon Borough Council.

Grant assistance of £3,490 given towards: Repairs to chimneys. Roof repairs to Fairview House. Re-slating using asbestos-cement slate to Mill House. Replacement external doors in original style. Treatment of wood rot. Internal re-plastering. Repairs to timber floors. Installation of damp-proof solid floors.

Approximate cost of work: £44,060. Carried out in 1979 and 1980.

Contractor: B. J. McAnallen, Dungannon.

The Bishop's Palace, Armagh.

The Palace, commanding a spectacular view of the city, was designed by Thomas Cooley for Archbishop Richard Robinson in 1770. In 1825 Lord George Beresford added another storey and new octagonal entrance porch giving it it's present appearance of nine-bays by three-storeys on a high basement. The roof is hipped and slated with projecting, bracketted eaves, walls are of limestone ashlar and windows have Georgian-glazed sashes. The Palace has now been restored and converted for use as council offices.

Recipient of grant: Armagh District Council.

Grant assistance of £15,250 given towards: Repairs to roof structure. Replacement sash windows in original style. Treatment of extensive dry rot. Installation of damp-proof course. Internal re-plastering. Repairs to timber floors. Insertion of new lintels over structural openings.

Approximate cost of work: £30,502. Carried out in 1977.

Architect: Ian Donaldson, Armagh.

Quantity Surveyor: F. H. Wright & Partners, Belfast, Coleraine and Omagh.

Contractor: O'Hanlan Brothers, Coalisland.

Public Library, Abbey Street, Armagh.

A fine two-storey building in Renaissance style with hipped slated roof and dressed limestone walls. The building was designed by Thomas Cooley and built in 1771 for Primate Robinson. It was extended and partly rebuilt in 1845.

Recipient of grant: Board of Trustees.

Grant assistance of £2,430 given towards: Treatment of extensive dry rot and subsequent reinstatement.

Approximate cost of work: £4,595. Carried out in 1979.

Architect: W. A. Johnston, Armagh.

Contractor: A. C. Simpson & Partners Ltd., Armagh.

Timber treatment by: Rentokil Ltd., Belfast.

Community Centre, 61 Dominic Street, Newry.

A three-bay, three-storey early-19th century house. The roof is slated and gabled, walls are roughcast, windows have Georgian-glazed sashes and the panelled entrance door has sidelights and decorative semi-circular fanlight and is approached by steps.

Recipient of grant: Newry and Mourne District Council.

Grant assistance of £2,300 given towards: Repairs to chimneys. Re-slating using natural slate. Replacement metal rainwater goods. Replacing slate-hanging to gable wall.

Approximate cost of work: £7,932. Carried out in 1982.

Contractor: W. A. Coulter, Kilkeel.

Old Technical School, Downshire Road, Banbridge.

A two- and three-storey, irregularly planned Elizabethan style building. The roof is slated with half-timbered gables and gablets and the walls are of red brick. A square porch with pointed archway, part-balustraded parapet and finely moulded brick detailing, projects centrally on the main front.

Recipient of grant: Banbridge District Council.

Grant assistance of £480 given towards: External redecoration.

Approximate cost of work: £1,465. Carried out in 1980.

Painting by: Ivan J. Gault, Banbridge.

Town Hall, Market Square, Dromore.

Formerly the market house. Built in 1886 it is a red-brick building with 'L' shaped plan. The entrance front is of three-bays and two storeys with a subtle arrangement of door and window openings rising to an occulus window in the gable which is surmounted by an attractive but out-of-place timber pedimented cupola, containing a clock.

Recipient of grant: Banbridge District Council.

PHASE ONE

Grant assistance of £3,130 given towards: Re-slating usual natural slate.

Approximate cost of work: £8,435. Carried out in 1978.

Architect: M. H. Ferguson, Banbridge.

Contractor: A. Malcolmson, Rathfriland.

PHASE TWO

Grant assistance of £2,200 given towards: Cleaning and re-pointing of brickwork.

Approximate cost of work: £6,670. Carried out in 1979.

Contractor: Alexander Greer Ltd., Lurgan.

PHASE THREE

Grant assistance of £200 given towards: External redecoration.

Approximate cost of work: £620. Carried

out in 1980.

Painting by: Ivan J. Gault, Banbridge.

Tower House, Quay Street, Bangor.

A two-storey house with attic with a four-storey tower at its north west corner, built in 1637 as the Customs House. The roof to the house is slated with a crow-stepped gable to the north, the tower and stair turret are battlemented with a flat roof. Walls are of split stone rubble with sandstone dressings and quoins. Original window openings are square-headed with quirked aris-rolls to the surrounds and are grooved to receive glass. The tower house has been the subject of a superb restoration scheme and is now a tourist information and exhibition centre.

Recipient of grant: North Down Borough Council.

Grant assistance of £45,000 given towards: Reconstruction of chimney, parapets and crow-stepped gable. Re-roofing using natural slate. Re-covering of flat roof to tower. Replacement metal rainwater goods. Structural repairs to masonry. Re-pointing of stonework. Repairs to external render. Replacement windows in original style. Replacement external doors in original style. Treatment of wood rot. Stripping of internal plaster. Repairs to timber floors. Replacement of internal panelled doors. Replacement timber staircase. Professional fees.

Approximate cost of work: £152,726. Carried out in 1981 and 1982.

Architect: Larry Thompson & Partners, Belfast.

The Castle, Bangor.

Quantity Surveyor: Andrew G. Crawford & Co., Belfast.

Contractor: Pilot Construction Ltd., Belfast.

Timber treatment by: Radication Ltd., Dunmurry, Belfast.

Stone repair by: J. Rainey & Co. Ltd., Belfast.

The Castle, Bangor.

A fine Scrabo stone building of one-, two- and three-storeys built in 1852 by R. E. Ward. The slated roof is multi-gabled with decorated parapets and balustrades and small gabled dormers. A rectangular tower rises by the main entrance surmounted on one corner by a square clock turret. Windows are mullioned and transomed and contain plain sashes. The building, now a town hall, has been extensively and well restored.

Recipient of grant: North Down Borough Council.

PHASE ONE

Grant assistance of £350 given towards: Re-pointing of tower. Provision of new weathervane.

Approximate cost of work: £756. Carried out in 1975.

Contractor: John McQuillan, Bangor.

PHASE TWO

Grant assistance of £50,000 given towards: Partial re-roofing using natural slate. Replacement leadwork. Repairs to rainwater goods. Underpinning of walls. Stone cleaning. Repairs to stonework. Repairs to windows. Treatment of wood rot. External redecoration.

Approximate cost of work: £158,507. Carried out in 1981 and 1982.

Architect: Larry Thompson & Partners, Belfast.

Quantity Surveyor: Andrew G. Crawford & Co., Belfast.

Contractor: McLaughlin & Harvey Ltd., Newtownabbey.

Timber treatment by: Timbertreat Services Ltd., Belfast.

Stone repair by: Alexander Greer Ltd., Lurgan.

Market House, Market Square, Portaferry.

A pleasant four-bay, two-storey Georgian market house built in 1752. The roof is low pitched and hipped, surmounted by a bell and sailing-ship windvane and with a simple pediment containing a clock. The walls are smooth rendered with moulded quoins and the windows have Georgian-glazed sashes. The building has been well restored from dereliction by the Borough Council.

Recipient of grant: Ards Borough Council.

Grant assistance of £620 given towards: Repair of cage frame clock (c 1850).

Approximate cost of work: £2,148. Carried out in 1982 and 1983.

Clock repairs by: J. B. Joyce & Co. Ltd. Whitchurch.

Tower on Motte, Moat Street, Donaghadee.

A castellated tower built as a powder magazine when the harbour was being reconstructed in 1821. The walls are of rendered rubble and brick.

Recipient of grant: Ards Borough Council.

Grant assistance of £5,500 given towards: Exposing and pointing stonework.

Re-rendering of walls. Provision of external stone buttresses. Provision of two portculli.

Approximate cost of work: £16,700. Carried out in 1979 and 1980.

Contractor: Johnston-Orr Construction, Bangor.

Gillespie's Monument, The Square, Comber.

A tall square stone pillar on a panelled pedestal surmounted by a statue of Major General Robert Rolls Gillespie. Erected in 1845.

Recipient of grant: Ards Borough Council.

Grant assistance of £1,100 given towards: Cleaning of monument using sand-blasting and chemical techniques. Restoration of stonework.

Approximate cost of work: £3,930. Carried out in 1979.

Stone repair by: John McQuillan, Bangor.

Old Corn Market, The Diamond, Lisnaskea.

A paved market yard flanked by two, three-bay Tudoresque side pavilions (one of which has now been demolished) and linked at the rear by a cloister carried on cast-iron columns. The cloistered building dates from 1841 while the side buildings are probably earlier. The group has been restored.

Recipient of grant: Lisnaskea Fairs and Markets Committee.

Grant assistance of £26,000 (including Environment Improvement Grant of £6,500) given towards: Re-slating using natural slate. Replacement metal rainwater goods. Sandblasting and

Town Hall, The Diamond, Enniskillen.

re-pointing of stonework. Replacement external doors in original style. Repairs to railings. Re-location of market cross in central position. Professional fees.

Approximate cost of work: £51,945. Carried out in 1980.

Agent: Garnet V. Mills, Lisnaskea.

Contractor: T. Chambers & Sons (E.) Ltd., Enniskillen.

Town Hall, The Diamond, Enniskillen.

Completed in 1901 to a competition winning design by William Scott of Drogheda, the Town Hall is an imposing building dominating the east end of the town. The tall clock tower with its niches, clocks, belfry and cupola stands on the corner between the five-bay, two-storey front and taller six-bay side. Both have columned entrance porches and balustrades at roof level. The walls of pale Carrickreagh stone are rusticated on the ground floor and ashlar at first floor level. The building has been restored and refurbished following severe bomb damage incurred in 1971.

Recipient of grant: Fermanagh District Council.

Grant assistance of £22,500 given towards: Roof repairs. Extensive stonework repairs. Replacement leadwork. Repairs to timberwork of cupola.

Further financial assistance received from: Northern Ireland Office as bomb damage compensation.

Approximate cost of work: £423,708. Carried out from 1978 to 1979.

Architect: H. A. Patton & Partners, Bangor.

Quantity Surveyor: John F. Kerr, Belfast.

Contractor: John Paul & Co. (Northern Ireland) Ltd., Hillsborough.

Commercial Buildings

125 Ormeau Road, Belfast.

A three-bay, three-storey terrace property built in 1846. The roof is slated, the frontage is smooth rendered to the upper floors and deeply lined to the ground floor and the windows have plain sashes. The panelled entrance door is flanked by Ionic columns and set under a decorative elliptical fanlight all contained within a moulded archivolt.

Recipients of grant: Messrs. Henderson & Donnelly.

Grant assistance of £2,820 given towards: Rebuilding of chimney. Re-slating using natural slate. Repairs to rainwater goods. Repairs to windows. Repairs to external render. Repairs to entrance steps.

Approximate cost of work: £8,933. Carried out in 1978.

Architects: H. A. Patton & Partners, Belfast.

Contractor: W. C. Hodgen Ltd., Belfast.

12 Upper Crescent, Belfast.

One of ten, three-storey rendered houses in a concave row comprising the finest Neo-Classical terrace in Northern Ireland. The group was built in 1846 by James Corry possibly to designs by Charles Lanyon, the centre and ends are emphasised by attached giant order Corinthian columns and high balustraded attics.

Recipient of grant: Nat. Joseph Ltd.

Grant assistance of £360 given towards: Repairs to external render.

Approximate cost of work: £1,100. Carried out in 1979.

Plastering by: Raymond P. Smyth, Belfast.

13 Upper Crescent, Belfast.

One of ten, three-storey rendered houses in a concave row comprising the finest Neo-Classical terrace in Northern Ireland. The group was built in 1846 by James Corry possibly to designs by Charles Lanyon, the centre and ends are emphasised by attached giant order Corinthian columns and high balustraded attics.

Recipient of grant: Mr. W. L. McConville.

Grant assistance of £430 given towards: Repairs to external render.

Approximate cost of work: £1,300. Carried out in 1980.

Plastering by: Raymond P. Smyth, Belfast.

Scottish Provident Building, Donegall Square West, Belfast.

A huge, pale sandstone, classically detailed office block built between 1899 and 1902 to designs by the Belfast architects Young & Mackenzie. The building is of six storeys, heavily decorated with rusticated ground first and second floors, engaged Corinthian columns running through the third, fourth and fifth floors and a balustraded parapet at roof level. The central bowed section has paired columns and a raised attic supporting a huge pediment and the ends are terminated by tall octagonal domed towers. The building has been painstakingly stabilised and restored.

Recipient of grants: Scottish Provident Institution.

PHASE ONE – STRUCTURAL STABILISATION

Grant assistance of £59,700 given towards: Underpinning of foundations. Repairs to pediment wall at sixth floor. Professional fees.

Scottish Provident Building, Donegall Square West, Belfast.

Commercial Buildings

Approximate cost of work: £142,018. Carried out in 1979 and 1980.

Structural Engineers: McAuley & Browne, Belfast.

Contractor: H. & J. Martin Ltd., Belfast.

PHASE TWO – ROOF

Grant assistance of £19,350 given towards: Repairs to central pediment roof including new covering, box gutters and rainwater goods. Treatment of wood rot.

Approximate cost of work: £45,038. Carried out in 1980.

Architects: Young & Mackenzie, Belfast.

Quantity Surveyor: John F. Kerr, Belfast.

Contractor: H. & J. Martin Ltd., Belfast.

Roof work by: Maurice McCavery, Dromara.

Timber treatment by: Timbercare (N.I.) Lisburn.

PHASE THREE – RESTORATION AND REFURBISHMENT

Grant assistance of £125,000 given towards: Repairs to main roof. Re-pointing and repair of stonework. Replacement and repair of existing sash windows. Treatment of dry rot and subsequent reinstatement. Restoration of corridor tiling. Provision of panelled doors to corridors.

Approximate cost of work: £1,045,311. Carried out in 1981.

Architects: Young & Mackenzie, Belfast.

Quantity Surveyor: John F. Kerr, Belfast.

Contractor: Jamison & Sloan, Belfast.

Ocean Buildings, 3 Donegall Square East, Belfast.

A five-storey asymmetrical Scottish-Baronial-Tudor style sandstone office block built in 1902 to designs by Young & Mackenzie. The building is richly decorated with carved grotesques and gargoyles and over the splayed corner doorway dangle the heads of Edward VII, Queen Victoria and Queen Alexandra.

Recipient of grant: Pearl Assurance Company Limited.

Grant assistance of £19,000 given towards: Roof repairs. Repairs to leadwork. Repairs to rainwater goods. Stone cleaning and re-pointing. Cleaning of and repairs to faience tiling. Replacement of carved stone gargoyle. Repairs to windows. External redecoration. Treatment of wood rot and subsequent reinstatement. Professional fees.

Approximate cost of work: £69,600.

Architects: Young & Mackenzie, Belfast.

Contractor: H. & J. Martin Ltd., Belfast.

Timber treatment by: Timbercare (N.I.), Lisburn.

Roof work by: Rainey & Co., Belfast.

7 and 9 Chichester Street, Belfast.

Two three-bay, four-storey, late-Georgian houses with basements forming part of what was once a longer terrace built in 1804. Roofs are slated with shallow parapet and projecting eaves cornice, the frontage is brick-faced, windows have Georgian-glazed sashes and the flush panelled entrance doors are flanked by sandstone Doric-columns with frieze and semi-circular fanlights over, all set within moulded archivolts. The entrances are approached by stone steps and cast-iron railings protect the basements.

Recipient of grant: Mr. C. E. B. Brett and Mr. H. E. Pierce.

Grant assistance of £845 given towards: Re-slating using natural slate. Professional fees.

Approximate cost of work: £1,960. Carried out in 1979.

Architects: Robert McKinstry & Melvyn Brown, Belfast.

Roof work by: Thomas Flynn, Belfast.

11 Chichester Street, Belfast.

A three-bay, four-storey, Late-Georgian house forming part of what was once a longer terrace built in 1804. The roof is slated and has a shallow parapet and projecting eaves cornice, the frontage is brick-faced and the windows have Georgian-glazed sashes. The building has been restored and a Georgian-styled period shopfront has been added.

Recipient of grant: Dunleady Properties Limited.

Grant assistance of £11,350 given towards: Repairs to roof structure. Re-slating using natural slate. Repairs to windows. Removal of existing shopfront. Rebuilding of defective wall at rear of property. Redecoration of remedial items. Professional fees.

Approximate cost of work: £21,273. Carried out in 1980.

Architects: Robert McKinstry & Melvyn Brown, Belfast.

Quantity Surveyors: V. B. Evans & Co., Belfast.

Contractor: Kelly, McEvoy & Brown, Dundrum.

Commercial Buildings

14 College Square East, Belfast.

An early 19th-century four-storey smooth rendered building with Georgian-glazed sash windows and a ground floor shop front.

Recipient of grant: Belfast Scout Council.

PHASE ONE

Grant assistance of £117 given towards: Replacement of sash windows in original style.

Approximate cost of work: £407. Carried out in 1977.

Architect: W. Finlay Reid, Belfast.

Contractor: Jamison & Sloan, Belfast.

PHASE TWO

Grant assistance of £1,270 given towards: Rebuilding of chimney. Repairs to roof structure. Re-slating using natural slate.

Approximate cost of work: £4,925. Carried out in 1981.

Contractor: Kerr & Wallace, Belfast.

60 to 64 Wellington Place and 12 College Square East, Belfast.

A four-storey mid-19th century building occupying a corner site. The roof is slated and walls are smooth rendered with moulded quoins. The ground floor is occupied by shops which project on the Wellington Place frontage.

Recipient of grant: Mr. J. D. Caskey.

Grant assistance of £5,000 given towards: Repairs to roof structure. Re-slating using natural slate to front slopes and asbestos-cement to rear. Replacement leadwork. Treatment of wood rot. Repairs to internal plasterwork. Repairs to timber floors. Professional fees.

Approximate cost of work: £15,538. Carried out in 1980 and 1981.

Architects: Houston, Bell & Kennedy, Belfast.

Structural Engineers: Kirk, McClure & Morton, Belfast.

Contractor: Danlor Services, Belfast.

16 College Square East, Belfast.

An early-19th century four-storey house reputed to be the birthplace of Lord Kelvin. The roof is slated, walls are smooth rendered and the ground floor is occupied by a shop.

Recipient of grant: Trustees of T. Y. Moore.

Grant assistance of £2,000 given towards: Treatment of wood rot. Repairs to roof structure. Repairs to internal plasterwork. Repairs to timber floors.

Further financial assistance received from: Northern Ireland Office.

Approximate cost of work: £25,347. Carried out in 1981 and 1982.

Architects: Brian Emerson Associates, Hillsborough.

Quantity Surveyors: W. H. Stephens & Sons, Belfast.

Contractor: M. E. Crowe, Lisburn.

Timber treatment by: Rentokil Ltd., Belfast.

St. Malachy's School, 21 Oxford Street, Belfast.

A tiny Victorian Gothic two-storey, sandstone-faced and steeply gabled building squeezed between two, much larger, blocks. Built in 1874, to designs by Alexander McAllister, it became a derelict shell for some years before adaption to its present commercial use.

Recipient of grant: Mr. D. S. Rana.

Grant assistance of £7,860 given towards: Re-roofing using asbestos-cement slate. Replacement metal rainwater goods. Restoration of stonework to frontage. Replacement windows in original style. Installation of electro-osmotic damp-proof course. Repair of gates, railings and plinth walls. Redecoration of remedial items.

Approximate cost of work: £56,900. Carried out in 1980 and 1981.

Architect: Peter G. M. Shaw, Londonderry.

Contractor: Marlborough Building Works, Finaghy.

Masonic Hall, Arthur Square, Belfast.

A Gothic style, smooth rendered building, completed in 1869, possibly by Sir Charles Lanyon and if so, certainly one of his last designs.

Recipient of grant: Trustees, Freemasons Hall.

Grant assistance of £2,400 given towards: Repairs to chimney. External re-rendering.

Approximate cost of work: £9,191. Carried out in 1981.

Contractors: Boland, Reilly Ltd., Bangor and Edward Wilson & Co. Ltd., Newtownabbey.

Head Line Buildings, 10 to 14 Victoria Street, Belfast.

A three-storey Italianate-style building with basement occupying an island site and designed by Thomas Jackson in 1863. The slated roof is concealed behind a parapet, the main facades are of sandstone and elsewhere yellowish brick facing has been adopted. The windows have plain sashes, curved, at the corners of the main front.

Commercial Buildings

Recipient of grant: G. Heyn & Sons Ltd.

Grant assistance of £7,080 given towards: Replacement sash windows in original style.

Further financial assistance received from: Northern Ireland Office.

Approximate cost of work: £22,380. Carried out in 1979.

Agent: Thomas P. Pentland & Co., Ballyclare.

Contractor: McLaughlin & Harvey Ltd.

The Northern Bank, Waring Street, Belfast.

Charles Lanyon's 1845 reconstruction of the old Exchange and Assembly Rooms is one of the first and best examples of the Italianate palazzo style in Belfast. The remodelled building is rendered with a part-balustraded parapet, bold bracketted eaves cornice, pedimented aedicules to first floor windows, vermiculated quoins and rusticated ground floor. The windows have plain sashes and the entrance has a tall porch with two Doric columns supporting a plain frieze, cornice and coat-of-arms. Lanyon carefully preserved as much of the original interior as possible but it was completely lost when further alterations were carried out by his partner, W. H. Lynn, in 1895.

Recipient of grant: The Northern Bank Ltd.

Grant assistance of £16,500 given towards: Repairs to parapet. Protection of banking hall ceiling. Repairs to roof structure. Treatment of extensive dry rot. Repairs to internal plasterwork. Repairs to decorative plasterwork.

Approximate cost of work: £53,780. Carried out in 1978.

The Northern Bank, Waring Street, Belfast.

Commercial Buildings

Architects: Samuel Stevenson & Sons, Belfast.

Contractor: William Dowling Ltd., Belfast.

Mayfair Building, Arthur Square, Belfast.

A five-storey, multi-gabled, brick building with sandstone dressings built in 1906 to designs by P. M. Jury. The windows have a mixture of plain sashes and casements and the ground floor is occupied by shops.

Recipient of Grant: Arthur Square Development Company Ltd.

Grant assistance of £900 given towards: Stone restoration adopting 'plastic' in-situ technique.

Approximate cost of work: £3,155. Carried out in 1982.

Stone repair by: Alexander Greer Ltd., Lurgan.

Bank Buildings, Royal Avenue, Belfast.

Built at the turn of the century the Bank Buildings stands on an island site and is one of the first iron-framed buildings in the city and also one of the last buildings designed by W. H. Lynn. The structure faced in sandstone is of four storeys with a basement, the upper storeys are classical in style and the ground floor displays large expanses of plate glass. The building has been drastically converted for use as a chain store.

Recipient of grant: Primark Limited.

Grant assistance of £20,000 given towards: Roof repairs. Repairs to rainwater goods. Replacement leadwork. Cleaning and restoration of stone facade. Restoration of clock. Repairs to

windows. Repairs to floors.

Approximate cost of work: £3,000,000. Carried out in 1979 and 1980.

Architects: Dupree Partnership Ltd., London.

Quantity Surveyor: J. J. Riordan, Belfast.

Contractor: H. & J. Martin Ltd., Belfast.

Stone cleaning and stone repairs by: J. Rainey & Co., Ltd., Belfast.

Glazing by: T. McClune & Sons Ltd., Belfast.

Rainwater installation by: Haypark Heating Ltd., Belfast.

Clock repairs by: Rotary Services Ltd., Newtownabbey and W. J. Briggs Ltd., Newtownards.

Railway Station, Portrush.

An unusual redbrick, half-timbered building in mock Tudor style. A low square clock tower occupies one corner. Built in 1893 to designs by Berkley Wise the B.N.C.R. engineer. The station fell into disuse until being converted for use as an amusement centre.

Recipient of grant: Mr. R. Crawford.

Grant assistance of £4,976 given towards: Roof repairs. Repairs to leadwork. Repairs to ornamental barge boards, facias and finials. Repairs to rainwater goods. Repairs to timber framing. External redecoration.

Approximate cost of work: £225,000. Carried out in 1977 and 1978.

Architects: Dalzell & Campbell, Coleraine/Portrush/Belfast/ Londonderry.

Contractor: David Patton & Sons (N.I.) Ltd. Ballymena.

Railway Station, Portrush.

Commercial Buildings

6, 8 Bath Street, Portrush.

A pair of late-19th century semi-detached, three-storey houses with basements and full height canted bay windows. Roof is slated with eaves supported on corbel brackets, walls are rendered, windows have plain sashes and the panelled entrance doors are flanked by pilasters with scroll brackets, frieze, fanlight and pedimented overdoors.

Recipient of grant: Mr. N. E. Campbell.

Grant assistance of £1,000 given towards: Repairs to external render. External redecoration.

Approximate cost of work: £3,930. Carried out in 1982.

Contractor: John Rainey & Co., Portrush.

23 Mill Street, Cushendall.

A three-storey terrace property with good pub front with applique lettering and a coach arch.

Recipient of grant: Mr. P. J. McCollam.

Grant assistance of £2,240 given towards: Rebuilding of chimneys. Re-slating using natural slate. Replacement metal rainwater goods.

Approximate cost of work: £5,510. Carried out in 1981.

Contractor: Martin Jamieson, Ballycastle.

105 Main Street, Bushmills.

A small two-storey terrace property with slated roof, plain sashed first floor windows and three-light shop windows.

Recipient of grant: Mr. J. Creelman.

Grant assistance of £960 given towards: Rebuilding of chimney. Roof repairs. Repairs to leadwork. Replacement

metal rainwater goods. Replacement sash windows in original style. Replacement back door in original style.

Approximate cost of work: £2,894. Carried out in 1982.

Contractor: Robert McCrellis, Dervock, Ballymoney.

41 Main Street, Bushmills.

A two-storey, terrace property with slated roof, rendered walls, half-glazed four panel entrance door, exposed box plain sash windows and coach arch.

Recipient of grant: Mrs. E. Patterson.

Grant assistance of £95 given towards: Repairs to chimney. Re-slating using natural slate. Repairs to rainwater goods. Replacement external doors in original style. Repairs to internal plasterwork.

Further financial assistance received from: Northern Ireland Housing Executive.

Approximate cost of work: £2,178. Carried out in 1983.

Contractor: David Horner, Bushmills.

72 Castle Street, Ballycastle.

A pleasing three-bay, two-storey house making worthy contribution to the streetscape. Georgian-glazed with a good pilastered shop-front, signwriting and doorcase.

Recipient of grant: Mr. G. McKinley.

Grant assistance of £250 given towards: Roof repairs. Replacement metal rainwater goods. Repairs to internal plasterwork. Redecoration of remedial items.

Approximate cost of work: £749. Carried out in 1981.

Roof work by: McMahon & Co., Belfast.

10 and 12 Bridge Street, Carnlough.

A most peculiar, slightly tipsy, little group of two-storey rendered buildings leaning at the corner of Bridge Street and Waterfall Road. It might well incorporate part of the old corn-mill which formerly occupied this site.

Recipient of grant: Mr. P. McAuley.

Grant assistance of £1,700 given towards: Repairs to chimney. Repairs to roof structure. Re-slating using natural slate. Repairs to rainwater goods. Repairs to windows. Redecoration of remedial items.

Approximate cost of the work: £6,308. Carried out in 1982.

Contractor: James Caves, Cullybackey.

135 and 137 Church Street, Ballymena.

Part of a long thirteen-bay rendered terrace of shops with dwellings over given a classical feeling by the treatment of the upper floors.

Recipient of grant: Messrs. Dunlop & Carson.

Grant assistance of £200 given towards: Replacement sash windows in original style.

Further financial assistance received from: Northern Ireland Office.

Approximate cost of work: £1,131. Carried out in 1980.

Contractor: Robert Wilson, Ballymena.

Lower Ballinderry School, Lisburn.

A five-bay, two-storey harled and whitened school house with small central gable at front, Georgian-glazed windows and a lean-to porch at road level. The school house has been converted for use as a home bakery

Commercial Buildings

and shop.

Recipient of grant: Mr. J. McK. Andrews.

Grant assistance of £2,580 given towards: Repairs to chimney. Roof repairs. External re-rendering. Replacement external doors in original style. Restoration of gates and railings. Treatment of wood rot. Installation of electro-osmotic damp-proof course. Repairs to internal plasterwork. Installation of damp-proof solid floors. Repairs to timber floors.

Approximate cost of work: £7,620 (materials only). Carried out in 1981.

Work carried out using own and direct labour.

Timber treatment by: Radication Ltd., Dunmurry, Belfast.

Lower Ballinderry School, Lisburn.

Castle Buildings, 1 Castle Street, Lisburn.

A three-storey corner block of shops and offices built in 1890 to designs by George Sands. The roof is hipped and slated behind a parapet balustrade, the upper walls are of brick and the ground floor shop fronts have full-height pilasters.

Recipient of grant: Alexander Boyd & Co., Ltd.

Grant assistance of £1,500 given towards: Repairs to chimneys. Roof repairs. Repairs to leadwork. Repair of parapet balustrade including replacement balusters. Treatment of wood rot, and subsequent reinstatement. Professional fees.

Approximate cost of work: £4,718. Carried out in 1980 and 1981.

Architects: McKee & Kirk Partnership, Lisburn.

Contractor: Timbercure Services Ltd., Lisburn.

2 Main Street, Randalstown.

A handsome, pre-1857 five-bay, two-storey building now car showrooms and a garage but formerly a hotel. The roof is parapeted and walls are smooth rendered with bold moulded details including pediments over the first-floor windows.

Recipient of grant: Robert Moore & Son.

Grant assistance of £1,960 given towards: Repairs to leadwork. Repairs to external render. Repairs to windows. External redecoration. Professional fees.

Approximate cost of work: £5,830. Carried out in 1979.

Architects: W. D. R. & R. T. Taggart, Belfast.

Work carried out using direct labour.

13 and 15 Market Square, Antrim.

A four-bay, three-storey shop with gabled slated roof, basalt walls and recently restored Georgian-glazed sash windows and traditional shop front.

Recipient of grant: J. W. Craig & Son (Antrim) Ltd.

Grant assistance of £1,122 given towards: Restoration of sash windows. Provision of appropriate shopfront and fascia.

Approximate cost of work: £3,367. Carried out in 1980.

Contractor: W. A. Gawn, Templepatrick.

Commercial Buildings

37 High Street, Antrim.

A three-storey building, part of an early-19th century group of reasonable quality. The upper floors have Georgian-glazed sash windows.

Recipient of grant: Mr. J. T. Erwin.

Grant assistance of £1,200 given towards: Repairs to roof structure and re-slating. External re-rendering. Repairs to internal plasterwork. Repairs to timber floors. Provision of new hand-painted fascia.

Approximate cost of work: £7,000. Carried out in 1980.

Contractor: Robert McIlvenna, Upperlands, County Londonderry.

38 High Street, Portadown.

Formerly a bank now converted for building society and shop use. The building incorporates two, mid-19th century, three-storey classically detailed houses. The roof is slated and gabled behind a parapet, the facade is smooth rendered on the upper floors and lined on the ground floors, with moulded quoins. All windows have plain sashes and moulded surrounds; the first floor windows have canopys supported on console brackets. The panelled entrance door with rectangular fanlight over is set within a columned portico.

Recipient of grant: Anglia Building Society.

Grant assistance of £4,600 given towards: Repairs to chimneys. Roof repairs. Repairs to rainwater goods. Strengthening of foundations. Restoration of rendered front facade. Repairs to internal plasterwork. External redecoration. Professional fees.

Approximate cost of work: £96,668. Carried out in 1981 and 1982.

Architects: Hobart & Heron, Belfast.

Quantity Surveyors: W. H. Stephens & Sons, Portadown.

Contractor: R. Hollingsworth & Son, Portadown.

2–4 Church Street, Portadown.

A four-bay, three-storey commercial property. The facade is rendered, with Georgian-glazed windows to the upper floors.

Recipient of grant: Mr. W. J. Grant.

Grant assistance of £1,120 given towards: Re-slating using natural slate to front slope and asbestos-cement to back. Repairs to rainwater goods.

Approximate cost of work: £4,058. Carried out in 1983.

Contractor: Whitten Bros. & Leeman, Portadown.

10 and 12 Church Street, Portadown.

Two, three-storey, brick terrace houses. Roofs are slated with fire-break party walls and gablet dormers. Eaves are plastered, with heavy moulded brackets. Windows to the upper floors have vertically divided sashes. At ground floor each house has a single-storey canted bay. The houses have been combined and converted for use as a bank.

Recipient of grant: Allied Irish Bank Ltd.

Grant assistance of £4,000 given towards: Repairs to chimneys. Repairs to roof structure. Re-slating using natural slate. Replacement metal rainwater goods. Re-pointing of brickwork. Replacement sash windows in original style. Treatment of wood rot. Repairs to internal plasterwork. Repairs to timber floors.

Approximate cost of work: £168,876. Carried out in 1981 and 1982.

Architects: Dennis McIntyre & Devon, Belfast.

Quantity Surveyors: Robert J. Love & Partners, Belfast.

Contractor: Henry Coary & Sons Ltd., Dungannon.

Timber treatment by: Timbercare (N.I.), Lisburn.

14 Church Street, Portadown.

A three-storey brick terrace house with slated roof, fire-break party walls and gablet dormer. Eaves are plastered, with heavy moulded brackets. There is a single-storey ground floor canted bay window. All windows have vertically divided sashes.

Recipient of grant: Carleton, Atkinson & Sloan.

Grant assistance of £2,170 given towards: Roof repairs. Repairs to rainwater goods. Re-pointing of brickwork. Repairs to external render. Repairs to windows. Treatment of wood rot. Replacement of front entrance steps and paving. Repairs to doors. Internal plastering. Redecoration of remedial items.

Approximate cost of work: £10,182. Carried out in 1981 and 1982.

Contractor: D. Chambers, Banbridge.

Timber treatment by: Lacey Timbertreatments, Belfast.

Old Cinema, 48 Church Street, Portadown.

A three-storey building formerly a cinema now converted for use as offices. The upper floors are of variegated brickwork and the ground floor is decorated with faience tiling.

Recipient of grant: Mr. B. Campbell.

Grant assistance of £2,060 given towards: Roof repairs. Repairs to windows. Repairs to facade.

Approximate cost of work: £25,690. Carried out in 1979.

Architect: J. G. O'Neill, Lurgan.

Quantity Surveyors: McFarlane & Partners, Belfast.

Contractor: F. Reynolds, Lurgan.

56 Main Street, Loughall.

A two-bay, two-storey end of terrace shop built, possibly, in the mid-19th century. The roof is slated and gabled, walls are roughcast, first floor windows have Georgian-glazed sashes and the ground floor shop front has been restored.

Recipient of grant: Mr. T. G. Jameson.

Grant assistance of £1,210 given towards: Restoration of shop front.

Approximate cost of work: £3,634. Carried out in 1980.

Contractor: S. A. Hawthorne, Newtownhamilton.

11 College Street, Armagh.

A two-bay, three-storey pre-1835 mid-terrace house. The roof is slated, walls are of random rubble and windows have Georgian-glazed sashes with a tri-partite window to both ground and first floors. The panelled entrance door is set under a semi-circular fanlight all in a Gibbsian stone surround. The house has been restored subsequent to bomb damage.

Recipient of grant: Mr. J. McAllister.

Grant assistance of £220 given towards: Treatment of wood rot. Repairs to internal plasterwork. Repairs to timber floors.

Approximate cost of work: £815. Carried

out in 1981.

Work carried out using direct labour.

Timber treatment by: Protim Services, Lisburn.

28 Scotch Street, Armagh.

A two-bay, three-storey mid-terrace building with slated roof, coursed limestone facade, Georgian-glazed sash windows to the upper floors and a shopfront to the ground floor. Part of a block designed before 1835 by Francis Johnston. One of a group of buildings rescued from dereliction and successfully restored.

Recipient of grant: Mr. P. J. Wilson.

Grant assistance of £1,250 given towards: Roof repairs. Replacement metal rainwater goods. Stabilising of front wall. Replacement sash windows in original style. Re-pointing of stonework. Repairs to timber floors. Installation of damp-proof solid floors. Provision of new 'period' shopfront.

Further financial assistance received from: Northern Ireland Office.

Approximate cost of work: £7,705. Carried out in 1982.

Structural Engineers: Armstrong & Shaw, Belfast.

Work carried out using direct labour.

32 Scotch Street, Armagh.

A single-bay, two-storey mid-terrace property, part of a block designed by Francis Johnston. The roof is slated, walls are of coursed limestone and the first floor window has Georgian-glazed sashes. The property was derelict as a result of bomb damage before it was restored to its present condition.

Recipient of grant: Mr. D. Hutchinson.

Grant assistance of £1,275 given towards:

Repairs to chimney. Cleaning and re-pointing of stonework. Provision of new 'period' shopfront. Repairs to internal plasterwork.

Approximate cost of work: £4,091. Carried out in 1982.

Contractors: Malachy P. O'Neill & Sons, Dungannon.

34 Scotch Street, Armagh.

A single-bay, two-storey end-of-terrace property, forming part of a block designed by Francis Johnston before 1835. The roof is hipped and slated, walls are of coursed limestone and the first floor window has Georgian-glazed sashes. The cut stone urn at the corner of the roof balances that on number 38 at the other side of the adjacent recessed bank property. The property has been restored following bomb damage and has a period shop-front with a good hand-painted sign.

Recipient of grant: Mr. R. Paynter.

Grant assistance of £425 given towards: Rebuilding of chimney. Provision of new hand-painted shop sign.

Approximate cost of work: £1,275. Carried out in 1983.

Contractors: Malachy P. O'Neill & Sons, Dungannon.

42 Scotch Street, Armagh.

A two-bay, three-storey end-of-terrace, pre-1835 building. The roof is gabled and slated, walls are of coursed limestone and windows have Georgian-glazed sashes. The building has been well restored following bomb damage, the new period shop-front being of particularly high quality.

Recipient of grant: Mr. & Mrs. W. G. I. Wilson.

Commercial Buildings

42 Scotch Street, Armagh.

Grant assistance of £1,160 given towards: Additional cost of restoration because of historic significance of building.

Further financial assistance received from: Northern Ireland Office.

Approximate cost of work: £49,744. Carried out in 1980.

Work carried out using direct labour.

14 Dobbin Street, Armagh.

Part of a two-storey curved terrace believed to have been built to designs by Francis Johnston in 1811. The roof is slated and walls are of roughly squared limestone. The property has been restored following fire damage in 1981.

Recipient of grant: Armadale Veterinary Group.

Grant assistance of £2,300 given towards: Repairs to chimney. Re-roofing using natural slate. Replacement metal rainwater goods. Re-pointing of stonework. Replacement sash windows in original style. Replacement panelled entrance door. Internal re-plastering. Replacement timber floors. Installation of damp-proof solid floors.

Further financial assistance received from: Insurance company.

Approximate cost of work: £34,847. Carried out in 1981 and 1982.

Architect: J. Ross Campbell, Armagh.

Quantity Surveyors: J. B. Kingston & Partners, Armagh.

Work carried out using direct labour.

5 Downshire Place, Downshire Road, Newry.

A three-bay, two-storey, early-19th century end-of-terrace house in the manner of Thomas Duff. The roof is hipped and slated, walls are smooth rendered, windows have Georgian-glazed sashes and decorative rectangular fanlight is set in a pilastered and bracketed doorcase with flat entablature.

PHASE ONE

Recipient of grant: Mr. K. J. Kenny.

Grant assistance of £115 given towards: Repairs to chimney. Repairs to rainwater goods. Repairs to external render.

Approximate cost of work: £205. Carried out in 1980 and 1981.

Work carried out using direct labour.

PHASE TWO

Recipient of grant: Mr. J. Lynam.

Grant assistance of £6,100 given towards: Rebuilding of chimneys. Re-slating using natural slate. Replacement metal rainwater goods. External re-rendering. Sandblasting granite columns at entrance. Repairs to windows. External redecoration. Repairs to internal plasterwork.

Commercial Buildings

Repairs to timber floors. Installation of damp-proof solid floors. Provision of concrete lintels over structural openings.

Approximate cost of work: £21,284. Carried out in 1983.

Architects: J. Lynam & Associates, Newry.

Contractors: Reavey Bros. Ltd., Drumheriff, Whitecross.

2 and 4 Sugar Island, Newry.

A mid-19th century four-bay, three-storey building with Ionic columned twin-shop fronts and rendered upper floors.

Recipient of grant: Mr. D. McCarten.

Grant assistance of £1,002 given towards: Roof repairs. Repairs to external render. Restoration of shop frontage. Redecoration of remedial items.

Further financial assistance received from: Northern Ireland Office.

Approximate cost of work: £30,000. Carried out in 1976.

Agent: J. L. O'Hagan & Co., Newry.

Contractor: C. Meehan, Poyntzpass, Newry.

Northern Bank, 58 Hill Street, Newry.

A fine three-storey, Gothic-style building with tall gabled attics, occupying a corner site and built in the mid-19th century to designs by W. J. Watson. The attics and second floor have bracketted balconies, a cantilevered canted bay projects at first floor of the Hill Street elevation and also on this elevation the entrance is contained in an elaborate bracketted canopy. The plain sash windows are set in pointed arch openings. The

building has been extensively restored.

Recipient of grant: Northern Bank Ltd.

Grant assistance of £13,225 given towards: Repairs to leadwork. Repairs to rainwater goods. Repairs to metalwork of balconies. Repairs to stonework. Repairs to external render. Repairs to windows. Treatment of extensive dry rot. Professional fees.

Approximate cost of work: £88,982. Carried out in 1981.

Architects: John Neill and Partners, Belfast.

Quantity Surveyor: H. M. Blamphin, Belfast.

Contractors: Gilbert Ash (N.I.) Ltd., Warrenpoint.

22 Kilmorey Street, Newry.

Formerly two mid-19th century, two-storey Georgian town houses with a central coach arch now converted for use as architect's offices.

Recipients of grant: Messrs. J. Smith and P. J. Fay.

Grant assistance of £3,400 given towards: Rebuilding of chimney. Repairs to roof structure. Re-slating using natural slate. Replacement metal rainwater goods. Re-pointing and repair of stonework. Re-pointing of brickwork. External re-rendering. Replacement sash windows in original style. Replacement external doors in original style. Internal re-plastering. Redecoration of remedial items.

Approximate cost of work: £12,895. Carried out in 1982.

Architects: Smith & Fay, Newry.

Contractors: O'Hagan & Madden, Newry.

67 Bridge Street, Banbridge.

A three-bay, three-storey, brick-faced building built about 1840.

Recipient of grant: Mr. W. S. Vaughan.

Grant assistance of £2,961 given towards: Rebuilding of chimney Re-slating using natural slate. Replacement metal rainwater goods. Repairs to external render.

Approximate cost of work: £8,500. Carried out in 1982.

Architects: Rooney & McConville, Belfast.

Contractor: McParland & Gordon Ltd., Banbridge.

72 and 74 Main Street, Saintfield.

A plain, four-bay, two-storey terrace dwelling with a ground floor shop front to one side. The roof is slated, walls are smooth rendered and windows have vertically divided sashes.

Recipient of grant: Mr. D. A. Marshall.

PHASE ONE

Grant assistance of £250 given towards: Treatment of wood rot. Installation of damp-proof solid floors.

Approximate cost of work: £1,015. Carried out in 1981.

Contractor: Robert McKenzie, Saintfield.

PHASE TWO

Grant assistance of £640 given towards: Repairs to external render. Replacement window in original style. Treatment of wood rot and subsequent reinstatement. External redecoration.

Approximate cost of work: £2,395. Carried out in 1982.

Contractor: Robert McKenzie, Saintfield.

Commercial Buildings

4 and 6 Kildare Street, Ardglass.

Two pre-1833 three-storey properties with a small, three-light, shop window to one side. The roof is slated and gabled, walls are smooth rendered with raised quoins and windows have Georgian-glazed sashes.

Recipient of grant: Mrs. E. J. Byrne.

Grant assistance of £3,500 given towards: Repairs to chimneys. Roof repairs. Repairs to rainwater goods. Repairs to external render. Replacement sash windows in original style. Replacement external doors in original style. Repairs to internal plasterwork. Repairs to timber floors.

Approximate cost of work: £8,870. Carried out in 1980.

Contractor: Patrick K. Braniff, Downpatrick.

Las Vegas and the Pheasant Inn, 36 Main Street, Castlewellan.

A three-storey building occupying a corner site. The roof is hipped and slated, walls are smooth rendered with moulded details and windows are paired and have plain sashes, segmentally-headed to the ground and second floors. A corbelled octagonal turret is located on the corner.

Recipient of grant: S. P. Stranney & Co.

Grant assistance of £425 was given towards: Replacement shop windows in an appropriate style.

Approximate cost of work: £1,275. Carried out in 1982.

Contractor: P. & M. O'Hare, Ballynahinch.

24 Main Street, Hillsborough.

A wide two-storey terrace house built before 1833. The roof is slated, walls are roughcast and first floor windows have plain sashes.

Recipient of grant: Mr. P. Sigaroudinia.

Grant assistance of £1,340 given towards: Re-slating using natural slate. External re-rendering. Repairs to windows. Replacement panelled entrance door. Repair of railings. Redecoration of remedial items.

Approximate cost of work: £5,767. Carried out in 1979.

Architect: Peter Crowther & Associates, Belfast.

Contractor: H. & S. Press Ltd., Belfast.

32 Main Street, Hillsborough.

A three-bay, three-storey red-brick terrace house with a slightly convex front, Georgian-glazed sash windows, good plain doorcase and coach arch.

Recipient of grant: Mr. D. R. S. Kingen.

Grant assistance of £605 given towards: Repairs to chimneys. Roof repairs. Re-pointing of brickwork. Repairs to windows.

Approximate cost of work: £1,913. Carried out in 1980.

Contractors: E. Wilkinson & Sons, Hillsborough.

Trevor House, 9 The Square, Hillsborough.

A three-bay, three-storey late-18th century house with basement on the south side of the Square. The roof is slated and gabled, walls are of rendered rubble with raised quoins, windows have Georgian-glazed sashes and the panelled entrance door with semi-circular fanlight is approached by steps. Railings protect the basement.

Recipient of grant: Mr. J. B. Emerson.

Grant assistance of £550 given towards: Replacement sash windows in original style. Damp-proofing of front wall. Repairs to internal plasterwork. Strengthening of timber ground floor. Installation of damp-proof solid floors in basement.

Approximate cost of work: £2,627. Carried out in 1981.

Architects: Brian Emerson Associates, Hillsborough.

Contractors: Lesmar Developments Ltd., Hillsborough.

G. & H. Bell Ltd., 4 and 6 Lisburn Street, Hillsborough.

A three-storey block of shops with slated gabled roof, roughcast walls, Georgian-glazed sash windows and an asymmetrically positioned doorway between shopfronts with a carved canopy over.

Recipient of grant: G. & H. Bell Ltd.

Grant assistance of £2,575 given towards: Repairs to external render. Stabilisation of front wall. Replacement of sash windows in original style. Replacement panelled entrance door. Provision of new shop window to match existing traditional window. Repairs to internal plasterwork.

Approximate cost of work: £8,885. Carried out in 1979 and 1980.

Architects: Hobart & Heron, Belfast (part service).

Contractors: Lesmar Developments Ltd., Hillsborough.

Northern Bank, Main Street, Bangor.

A two-storey building built in 1780 as a market house. The main front has five bays of which the central three project slightly and are surmounted by

Commercial Buildings

The Northern Bank, Main Street, Bangor.

a pediment containing a clock in the tympanum. The slated roofs are concealed behind a balustraded parapet. Walls are smooth rendered with moulded details. Windows to the first floor are square-headed and have Georgian-glazed sashes and to the ground floor have semi-circular heads. The building has been extensively restored.

Recipient of grant: Northern Bank Ltd.

Grant assistance of £20,000 given towards: Treatment of extensive dry rot. Rebuilding of chimney. Repairs to roof structure. Re-slating using natural slate. Replacement leadwork. External re-rendering. External redecoration. Installation of silicone injection damp-proof course. Professional fees.

Approximate cost of work: £86,986. Carried out in 1979.

Architects: Brian Emerson Associates, Hillsborough.

Quantity Surveyors: W. H. Stephens & Sons, Belfast.

Contractor: William Dowling Ltd., Belfast.

Roof work by: Thomas S. Dixon & Co. Ltd., Belfast.

Timber treatment by: Protim Services, Lisburn.

Damp-proof course by: Alexander Greer Ltd., Lurgan.

Painting by: McBurney & Cowan, Belfast.

33 Shore Road, Holywood.

A two-storey 19th century terrace property. The roof is slated, walls are smooth rendered, windows are tripartite, with Georgian glazing, and the panelled entrance door is flanked by narrow pilasters supporting a flat cornice hood. A square coachway leads to the rear of the property. The house has been successfully converted for use as offices.

Commercial Buildings

Recipient of grant: Mr. J. D. Warwick.

Grant assistance of £9,000 given towards: Rebuilding of chimneys. Re-roofing using natural slate. External re-rendering. Replacement sash windows in original style. Internal re-plastering. Replacement timber floors. Professional fees.

Approximate cost of work: £27,851. Carried out in 1981.

Architect: Alan James Jones, Craigavad.

Contractor: H. S. Warwick, Ltd., Holywood.

16 and 17 The Square, Portaferry.

An important three-bay, three-storey building built about 1850 and saved from almost total dereliction when restored in the early eighties. Walls are rendered with moulded dressings and rise to an ornate parapet. Windows are tripartite to the upper floors with Georgian-glazed sashes. The entrance door is set within an Ionic columned porch.

Recipient of grant: Mr. & Mrs. J. D. McDermot.

Grant assistance of £1,540 given towards: Repairs to chimneys. Re-modelling of parapet gutter. Repairs to external render. Repairs to windows. Replacement panelled entrance door. Re-positioning of electricity supply cables.

Approximate cost of work: £4,864. Carried out in 1981.

Work carried out using direct labour.

Painting by: Thomas Adair, Kircubbin.

35 Market Square, Portaferry.

A two-storey terrace property built before 1834. The roof is slated and has a projecting dormer, walls are smooth

16 and 17 The Square, Portaferry.

Commercial Buildings

rendered and windows have moulded architraves and plain sashes.

Recipient of grant: Mr. & Mrs. J. Birch.

Grant assistance of £170 given towards: Roof repairs. Replacement metal rainwater goods. External re-rendering. Replacement sash windows in original style. Redecoration of remedial items. Signwriting to shopfront.

Further financial assistance received from: Northern Ireland Housing Executive.

Approximate cost of work: £1,959. Carried out in 1980.

Contractor: Coleman Bros., Portaferry.

16 Warren Road, Donaghadee.

A good five-bay by six-bay, L-shaped, two-storey, mid-19th century house. Walls are rendered, windows have Georgian-glazed sashes and the entrances are offset in a fine stone door surround.

Recipient of grant: Mr. D. R. Patterson.

Grant assistance of £3,400 given towards: Repairs to chimneys. Repairs to roof structure. Re-slating using natural slate. Repairs to external render. Repairs to windows. Replacement external doors in original style. Repairs to internal plasterwork. Repairs to timber floors. Installation of damp-proof solid floors.

Approximate cost of work: £10,641. Carried out in 1981 and 1982.

Contractor: Century Construction Co., Bangor.

29 High Street, Donaghadee.

A four-bay, two-storey late-Georgian end-of-terrace property. The roof is tiled with modern pantiles fortunately largely hidden by a parapet. The walls

are smooth rendered. At ground floor the panelled entrance door, with semi-circular fanlight is set in a doorcase with open pediment, to one side of the frontage with a Palladian window to the other side with a normal Georgian sash window positioned between the two. At first floor the four Georgian-paned sash windows are equally spaced. The house is fronted by good cast-iron spear headed railings.

Recipient of grant: Miss E. Craig.

Grant assistance of £2,057 given towards: Reconstruction of return building at rear of property. Lining of parapet gutter with glass-reinforced plastic.

Approximate cost of work: £6,092. Carried out in 1981 and 1982.

Architects: Dragon Tower Architects, Donaghadee.

Contractor: Orion Construction Ltd., Greyabbey.

Repairs to gutter by: Timbercure Services Ltd., Lisburn.

23 and 25 High Street, Donaghadee.

A two-storey, late-Georgian double-house composition which has been restored from dereliction by the present owner. Each house is two-bays wide, rendered, with two tripartite windows upstairs and a single tripartite window on the ground floor next to the front door which has a rusticated stone surround. Between the two doors is a coach arch leading to the rear of the premises.

Recipient of grant: Mr. J. Shields.

Grant assistance of £12,000 given towards: Rebuilding of chimneys. Re-roofing using natural slate. Replacement metal rainwater goods. External re-rendering. Repairs to windows.

Internal re-plastering. Repairs to timber floors. Installation of damp-proof solid floors.

Approximate cost of work: £80,000. Carried out in 1979 and 1980.

Work carried out using direct labour.

12 The Parade, Donaghadee.

A five-bay, three-storey mid-Georgian rendered house with central doorway with elliptical fanlight.

Recipient of grant: Mr. M. W. Connell.

Grant assistance of £4,000 given towards: Re-slating using natural slate. Replacement metal rainwater goods. External re-rendering. Replacement sash windows in original style. Restoration of doorcase. Re-laying of stone tiled floor in hall. Repairs to timber floors.

Approximate cost of work: £15,000. Carried out from 1979 to 1983.

Architect: Brian T. Knox, Bangor (part service only).

Contractors: K. & S. Builders, Donaghadee and Nat. McKibben, Donaghadee.

2 William Street, Newtownards.

A three-bay, two-storey, mid-19th century, end-of-terrace property. The roof is slated and gabled, walls are of sandstone, windows have Georgian-glazed sashes and the panelled entrance door is offset to one side under a semi-circular decorative fanlight and has a cut stone surround.

Recipient of grant: Mr. A. J. P. Bradley.

Grant assistance of £884 given towards: Treatment of dry rot and subsequent reinstatement. Professional fees.

Approximate cost of work: £2,975. Carried out in 1981.

Agent: Henry L. Taggart, Donaghadee.

Contractor: Amberson & Kennedy Ltd., Newtownards.

Timber treatment by: Timbertreat Services Ltd., Belfast.

69 Court Street, Newtownards.

A four-bay, two-storey, mid-19th century terrace property. The roof is slated, frontage is smooth rendered, windows have Georgian-glazed sashes and the panelled entrance door with sidelights is set under a segmental fanlight. A coach arch leads to the rear.

Recipient of grant: Mrs. V. R. Morrison.

Grant assistance of £1,820 given towards: Repairs to rainwater goods. Repairs to windows. Repairs to panelled entrance door. External redecoration. Treatment of wood rot. Installation of silicone-injection damp-proof course. Repairs to internal plasterwork. Repairs to timber floors. Installation of damp-proof solid floors. Repairs to staircase.

Approximate cost of work: £5,990. Carried out in 1982.

Architect: Mervyn Walker Morrison, Newtownards.

Contractor: William D. Jordan & Son, Saintfield.

Damp-proof course by: Jack Turner, Son & Co. (Construction) Ltd., Belfast.

Painting by: John O'Lone, Newtownards.

Regent House, Regent Street, Newtownards.

A six-bay, by four-bay, two-storey house built about 1820 in a neo-Greek style. Formerly Regent House School

the house is now a car showroom. The hipped and slated roof is concealed behind a parapet and cornice. The walls of the south front are of ashlar Scrabo stone and the central two bays are set forward slightly and are fronted by a single-storey portico with two pairs of fluted Ionic Columns. The portico does not contain the entrance (which is on the west side) but a three-light window composition. All other windows have Georgian-glazed sashes and moulded architraves. A fine glazed cupola lights the main staircase.

Recipient of grant: M. Ferguson (Newtownards) Ltd.

Grant assistance of £8,000 given towards: Repairs to chimneys. Treatment of extensive dry rot. Repairs to roof structure. Repairs to leadwork. Repairs to stone parapet including replacement of cramps and re-pointing. Repairs to internal plasterwork. Professional fees.

Approximate cost of work: £25,103. Carried out in 1977 and 1978.

Architect: Henry L. Taggart, Donaghadee.

Contractor: B. Mullan & Sons, Ballygowan.

Timber treatment by: Timbertreat Services Ltd., Belfast.

Fermanagh Times Office, 14 Townhall Street, Enniskillen.

A three-bay, three-storey building with an elaborate high Victorian rendered facade.

Recipient of grant: Mr. & Mrs. R. H. Ritchie.

Grant assistance of £830 given towards: Taking down defective cornice at roof level and replacing with fibreglass replica.

Approximate cost of work: £2,729. Carried out in 1979.

Architect: Richard H. Pierce, Enniskillen.

Contractor: Irvine Bros., Enniskillen.

Painting by: R. W. Molloy & Sons, Enniskillen.

Star Factory, Foyle Road, Londonderry.

A small but impressive factory built in sandstone to a design by Daniel Conroy in 1899. The main facade is ten windows wide and four-storeys high with a squat central clock tower. Each window has a segmental head. Now sadly derelict.

Recipient of grant: Bayview Garments Ltd.

Grant assistance of £420 given towards: Repairs to rainwater goods.

Approximate cost of work: £974. Carried out in 1980.

Contractor: John Hutton, Londonderry.

Austin's Department Store, The Diamond, Londonderry.

Rebuilt after a fire in 1906 to a design by M. A. Robinson in an imaginative Edwardian Baroque style. A corner tower terminates in a copper-covered cupola.

Recipient of grant: Austin & Co. Ltd.

Grant assistance of £746 given towards: Repairs to balconies. Low pressure sand blasting of rendered exterior detail. Part of a general face-lift scheme.

Further financial assistance received from: Face-lift Scheme.

Approximate cost of work: £9,392. Carried out in 1979.

Commercial Buildings

Architects: Liam McCormick & Partners, Londonderry.

Contractor: Cleanstone Co., Dungannon.

Balcony repairs by: City Asphalt, Londonderry.

15, The Diamond, Londonderry.

A seven-bay, three-storey building with roof concealed behind a decorative balustrade and projecting bracketed cornice. The walls are smooth rendered, lined on ground floor and with moulded strings, quoins and architraves. Windows generally have plain sashes and the panelled entrance door with plain rectangular fanlight has a moulded architrave and segmental canopy supported on console brackets.

Recipient of grant: Troy Estate Ltd.

Grant assistance of £120 given towards: External redecoration.

Painting by: M. A. White, Londonderry.

6 Shipquay Street, Londonderry.

A three-storey brick-faced Georgian terrace house built about 1770.

Recipient of grant: Mr. J. Mulheron.

Grant assistance of £235 given towards: External redecoration.

Approximate cost of work: £660. Carried out in 1982.

Painting by: D. V. Ferry, Londonderry.

Allied Irish Bank, 15–17 Shipquay Street, Londonderry.

The original three-storey building on this site, built to designs by E. J. Toye in 1896, was threatened with total demolition as part of the comprehensive redevelopment of the

Austin's Department Store, Londonderry.

Commercial Buildings

Allied Irish Bank, Shipquay Street, Londonderry.

surrounding area. However, on the advice of the Historic Building's Council, the interior was gutted and rebuilt and the Victorian facade has been preserved, improved and extended over an adjoining property and now makes an important contribution to the streetscape. The completed scheme received a Civic Trust commendation in 1982.

Recipient of grant: Allied Irish Banks Ltd.

Grant assistance of £30,000 given towards: Provision of temporary steel work to support facade. Re-roofing using natural slate. External re-rendering. Replacement panelled entrance doors. Replacement windows in original style. External redecoration.

Approximate cost of work: £581,641. Carried out between 1978 and 1979.
Architects: F. M. Corr & Associates, Belfast and Londonderry.
Quantity Surveyor: J. J. Riordan, Belfast.
Structural Engineers: Dr. I. G. Doran & Partners, Belfast.
Contractor: C. V. McWilliams Ltd., Londonderry.

Northern Bank, Shipquay Place, Londonderry.

Built in 1866 to a palazzo-style by Thomas Turner. Occupies an end of island site opposite the Guildhall. Three-storeys high with a six-bay frontage and four-bay returns to either side. Walls of Scottish sandstone with rusticated ground floor and ashlar upper floors. Ground floor windows have semi-circular heads and first floor windows have Roman aedicules with curved pediments. Above is a strong entablature of frieze and cornice surmounted by balustrading.
Recipient of grant: Northern Bank Ltd.
Grant assistance of £1,000 given towards: Treatment of wood rot.
Approximate cost of work: £3,051. Carried out in 1980.
Architects: Dalzell & Campbell, Coleraine, Portrush, Belfast and Londonderry.
Timber treatment by: Rentokil Ltd., Belfast.

Ivy House, 34 Strand Road, Londonderry.

A fine four-storey, four-bay, brick-faced Georgian building built around 1855. The panelled entrance door is flanked by Doric columns and has a simple fanlight over.

Recipient of grant: Robert Keys Ltd.

Grant assistance of £478 given towards: Re-pointing of brickwork. Repairs to windows. External redecoration.

Further financial assistance received from: Face-lift Scheme.

Contractor: Derry Construction Ltd., Londonderry.

Painting by: J. Toland, Londonderry.

Brickwork repairs: Alexander Greer Ltd., Lurgan.

18 Crawford Square, Londonderry.

A pre-1871 three-storey terrace house paired with its neighbour. The facade is rendered with a two-storey canted bay, windows are plain sashed with segmented heads and the panelled entrance door and fanlight are set under a semi-circular archivolt supported on console brackets.

Recipient of grant: The Eagle Investment Trust Ltd. and B. M. Wright & Partners.

Grant assistance of £110 given towards: External redecoration.

Approximate cost of work: £385. Carried out in 1980.

Painting by: M. A. White, Londonderry.

13 Queen Street, Londonderry.

A dignified three-storey, three-bay brick Georgian terrace house with attic and basement, built before 1873. The panelled entrance door, flanked by columns with fanlight over, is set in an elliptical arched opening and approached by a flight of steps. A slated dormer projects from the roof.

Recipient of grant: Lombard & Ulster Banking Ltd.

Grant assistance of £6,100 given towards: Roof repairs. Repairs to rainwater goods. Re-pointing of brickwork. Repairs to windows. Replacement external doors in original style. Repairs to entrance steps and railings. Treatment of wood rot. Repairs to internal plasterwork. Repairs to decorative plasterwork. Repairs to staircase.

Approximate cost of work: £39,544. Carried out in 1980 and 1981.

Architects: McCormick, Tracey, Mullarkey, Londonderry.

Contractor: Samuel Anthony & Sons Ltd., Londonderry.

Timber treatment by: Rentokil Ltd., Belfast.

Northern Bank, Shipquay Place, Londonderry.

31

Commercial Buildings

13 Queen Street, Londonderry.

Painting by: P. B. McLaughlin, Londonderry.

14 Clarendon Street, Londonderry.

A fine, three-storey, mid-19th century red brick terrace house with Georgian-glazed sash windows and panelled entrance door with flanking columns and fanlight set in an elliptically arched opening.

Recipient of grant: Mr. B. Kearney.

Grant assistance of £590 given towards: Cleaning and re-pointing brickwork. Replacement sash windows in original style. Redecoration of remedial items.

Approximate cost of work: £1,942. Carried out in 1980 and 1981.

Contractor: R.Q. Construction, Londonderry.

Brick cleaning by: Derry Sandblasting & Scaffolding Co. Ltd., Londonderry.

Painting by: Dermot Coyle, Londonderry.

83–89 Main Street, Garvagh.

A thirteen-bay, three-storey terrace with modern ground-floor shop-fronts. Walls are of blackstone with red brick dressings. First and second-floor windows are mainly Georgian-glazed sashes.

Recipient of grant: Mr. A. S. Clyde.

Grant assistance of £1,920 given towards: Re-slating using natural slate to front slopes and asbestos-cement to rear.

Approximate cost of work: £11,812. Carried out in 1979.

Contractor: S. J. Linton, Garvagh.

15 Kingsgate Street, Coleraine.

A late-19th century three-storey rendered terrace property with modern ground floor shopfront and plain sash windows with moulded architraves to the upper floors.

Recipient of grant: Messrs. E. F. W. and P. C. Orr.

Grant assistance of £2,250 given towards: Repairs to roof structure. Re-slating using natural slate to front slope. Replacement metal rainwater goods. Treatment of wood rot. Repairs to internal plasterwork.

Approximate cost of work: £14,606. Carried out in 1981 and 1982.

Architects: W. & M. Given, Coleraine.

Contractor: J. S. Dunlop, Ballymoney.

Timber treatment by: Timbercare (N.I.) Ltd., Lisburn.

2 Lodge Road, Coleraine.

An end-of-terrace three-storey rendered house with dormered attics built after 1831.

Recipient of grant: PDC Estates.

PHASE ONE – REPAIRS

Grant assistance of £2,030 given towards: External re-rendering. Replacement sash windows in original style. Treatment of wood rot. Repairs to internal plasterwork. Repairs to internal joinery work.

Approximate cost of work: £6,638. Carried out in 1979 and 1980.

Contractor: L. M. Acheson (Construction) Ltd., Coleraine.

Timber treatment by: Radication Ltd., Dunmurry, Belfast.

PHASE TWO – REPAIRS

Grant assistance of £2,530 given towards: Re-slating using natural slate. Rebuilding of dormer window. Repairs to internal plasterwork. Redecoration of remedial items.

Commercial Buildings

Approximate cost of work: £7,590. Carried out in 1982.

Contractor: E. Mooney, Coleraine.

6 Lodge Road, Coleraine.

A three-story rendered house built after 1831.

Recipient of grant: Mr. F. H. Wright.

Grant assistance of £690 given towards: Repairs to windows. Treatment of wood rot. Repairs to internal plasterwork. Repairs to timber floors. Redecoration of remedial items.

Approximate cost of work: £2,077. Carried out in 1979.

Quantity Surveyors: F. H. Wright & Partners, Coleraine.

Contractor: William Harte, Coleraine.

Timber treatment by: Rentokil Ltd., Belfast.

28 Bridge Street, and 2 Hanover Place, Coleraine.

Part of a four-storey Georgian-glazed corner block now rendered but originally brick-faced.

Recipient of grant: Mr. J. O'Kane.

Grant assistance of £11,320 given towards: Roof repairs. Repairs to external render. Repairs to windows. External redecoration.

Approximate cost of work: £3,632. Carried out in 1980.

Contractor: William Scott, Bushmills.

Painting by: Paintall Decorators, Londonderry.

Northern Bank, Old Market House, High Street, Moneymore.

The bank occupies one wing of the Market House built in 1818 to designs by Jesse Gibson, the Drapers' Company's surveyor. It is the least sophisticated element in the Company's 20-year redevelopment of the town. The building consists of a three-bay, crudely pedimented central block surmounted by a Victorian bell turret, linked by single-bay, two-storey sections to two four-bay blocks each with Tuscan columned porches approached by stone steps.

Recipient of grant: Northern Bank Ltd.

Grant assistance of £12,900 given towards: Re-roofing using natural slate. Restoration of parapet wall and stonework generally. Replacement sash windows in original style. Restoration of railings. Treatment of extensive dry rot. Installation of damp-proof course. Internal re-plastering. Provision of reinforced concrete first floor. Installation of damp-proof solid floors.

Approximate cost of work: £83,000. Carried out in 1978 and 1979.

Architects: Smyth Cowser & Partners, Belfast (now Brian Emerson Associates, Hillsborough).

Quantity Surveyors: Ferris, Craig & Moore, Belfast.

Contractor: Benson Bros. Ltd., Cookstown.

Northern Bank, Moneymore.

Old Market House, High Street, Moneymore.

Part of the Market House built in 1818 to designs by Jesse Gibson, the Drapers' Company's surveyor. It is the least sophisticated element in the company's 20-year redevelopment of the town. The building consists of a three-bay crudely pedimented central block surmounted by a Victorian bell turret, linked by single-bay, two-storey sections to two four-bay blocks each with Tuscan columned porches approached by stone steps.

Recipient of grant: The Manor of Drapers Charity.

Grant assistance of £1,790 given towards: Re-roofing using natural slate. Replacement sash windows in original style. Treatment of extensive dry rot. Internal re-plastering. Provision of reinforced concrete first floor. Installation of damp-proof solid floors.

Approximate cost of work: £6,680. Carried out in 1979.

Architects: Smyth Cowser & Partners, Belfast (now Brian Emerson Associates, Hillsborough).

Quantity Surveyors: Ferris, Craig & Moore, Belfast.

Contractors: Benson Bros. Ltd., Cookstown.

Public Houses, Hotels and Restaurants

The Crown Bar, 46 Great Victoria Street, Belfast.

A superb High Victorian public house, possibly one of the finest of its kind in the British Isles. The slated roof is concealed behind a parapet, the upper floors are rendered and have four truncated Corinthian pilasters, the ground floor is a wonderful profusion of coloured glass and tile. The interior is exceptionally rich, with moulded and brightly coloured tiles, carved and panelled snugs, marble bar top, glittering mirrors, arcaded backbar and a high relief patterned ceiling supported by hexagonal wooden columns with carved Corinthian capitals and feathered ornament. The Crown has been fully restored to its former brilliance including the installation of gas lighting.

Recipient of grant: The National Trust.

Grant assistance of £61,250 given towards: Repairs to chimneys. Roof repairs. Repairs to leadwork. Repairs to rainwater goods. Repairs to external render. Replacement windows in original style. Replacement decorative glazing. Repair and replica replacement of decorative tiling. External redecoration. External sign writing. Repairs to internal plasterwork. Reinstatement of gas lighting. Professional fees.

Approximate cost of work: £150,481. Carried out from 1979 to 1981.

Architects: Robert McKinstry & Melvyn Brown, Belfast.

Quantity Surveyors: Hastings & Baird, Belfast.

Contractor: H. & J. Martin Ltd., Belfast.

Painting by: John Hamilton Ltd., Newtownabbey.

Decorative glass by: Joseph McManus Ltd., Belfast.

Decorative tiling made by: Jackfield Tile Workshop, Ironbridge, Shropshire.

Gas lighting by: Calor Kosangas Limited, Belfast.

Decorative plasterwork by: Nicholl Plaster Mouldings, Belfast.

Upholstery by: Edwards Upholsterers, Belfast.

Brasswork by: James Healy Ltd., Dublin.

Wood carving by: Grace Church Furniture, Moneyrea.

The Gamble Bar, 19 Gamble Street, Belfast

A three-storey, rendered and painted building with foliated pilastered pub front and aediculed windows on the upper floors.

Recipient of grant: Mr. B. Kerr.

Grant assistance of £2,320 given towards: Re-slating using natural slate. Replacement leadwork. Replacement metal rainwater goods. Repairs to external render. External redecoration.

Approximate cost of work: £8,317. Carried out in 1980.

Contractor: Hugh Lavery, Belfast.

Roof work by: V. Parker & Co., Belfast.

Painting by: Sullivan Bros., Belfast.

The Windsor Guest House, 67–69 Main Street, Portrush.

Two three-storey villas with attics and canted bay windows.

Recipient of grant: Mrs. E. Knox.

PHASE ONE – REPAIRS

Grant assistance of £880 given towards:

The Crown Bar,
46 Gt. Victoria Street, Belfast.

Roof repairs. Repairs to external render. Repairs to bay windows.
Approximate cost of work: £2,666. Carried out in 1979 and 1980.
Contractor: S. M. Oliver, Coleraine.

PHASE TWO – RESTORATION

Grant assistance of £2,190 given towards: Removal of shopfront and restoration of bay to match adjoining property.
Approximate cost of work: £6,570. Carried out in 1981.
Architects: Dalzell & Campbell, Coleraine/Portrush/Balfast/Londonderry.
Contractor: J. Elliott, Portrush.
Painting by: Malcolm Elliott, Portrush.

Magheramorne House, Larne.

A major conversion and extension of an old persons house to form a hotel. The project involved conversion of the main house and stable block and restoration of the formal garden. It was complicated by fire damage which occurred during the contract.
Recipient of grant: Atlantic Steam Navigation Company.
Grant assistance of £32,400 given towards: In the main house; Repairs to chimneys. Repairs to roof structure. Re-slating using natural slate. Replacement leadwork. Repairs to stonework. Repairs to windows and replacement sash windows in original style. Treatment of wood rot. Installation of electro-osmotic damp-proof course. Internal re-plastering. Installation of damp-proof solid floors in basement. Professional fees. In the stables: Repairs to chimneys. Roof repairs. Replacement leadwork. Replacement metal rainwater goods. Repairs to

stonework. Treatment of wood rot. Repairs to timber floors. Installation of damp-proof solid floors. Professional fees. In the grounds: Restoration of the formal gardens.
Further financial assistance received from: Insurance company and from a Department of Commerce Grant.
Approximate cost of work: £905,401. Carried out in 1980 and 1981.
Architects and Structural Engineers: Brian A. Morton & Partners, London and Milton Keynes.
Quantity Surveyors: Henry Cooper & Sons, Milton Keynes.

PRELIMINARY INVESTIGATIVE CONTRACT

Contractors: McLaughlin & Harvey, Belfast and Edward Wilson & Co., Ltd. (Steeplejacks), Newtownabbey.

MAIN CONTRACT

Contractor: Martin & Hamilton Ltd., Ballymena.
Timber treatment and damp-proof course by: Radication Ltd., Dunmurry, Belfast.

The Thatch Inn, 57 Main Street, Broughshane.

A two-storey, six-bay, 18th century thatched house with Georgian glazed windows.
Recipient of grant: Mrs. I. Graham.
Grant assistance of £2,070 given towards: Repairs to thatch.
Approximate cost of work: £2,675. Carried out in 1978.
Thatching by: Gerald Agnew, Ahoghill.

Crosskey's Inn, 40 Grange Road, Toomebridge.

An 'L' shaped roughcast and thatched inn built before 1832.

PHASE ONE

Recipient of grant: Mr. J. Stinson.
Grant assistance of £2,000 given towards: Re-thatching.
Approximate cost of work: £4,208. Carried out in 1978 and 1979.
Work carried out using direct labour.

Crosskey's Inn, Toomebridge.

Public Houses, Hotels and Restaurants

PHASE TWO
Recipient of grant: Mr. E. Stinson.
Grant assistance of £469 given towards:
Repairs to thatch.
Approximate cost of work: £1,407.
Carried out in 1982.
Thatching by: Gerald Agnew, Ahoghill.

Montgomery's Shop, 25–29 High Street, Ballymena.

Boasting what was arguably one of the best remaining shop fronts of its period in Ireland, Montgomery's shop was threatened with total demolition as part of the major redevelopment of the town centre in the early 1980's. However the frontage was eventually saved by being carefully dismantled and reconstructed on the same site now providing an important link with the past at one entrance to a modern shopping precinct. The frontage is of basalt with brick dressings, five bays wide and three storeys high. The shop front is of finely detailed classical design consisting of a long entablature supported on five irregularly spaced fluted Ionic columns. Between the columns are tripartite Georgian windows, a fine panelled door in a curved segmental recess, and the entrance door with curved glazing to either side. The upper floors have Georgian glazed sash windows.

Recipient of grant: W. C. S. Holdings (N.I.) Ltd.
Grant assistance of £55,000 given towards:
Reconstruction of frontage.
Professional fees.
Approximate cost of work: £200,760.
Carried out in 1982.
Architects: Design Service Associates, Belfast.

Montgomery's Shop, Ballymena.

Quantity Surveyors: Bailie Connor Partnership, Belfast.
Structural Engineers: Armstrong & Shaw, Belfast.
Contractor: R. E. Linton & Co. (Construction) Ltd., Coleraine.

Prospect House, Woodburn Road, Carrickfergus.

A two-storey house with attics and half-basement, built about 1760. The roof is slated and gabled with hipped projections over full-height central bays, walls are of roughly coursed and galleted blackstone blocks and windows have Georgian-glazed sashes to first floor and plain casements to ground floor. The panelled entrance door with flanking Doric columns and side-lights is set under a massive semi-circular fanlight and approached by sweeping stone steps with cast-iron railings. Over the entrance a Palladian

window gives access to a cantilevered wrought-iron balcony. The house has been converted for use as a licensed restaurant.

Recipient of grant: Basket Developments Ltd.

Grant assistance of £3,000 given towards: Roof repairs. Repairs to windows. Repairs to internal plasterwork. Repairs to decorative plasterwork. Repairs to timber floors. Installation of damp-proof solid floors in basement. Repairs to internal panelled doors. Repairs to staircase.

Approximate cost of work: £19,764. Carried out in 1975 and 1976.

Architects: John Neil & Partners, Belfast.

Quantity Surveyors: Hastings & Baird, Belfast.

Contractor: McKnight Construction Co. Ltd., Holywood.

Dufferin Arms, 35 High Street, Killyleagh.

A fine three-bay, two-storey rendered building built about 1830. The ground floor is rusticated with moulded details.

Recipient of grant: Miss S. Orr.

Grant assistance of £160 given towards: External redecoration.

Approximate cost of work: £886. Carried out in 1982.

Painting by: S. W. Taylor, Downpatrick.

Castlewellan Castle, Castlewellan.

Built between 1856 and 1858 by Lord Annesley to designs by William Burns, the castle is of three- and four-storeys with square and round towers and a profusion of turrets and gabled

Castlewellan Castle, Castlewellan.

Public Houses, Hotels and Restaurants

dormers. The roof is of graded slate, walls are of squared random granite blocks with ashlar dressings, castellated parapets and crow-stepped gables and windows mainly have plain sashes. The castle is cut into the hillside with a terrace on the south side overlooking the lake and mountains. It was rescued from dereliction in the early 1970's when it found a new use as a Christian conference centre.

Recipient of grant: Cloverley Hall Conference Centre.

Grant assistance of £19,000 given towards: Repairs to chimneys. Roof repairs. Repairs to leadwork. Re-pointing of stonework. Replacement sash windows in original style. Treatment of wood rot. Repairs to internal plasterwork. Repairs to timber floors. Restoration of main staircase. Restoration of detailed carving and joinery in Library.

Further financial assistance received from: Department of Commerce.

Approximate cost of work: £179,900. Carried out from 1975 to 1981.

Architects: McCormick & Co., Belfast and Lurgan.

Quantity Surveyor: William H. Hughes, Belfast.

Contractor: Joseph McClune & Son, Dundrum.

Work carried out using direct labour.

Roof work by: E. Wilson & Co., Whiteabbey.

Timber treatment by: Timbertreat Services Ltd., Belfast.

The Station Building, Station Square, Helen's Bay.

A single-storey station building built in 1863 in an exuberant Scottish baronial style to designs by Benjamin Ferrey for the Baron Dufferin and

Clandeboye. The roof is slated with crow-stepped gables. The walls are of rubble masonry locally quarried with pointed, lancet windows and moulded arches, all with limestone dressings. A squat circular tower occupies the north-west corner of the building, this originally had a conical roof which sadly is now missing. The station, no longer used by Northern Ireland Railways, has been leased for use as a restaurant.

Recipient of grant: Mr. J. A. McKenna.

Grant assistance of £41 given towards: Roof repairs. Repairs to rainwater goods.

Approximate cost of work: £94. Carried out in 1976.

Contractor: R. A. Gillespie, Helen's Bay.

Portaferry Hotel, The Strand, Portaferry.

Two two-storey properties, probably both 18th century, which have been combined to form the hotel. The roofs are slated, walls are rendered and windows (tripartite in the house to the south) have Georgian-glazed sashes. The hotel has been extensively refurbished.

Recipient of grant: Mr. & Mrs. J. Herlihy.

Grant assistance of £5,000 given towards: Repairs to chimneys. Re-slating using natural slate. Replacement metal rainwater goods. Repairs to external render. Replacement sash windows in original style. Replacement external doors in original style. External redecoration. Professional fees.

Further financial assistance received from: Department of Economic Development.

Approximate cost of work: £23,118. Carried out in 1982.

Architects: Diarmind Herlihy & Associates, Dublin.

Contractor: Joseph McClune & Son, Dundrum.

Painting by: Brian Kelly, Kircubbin.

Stable Block, Blessingbourne, Fivemiletown.

The stable block belonging to a large, well executed Elizabethan manor built in 1874 to the designs of F. P. Cockerell. The stables have been converted to provide self-catering flats.

Recipient of grant: Captain R. H. Lowry.

Grant assistance of £2,820 given towards: Re-slating using natural slate. Replacement metal rainwater goods. Repairs to external render. Replacement windows in original style. Repairs to stone dressings on outer elevation. Reinstatement of cobbled yard. Reconstruction of floors. Professional fees.

Further financial assistance received from: Department of Commerce.

Approximate cost of work: £45,533. Carried out in 1979.

Agent: Norman Coulter, Omagh.

Work carried out using direct labour.

The Parks, 31 Collon Lane, Shantallow, Londonderry.

A three-bay, one-and-a-half-storey mid-19th century house with classical rendered facade. Possibly designed by Stewart Gordon, the house incorporates an earlier building to the rear. It has now found a new use as a restaurant.

The Parks, Shantallow, Londonderry.

Recipient of grant: Mr. J. Lamberton.

Grant assistance of £2,330 given towards: Roof repairs. Rebuilding of chimneys. Repairs to rainwater goods. Insertion of new lintels over openings. Repairs to external render. Installation of electro-osmotic damp-proof course. Repairs to internal plasterwork. Redecoration of remedial items.

Approximate cost of work: £11,832. Carried out in 1978.

Work carried out using direct labour.

Damp-proof course by: Rentokil Ltd., Belfast.

Ballymaclary House, Magilligan.

Built in mid-18th century and described by Alistair Rowan as 'a charming and surprisingly well finished gentleman's house on a miniature scale.' The front elevation is of one-and-a-half-storeys and five bays wide. Walls are rendered but with fine sandstone detailing. The central bay projects slightly with the entrance door flanked by Ionic half columns, sash windows and Ionic pilasters all with entablature and central pediment over. The house has been restored and converted for use as a restaurant.

Recipient of grant: Mr. S. McLaughlin.

PHASE ONE

Grant assistance of £5,520 given towards: Repairs to chimneys. Repairs to stonework at entrance. Repairs to external render. Replacement panelled entrance door. Treatment of wood rot. Restoration of fine 18th century dog-leg staircase.

Approximate cost of work: £19,900. Carried out in 1976 and 1977.

Contractor: Tony McGarvey, Articlave, Castlerock.

Stone repair by: Alexander Greer Ltd., Lurgan.

PHASE TWO

Grant assistance of £1,600 given towards: Roof repairs. Replacement sash windows in original style. External redecoration. Repairs to internal plasterwork.

Approximate cost of work: £4,820. Carried out in 1979.

Contractor: Tony McGarvey, Articlave, Castlerock.

The Manor House, 30 Main Street, Moneymore.

A five-bay, three-storey classical house built about 1840. The central three bays of the rendered front project and rise to a balustrade while the end bays have solid parapets. Windows are plain sashes, tripartite on the end bays. The square porch contains a semi-circular arching opening. The building has been converted for use as a licensed restaurant.

Recipient of grant: Mr. J. Dunlop.

Grant assistance of £3,450 given towards: Rebuilding of chimneys. Roof repairs. Repairs to rainwater goods. Repairs to external render.

Approximate cost of work: £11,692. Carried out in 1982.

Architects: Dawson, Pentland & Kay, Magherafelt.

Contractor: McCullough Bros., Moneymore.

Roof work by: Roof Sealers (N.I.) Ltd., Magherafelt.

40

Public Houses, Hotels and Restaurants

Hanover House, Hanover Square, Coagh.

A five-bay, two-storey Georgian style house which has been converted for use as a restaurant. The roof is gabled and slated, walls are of blackstone with brick dressings, windows have Georgian-glazed sashes and the panelled entrance door with flanking pilasters is set under a semi-circular fanlight and moulded archivolt.

Recipient of grant: Mr. T. B. Gibson.

Grant assistance of £100 given towards: Preservative treatment of roof and floor timbers.

Approximate cost of work: £324. Carried out in 1978.

Agent: Trevor Morgan, Stewartstown.

Timber treatment by: Rentokil Ltd., Belfast.

Glenavon House Hotel, Drum Road, Cookstown.

A two-storey ashlar Victorian house carefully detailed in a restrained Italianate classical style.

Recipient of grant: Mr. P. J. McCullagh.

Grant assistance of £2,580 given towards: Repairs to roof and tower using natural slate.

Approximate cost of work: £7,740. Carried out in 1981.

Agent: Associated Architectural Consultants, Omagh.

Contractor: Peter Conway, Omagh.

The Artic Star, 1 Castle Lane, Caledon.

A two-storey stone Georgian building in keeping with the streetscape.

Recipient of grant: Mr. H. Donnelly.

Grant assistance of £3,180 given towards: Re-slating using natural slate. Replacement metal rainwater goods. Re-pointing of stonework. Replacement windows in original style. Replacement external doors in original style. Professional fees.

Approximate cost of work: £22,500. Carried out in 1979 and 1980.

Architect: Marshall & Ryan, Dungannon.

Contractor: Kevin Mohan, Castleshane, Co. Monaghan.

Hanover House, Coagh.

Educational Buildings

Union Theological College, Botanic Avenue, Belfast.

The main block was built from 1852 to 1855 to designs by Sir Charles Lanyon. Forming an appropriate vista stop to University Square the building is in a rather unusual Italianate style of two-storeys with a taller central portico with four massive attached Tuscan columns and a square attic above. The construction is of Scrabo stone, rusticated on the ground floor. Windows are square-headed to the first floor and to the ground floor have semi-circular heads with Venetian windows to the slightly projecting end bays. Behind the main block, the south wing was added by Young and Mackenzie in 1869 and the north wing and chapel by John Lanyon in 1878.

Recipient of grant: The Presbyterian Church in Ireland.

Grant assistance of £300 given towards: Roof repairs. Repairs to rainwater goods.

Approximate cost of work: £3,028. Carried out in 1981.

Contractor: Sloan Bros. (c) Ltd., Belfast.

38 and 40 University Road and 1 Mount Charles, Belfast.

The present building is virtually a reconstruction of the original four-bay, three-storey, rendered Italianate style block which stood on this site until demolition in 1978.

Recipient of grant: The Open University.

Grant assistance of £1,150 given towards: Provision of fibre-glass facsimile chimney stack.

Approximate cost of work: £2,373.

Carried out in 1982 and 1983.

Architects: Robert McKinstry & Melvyn Brown, Belfast.

Contractor: William Dowling Ltd., Belfast.

14 Upper Crescent, Belfast.

Two of ten, three-storey rendered houses in a concave row comprising the finest Neo-Classical terrace in Northern Ireland. The group was built in 1846 by James Corry possibly to designs by Charles Lanyon, the centre and ends are emphasised by attached giant order Corinthian columns and high balustraded attics.

Recipient of grant: The Queen's University of Belfast.

Grant assistance of £1,620 given towards: Rebuilding of chimneys.

Approximate cost of work: £4,866. Carried out in 1982.

Contractor: F. B. McKee Ltd., Belfast.

Elmwood Hall, Elmwood Avenue, Belfast.

Built in 1862 in a pleasantly eclectic style by the amateur architect John Corry, Elmwood Presbyterian Church was one of Northern Ireland's best High Victorian church designs. The arcaded facade in polychromatic freestone is Italianate in style and the tower, added in 1870, rises in three multi-columned stages to a French needle spire. The building has been successfully converted to a new use as a concert and examination hall. The phased restoration of the tower and spire by McLaughlin & Harvey was proceeding at the time of writing.

Recipient of grant: The Queen's University.

Elmwood Hall, Elmwood Avenue, Belfast.

Educational Buildings

PHASE ONE – TOWER AND SPIRE

Grant assistance of £1,000 given towards: Repairs to stonework. Repairs to wrought-iron work. Repairs to weathercock.

Approximate cost of work: £3,432. Carried out in 1975.

Architects: H. A. Patton & Partners, Bangor.

Quantity Surveyors: W. H. Stephens & Sons, Belfast.

Contractor: E. Wilson & Co., Newtownabbey.

PHASE TWO – TOWER AND SPIRE

Grant assistance of £11,000 given towards: Purchase and erection of scaffolding to assist in preliminary survey and for phased restoration.

Royal Belfast Academical Institution.

Approximate cost of work: £49,401. Carried out in 1981.

Architects: H. A. Patton & Partners, Bangor.

Quantity Surveyors: W. H. Stephens & Sons, Belfast.

Contractor: McCrory Scaffolding (N.I.) Ltd., Lurgan.

Royal Belfast Academical Institution, College Square East, Belfast.

The main block of the present school was completed in 1814 probably designed by Sir John Soane and certainly the result of severe cost cutting from his original and much more elaborate scheme. The long, three-storey, brick facade is relieved by smooth rendering consisting of four pairs of plain pilasters, a continuous first floor sill course and a parapet, cornice and frieze at roof level. Windows have Georgian-glazed sashes with semi-circular heads to the ground floor and square heads to the upper floors. The entrance doorcase is deeply recessed at the back of a Doric columned porch.

Recipient of grant: Royal Belfast Academical Institution.

PHASE ONE – EXTERIOR DECORATION

Grant assistance of £592 given towards: External redecoration.

Approximate cost of work: £1,183. Carried out in 1976.

Painting by: McBurney & Cowan, Belfast.

Educational Buildings

PHASE TWO — DRY ROT

Grant assistance of £530 given towards:
Treatment of dry rot. Installation of silicone injection damp-proof course.

Approximate cost of work: £1,050. Carried out in 1980.

Timber treatment and damp-proof course by: Timbercare (N.I.) Lisburn.

PHASE THREE — ROOF

Grant assistance of £28,500 given towards:
Repairs to chimneys. Repairs to roof structure. Re-slating using natural slate. Replacement leadwork. Repairs to rainwater goods. Repairs to parapet. Professional fees.

Approximate cost of work: £55,970. Carried out in 1981.

Architects: Samuel Stevenson & Sons, Belfast.

Contractor: H. & J. Martin Ltd., Belfast.

St. Louis Convent School, Cullybackey Road, Ballymena.

A two-storey house with attics built about 1860 in a neo-Jacobean style for the Young family. The house is of an asymmetrical design with high curved gables, a square tower with ogee cupola, balustraded ground floor porch and bay windows all in broached sandstone with ashlar dressings. The windows are plain sashes.

Recipient of grant: St. Louis Grammar School.

Grant assistance of £7,150 given towards:
Repairs to chimneys. Re-slating using natural slate.

Approximate cost of work: £21,473. Carried out in 1976 and 1977.

Architects: P. & B. Gregory, Belfast.

Quantity Surveyor: W. H. McEvoy, Belfast.

Contractor: Hugh Griffin, Portglenone.

The Royal School, College Hill, Armagh.

A group of two- and three-storey buildings gathered around an enclosed courtyard and built to designs by Thomas Cooley in 1774 and enlarged in 1849. The roofs are hipped and slated, walls are of rubble stonework with crenellated parapets and windows have Georgian-glazed sashes.

Recipient of grant: Board of Governors.

REPAIRS TO EAST DORMITORY AND ADMINISTRATIVE WING

Grant assistance of £8,000 given towards:
Repairs to windows. Treatment of extensive dry rot. Repairs to internal plasterwork. Repairs to timber floors. Professional fees.

Approximate cost of work: £27,339. Carried out in 1982 and 1983.

Architect: Ian Donaldson, Armagh.

Quantity Surveyors: J. B. Kingston & Partners, Armagh.

Contractors: Philip Hobson & Co., Moy.

Rockport School, Craigavad.

A five-bay, two-storey, classically-styled 19th century house. The sea front is of three storeys. The roof is hipped and slated with modillioned eaves, walls are smooth rendered, with stone dressings, windows have Georgian-glazed sashes and the entrance is set in as ashlar, flat-roofed, portico. There are many later additions.

Recipient of grant: Rockport School Trust.

Grant assistance of £1,460 given towards:
Re-covering of porch and dormer roofs. Repairs to inner slopes of main roof using natural slate. Repairs to leadwork. Professional fees.

Approximate cost of work: £4,192. Carried out in 1980.

Architects: The Robinson Patterson Partnership, Bangor.

Roof work by: Hugo Clarke, Newtownards.

9, 11 and 13 The Strand, Portaferry.

Three properties comprising the Queen's University Marine Biology Station. Number nine is a two-storey rendered house, number eleven is also two-storey and rendered but grander and built about 1850 and number thirteen is a three-bay, two-storey house with basement built about 1830, rendered, with later bay windows and an excellent doorcase with wreaths and incised Greek-key pattern. All three properties have been repaired and restored.

Recipient of grant: The Queen's University of Belfast.

Grant assistance of £8,000 given towards:
Repairs to roof structure. Re-slating using natural slate. Replacement metal rainwater goods. Repairs to external render. External redecoration. Treatment of wood rot. Repairs to internal plasterwork. Damp-proofing of walls.

Approximate cost of work: £38,432. Carried out in 1980 and 1981.

Contractor: Joseph McClune & Son, Dundrum.

Roof work by: McMahon (Roofing) & Co., Belfast.

Timber treatment by: Timbercare (N.I.), Lisburn.

9, 11, 13, The Strand, Portaferry.

Educational Buildings

Plastering by: Raymond P. Smyth, Belfast.

Painting by: E. Adamson Ltd., Finaghy.

Portora Royal School, Enniskillen.

The original house, built in 1777 was seven bays wide and three storeys high with a basement. Colonnades and wings were added in 1837–8 and to increase accommodation, two-storey blocks were added behind the colonnades in 1859–61.

Recipient of grant: Fermanagh Protestant Board of Education.

Grant assistance of £20,000 given towards: Repairs to chimneys. Repairs to roof structure. Re-slating using natural slate. Replacement leadwork. Replacement metal rainwater goods. Treatment of woodrot. Repair to internal plasterwork. Professional fees.

Further financial assistance received from: Department of Education.

Approximate cost of work: £93,500. Carried out in 1982.

Architects: Robert McKinstry & Melvyn Brown, Belfast.

Contractor: McAleer & Teague, Dromore, Co. Tyrone.

St. Joseph's Primary School, Artillery Street, Londonderry.

Built in 1911 to designs by E. J. Toye the school is an imposing three-storey building, heavily moulded in smooth render. The entrance gateway is pedimented, as are the square-headed ground floor windows. The first floor windows are round-headed with three-quarter columns between rising to a second floor entablature containing square-headed windows.

Recipient of grant: Sisters of Mercy.

Grant assistance of £2,730 given towards: Repairs to flat roof. Repairs to parapet walls. External re-rendering. Internal re-plastering. Professional fees.

Approximate cost of work: £7,828. Carried out in 1979 and 1980.

Architect: Charles Hegarty, Londonderry.

Contractor: McCloskey & Co., Londonderry.

Old Foyle College, Lawrence Hill, Strand Road, Londonderry.

A simple Regency style building opened in 1814 to a design by John Bowden. A central five-bay, three-storey block is flanked by slightly projecting single-bay, two-storey wings. The links between the central block and the wings each contain tripartite door surrounds surmounted by large fanlights. Both wings have tripartite ground floor windows and pedimental gables. The walls are in whinstone. The college closed in 1968 and is now gradually being restored from virtual dereliction by the Derry Youth and Community Workshop.

Recipient of grant: Londonderry City Council.

Grant assistance of £17,860 given towards: Emergency first-aid repairs. Repairs to internal joinery work. Repairs to windows. Repairs to internal plasterwork.

Further financial assistance received from: Department of Manpower Services towards labour content.

Approximate cost of work: £42,864 (materials only). Carried out in 1979 and 1980.

Architect: Charles Hegarty, Londonderry.

Work carried out using own labour.

34 Catherine Street, Limavady.

A fine three-bay, three-storey brick Georgian terrace house. The panelled entrance door set in a concave recess is flanked by slender fluted columns with Doric capitals with a segmented decorative fanlight over.

The ground floor, now a nursery school, has been restored and a totally inappropriate modern shop front has been removed.

Recipient of grant: Mrs. M. L. Boyle.

Grant assistance of £800 given towards: Re-pointing of brickwork.

Approximate cost of work: £2,032. Carried out in 1978.

Contractor: Deans & Hylands Ltd., Limavady.

Dungannon Royal School, Ranfurly Road, Dungannon.

A five-bay, three-story rendered Georgian house built by Primate Robinson in 1786. Two-storey gabled wings flush with the front of the main block extend backwards to form an enclosed garden. The back ends of the wings were later linked by a cloistered arcade. John McCurdy was responsible for the large-scale Italianate extensions to the south.

Recipient of grant: Board of Governors.

Grant assistance of £2,545 given towards: Replacement sash windows in original style.

Approximate cost of work: £7,633. Carried out in 1978 and 1979.

Contractor: McAleer & Teague, Dromore, Co. Tyrone.

Church Halls, Clubs and Institutions

Clifton House, Clifton Street, Belfast.

The Poorhouse, now Clifton House, opened in 1774, and remains a sanctuary of peace in a sea of urban change. The original building, to designs by amateur architect Robert Joy, fronts North Queen street and comprises a five-bay, two-storey pedimented central block, four-bay, single-storey wings and projecting pedimented end pavilions, all in red brick with stone dressings and set on a half basement. The handsome octagonal central spire is of stone, windows have Georgian glazing with square-headed openings in the central block and semi-circular-headed openings in the wings and the panelled entrance door approached by a broad sweeping flight of steps is set in a pedimented stone doorcase. Later additions from 1820 onwards are fortuitously congruous.

Recipient of grant: Belfast Charitable Society.

PHASE ONE — EXTERIOR

Grant assistance of £300 given towards: Re-pointing of stonework. Professional fees.

Approximate cost of work: £601. Carried out in 1977.

Architects: Smyth Cowser & Partners, Belfast.

Contractor: McRoberts & Crockard, Belfast.

PHASE TWO — DRY ROT

Grant assistance of £1,858 given towards: Treatment of extensive dry rot. Repairs to roof structure. Repairs to leadwork. Repairs to brickwork. Repairs to internal plasterwork. Professional fees.

Approximate cost of work: £3,715. Carried out in 1977.

Architects: Smyth Cowser & Partners, Belfast.

Contractor: Timbercare (N.I.) Lisburn.

PHASE THREE — EXTERIOR

Grant assistance of £390 given towards: Re-pointing of brickwork in courtyard.

Approximate cost of work: £783. Carried out in 1978.

Contractor: McRoberts & Crockard, Belfast.

PHASE FOUR — DRY ROT

Grant assistance of £3,774 given towards: Treatment of extensive dry rot including Chapel roof. Repairs to roof structure. Subsequent reinstatement of finishes.

Approximate cost of work: £7,548. Carried out in 1978 and 1979.

Architects: Smyth Cowser & Partners, Belfast.

Contractor: Timbercare (N.I.) Lisburn.

PHASE FIVE — EXTERIOR

Grant assistance of £1,196 given towards: Replacement metal rainwater goods. Professional fees.

Approximate cost of work: £2,166. Carried out in 1978 and 1979.

Architects: Smyth Cowser & Partners, Belfast.

Contractor: McRoberts & Crockard, Belfast.

PHASE SIX — EXTERIOR

Grant assistance of £5,431 given towards: Repairs to chimneys. Repairs to external render. Replacement of defective stone window sills. External redecoration. Professional fees.

Clifton House, Clifton Street, Belfast.

Approximate cost of work: £10,965.
Carried out in 1980.
Architects: Barnes McCrum
Partnership, Belfast.
Contractor: McRoberts & Crockard
Ltd., Belfast.
Painting by: R. McClughan, Dromore,
Co. Down.

PHASE SEVEN – DRY ROT

Grant assistance of £619 given towards:
Treatment of wood rot and subsequent
reinstatement. Professional fees.
Approximate cost of work: £1,196.
Carried out in 1980.
Architects: Barnes McCrum
Partnership, Belfast.
Contractor: McRoberts & Crockard
Ltd., Belfast.

PHASE EIGHT – WARD 5

Grant assistance of £4,100 given towards:
Repairs to roof structure. Roof repairs.
Replacement leadwork. Repairs to
internal plasterwork. Professional fees.
Approximate cost of work: £8,576.
Carried out in 1982.
Architects: Barnes McCrum
Partnership, Belfast.
Contractor: McRoberts & Crockard
Ltd., Belfast.

PHASE NINE – HALL, MAIN STAIRS,
LANDING

Grant assistance of £5,550 given towards:
Internal re-plastering. Professional fees.
Approximate cost of work: £10,884.
Carried out in 1983.
Architects: Barnes McCrum
Partnership, Belfast.
Contractor: McRoberts & Crockard
Ltd., Belfast.

Victoria Memorial Hall, 12 May Street, Belfast.

A classically styled rendered building
built in 1840 as a music hall, latterly a
church and now, sadly, demolished
after a period of redundancy.
Recipient of grant: Trustees of Victoria
Memorial Hall.

PHASE ONE

Grant assistance of £285 given towards:
Preparation of structural report.
Approximate cost of work: £285. Carried
out in 1975.
Structural Engineers: Taylor & Boyd,
Belfast.
Contractor: McKnight Construction
Co. Ltd., Belfast.

PHASE TWO

Grant assistance of £200 given towards:
Vandal-proofing of building.
Approximate cost of work: £200
(materials only). Carried out in 1977.
Work carried out using own labour.

Ulster Institute for the Deaf, 5 and 6 College Square North, Belfast.

Two early-19th century tall
three-storey houses with basements
and attics which have been combined
to form one building. The slated
gabled roof is concealed behind an attic
parapet and the seven-bay frontage is
smooth rendered with a rusticated
ground floor. The two end bays on
each side project slightly and are
delineated by flat, panelled, pilasters.
Windows have Georgian-glazed sashes
and the original moulded entrance
door surrounds also contain windows
while the new central entrance is a
totally inappropriate addition set in a

wide square-headed opening.
Recipient of grant: Ulster Institute for
the Deaf.

PHASE ONE

Grant assistance of £3,764 given towards:
Treatment of extensive dry rot and
subsequent reinstatement.
Approximate cost of work: £4,529.
Carried out in 1977.
Timber treatment by: Timbertreat
Services Ltd., Belfast.
Plastering by: T. J. Caulfield,
Glengormley.

PHASE TWO

Grant assistance of £115 given towards:
Repairs to chimney. Roof repairs.
Approximate cost of work: £350. Carried
out in 1980.
Contractor: Thomas Hanvey, Belfast.

Ulster Reform Club, 4 and 6 Royal Avenue, Belfast.

A fine three-storey sandstone corner
building built in 1883 by Maxwell and
Tuke of Manchester. The main front
has three canted bays with first floor
cast-iron balconies and second floor
stone balustrading, a mansard roof
rises behind the frontage parapet.
Windows have plain sashes set in a
variety of openings and the marble
columned entrance is set within the
quadrant corner which rises to a
circular, metal-clad, cupola.
Recipient of grant: Ulster Reform Club
Building Co. Ltd.

PHASE ONE

Grant assistance of £6,710 given towards:
Roof repairs. Repairs to rainwater
goods. Replacement of decayed stone
balustrading. Treatment of extensive
dry rot in library, bar and dining room

and subsequent reinstatement.

Approximate cost of work: £29,480. Carried out in 1978 and 1979.

Architects: Samuel Stevenson and Sons, Belfast.

Quantity Surveyors: W. H. Stephens & Sons, Belfast.

Contractors: McRoberts & Crockard, Belfast; Thomas T. Gray, Belfast and Edward Wilson & Co. Ltd., Newtownabbey.

PHASE TWO

Grant assistance of £12,300 given towards: Treatment of extensive dry rot in dining room, billiard room and kitchen and subsequent reinstatement including timber panelling.

Approximate cost of work: £37,157. Carried out from 1979 to 1981.

Architects: Samuel Stevenson & Sons, Belfast.

Quantity Surveyors: W. H. Stephens & Sons, Belfast.

Contractor: McLaughlin & Harvey Ltd., Belfast.

Timber treatment by: Protim Services Ltd., Lisburn.

PHASE THREE

Grant assistance of £6,000 given towards: Repairs to roof structure. Replacement leadwork. Treatment of extensive dry rot in billiard room and bedrooms and subsequent reinstatement.

Approximate cost of work: £48,000. Carried out in 1983.

Architects: Samuel Stevenson & Sons, Belfast.

Quantity Surveyors: W. H. Stephens & Sons, Belfast.

Contractors: H. & J. Martin Ltd., Belfast and Jamison & Sloan Ltd., Belfast.

Clough Masonic Hall, Clough.

A strange, mainly plain, roughcast two-storey building with a classical facade consisting of an out-of-scale pediment over a heavy cornice and architrave all supported on two pairs of unfluted Corinthian columns.

Recipient of grant: Trustees, Clough Masonic Hall.

Grant assistance of £1,555 given towards: Restoration of entablature.

Approximate cost of work: £4,343. Carried out in 1979.

Contractor: David Patton & Sons, Ballymena.

Craigs Church Hall, Craigs, Cullybackey.

Formerly Craigs Parochial School built in 1841 probably to designs by Charles Lanyon. Walls are of basalt with sandstone trim. The symmetrical facade is terminated with projecting shouldered gables. An onion-shaped roof ventilator surmounts the central block and the pointed entrance doorway has a hood moulding. The grant aided repairs were included with an extension scheme.

Recipient of grant: Craigs Parish Church.

Grant assistance of £4,900 given towards: Repairs to chimney. Roof repairs. Repair of roof ventilator. Replacement leadwork. Replacement windows in original style. Treatment of wood rot. Professional fees.

Approximate cost of work: £50,600. Carried out in 1982.

Agent: Joseph E. McKernan, Ballymena.

Contractor: Charles Johnston, Cullybackey.

Parish Hall, Lylehill Road/Coach Road, Templepatrick.

A single-storey hall three bays by one built in 1835 by John Henry Upton. The roof is slated and gabled and the walls are of coursed basalt rubble with dressed quoins and surrounds to the lofty Y-traceried windows. A large, square, flat-roofed porch clumsily projects from one end.

Recipient of grant: The Church of Ireland.

Grant assistance of £100 given towards: Repairs to windows.

Approximate cost of work: £465. Carried out in 1981.

Contractor: Antrim Aluminium and Glass Co. Ltd., Templepatrick.

St. Patrick's Parochial Hall, Downshire Road, Newry.

A rectangular building, with buttressed, pinnacled and crenellated gabled facade; built in 1846 to designs by Thomas Duff.

Recipient of grant: Select Vestry, St. Patrick's Church.

Grant assistance of £1,900 given towards: Re-slating using natural slate. Repairs to leadwork. Replacement metal rainwater goods.

Approximate cost of work: £5,793. Carried out in 1982.

Contractors: McDonald Bros., Newry.

1 Trevor Hill, Newry.

A five-bay, three-storey house with attic and basement, built about 1770 for Andrew Thompson, a Newry merchant. The roof is slated and has a moulded eaves cornice, the frontage is of roughly dressed rubble with granite

1 Trevor Hill, Newry.

Approximate cost of work: £1,221. Carried out in 1975.

Work carried out using direct labour.

PHASE TWO

Grant assistance of £49 given towards: Strengthening of defective timber roof beam.

Approximate cost of work: £98. Carried out in 1980.

Contractor: Stephen Fearon, Newry.

Aghaderg Parish Hall, Drumnahare, Loughbrickland.

A long narrow single-storey former school built in 1824. The roof is hipped and slated with a central gable over the entrance, walls are of blackstone and windows have Georgian-glazed sashes. The ends contain blind elliptically-arched recesses.

Recipient of grant: Select Vestry, Aghaderg Parish Church.

Grant assistance of £4,730 given towards: Re-roofing using natural slate. Repairs to rainwater goods. Repairs to

dressings and windows have Georgian-glazed sashes. The central panelled entrance door with semi-circular fanlight and flanking sidelights is surmounted at first floor level by a Venetian window and at second floor level by a semi-circular headed window. An elliptically arched coachway to one side, leads to the rear.

Recipient of grant: Newry Republican Social Club.

PHASE ONE

Grant assistance of £610 towards: Provision of lintels over structural openings.

Aghaderg Parish Hall, Drumnahare, Loughbrickland.

stonework and brick dressings. Repairs to windows and doors. Redecoration of remedial items.

Approximate cost of work: £29,811. Carried out in 1981.

Architect: M. H. Ferguson, Banbridge.

Contractor: D. C. McCready, Gilford.

9 Catherine Street, Killyleagh.

A large four-bay, two-storey pre-1834 terrace property. The roof is slated and gabled, walls are smooth rendered, windows have Georgian-glazed sashes and the panelled entrance door with decorative sidelights and fanlight is recessed in an elliptically arched opening and approached by stone steps. An arched coachway leads to the rear of the property.

Recipient of grant: The Royal British Legion.

Grant assistance of £1,200 given towards: Repairs to chimney. Re-slating front slope of roof using natural slate. Replacement sash windows in original style.

Approximate cost of work: £3,900. Carried out in 1982.

Contractor: Richard Edgar, Downpatrick.

Club House, Ardglass Golf Club (formerly Ardglass Castle).

Originally a range of two-storey early-15th century fortified warehouses with three three-storey towers overlooking the harbour. A large part of the building was converted to a mansion about 1790 perhaps to designs by Charles Lilly. It found another new use, as a club-house, early in this century. The roofs are slated and gabled and the walls are of split-stone rubble, roughcast and with castellated

parapets.

Recipient of grant: Ardglass Golf Club.

PHASE ONE – MAIN ROOF

Grant assistance of £3,750 given towards: Re-slating using natural slate.

Approximate cost of work: £12,936. Carried out in 1979.

Architects: Ferguson & McIlveen, Belfast.

Roof work by: Raymond Burke, Ardglass.

PHASE TWO – REPAIR AND CONVERSION OF FIRST AND SECOND FLOORS

Grant assistance of £6,290 given towards: Treatment of wood rot. Strengthening and repair of timber floors. Repairs to internal plasterwork. Repairs to decorative plasterwork. Repairs to staircase.

Approximate cost of work: £57,500. Carried out in 1980 and 1981.

Architects: Ferguson and McIlveen, Belfast.

Quantity Surveyor: D. A. Carville, Ardglass.

Contractor: Commercial Construction, Saintfield.

PHASE THREE – MISCELLANEOUS REPAIRS

Grant assistance of £6,000 given towards: Re-slating of west wing roof using natural slate. External re-rendering. Replacement windows in original style. Re-modelling of entrance porch roof. Re-location of coat-of-arms to a position inside the club-house.

Approximate cost of work: £22,027. Carried out from 1980 to 1982.

Architects: Ferguson & McIlveen, Belfast.

Contractor: Raymond Burke, Ardglass.

Timber treatment by: Timbercare (N.I.), Lisburn.

3 Castle Place, Ardglass.

One of a terrace of four tall three-storey houses built in 1820. The walls are rendered, windows have Georgian-glazed sashes and the panelled entrance door has barley-sugar half-columns and a decorative fanlight.

Recipient of grant: The Royal British Legion.

Grant assistance of £1,400 given towards: Repairs to chimney. Repairs to leadwork. Repairs to rainwater goods. Repairs to external render. Replacement of defective timber beam. Repairs to internal plasterwork.

Approximate cost of work: £8,471. Carried out in 1981 and 1982.

Contractor: Joseph M. Blaney, Downpatrick.

Club House, Royal County Down Golf Club, Newcastle.

A two-storey building with an entrance porch at first floor level approached by steps. The roof is tiled, upper walls are roughcast and the lower walls are of granite. The club house was built about 1890 by the Belfast and County Down Railway Co.

Recipient of grant: Royal County Down Golf Club.

PHASE ONE – REPAIRS

Grant assistance of £440 given towards: Repairs to chimney. Roof repairs including central roof area. Repairs to rainwater goods. Replacement of two timber moulded uprights in porch.

Approximate cost of work: £1,216. Carried out in 1978.

Architects: Hobart & Heron, Belfast.

Contractor: Joseph McClune & Son, Dundrum.

Grant assistance of £560 given towards: Repairs to chimneys. Roof repairs. Repairs to leadwork. Repairs to rainwater goods. Repairs to windows.

Approximate cost of work: £1,680. Carried out in 1980 and 1982.

Contractor: McLaughlin & Harvey Ltd., Newtownabbey.

Window repairs by: R. J. McCall & Sons, Downpatrick.

Southwell Charity School and Almshouses, English Street, Downpatrick.

A group of three buildings, typical of Irish Palladianism, founded in 1733 by Edward Southwell as an almshouse and school for the poor. The main block consists of a central coach arch surmounted by a tall semi-circular headed window, pediment and quadrangular sandstone cupola; with five-bay two-storey almshouses to either side and terminated by slightly projecting two-bay, two storey schoolrooms. Two three-bay, two-storey teacher's houses sit well forward from the main block and are linked to it by low quadrant walls. The impact of the group has been somewhat subjugated by the raising of the level of English Street by some five metres in 1790. Roofs are hipped and slated and the frontage is of brick with sandstone quoins and plinth. Windows to the almshouses are square-headed, the school rooms have large semi-circular headed windows and the teacher's houses each have a central ground floor semi-circular-headed window while the remainder are square-headed. All sashes have Georgian glazing.

Recipient of grant: Governors of the Southwell Charity.

PHASE ONE — REPAIRS

Grant assistance of £8,323 given towards: Roof repairs. Repairs to rainwater goods. Repairs to stonework. Repairs to brickwork. Repairs to windows. Redecoration of remedial items. Treatment of wood rot. Repairs to internal plasterwork.

Approximate cost of work: £13,874. Carried out in 1975 and 1976.

Architects: Houston, Bell & Kennedy, Belfast.

Contractor: C. A. Thompson & Co. Ltd., Killyleagh.

PHASE TWO — REPAIRS

Grant assistance of £483 given towards: Roof repairs. Repairs to rainwater goods.

Approximate cost of work: £1,025. Carried out in 1978.

Contractor: Alex Kennedy, Seaforde.

Southwell Charity School and Almshouses, English Street, Downpatrick.

Down Hunt Rooms, English Street, Downpatrick.

A low three-bay, two-storey building surmounted by an elementary full width pediment. The first floor windows have slim entablatures and an Adamesque porch projects into the street.

Recipient of grant: Down Hunt Club.

Grant assistance of £1,085 given towards: Repairs to chimney. Roof repairs. Repairs to windows. Treatment of wood rot. Repairs to internal plasterwork. Professional fees.

Approximate cost of work: £8,354. Carried out in 1980 and 1981.

Architects: Hobart & Heron, Belfast.

Contractor: Polly Bros. Ltd., Downpatrick.

Timber treatment by: Timbercare (N.I.), Lisburn.

St. Michael's Administration Centre, 99 Irish Street, Downpatrick.

A three-bay, three-storey house. The slated roof is concealed behind an eaves parapet, walls are of rough coursed rubble with brick dressings, windows have Georgian-glazed sashes and the panelled entrance door is flanked by attached columns with a plain segmental fanlight over. The house has recently been restored and converted for use as a parish recreational centre.

Recipient of grant: The Very Rev. Dr. J. Maguire.

Grant assistance of £11,750 given towards: Repairs to chimneys. Repairs to roof structure. Re-slating using natural slate. Replacement metal rainwater goods. Installation of new structural supports over openings. Replacement

sash windows to original style. Treatment of extensive dry rot. Internal re-plastering. Repairs to timber floors.

Approximate cost of work: £174,000. Carried out in 1981 and 1982.

Architects: McLean & Forte, Belfast and Newry.

Quantity Surveyor: D. A. Carville, Belfast.

Structural Engineer: Fergus Gilligan, Belfast.

Contractor: H. J. O'Boyle Ltd., Downpatrick.

Kilwarlin Moravian Church, 49 Kilwarlin Road, Hillsborough.

A group of adjoining buildings consisting of a two-storey manse, church hall and church, all with slated roofs and simple Georgian detailing. The manse has a gabled porch and a cantilevered projection to the rear known as Zola's hide.

Recipient of grant: Kilwarlin Moravian Church.

PHASE ONE – REPAIRS TO CHURCH HALL AND MANSE

Grant assistance of £1,720 given towards: Church Hall – Repairs to chimneys. Re-slating using natural slate. Replacement metal rainwater goods. Internal re-plastering. Manse – Repairs to chimneys. Re-slating using natural slate. Repairs to external render. Replacement metal rainwater goods. Repairs to internal plasterwork. Repairs to Zola's hide. Repairs to staircase.

Further financial assistance received from: Northern Ireland Housing Executive.

Approximate cost of work: £10,630. Carried out in 1979 and 1980.

Contractor: James Walsh Builders (N.I.) Ltd., Lisburn.

PHASE TWO – REPAIRS TO RETURN BUILDING

Grant assistance of £385 given towards: Re-slating using natural slate. Repairs to internal plasterwork. Installation of damp-proof solid floors.

Approximate cost of work: £2,075. Carried out in 1982.

Work carried out using own labour.

Orange Hall, 18 Hamilton Road, Bangor.

A two-storey building built in 1872. A central projecting gable to the frontage has a tall central window set in a pointed opening flanked by small pointed niches all with a label moulding over. The roof is slated and walls are smooth rendered.

Recipient of grant: Trustees Bangor Orange Hall.

Grant assistance of £65 given towards: Replacement panelled entrance door.

Approximate cost of work: £200. Carried out in 1981.

Contractor: William C. Mulholland, Bangor.

Club House, Royal Belfast Golf Club, Craigavad.

A two-storey, classically styled house built in 1881 by the Lord Dunleath. The roof is hipped and slated, with projecting eaves, the first floor is of smooth ashlar and the ground floor is rusticated; windows have segmental heads and Georgian-glazing and the entrance is approached through a columned and balustraded portico. The property has later additions.

Recipient of grant: Royal Belfast Golf Club.

PHASE ONE – REPAIRS

Grant assistance of £2,110 given towards: Repairs to west balcony. Replacement roof windows. Repairs to stonework. Re-pointing of stonework. Replacement sash windows in original style.

Approximate cost of work: £7,270. Carried out in 1979 and 1980.

Architect: L. G. D. Thompson, Belfast.

Contractor: Connor and Beattie Ltd., Lisburn.

Stone repair by: H. L. Stuart-Cox & Co. Ltd., Belfast.

PHASE TWO – SOUTH PORCH AND WEST ELEVATION

Grant assistance of £420 given towards: Stonework repairs.

Approximate cost of work: £1,380. Carried out in 1980.

Stone repair by: H. L. Stuart-Cox & Co. Ltd., Belfast.

Parochial Hall, Church Road, Holywood.

A single-storey, Gothic revival style church school built in 1877.

Recipient of grant: Holywood Parish Church.

Grant assistance of £1,035 given towards: Restoration of 17 coloured glass leaded window panes.

Approximate cost of work: £3,105. Carried out in 1979 and 1980.

Glazing by: Caldermac Studios, Belfast.

Old Orphanage, Comber Road, Ballygowan.

A gaunt three- and four-storey

Old Orphanage, Ballygowan.

blackstone building dominating the village and built in 1866 as an orphanage. The roof is slated, and the slightly projecting end bays have crow-stepped gables. The entrance at first floor level is approached by a long flight of steps and is contained in a tall square crenellated tower. The building has been extensively refurbished and is now in use as church halls.

Recipient of grant: Ballygowan Presbyterian Church.

Grant assistance of £30,000 given towards: Repairs to chimneys. Treatment of extensive dry rot. Repairs to roof structure. Re-slating using natural slate. Replacement leadwork. Replacement metal rainwater goods. Re-pointing of stonework. External re-rendering. Replacement windows in original style. Internal re-plastering. Replacement timber floors. Restoration of interior joinery work.

Approximate cost of work: £101,116. Carried out from 1980 to 1982.

Architect: Gordon McKnight, Holywood.

Contractor: A. & W. Joinery Works Ltd., Belfast and work carried out using own labour.

Orange Hall, East Bridge Street, Enniskillen.

Described by Alistair Rowan as 'a jaunty Italianate block'. The building presents four bays to the bridge and four to the street and is two-storeys on a high basement. A modillion bracketed eaves cornice is set over round-headed first floor windows and segmental-headed ground floor windows. The walls are rendered with heavy mouldings at windows and quoins.

Recipient of grant: Trustees of Orange Hall.

Grant assistance of £690 given towards: Roof repairs. Repairs to rainwater goods. Repairs to windows.

Further financial assistance received from: Face Lift Scheme.

Approximate cost of work: £8,039. Carried out in 1980.

Work carried out using direct labour.

Methodist Church Hall, Wesley Street, Enniskillen.

Built in 1887, stone walls with round-headed traceried windows.

Recipient of grant: The Methodist Church in Ireland.

PHASE ONE

Grant assistance of £820 given towards: Repairs to chimney. Repairs to leadwork. Treatment of wood rot. Repairs to internal plasterwork. Repairs to staircase.

Approximate cost of work: £5,209. Carried out in 1981.

Contractor: Wilson & Ward, Enniskillen.

PHASE TWO

Grant assistance of £1,540 given towards: Installation of damp-proof solid floors. Repairs to internal joinery work.

Approximate cost of work: £19,635. Carried out in 1983.

Architect: Walter J. Cox, Enniskillen.

Contractor: Irvine Bros., Enniskillen.

St. Macartan's Home, 74 Main Street, Clogher.

Formerly the Protestant bishop's palace, built by Archbishop Beresford in 1819. The main block, built into the hillside, is seven bays by three storeys high on the entrance front and six bays by four storeys high on the garden front. The construction is of plain ashlar. The central three bays of the entrance front are pedimented and have a single-storey Doric porch. The arcaded garden front is flanked by recessed two-storey wings with canted bay windows.

Recipient of grant: Sisters of Mercy.

Grant assistance of £3,270 given towards: Re-slating of Chapel and dining annex using natural slate. Repairs to leadwork.

Approximate cost of grant: £10,115. Carried out in 1980 and 1981.

Architect: M. Donnelly, Enniskillen.

Contractor: McAleer and Teague, Dromore, Co. Tyrone.

Northern Counties Club, 24 Bishop Street, Londonderry.

Remodelled in 1902 by Alfred Forman, is now a three-storey, five-bay rendered building with slated, dormered roof with steep pyramids over the end bays. The rusticated ground floor is surmounted by an entablature with scrolled pediments. The upper floors are divided by a giant order of Composite pilasters and half-columns.

Recipient of grant: Northern Counties Club.

Grant assistance of £1,580 given towards: Rebuilding of chimneys. Repairs to external render. Repairs to windows including dormers. Redecoration of remedial items.

Approximate cost of work: £10,199. Carried out between 1978 and 1980.

Architects: Albert Wallace & Partners, Londonderry.

Contractor: James M. Jefferson & Sons, Londonderry.

Roof work by: Alwyn Coyle & Co. Ltd., Londonderry.

Painting by: M. A. White, Londonderry.

St. Columb's Hall, Richmond Street, Londonderry.

Built in 1888 in a lavish Italianate and Gothic style to a design by architects Croom and Toye. The steeply sloping site dictates that the building is two storeys high at one end and three storeys at the other. The three-bay sandstone frontage has a central balconied portico and each bay has a group of three semi-circular-headed windows. The central attic pediment is surmounted by carved figures of Erin, Temperance and Vulcan carved by C. W. Harrison of Dublin. The roof line is balustraded.

Recipient of grant: The Committee of St. Columb's Hall.

Grant assistance of £120 given towards: Low-pressure sand-blasting of details. Part of a general face-lift scheme.

Further financial assistance received from: Face-lift Scheme.

Approximate cost of work: £12,268. Carried out in 1979.

Architects: Liam McCormick & Partners, Londonderry.

Stone repair by: Ulster Cleanstone Co., Dungannon.

Grant assistance of £3,500 given towards: Treatment of extensive dry rot and subsequent reinstatement.

Approximate cost of work: £12,064. Carried out in 1980 and 1981.

Contractor: Bernard Boyle, Londonderry.

Roof work by: City Asphalt, Londonderry.

Timber treatment by: Rentokil Ltd., Belfast and Protim Services, Lisburn.

35 Great James Street, Londonderry.

A three-storey end-of-terrace building with half basement. The three-bay entrance front is at right angles to the two-bay road frontage. The roof is hipped and slated, walls are smooth rendered with moulded quoins, strings and architraves, and windows have Georgian-glazed sashes. The panelled entrance door flanked by Ionic columns and with an elliptical decorative fanlight is set in a square, flat-roofed projecting porch approached by steps.

Recipient of grant: North West Council of Social Service.

Grant assistance of £70 given towards: Repairs to roof.

Approximate cost of work: £192. Carried out in 1981.

Architect: Charles Hegarty, Londonderry.

Contractor: McCloskey & Co., Londonderry.

5 Crawford Square, Londonderry.

A fine three-storey rendered terrace house built before 1871 to the designs of Robert Collins. A two-storey bay projects at the front.

Recipient of grant: Methodist Mission.

Grant assistance of £240 given towards: External redecoration.

Approximate cost of work: £720. Carried out in 1982.

Painting by: M. S. Dinsmore, Londonderry.

St. Mary's Church, Macosquin.

A 'T'-shaped, single-storey Sunday School with slated roof, decorative barge boards, blackstone walls with brick dressings and Georgian-glazed sash windows.

Recipient of grant: St. Mary's Church of Ireland Church.

Grant assistance of £1,750 given towards: Re-roofing using natural slate. Re-pointing of brickwork. Re-pointing of stonework. Repairs to windows. Replacement external doors in original style. Repairs to internal plasterwork. Redecoration of remedial items.

Approximate cost of work: £4,911. Carried out in 1980.

Contractor: S. W. W. McMullan, Coleraine.

St. David's Church Hall, Sion Mills.

A half-timbered building on a buttressed rubble base with tiled roof and brick bell-cote. Built in 1895.

Recipient of grant: Select Vestry, Sion Mills Parish Church.

Grant assistance of £3,000 given towards: Rebuilding of chimney. Re-tiling of roof. Replacement metal rainwater goods. Repairs to external render. Repairs to wall panelling. Installation of damp-proof solid floors. Redecoration of remedial items. Professional fees.

Approximate cost of work: £13,363. Carried out in 1982.

Architect: Caroline Dickson, Londonderry.

Quantity Surveyor: John D. D. O'Neill, Coleraine.

Contractor: J. J. Millar, Sion Mills.

Church Halls, Clubs and Institutions

St. David's Church Hall, Sion Mills.

Charles Shiel's Institution, 2, 6, 9, 10, 14, 15, 19, 21, 23 and 28 Circular Road, Dungannon.

A group of high-Victorian one-and-a-half-storey almshouses designed by Lanyon, Lynn & Lanyon in 1867. They are symmetrically laid out with a central louvred clock tower above a Gothic doorway with colonettes. The walls are of rubble sandstone with dressed sandstone and slate bands. The roofs are in patterned slate.

Recipient of grant: Board of Governors.

Grant assistance of £5,987 given towards: Rebuilding of chimneys. Re-slating using natural slate. Repairs to leadwork. Repairs to rainwater goods. Repairs to external render. Repairs to windows. Repairs to panelled entrance doors. Treatment of wood rot. Repairs to internal plasterwork. Repairs to timber floors. Installation of damp-proof solid floors. Repairs to staircase. Professional fees.

Further financial assistance received from: Northern Ireland Housing Executive.

Approximate cost of work: £65,883. Carried out from 1980 to 1982.

Architect: Ian Donaldson, Armagh – House numbers 2 and 28.

Architect: F. M. W. Schofield, Dungannon – House number 15.

Agent: P. McCaughey, Dungannon – House numbers 6, 9, 14, 19 and 23.

Contractor: Hugh Hughes, Dungannon.

Timber treatment by: Timbercare Services Ltd., Lisburn – House numbers 14, 19 and 21.

59

Residential
Cottages and Small Houses

47 Old Holywood Road, Belfast.

A small but attractive semi-detached, mid-19th century, one-and-a-half-storey house associated with nearby Glenmachan House. The roof is half-hipped with alternate bands of plain and fish-scale tiles, a tall decorative central brick chimney and sprocketed eaves. The upper portion of the walls are also tiled and the lower portions are of red brick with yellow and black bands. The windows have margined sashes with a single diamond pane in the centre of each upper sash. The panelled entrance door with rectangular fanlight is set under a bracketted lean-to canopy.

Recipient of grant: Mr. R. J. Sholdis.

Grant assistance of £1,200 given towards: Roof repairs. Repairs to rainwater goods. Replacement windows in original style. Repairs to entrance door. Repairs to internal plasterwork. Installation of damp-proof solid floors. Repairs to staircase.

Further financial assistance received from: Northern Ireland Housing Executive.

Approximate cost of work: Not known. Carried out in 1980.

Work carried out using direct labour.

49 Old Holywood Road, Belfast.

A small semi-detached house similar to number 47 described in the previous entry.

Recipient of grant: Miss J. M. Best.

Grant assistance of £680 given towards: Repairs to chimney. Roof repairs. Repairs to rainwater goods. Re-pointing of brickwork. Replacement windows in original style. Treatment of wood rot. Installation of damp-proof course.

Repairs to internal plasterwork. Installation of damp-proof solid floors. Replacement staircase.

Further financial assistance received from: Northern Ireland Housing Executive.

Approximate cost of work: £8,614. Carried out in 1979.

Work carried out using direct labour.

51 Old Holywood Road, Belfast.

A small semi-detached house similar to number 47 described above.

Recipient of grant: Mr. P. A. Saunders.

Grant assistance of £680 given towards: Repairs to chimney. Roof repairs. Repairs to rainwater goods. Re-pointing of brickwork. Replacement windows in original style. Treatment of wood rot. Installation of damp-proof course. Repairs to internal plasterwork. Installation of damp-proof solid floors. Replacement staircase.

Further financial assistance received from: Northern Ireland Housing Executive.

Approximate cost of work: £8,443. Carried out in 1979.

Work carried out using direct labour.

Lock-keeper's House, Drumbridge, Old Forge, Belfast.

A fine little, two-storey lock-keeper's house built in 1757 to designs by Thomas Omer, the Lagan Canal engineer. The roof is slated and gabled, walls are of rubble with sandstone dressings, the main elevations have brick-arched semi-circular-headed recesses extending into the upper storey. A platband extends around the building at first floor level. The windows have flush, exposed case, Georgian-glazed sashes

Lock-keeper's House, Drumbridge, Old Forge, Belfast.

61

and the panelled entrance door has a raised cut stone block surround with triple keystone. The house has been superbly restored.

Recipient of grant: Historic, Environmental and Architectural Rehabilitation Trust.

Grant assistance of £2,600 given towards: Repairs to roof structure. Re-slating using natural slate. Replacement metal rainwater goods. Extensive stonework repairs and re-pointing. Replacement sash windows in original style. Replacement panelled entrance door. Installation of damp-proof course. Internal re-plastering. Installation of damp-proof solid floors.

Further financial assistance received from: Northern Ireland Housing Executive and Insurance Company.

Approximate cost of work: £30,000. Carried out in 1982 and 1983.

Contractor: Jose Alves Areias, Belfast.

Rhubarb Cottage, 36 Ballysillan Road, Belfast.

A single-storey gate lodge lost in the middle of suburbia. The roof is hipped with hexagonally patterned slating, walls are smooth rendered and triple windows have segmental heads. The entrance is set in a gabled porch.

Recipient of grant: Mr. P. J. Emerson.

Grant assistance of £460 given towards: Re-slating using natural slate.

Approximate cost of work: £1,375. Carried out in 1982 and 1983.

Work carried out using own labour.

Main Gate Lodge, Belfast Castle, 554 Antrim Road, Belfast.

A Scottish Baronial style sandstone gate lodge designed by John Lanyon,

formerly belonging to the castle but now in private ownership and very successfully restored.

Recipient of grant: Mrs. K. Colgan.

Grant assistance of £1,330 given towards: Roof repairs. Repairs to leadwork. Replacement metal rainwater goods. Repairs to stonework. Installation of damp-proof course.

Approximate cost of work: £9,800. Carried out from 1980 to 1983.

Work carried out using direct labour.

Breezemount, Ballaghmore Road, Portballintrae.

A five-bay, single-storey thatched house sharing its gable at the left side with a two-storey slated dwelling. The house originally had pegged and roped thatch characteristic of North Antrim.

Recipient of grant: Mrs. I. Cochrane.

PHASE ONE – RESTORATION

Grant assistance of £2,792 given towards: Repairs to walls and gables. Renewing roof structure. Rebuilding of chimneys. Re-thatching. Replacement sash windows in original style. Replacement external doors in original style.

Approximate cost of work: £11,634. Carried out in 1976 and 1977.

Roof work by: Rankin & McShane, Coleraine.

Thatching by: Gerald Agnew, Ahoghill.

Joinery work by: Brian McBride & Ivan Cook, Armoy.

PHASE TWO – REPAIRS

Grant assistance of £8 given towards: Repairs to thatch.

Approximate cost of work: £24. Carried out in 1980.

Thatching by: Gerald Agnew, Ahoghill.

Rose Cottage, 19 Beach Road, Portballintrae.

A single-storey thatched house originally with pegged and roped thatch characteristic of North Antrim.

Recipient of grant: Dr. H. Armstrong.

Grant assistance of £1,794 given towards: Repairs to roof structure. Re-thatching.

Approximate cost of work: £2,760. Carried out in 1977.

Roof work by: J. McLernon, Portballintrae.

Thatching by: Gerald Agnew, Ahoghill.

Gardenvale House, 153 Ballinlea Road, Stranocum.

A single-storey rendered building with hipped, slated roof and round-headed windows. The entrance is recessed in a twin-arched, gabled porch.

Recipient of grant: Mr. B. Harkness.

Grant assistance of £993 given towards: Repairs to chimneys. Re-slating using natural slates. Replacement metal rainwater goods. Repairs to windows. Repairs to panelled entrance door. External redecoration. Repairs to internal plasterwork. Installation of damp-proof solid floors.

Further financial assistance received from: Northern Ireland Housing Executive.

Approximate cost of work: £12,108. Carried out in 1982.

Contractor: A. M. Christie, Ballymoney.

Carnfinton Cottage, 132 Barn Road, Rasharkin.

A charming single-storey harled thatched house with horizontally divided sash windows. Built before 1833.

Recipient of grant: Mrs. A. McCoy.

Grant assistance of £2,734 given towards: Repairs to chimneys. Repairs to roof structure. Re-thatching.

Approximate cost of work: £8,988. Carried out in 1982.

Thatching by: Gerald Agnew, Ahoghill.

Layd Schoolhouse, 63 Middlepark Road, Glenariff.

A small single-storey, Georgian-glazed cottage. A plaque above the door bears the inscription 'Layd Schoolhouse. Founded 11 September Anno Domini 1820 Samuel Boyd Esqr.'

Recipient of grant: Mr. A. Murray.

Grant assistance of £250 given towards: Roof repairs. Restoration of inscription over door. Replacement sash windows in original style. Replacement panelled entrance door.

Further financial assistance received from: Northern Ireland Housing Executive.

Approximate cost of work: £8,350. Carried out in 1979.

Contractor: Brian McAuley, Ballymena.

29 Port Road, Islandmagee.

A pre-1831 harled and whitened, single-storey thatched house.

Recipient of grant: Mr. A. Houston.

Grant assistance of £610 given towards: Cost of materials for re-thatching of cottage.

Work carried out using own labour.

Roselawn, 48 Middle Road, Islandmagee.

A harled single-storey house with thatched roof. Sheeted door and horizontally divided sash windows. Built before 1831.

Recipient of grant: Mrs. P. S. Ferguson.

Grant assistance of £300 given towards: Repairs to thatch.

Approximate cost of work: £561. Carried out in 1977.

Thatching by: Gerald Agnew, Ahoghill.

Gate Lodge, Drumalis Convent, Glenarm Road, Larne.

A late-19th century gate lodge with roughcast walls, smooth rendered dressings, hipped roof, gabled porch and wrought-iron trellis work.

Recipient of grant: Sisters of the Cross and Passion.

Grant assistance of £2,626 given towards: Repairs to chimneys. Roof repairs. Replacement metal rainwater goods. Repairs to external render. Repairs to windows. Repairs to entrance porch and door. Installation of damp-proof course. Repairs to iron trellis work. Redecoration of remedial items.

Further financial assistance received from: Northern Ireland Housing Executive.

Approximate cost of work: £15,475. Carried out in 1981.

Architects: Moody Hegan Partnership, Larne.

Contractor: David White, Larne.

49 Hillmount Road, Cullybackey.

One of two early-20th century one-and-a-half-storey blackstone cottages with brick dressings, gabled porch and margined sash windows.

Recipient of grant: Frazer & Haughton Ltd.

Grant assistance of £880 given towards: Repairs to chimney. Roof repairs. Re-pointing of brickwork around windows. Repairs to external render. Replacement sash windows in original

style. Replacement panelled entrance door. Repairs to internal plasterwork. Repairs to timber floors. Redecoration of remedial items.

Further financial assistance received from: Northern Ireland Housing Executive.

Approximate cost of work: £11,000. Carried out in 1981 and 1982.

Agent: Joseph E. McKernan, Ballymena.

Contractor: John Anderson, Cullybackey.

Dunminning Cottage, 147 Ballywatermoy Road, Glarryford.

A charming rendered thatched cottage with a Gothic arched door and small sash windows. It has an unusual roof window peering out from the thatch.

Recipient of grant: Mr. A. Hutchinson.

Grant assistance of £480 given towards: Re-thatching.

Approximate cost of work: £1,181. Carried out in 1977.

Thatching by: Gerald Agnew, Ahoghill.

Grant assistance of £1,810 given towards: Re-thatching.

Approximate cost of work: £2,414. Carried out in 1982.

Thatching by: P. Stevenson, Dungannon.

Twin Cottages, 64 and 65 Main Street, Cullybackey.

One of two low two-storey roughcast houses set back from the Main Street. The total frontage has eight bays. The panelled doors are set under curved timber porches, supported on cast-iron brackets. Windows have Georgian-glazed sashes.

Cottages and Small Houses

Dunminning Cottage, 147 Ballywatermoy Road, Glarryford.

Recipient of grant: Mrs. E. Y. Aiken.

Grant assistance of £460 given towards: Rebuilding of chimneys. Roof repairs. Replacement metal rainwater goods. Repairs to external render. Repairs to windows.

Approximate cost of work: £3,377. Carried out from 1978 to 1980.

Contractors: David R. Jamison, Randalstown and T. W. Erwin, Ballymena.

Former School, 2 Sand Road, Galgorm.

One of two picturesque cottages which were formerly the village school. They are of basalt with granite dressings and have steeply pitched roofs with decorative slating. The gables contain triple lancets. This building is probably the earlier of the two, dated 1878, and with its bell tower and spire, more closely resembles a church than a school.

Recipient of grant: Mr. D. Moore.

Grant assistance of £1,956 given towards: Repairs to chimney. Roof repairs. Repairs to leadwork. Repairs to leadwork of spire. Repair of structural crack in gable. Replacement metal rainwater goods. Replacement sash windows in original style. Replacement external doors in original style. Installation of damp-proof course. Internal re-plastering. External redecoration.

Further financial assistance received from: Northern Ireland Housing Executive.

Approximate cost of work: £18,135. Carried out in 1982 and 1983.

Agent: Watson & Davidson, Ballymena.

Contractor: D. Herbison, Cullybackey.

Audley Lodge, 29 Ballymoney Road, Ballymena.

A single-storey house with dormered attics built before 1857. The walls are roughcast with plain dressings, windows are Georgian-glazed and the Ionic columned entrance is set in an elliptical arched opening.

Recipient of grant: Dr. S. T. Armstrong.

Grant assistance of £1,310 given towards: Roof repairs. Treatment of wood rot. Replacement sash windows in original style.

Approximate cost of work: £3,953. Carried out in 1980.

Contractor: John Carson, Ballymena.

Timber treatment by: Protim Services, Lisburn.

Thatched Cottage, 4 Meeting House Road, Aghacarnan, Ballinderry Upper, Lisburn.

A one-and-a-half-storey thatched house with roof probably of oak butt-purlin construction, possibly dating from the late 17th century. Walls are harled and whitened and there is a slated entrance porch on the east gable.

Cottages and Small Houses

Recipient of grant: Mr. S. J. Tuft.
Grant assistance of £2,860 given towards:
Re-thatching.
Approximate cost of work: £3,820.
Carried out in 1983.
Thatching by: Gerald Agnew, Ahoghill.

1 Manor Drive, Lisburn.

A very good quality one-and-a-half
storey gate lodge built about 1855. The
roof is slated and gabled with
decorative carved barge boards, walls
are of dressed sandstone with
dripstones over the two- and
three-light pointed windows. There is
a carved stone plaque over the
entrance. The house has been restored
and extended.

Recipient of grant: Mr. P. D. Cheyne.
Grant assistance of £500 given towards:
Repairs to roof structure and
re-slating. Restoration of finials and
decorative barge boards. Replacement
of decayed stone dressings.
Damp-proofing of walls. Internal
re-plastering. Replacement timber
floors.
Further financial assistance received from:
Northern Ireland Housing Executive.
Approximate cost of work: £23,937.
Carried out in 1981 and 1982.
Architect: D. St. C. Cheyne, Lisburn.
Contractor: Raymond Carlisle,
Ballynahinch.

59 Cargin Road, Toomebridge.

A single-storey traditional thatched
house.
Recipient of grant: Miss R. Irvine.
Grant assistance of £4,496 given towards:
Re-thatching.

1 Manor Drive, Lisburn.

Approximate cost of work: £4,726.
Carried out in 1979.
Thatching by: Gerald Agnew, Ahoghill.

Moneynick Post Office, 120 Moneynick Road, Randalstown.

A single-storey, pre-1829 thatched
house with harled walls.
Recipient of grant: Mr. J. McKeever.

PHASE ONE — REPAIRS
Grant assistance of £20 given towards:
Repairs to thatch.
Approximate cost of work: £60. Carried
out in 1976.

Thatching by: Gerald Agnew, Ahoghill.

PHASE TWO — RE-THATCHING
Grant assistance of £180 given towards:
Re-thatching.
Approximate cost of work: £540. Carried
out in 1976 and 1977.
Work carried out using direct labour.

126 Staffordstown Road, Cranfield, Randalstown.

A single-storey, thatched house.
Recipient of grant: Mr. G. MacAteer.
Grant assistance of £2,740 given towards:

Re-thatching. Replacement sash windows in original style. Replacement external doors in original style. External redecoration.
Approximate cost of work: £8,213.
Carried out in 1982.
Thatching by: Gerald Agnew, Ahoghill.
Joinery by: John P. McElhone Ltd., Castledawson.

Ballygrooby Lodge, Shane's Castle, Randalstown.

A Tudor style rendered gate lodge with elaborate carved barge boards.
Recipient of grant: Shane's Castle Estate Co.,
Grant assistance of £1,740 given towards: Re-slating using natural slate.
Approximate cost of work: £3,789.
Carried out in 1982.
Roof work by: Derek A. Weir, Randalstown.

1 Shane's Street, Randalstown.

Part of a long, single-storey, row of estate cottages with gabled dormers. The walls are of finely cut basalt with brick dressings.
Recipient of grant: The Lord O'Neill.
Grant assistance of £673 given towards: Re-slating using natural slate. Re-pointing stonework. Replacement sash windows in original style. Repairs to internal plasterwork. Installation of damp-proof solid floors.
Further financial assistance received from: Northern Ireland Housing Executive.
Approximate cost of work: £9,694.
Carried out in 1980.
Contractor: Wilson Partners, Antrim.

The Antrim Gate Lodge, Shane's Castle, Randalstown.

A Tudor style gate lodge with elaborate barge boards, rendered walls, porchway and handsome iron gateway with piers surmounted by coronets.
Recipient of grant: The Lord O'Neill.

PHASE ONE – REPAIRS
Grant assistance of £130 given towards: External re-rendering, including running new mouldings.
Further financial assistance received from: Northern Ireland Housing Executive.
Approximate cost of work: £1,899.
Carried out in 1979.
Contractor: McNally Contractors (Randalstown) Ltd., Randalstown.

PHASE TWO – REPAIRS
Grant assistance of £1,230 given towards: Re-slating using natural slate. Repairs to rainwater goods. Repairs to panelled entrance door.
Approximate cost of work: £4,458.
Carried out in 1981.
Contractor: Derek A. Weir, Randalstown.

1 and 2 Edenduff Cottages, Shane's Castle, Randalstown.

Two single-storey workers' cottages which have been combined to form a single dwelling. The walls are of rubble basalt and windows were originally lattice-paned.
Recipient of grant: Mr. A. J. S. Haines.
Grant assistance of £1,115 given towards: Roof repairs. Replacement metal rainwater goods. Re-pointing of stonework. Replacement external doors in original style. External redecoration. Treatment of wood rot. Repairs to internal plasterwork.

Repairs to timber floors. Installation of damp-proof solid floors.
Further financial assistance received from: Northern Ireland Housing Executive.
Approximate cost of work: £12,000.
Carried out in 1979 and 1980.
Work carried out using direct labour.

13 and 14 Edenduff Cottages, Randalstown.

Two single-storey workers' cottages which have been combined to form a single dwelling. The walls are of rubble basalt and windows were originally lattice-paned.
Recipient of grant: Mrs. C. A. McClelland.
Grant assistance of £1,260 given towards: Re-slating using natural slate. Replacement metal rainwater goods. Re-pointing of stonework. Replacement external doors in original style. Installation of damp-proof course. Internal re-plastering. Installation of damp-proof solid floors.
Further financial assistance received from: Northern Ireland Housing Executive.
Approximate cost of work: £12,191.
Carried out from 1980 to 1982.
Contractor: Raymond Fry, Randalstown.

Clady Cottage, Straidballymorris, Dunadry, Antrim.

A beautifully situated, two-bay, single-storey thatched house with attic, built about 1780 and renovated in 1958. Recent additions have been carefully concealed. The thatched roof is half-hipped, walls are of rubble blackstone with brick dressings, the wide windows have unrecessed Georgian-glazed sashes and the panelled entrance door with decorative

Edenduff Cottages, Randalstown.

sidelights and fanlight is set in an elliptically-arched opening.

Recipient of grant: Mrs. J. E. P. Wilson.

Grant assistance of £405 given towards: Repairs to thatch.

Approximate cost of work: £1,195. Carried out in 1977 and 1978.

Thatching by: Gerald Agnew, Ahoghill.

41 Coach Road, Templepatrick.

A single-storey roughcast and thatched house with timber porch and lean-to extension to the north. The house was originally part of a three house terrace, the middle house of which has been demolished.

Recipient of grant: Mr. A. Sewell.

Grant assistance of £275 given towards: Repairs to roof structure. Re-thatching.

Approximate cost of work: £962. Carried out in 1977.

Contractor: F. C. Dubois & Co., Templepatrick.

Thatching by: Gerald Agnew, Ahoghill.

43 Coach Road, Templepatrick.

A single-storey roughcast and thatched house, originally part of a three house terrace, the middle house of which has been demolished.

Recipient of grant: Mrs. J. Adair.

Grant assistance of £205 given towards: Re-thatching.

Approximate cost of work: £614. Carried out in 1977.

Thatching by: Gerald Agnew, Ahoghill.

60 Abbeyview, Muckamore.

An attractive five-bay, single-storey pre-1780 cottage. The roof is hipped and slated, walls are dry-dashed with smooth plain dressings and windows have Georgian-glazed sashes. The panelled entrance door with plain sidelights and decorative fanlight, has barley sugar pilasters and is recessed in an elliptically-arched opening.

Recipient of grant: Mr. S. Mulholland.

Grant assistance of £700 given towards: Repairs to chimneys. Roof repairs. Repairs to leadwork. Repairs to rainwater goods. Replacement sash windows in original style. Repairs to doorcase. External redecoration. Damp-proofing of walls. Repairs to internal plasterwork. Installation of damp-proof solid floors. Repairs to internal joinery.

Further financial assistance received from: Northern Ireland Housing Executive.

Approximate cost of work: £7,874. Carried out in 1979 and 1980.

Contractor: James Rainey & Sons, Randalstown.

36 Derrycrush Road, Cloncore, Portadown.

A single-storey thatched house with an in-line range of outbuildings, sash windows and projecting porch with rounded quoins.

Recipient of grant: Mrs. M. J. Wilson.

Crabtree Cottage, 50 Farlough Road, Portadown.

PHASE ONE – REPAIRS

Grant assistance of £120 given towards: Repairs to thatch.

Approximate cost of work: £343. Carried out in 1977.

Thatching by: James J. Gray, Portadown.

PHASE TWO – REPAIRS

Grant assistance of £72 given towards: Repairs to thatch.

Thatching by: James J. Gray, Portadown.

PHASE THREE – REPAIRS

Grant assistance of £100 given towards: Repairs to thatch.

Approximate cost of work: £301. Carried out in 1980 and 1981.

Thatching by: Andrew Walker, Castletown, Omagh.

PHASE FOUR – REPAIRS

Grant assistance of £770 given towards: Repairs to thatch.

Approximate cost of work: £1,047. Carried out in 1982.

Thatching by: Andrew Walker, Castletown, Omagh.

PHASE FIVE – REPAIRS

Grant assistance of £150 given towards: Replacement sash windows in original style.

Approximate cost of work: £446. Carried out in 1983.

Contractor: The County Joinery Works Ltd., Portadown.

Crabtree Cottage, 50 Farlough Road, Portadown.

An early 19th century Ulster weaver's thatched house and barn.

Recipient of grant: Mr. and Mrs. R. E. Dickie.

Grant assistance of £370 given towards: Re-thatching.

Approximate cost of work: £3,098. Carried out in 1982 and 1983.

Thatching by: R. Stevenson, Mullenakill, Dungannon.

Lock House, Moneypenny's Lock, 30 Horseshoe Lane, Newry Canal, Portadown.

A one-and-a-half-storey 'T'-shaped house. The roof is slated with raised verges and gabled dormer windows, walls are of harled freestone, windows have plain sashes and the entrance door is set in a gabled porch.

Recipient of grant: The National Trust.

Grant assistance of £14,000 given towards: Purchase price of the property for ownership by the National Trust until 1992 or before, pending the emergence of a scheme to preserve the Newry Canal.

Approximate cost of work: £15,000. Carried out in 1982.

Cottages and Small Houses

Bloomvale House, 171 Plantation Road, Bleary, Craigavon.

A single-storey thatched house with galleted rubble walls and dressed stone openings.

Recipient of grant: Mr. D. Blane.

PHASE ONE – THATCHING

Grant assistance of £1,333 given towards: Re-thatching.

Approximate cost of work: £3,333. Carried out in 1979.

Thatching by: Gerald Agnew, Ahoghill.

PHASE TWO – REPAIRS

Grant assistance of £410 given towards: Replacement sash windows in original style. Replacement panelled entrance door. Repairs to internal plasterwork. Repairs to internal joinery. Installation of damp-proof solid floors.

Approximate cost of work: £1,134. Carried out in 1981.

Contractor: W. Scott, Bleary, Portadown.

36 Ballynagarrick Road, Portadown.

A single-storey, roughcast thatched house.

Recipient of grant: Miss M. D. McCullough.

Grant assistance of £216 given towards: Repairs to thatch.

Approximate cost of work: £647. Carried out in 1980.

Thatching by: Gerald Agnew, Ahoghill.

Drumnabreeze Post Office, Magheralin, Craigavon.

A single-storey estate cottage with slated roof, projecting gabled porch, roughcast walls and Georgian-glazed sash windows. The cottage has been extended and repaired.

The Lock House, Newry Canal, Portadown.

Recipient of grant: Col. E. H. Brush.

Grant assistance of £1,600 given towards: Repairs to chimneys. Re-slating using natural slate. Replacement metal rainwater goods. External re-rendering. Repairs to windows. Repairs to internal plasterwork. Installation of damp-proof solid floors.

Further financial assistance received from: Northern Ireland Housing Executive.

Approximate cost of work: £11,038. Carried out in 1980 and 1981.

Agent: Derek Hall, Lurgan.

Contractor: Hugh Bell, Ahorey, Richhill.

21 Seagoe Road, Portadown.

A long traditional, single-storey thatched house. Walls are harled and windows have vertically divided sashes.

Recipient of grant: Miss M. L. Best.

PHASE ONE

Grant assistance of £315 given towards: Repairs to chimneys. Repairs to thatch.

Approximate cost of work: £945. Carried out in 1979.

Contractor: Gerald Agnew, Ahoghill.

PHASE TWO

Grant assistance of £145 given towards: Repairs to external render. External redecoration.

Approximate cost of work: £558. Carried out in 1981.

Contractor: William Houston & Son, Portadown.

Painting by: G. Kelly, Portadown.

West Lodge, Knappagh House, 48 Knappagh Road, Killylea.

A single-storey, cross-gabled lodge with colonaded entrance front.

Recipient of grant: Messrs. Terris Partners.

Grant assistance of £3,221 given towards: Rebuilding of chimneys. Repairs to roof structure. Re-slating using natural slate. Replacement metal rainwater goods. External re-rendering. Replacement sash windows in original style. Replacement external doors in original style. Sandblasting of cast-iron columns. Internal re-plastering. Installation of damp-proof solid floors. External redecoration.

Further financial assistance received from: Northern Ireland Housing Executive.

Approximate cost of work: £18,163. Carried out in 1981 and 1982.

Contractor: S. F. Mullan, Bellaghy, Co. Armagh.

Riverside Cottage, 34 Water Street, Rostrevor.

One of a terrace of four, one-and-a-half-storey, early-19th century cottages. The roofs are slated, with gabled dormers and decorative barge boards. The windows have lattice-paned glazing.

Recipient of grant: Mr. J. Branagan.

Grant assistance of £605 given towards: Repairs to chimney. Re-slating using natural slate. Repairs to rainwater goods. Repairs to windows. Replacement panelled entrance door. Repairs to internal plasterwork. Installation of damp-proof solid floors. Redecoration of remedial items.

Further financial assistance received from: Northern Ireland Housing Executive.

Approximate cost of work: £10,500. Carried out in 1982.

Architects: Cole Partnership, Warrenpoint.

Contractor: P. Quinn, Rostrevor.

Dunbarton Lodge, 52 Dunbarton Street, Gilford.

A single-storey, late-19th century building. The roof is hipped and slated with modillioned eaves, walls are smooth rendered and windows have Georgian-glazed sashes. The panelled entrance door has a plain rectangular fanlight.

Recipient of grant: Mrs. S. Beggs.

Grant assistance of £550 given towards: Treatment of wood rot and subsequent reinstatement.

Approximate cost of work: £1,652. Carried out in 1978.

Contractor: A. A. Quinn Ltd., Tandragee.

Mutton Hill, 71 Dromore Road, Banbridge.

A one-and-a-half-storey cottage-orné style house built about 1840. The roof is slated, walls are roughcast and the windows have small-paned casements with external screens.

Recipient of grant: Mrs. D. J. Watson.

Grant assistance of £520 given towards: Re-slating using natural slate. Repairs to windows. Replacement external window screens. Repairs to internal plasterwork.

Approximate cost of work: £1,802. Carried out in 1979.

Contractor: Robert Heak Ltd., Tandragee.

Laburnum Cottage, 37 Edentiroory Road, Dromore.

A part-thatched and part-slated

single-storey cottage with roughcast walls.

Recipient of grant: Miss M. K. Boyce.

Grant assistance of £3,469 given towards: Repairs to chimneys. Re-thatching. Repairs to roof structure of slated roof. Re-slating using natural slate. Repairs to rainwater goods. External re-rendering.

Approximate cost of work: £3,877. Carried out in 1980.

Contractor: Kerr Bros., Banbridge.

Thatching by: Gerald Agnew, Ahoghill.

Ballyvicknacally School, 91 Ballynahinch Road, Dromore.

A single-storey schoolhouse built in 1885 with a later, lower addition of 1906. The roof is slated, chimneys are of yellow brick and walls are smooth rendered. The school has been converted for use as a dwelling.

Recipient of grant: Mr. M. R. McDowell.

Grant assistance of £3,850 given towards: Repairs to chimneys. Re-slating using natural slate. Repairs to rainwater goods. Restoration of original roof trusses and sheeted ceiling. Treatment of wood rot. Restoration of barrel stoves. External redecoration.

Further financial assistance received from: Northern Ireland Housing Executive.

Approximate cost of work: £20,500. Carried out in 1980.

Contractor: S. R. Cochrane Ltd., Belfast.

42 Quarterland Road, Rathgorman, Killinchy.

A single-storey, early-19th century, thatched house with whitened walls.

Recipient of grant: Mr. D. W. Wilson.

Grant assistance of £2,310 given towards: Re-thatching.

Approximate cost of work: £3,075. Carried out in 1980.

Thatching by: Gerald Agnew, Ahoghill.

40 Tullykin Road, Killyleagh.

A single-storey, slated and gabled dwelling built about 1800.

Recipient of grant: Mrs. L. Kulow.

Grant assistance of £3,234 given towards: Repairs to chimneys. Re-roofing using natural slate. External re-rendering. Internal re-plastering. Installation of damp-proof solid floors.

Further financial assistance received from: Northern Ireland Housing Executive.

Approximate cost of work: £26,320. Carried out in 1980 and 1981.

Architects: Diamond Redfern Anderson, Belfast.

Almshouse, 6 Churchtown Road, Ballyculter.

A single-storey, Tudor-cottage style, almshouse built in 1832 from an endowment of £365 by the Hon. Sophia Ward. The roof is slated, with three gables, walls are rendered and windows are mullioned with dripstones. The chimneys are extremely ornate.

Recipient of grant: Mrs. R. Walsh.

Grant assistance of £92 given towards: Replacement windows in original style.

Approximate cost of work: £276. Carried out in 1980.

Contractor: Joseph McClune & Son, Dundrum.

10 Castle Street, Killough.

Two, one-and-a-half-storey, pre-1833, cottages which have been combined to form one dwelling. The roof is slated with two gables to the smooth rendered frontage. Windows have plain sashes.

Recipient of grant: Mr. H. McKenna.

Grant assistance of £1,768 given towards: Repairs to chimneys. Re-slating using natural slate. Repairs to leadwork. Replacement rainwater goods. Repairs to external render. Replacement sash windows in original style. Treatment of wood rot. Internal re-plastering. Repairs to timber floors. Installation of damp-proof solid floors. Replacement of internal panelled doors. Repairs to staircase.

Further financial assistance received from: Northern Ireland Housing Executive.

Approximate cost of work: £14,713. Carried out from 1981 to 1983.

Contractor: Michael J. Hood, Belfast.

Timber treatment by: Radication Ltd., Dunmurry, Belfast.

16 Castle Street, Killough.

A one-and-a-half-storey terrace cottage with a single gable to the smooth rendered frontage.

Recipient of grant: Miss G. J. Rogan.

Grant assistance of £1,025 given towards: Provision of pitched roof to new extension using natural slate. Re-slating main roof using natural slate. Repairs to internal plasterwork.

Further financial assistance received from: Northern Ireland Housing Executive.

Approximate cost of work: £9,860. Carried out in 1981.

Contractor: John Gilchrist, Ardglass.

7 Bryansford Village.

A one-and-a-half-storey, late-19th century house with a central gabled

Cottages and Small Houses

timber porch and a flattish hipped half-dormer window offset on the main frontage. The roof is hipped and slated and the walls are of random rubble stonework,

Recipient of grant: Mr. J. N. Halford.

Grant assistance of £500 given towards: Roof repairs. Replacement windows in original style. Treatment of wood rot and subsequent reinstatement.

Further financial assistance received from: Northern Ireland Housing Executive.

Approximate cost of work: £8,945. Carried out in 1979.

Work carried out using direct labour.

Curragh-Ard Lodge, Newcastle.

A 'U'-shaped, five-bay, single-storey Regency house built about 1850 with basement and two-storey returns. The roof is hipped and slated, walls are rendered with moulded dressings, windows have Georgian-glazed sashes and the pedimented porch contains semi-circular-headed windows and the entrance door with radial fanlight over.

Recipient of grant: Mrs. M. H. Kirkpatrick.

Grant assistance of £153 given towards: External redecoration.

Approximate cost of work: £460. Carried out in 1975.

Painting by: R. Kendal, Newcastle.

161 and 163 South Promenade, Newcastle.

Two one-and-a-half-storey widows' terrace cottages built about 1850. The roofs are slated, with overhanging eaves and gabled over the single first floor windows. The frontage is of roughcast rubble stonework.

Recipients of grant: Miss P. A. Y. Speedy (Number 161) and Mr. H. A. Speedy (Number 163).

Grant assistance of £1,267 given towards: Repairs to chimney. Re-slating using natural slate. Repairs to fascia and barge boards. Replacement metal rainwater goods. External re-rendering. Replacement windows in a style similar to original. Replacement external doors in original style. Redecoration of remedial items. Repairs to internal plasterwork. Installation of damp-proof solid floors.

Further financial assistance received from: Northern Ireland Housing Executive.

Approximate cost of work: £18,860. Carried out in 1980 and 1981.

Contractor: John Rodgers, Annalong.

175 South Promenade, Newcastle.

A one-and-a-half-storey widows terrace cottage built about 1850. The roof is slated, with overhanging eaves and gabled over the single first floor window. The walls are of roughcast rubble stonework and windows have small panes.

Recipient of grant: Mr. A. Adair.

Grant assistance of £530 given towards: Re-slating. Replacement rainwater goods. External re-rendering. Replacement windows in original style. Repairs to internal plasterwork. Installation of damp-proof solid floors.

Further financial assistance received from: Northern Ireland Housing Executive.

Approximate cost of work: £7,198. Carried out in 1981.

Contractor: Kane & McAuley, Newcastle.

Rockmore, 163 Central Promenade, Newcastle.

A pretty, single-storey, Regency house with rendered walls, round-headed windows and a canted Victorian bay to one end. The house has a basement.

Recipient of grant: Mr. W. A. Campbell.

PHASE ONE — DRY ROT

Grant assistance of £1,050 given towards: Treatment of wood rot and subsequent reinstatement.

Approximate cost of work: £3,963. Carried out in 1978.

Architects: Ferguson & McIlveen, Belfast.

Timber treatment by: McLaughlin & Harvey Ltd., Newtownabbey.

PHASE TWO — DRY ROT

Grant assistance of £575 given towards: Treatment of wood rot and subsequent reinstatement.

Approximate cost of work: £1,725. Carried out in 1981.

Timber treatment by: Rentokil Ltd., Belfast.

PHASE THREE — REPAIRS

Grant assistance of £2,100 given towards: Repairs to roof structure. Re-slating using natural slate. Replacement metal rainwater goods. Repairs to external render. Replacement windows in basement in original style. Repairs to panelled entrance door. Repairs to internal plasterwork.

Approximate cost of work: £8,323. Carried out in 1981.

Contractor: F. J. Charleton, Ballymartin. Kilkeel.

Cottages and Small Houses

3 Blackstaff Road, Clough.

A single-storey vernacular dwelling, formerly part of a larger block.

Recipient of grant: Mrs. M. Johnston.

Grant assistance of £1,336 given towards: Repairs to chimneys. Re-roofing using natural slate. Replacement metal rainwater goods. Replacement sash windows in original style. Replacement entrance door. Installation of electro-osmotic damp-proof course. Installation of damp-proof solid floors.

Further financial assistance received from: Northern Ireland Housing Executive.

Approximate cost of work: £6,590. Carried out in 1981 and 1982.

Contractor: Tumelty Building Contractors, Dundrum.

Damp-proof course by: Rentokil Ltd., Belfast.

Shamrock Ville, 33 Sprucefield Road, Blaris, Lisburn.

A 'U'-shaped, single-storey, early-19th century house with basement becoming two storeys at rear. The main front is to the south and is three bays wide, the side bays, containing shallow bow, break forward slightly from the central bay and have tripartite windows. The roof is hipped and slated, walls are rendered, windows have Georgian-paned sashes and the entrance door with sidelights is set under an elliptical fanlight on the west side of the house.

Recipient of grant: Mr. W. M. Robinson.

Grant assistance of £2,500 given towards: Repairs to chimneys. Repairs to rainwater goods. External re-rendering. Replacement sash

windows in original style. Replacement external doors in original style. Redecoration of remedial items.

Approximate cost of work: £8,380. Carried out in 1978 and 1979.

Contractor: G. B. Smith, Maze.

Painting by: T. Foster & Son, Derriaghy.

Gate Lodge, St. Malachy's Parish Church, Main Street, Hillsborough.

A delightful single-storey long, low pavilion set at right angles to the road and forming part of the symmetrical composition of the gate screen at the entrance to the two parallel driveways leading to the church. The roof is slated, with three little Gothic spirelets to the gable facing the road. Walls are of rubble with sandstone dressings. The two tall, narrow diamond-paned windows and the door opening to the gable have two-centered arched openings.

Recipient of grant: The Church of Ireland.

Grant assistance of £1,330 given towards: Repairs to chimney. Roof repairs. Repairs to rainwater goods. Re-pointing of stonework. Replacement of windows with diamond-paned replicas. Installation of damp-proof solid floors. Damp-proofing of walls.

Approximate cost of work: £2,674. Carried out in 1979.

Contractor: Lockwoods Construction (N.I.) Ltd., Lisburn.

3 Arthur Street, Hillsborough.

One of a terrace of potentially attractive one-and-a-half-storey cottage orné style houses, built about 1850.

The roof is slated and walls are of blackstone with brick and sandstone dressings.

Recipient of grant: Mrs. M. P. White.

Grant assistance of £1,321 given towards: Replacement metal rainwater goods. Replacement casement windows in original style. Restoration of dormer. Replacement sheeted entrance door. Installation of damp-proof course. Repairs to internal plasterwork.

Further financial assistance received from: Northern Ireland Housing Executive.

Approximate cost of work: £11,500. Carried out in 1981.

Contractor: Stanley W. Gilmore, Lisburn.

7 Arthur Street, Hillsborough.

One of a terrace of potentially attractive one-and-a-half-storey cottage orné style houses, built about 1850. The roof is slated and walls are of blackstone with brick and sandstone dressings.

Recipient of grant: Mrs. E. J. Steer.

Grant assistance of £54 given towards: Re-slating using natural slate.

Further financial assistance received from: Northern Ireland Housing Executive.

Approximate cost of work: £6,149. Carried out in 1979.

Agent: S. V. W. McCready & Co., Lisburn.

Contractor: E. V. Bryans. Hillsborough.

Eden Cottage, 19 Pine Hill, Lisburn.

A three-bay, single-storey traditional thatched house.

Recipient of grant: Miss A. E. Weir.

Grant assistance of £3,315 given towards:
Re-thatching.
Approximate cost of work: £3,685.
Carried out in 1981.
Thatching by: Gerald Agnew, Ahoghill.

Ballyskeagh Lock-house, 1 Ballyskeagh Road, Lambeg.

A small square, two-storey lock-keepers house built about 1760 to designs by Thomas Omer, engineer for the Lagan Canal. The roof is slated and gabled, walls are of cement-washed rubble with cut stone dressings including a continuous platband at first floor level. Each elevation has a central recessed semi-circular-headed arch and on the north this contains the entrance door with block architrave and square head formed of stepped and projecting voussoirs. The house is derelict and attempts have been made to inspire restoration.
Recipient of grant: Mr. W. McCue.
Grant assistance of £6,283 given towards: Professional fees involved in feasibility study for re-use developed to tender stage.
Approximate cost of work: £9,043.
Carried out from 1981 to 1983.
Architects: Robert McKinstry & Melvyn Brown, Belfast.
Structural Engineers: Kirk, McClure & Morton, Belfast.

113 and 115 Hillhall Road, Lisburn.

Part of a group of roadside pre-1833 single-storey houses.
Recipient of grant: Mrs. S. Bingham.
Grant assistance of £2,800 given towards: Repairs to chimneys. Re-thatching. Repairs to external render.

Replacement sash windows in original style. Replacement external doors in original style. Repairs to internal plasterwork. Installation of damp-proof solid floors.
Further financial assistance received from: Northern Ireland Housing Executive.
Approximate cost of work: £18,000.
Carried out in 1980.
Contractor: M. & S. Building Contractors, Belfast.
Thatching by: Gerald Agnew, Ahoghill.

Thatch Cottage, 31 Halfpenny Gate Road, Broomhedge, Moira.

A six-bay, single-storey thatched house built before 1833. The walls are roughcast, windows have horizontal divided sashes and a porch with corrugated iron roof projects.
Recipient of grant: Mr. J. B. Ross.

PHASE ONE – REPAIRS TO THATCH
Grant assistance of £350 given towards: Repairs to thatch.
Approximate cost of work: £1,376.
Carried out in 1977.
Thatching by: Irish Thatchers Ltd., Dungannon.

PHASE TWO – RETHATCHING
Grant assistance of £3,400 given towards: Re-thatching.
Approximate cost of work: £4,565.
Carried out in 1981.
Thatching by: Gerald Agnew, Ahoghill.

5 Coastguard Cottages, Coastguard Avenue, Helen's Bay.

Part of a terrace of late-19th century two-storey cottages. Two properties have been combined to form one dwelling. The roof is slated, with tall chimneys and the walls are of decorative poly-chromatic brickwork.
Recipient of grant: Mr. P. G. Thallon.
Grant assistance of £2,450 given towards: Repairs to chimneys. Re-slating using natural slate. Repairs to metal framed diamond-paned windows. Replacement external doors in original style. Installation of damp-proof solid floors. Replacement of internal panelled doors.
Further financial assistance received from: Northern Ireland Housing Executive.
Approximate cost of work: £8,487.
Carried out in 1979 and 1980.
Contractor: James Rice & Co., Helen's Bay.

1 Coastguard Cottages, Farmhill Road, Marino.

One of a delightful asymmetrically planned terrace. The house is based around a square tower with pyramid roof and cut stone angular oriels at first floor level. Roofs are slated and walls are of variegated brickwork.
Recipient of grant: Mrs. M. Penpraze.
Grant assistance of £2,290 given towards: Repairs to weathercock. Re-slating using natural slate. Replacement metal rainwater goods. Re-pointing of brickwork.
Approximate cost of work: £6,897.
Carried out in 1983.
Contractor: Jonor Estates Ltd., Holywood.

West Gate Lodge, Ballywalter Park, 124 Greyabbey Road, Ballywalter.

A single-storey gate lodge, rendered, with classical detailing to gables and porch.

Cottages and Small Houses

Recipient of grant: The Lord Dunleath.

Grant assistance of £280 given towards: Repairs to chimney. Re-slating using natural slate. Repairs to rainwater goods. External re-rendering. Replacement sash windows in original style. Replacement external doors in original style. External redecoration. Repairs to internal plasterwork.

Further financial assistance received from: Northern Ireland Housing Executive.

Approximate cost of work: £6,595. Carried out in 1980 and 1981.

Work carried out using direct labour.

West Gate Lodge, Mount Stewart, Greyabbey.

One of a pair of tiny single-storey gate lodges with hipped slated roofs, dark stone walls and pointed-arch windows with decorative Georgian glazing.

Recipient of grant: Lady Mairi Bury.

Grant assistance of £216 given towards: Replacement windows in original Gothic style.

Approximate cost of work: £648. Carried out in 1981.

Work carried out using direct labour.

Cunningburn Mill Group, Newtownards.

A late-18th century, single-storey, thatched house with harled and whitened walls and Georgian-glazed sash windows.

Recipient of grant: Mr. F. Warden.

Grant assistance of £1,350 given towards: Repairs to chimneys. Re-thatching. External re-rendering.

Approximate cost of work: £4,049. Carried out in 1981.

Thatching by: Gerald Agnew, Ahoghill.

35 Thornyhill Road, Killinchy.

A single-storey whitewashed and thatched house with attic, built about 1784. The windows have Georgian-glazed sashes and the panelled door is set in an elliptically arched opening, with sidelights and fanlight.

Recipient of grant: Miss M. A. Craig.

PHASE ONE – REPAIRS

Grant assistance of £47 given towards: Repairs to thatch.

Approximate cost of work: £117. Carried out in 1976.

PHASE TWO

Grant assistance of £1,010 given towards: Re-thatching.

Approximate cost of work: £2,995. Carried out in 1980.

Thatching by: Gerald Agnew, Ahoghill.

35 Thornyhill Road, Killinchy.

Clongowna Cottage, 68 Cavan Road, Newtownbutler.

A traditional single-storey thatched house.

Recipient of grant: Mr. & Mrs. E. McEniff.

Grant assistance of £316 given towards: Repairs to external render. Provision of sash window in original style. Replacement panelled entrance door. Repairs to internal plasterwork. Installation of damp-proof solid floors.

Further financial assistance received from: Northern Ireland Housing Executive.

Approximate cost of work: £5,660. Carried out in 1982.

Work carried out using direct labour.

Thatched Cottage, Derryadd, Lisnaskea.

A three-bay one-and-a-half-storey thatched house.

Recipient of grant: Miss D. Plunkett.

Grant assistance of £430 given towards: Repairs to roof structure. Repairs to thatch. Repair to gate piers.

Further financial assistance received from: Northern Ireland Housing Executive.

Approximate cost of work: £4,370. Carried out in 1978 and 1979.

Contractor: Wilson & Ward, Enniskillen.

Thatching by: Kevin Mulhern, Belleek.

Stonepark Cottage, 4 Colebrooke Park Road, Eskragh, Brookeborough.

A single-storey cottage with attic. The roof is slated and gabled. Walls are roughcast with stone dressings and the windows have diamond-pane glazing.

Thatched Cottage, Derryadd, Lisnaskea.

Recipient of grant: Mrs. M. Hamill Smythe.

Grant assistance of £116 given towards: Repairs to windows. Replacement front door in original style.

Approximate cost of work: £310. Carried out in 1978.

Contractor: Norman Kerr, Fivemiletown.

49 Main Street, Brookeborough.

One of a block of three, mid-19th century, single-storey houses with slated roofs, roughcast walls and Georgian-glazed sash windows.

Recipient of grant: Mr. A. E. Gale.

Grant assistance of £4,414 given towards: Repairs to chimneys. Re-slating using natural slate. Replacement metal rainwater goods. Repairs to external render. Repairs to windows. Replacement panelled entrance door. Treatment of wood rot. Installation of damp-proof course. Repairs to internal plasterwork. Repairs to timber floors.

Further financial assistance received from: Northern Ireland Housing Executive.

Approximate cost of work: £15,180. Carried out in 1981.

Contractor: John Johnston, Fivemiletown.

47 Main Street, Brookeborough.

One of a block of three, mid-19th century, single-storey houses with slated roofs, roughcast walls and Georgian-glazed sash windows.

Recipient of grant: Mr. P. Lynch.

Grant assistance of £1,760 given towards: Rebuilding of chimneys. Re-slating using natural slate. Provision of decorative barge board to gable. Replacement metal rainwater goods. External re-rendering. Replacement sash windows in original style. Replacement external doors in original style. Repairs to internal plasterwork. Installation of damp-proof solid floors.

Further financial assistance received from: Northern Ireland Housing Executive.

Approximate cost of work: £14,500. Carried out in 1981.

Agent: Eugene Howe, Tempo.

Contractor: Michael King, Trillick.

Bannagh Lodge, 106 Pettigo Road, Kesh.

A single-storey, stone-built, estate dwelling.

Recipient of grant: Rev. L. Bryan.

Grant assistance of £3,114 given towards: Repairs to chimneys. Repairs to roof structure. Re-slating using natural slate. Replacement of stone ridge tiles. Repairs to bracketted soffit of roof eaves. Repairs to cast-iron windows. Re-pointing of stonework. Treatment of wood rot. Installation of electro-osmotic damp-proof course. Internal re-plastering. Replacement of internal doors with second-hand panelled doors. Internal joinery repairs. Professional fees.

Further financial assistance received from:

Northern Ireland Housing Executive.

Approximate cost of work: £17,800. Carried out in 1981 and 1982.

Agent: Brian Cooke Design, Enniskillen.

Contractor: G. Ferguson & Sons, Belcoo.

Timber treatment by: Rentokil Ltd., Belfast.

Gate Lodge, Necarne Castle, Irvinestown.

A neat three-bay lodge in an Elizabethan style echoing the main house. The chimneys are diagonally set.

Recipient of grant: Mr. R. B. McCartney.

Grant assistance of £2,013 given towards: Re-slating using natural slate to front slopes. Replacement metal rainwater goods. Repairs to external render. Replacement windows in original style. Repairs to internal plasterwork. Installation of damp-proof solid floors.

Further financial assistance received from: Northern Ireland Housing Executive.

Approximate cost of work: £12,757. Carried out in 1981.

Contractor: John Gray, Enniskillen.

West Gate Lodge, Castle Coole, Enniskillen.

A single-storey gate lodge with part basement built about 1850 possibly to designs by Charles Lanyon. The roof is hipped and slated with decorative chimney pots set on stone bases. Walls are of coursed sandstone ashlar.

Recipient of grant: The National Trust.

Grant assistance of £270 given towards: Provision and installation of replica decorative chimney pots.

Approximate cost of work: £809. Carried out in 1980.

Contractor: Wilson & Ward, Enniskillen.

Pots manufactured by: McClurg Developments Ltd., Hillsborough.

West Gate Lodge,
Castle Coole, Enniskillen.

Cottages and Small Houses

Gate Lodge, Blessingbourne, Fivemiletown.

A picturesque, symmetrically planned single-storey lodge with verandah at front and diamond-paned windows. The lodge has been restored and extended.

Recipient of grant: Captain R. H. Lowry.

Grant assistance of £1,025 given towards: Rebuilding of chimneys. Re-slating using natural slate. External re-rendering. Replacement panelled entrance door. Treatment of wood rot. Installation of silicone injection damp-proof course.

Further financial assistance received from: Northern Ireland Housing Executive.

Approximate cost of work: £8,940. Carried out in 1981.

Work carried out using direct labour.

Gate Lodge, St. Macartan's Home, 72 Main Street, Clogher.

A small single-storey gate lodge built about 1819 with slated gabled roof, rendered walls with stone dressings and central Doric portico.

Recipient of grant: Sisters of Mercy.

Grant assistance of £140 given towards: Cleaning and repair of sandstone dressings.

Approximate cost of work: £429. Carried out in 1980 and 1981.

Architect: M. Donnelly, Enniskillen.

Contractor: McAleer & Teague, Dromore, Co. Tyrone.

The Lodge, Ballykelly Presbyterian Church, Ballykelly.

A small single-storey, three-bay lodge of ashlar sandstone construction with hipped slated roof. Built in 1827 at the same time as the church to the designs of Richard Suitar, the Fishmonger's Company surveyor.

Recipient of grant: Ballykelly Presbyterian Church.

Grant assistance of £425 given towards: Re-slating using natural slate.

Approximate cost of work: £825. Carried out in 1978.

Contractor: Deehan & Glass, Limavady.

85 Aghanloo Road, Drumbane, Limavady.

A nine-bay, single-storey, thatched house with plain sashed windows and modern porch.

Recipient of grant: Miss E. Love.

Grant assistance of £1,025 given towards: Repairs to thatch.

Approximate cost of work: £3,246. Carried out in 1978.

Thatching by: Gerald Agnew, Ahoghill.

40 Glen Road, Garvagh.

A single-storey thatched house built before 1832.

Recipient of grant: Mrs. E. O'Kane.

Grant assistance of £3,898 given towards: Repairs to roof structure. Re-thatching. External re-rendering. Replacement sash windows in original style. Replacement external doors in original style.

Approximate cost of work: £4,033. Carried out in 1981 and 1982.

Contractor: Brendan Boylan, Garvagh.

Thatching by: Gerald Agnew, Ahoghill.

Black Glen Lodge, 30 Tunnel Brae, Castlerock.

A single-storey blackstone cottage with projecting open lean-to entrance porch. Formerly a gate lodge to the Downhill Estate.

Recipient of grant: Mr. C. Houston.

PHASE ONE – REPAIRS

Grant assistance of £100 given towards: Treatment of woodworm. Installation of electro-osmotic damp-proof course.

Approximate cost of work: £352. Carried out in 1979.

Timber treatment and damp-proof course by: Rentokil Ltd., Belfast.

PHASE TWO – REPAIRS

Grant assistance of £140 given towards: Repairs to internal plasterwork.

Approximate cost of work: £430. Carried out in 1980.

Work carried out using direct labour.

12 School Lane, Castlerock.

One of a pair of blackstone single-storey cottages with stone dressings and decorative barge boards.

Recipient of grant: Mrs. H. Corrigan.

Grant assistance of £274 given towards: Replacement windows and doors in original style. Treatment of woodworm. Installation of damp-proof solid floors.

Further financial assistance received from: Northern Ireland Housing Executive.

Approximate cost of work: £2,648. Carried out in 1981.

Contractor: Adam Anderson, Castlerock.

Timber treatment by: Rentokil Ltd., Belfast.

Hazlett House, Liffock, Castlerock.

Cottages and Small Houses

14 School Lane, Castlerock.

One of a pair of blackstone single-storey cottages with stone dressings and decorative barge boards.

Recipient of grant: Mr. T. McCarron.

Grant assistance of £105 given towards: Rebuilding of chimney. Roof repairs. Repairs to rainwater goods.

Further financial assistance received from: Northern Ireland Housing Executive.

Approximate cost of work: £2,133. Carried out in 1980.

Contractor: Adam Anderson, Castlerock.

Woodland Cottage, 30 Springbank Road, Castlerock.

A five-bay traditional thatched single-storey house.

Recipient of grant: Mr. J. Brewster.

PHASE ONE – THATCHING
Grant assistance of £2,843 given towards: Re-thatching.

Approximate cost of work: £3,165. Carried out in 1978.

Thatching by: Gerald Agnew, Ahoghill.

PHASE TWO – REPAIRS TO THATCH
Grant assistance of £2,145 given towards: Repairs to thatch following partial collapse of roof.

Approximate cost of work: £2,445. Carried out in 1980.

Thatching by: Gerald Agnew, Ahoghill.

Hazlett House, Liffock, Castlerock.

A long, single-storey, thatched cottage with an attic and cruck truss roof, built in 1691 possibly as a clergyman's residence. Walls are battered and rough-cast. There is a decorative rectangular fanlight over the sheeted entrance door. The Georgian-paned sash windows are a later addition.

Recipient of grant: The National Trust.

Grant assistance of £20,000 (to date) given towards: Restoration of cruck framed oak roof structure. Repairs to chimneys. Re-thatching. Treatment of wood rot.

Approximate cost of work: £75,865. Carried out in 1982 and 1983.

Quantity surveyors: V. B. Evans & Co., Coleraine/Belfast.

Contractor: Hugh Taggart & Sons, Ballymoney.

Thatching by: Gerald Agnew, Ahoghill.

Lindesay Ville, Tullaghogue, Cookstown.

Ardvarners Cottage, Macosquin, Coleraine.

A one-and-a-half-storey rendered building built about 1800. A rectangular entrance porch projects to the south.

Recipient of grant: Dr. A. C. Hepburn.

Grant assistance of £325 given towards: Repairs to chimneys. Replacement metal rainwater goods. Repairs to external render. Restoration of fanlight over entrance door.

Further financial assistance received from: Northern Ireland Housing Executive.

Approximate cost of work: £4,500. Carried out in 1976 and 1977.

Architects: Liam McCormick & Partners, Londonderry.

Work carried out using direct labour.

Thatched Cottage, 28 Oldtown Road, Deerpark, Bellaghy.

A one-and-a-half-storey harled and whitened thatched cottage with unrecessed Georgian-glazed sash windows at front.

Recipient of grant: Miss K. McKenna.

Grant assistance of £2,120 given towards: Re-thatching.

Further financial assistance received from: Northern Ireland Housing Executive.

Approximate cost of work: £3,498. Carried out in 1979.

Thatching by: Gerald Agnew, Ahoghill.

48 and 50 Lindesay Ville, Tullaghogue, Cookstown.

Two cottages combined to form one dwelling. They are part of an attractive single-storey row of four. The slated roofs have wide, overhanging eaves, tiny dormers buried under heavy gabled roofs and decorative barge boards. The walls are of rubble and the window sashes have single glazing bars. The tall octagonal brick chimneys are a well known feature in the area.

Recipient of grant: Mrs. E. Henry.

Grant assistance of £1,548 given towards: Repairs to chimneys. Repairs to roof structure. Re-slating using natural slate. Repair of dormers. Repairs to windows. Treatment of wood rot. Installation of damp-proof course. Repairs to timber floors.

Further financial assistance received from: Northern Ireland Housing Executive.

Approximate cost of work: £11,732. Carried out in 1981.

Agent: Uel Henry, Cookstown.

Contractor: Megaw & Ferguson, Stewartstown.

Kingsmill Farm, Edernagh, Stewartstown.

A single-storey, harled and thatched house built in 1743 still retaining original internal doors and fireplace.

Recipient of grant: Mr. W. Reynolds.

Grant assistance of £5,910 given towards: Rebuilding of chimneys. Re-thatching. Replacement sash windows in original

style. Replacement external doors in original style.

Approximate cost of work: £7,876. Carried out in 1981.

Contractor: Victor Ferguson, Stewartstown.

Thatching by: Gerald Agnew, Ahoghill

66 Drumhubbert Road, Dungannon.

A single-storey harled and thatched house with projecting thatched porch.

Recipient of grant: Mr. R. Abernethy.

Grant assistance of £1,160 given towards: Repairs to chimneys. Re-thatching. Repairs to external render. Replacement sash windows in original style.

Further financial assistance received from: Northern Ireland Housing Executive.

Approximate cost of work: £5,355. Carried out in 1980.

Contractors: Harkness & Ferguson, Stewartstown.

Thatching by: Irish Thatchers Ltd., Dungannon.

Rock Cottage, Baronscourt Estate, Newtownstewart.

Built about 1791 in a charming cottage orné style with diamond brick chimneys, decorative barge boards and rock boulder walls. Attributed to Sir John Soane but the design was probably modified by Robert Woodgate, Soane's assistant.

Recipient of grant: Abercorn Estates.

Grant assistance of £1,760 given towards: Rebuilding of chimney. Re-slating using natural slate. Repairs to rainwater goods. Cleaning and re-pointing of stonework. Repair of diamond-pane windows. Provision of

new replica 'dummy' front door. Redecoration of remedial items.

Further financial assistance received from: Northern Ireland Housing Executive.

Approximate cost of work: £12,762. Carried out in 1978 and 1979.

Architects: Robert McKinstry & Melvyn Brown, Belfast.

Contractor: Jack Lynch, Castlederg.

Carleton's Cottage, 13 Springtown Road, Clogher.

A single-storey thatched house, the home of William Carleton, poet and novelist (1794–1869).

Recipient of grant: Mrs. A. McKenna.

Grant assistance of £2,985 given towards: Repairs to chimneys. Re-thatching. Repairs to external render. Repairs to internal plasterwork.

Approximate cost of work: £3,015. Carried out in 1978 and 1979.

Thatching by: Thomas Donnelly, Dernascobe, Augher.

Gate Lodge, Parkanaur House, Castlecaulfield.

A one-and-a-half-storey picturesque lodge in a Tudor Gothic style.

Recipient of grant: Thomas Doran Training Centre.

Grant assistance of £220 given towards: Repairs to chimneys. Roof repairs. Repairs to barge boards.

Further financial assistance received from: Northern Ireland Housing Executive.

Approximate cost of work: £14,024.

Architect: F. M. W. Schofield, Dungannon.

Contractor: Kilwe Construction, Dungannon.

Residential
Modest Houses

32 The Mount, Mountpottinger, Belfast.

A five-bay, two-storey terrace house which has been restored and converted for use as flats. The roof is hipped and slated and walls are smooth rendered with classical detailing.

Recipient of grant: Kendal Ltd.

Grant assistance of £3,800 given towards: Repairs to chimney. Roof repairs. Repairs to rainwater goods. External re-rendering. Replacement sash windows in original style. Replacement external doors in original style. Treatment of wood rot. Internal re-plastering.

Approximate cost of work: £13,809. Carried out from 1980 to 1982.

Quantity Surveyor: H. M. Blamphin, Belfast.

Work carried out using own labour.

36 The Mount, Mountpottinger, Belfast.

A five-bay, two-storey terrace house which has been restored and converted for use as flats. The roof is hipped and slated and walls are smooth rendered with classical detailing.

Recipient of grant: Mrs. E. Howard.

Grant assistance of £500 given towards: Repairs to chimney. Roof repairs. Repairs to rainwater goods. Repairs to external render. Repairs to windows. Repairs to internal plasterwork.

Approximate cost of work: £4,767. Carried out in 1981.

Contractor: Hugh P. Martin, Belfast, and work carried out using direct labour.

4 College Green, Belfast.

A two-storey High Victorian house

Bessvale, 63 Ballinderry Road, Lisburn.

with dormered attic. The roof is slated, with a heavy bracketted eaves cornice. The frontage is of brick, with smooth rendered, elaborately moulded, details. The panelled entrance door with plain semi-circular fanlight is set in a good Venetian canopy supported on flanking columns.

Recipient of grant: Miss. E. O. Bullick.

Grant assistance of £300 given towards: Roof repairs. Replacement leadwork. Repairs to rainwater goods.

Approximate cost of work: £903. Carried out in 1980.

Contractor: McRoberts & Crockard, Belfast.

14 Mill Street, Cushendall.

An end-of-terrace, three-bay, late-19th century town house. The gabled roof is slated, walls are smooth rendered and the sash windows are horizontally sub-divided and have moulded architraves to the first floor.

Recipient of grant: Mr. P. J. McKeegan.

Grant assistance of £1,403 given towards: Re-slating using natural slate. Replacement metal rainwater goods. External re-rendering. Replacement sash windows in original style. Replacement external doors in original style. Installation of damp-proof course. Internal re-plastering. Installation of damp-proof solid floors. Redecoration of remedial items.

Further financial assistance received from: Northern Ireland Housing Executive.

Approximate cost of work: £12,710. Carried out in 1982.

Contractor: Patrick J. O'Mullan, Cloughmills.

107 Main Street, Bushmills.

A two-storey terrace house with slated

roof, rendered walls and plain sash windows.

Recipient of grant: Mr. J. Crooks.

Grant assistance of £1,716 given towards: Rebuilding of chimney. Re-slating using natural slate. Replacement metal rainwater goods. Replacement sash windows in original style. Replacement panelled entrance door. External redecoration. Installation of damp-proof course. Internal re-plastering. Installation of damp-proof solid floors.

Further financial assistance received from: Northern Ireland Housing Executive.

Approximate cost of work: £15,602. Carried out in 1983.

Contractor: L. M. Acheson (Construction) Ltd., Coleraine.

Timber treatment and damp-proof course by: Rentokil Ltd., Belfast.

97 Main Street, Bushmills.

A small two-storey terrace house with slate roof, rendered walls and plain sashed windows.

Recipient of grant: Mr. D. J. Duthie.

Grant assistance of £789 given towards: Rebuilding of chimney. Re-slating using natural slate. Replacement metal rainwater goods. External re-rendering. Replacement sash windows in original style. Replacement external doors in original style. Internal re-plastering. Redecoration of remedial items.

Further financial assistance received from: Northern Ireland Housing Executive.

Approximate cost of work: £11,440. Carried out in 1982 and 1983.

Contractor: Boyd McIntyre, Bushmills.

1 Klondyke Terrace, Bushmills.

Part of a late-19th century symmetrical

terrace with half-timbered projecting end gables, dormer windows and lean-to porches.

Recipient of grant: Mrs. R. Kane.

Grant assistance of £722 given towards: Roof repairs. Replacement metal rainwater goods. External re-rendering. Restoration of bay window. Repairs to windows. Redecoration of remedial items.

Further financial assistance received from: Northern Ireland Housing Executive.

Approximate cost of work: £4,166. Carried out in 1981.

Contractor: McMullan & Montgomery, Bushmills.

2 Klondyke Terrace, Bushmills.

Part of a late-19th century one-and-a-half-storey symmetrical terrace with half-timbered projecting end gables, dormer windows and lean-to porches.

Recipient of grant: Mrs. R. Kane.

Grant assistance of £80 given towards: Repairs to rainwater goods. Repairs to external render. Redecoration of remedial items.

Approximate cost of work: £465. Carried out in 1981.

Contractor: McMullan & Montgomery, Bushmills.

5 High Street, Carnlough.

A two-storey rendered house.

Recipient of grant: Mrs. E. McDonnell.

Grant assistance of £2,086 given towards: Re-slating using natural slate. Repairs to rainwater goods. Repairs to external render. Replacement sash windows in original style. Replacement panelled entrance door. Installation of damp-proof course. Repairs to internal

plasterwork. Installation of damp-proof solid floors.

Further financial assistance received from: Northern Ireland Housing Executive.

Approximate cost of work: £16,300. Carried out in 1982.

Contractors: McGarel Bros., Carnlough.

14 Castle Street, Glenarm.

A two-storey terrace house built in 1830 by Adam Ellison. The roof is slated, walls roughcast and windows Georgian-glazed sashes.

Recipient of grant: Mr. & Mrs. R. Hunter.

Grant assistance of £804 given towards: Repairs to chimney. Roof repairs. Replacement metal rainwater goods. External re-rendering. Replacement sash windows in original style. Replacement panelled entrance door. Treatment of wood rot. Installation of damp-proof course. Installation of damp-proof solid floors.

Further financial assistance received from: Northern Ireland Housing Executive.

Approximate cost of work: £8,500. Carried out in 1981.

Contractor: H. Grange Contracts, Larne.

Turnly's Tower, Mill Street, Cushendall.

A four-storey, sandstone tower surmounted by battlements. One side is slate-hung. The windows project on each side of the upper storeys and the heavy door is set in a narrow, round headed opening. Described in the U.A.H.S.'s Glens of Antrim as 'a truly remarkable romantic building, providing at once the pivot and focus

Modest Houses

for the central crossing of the town'. It is now partly used as a dwelling but was built in 1809 by the eccentric Francis Turnly 'as a place of confinement for idlers and rioters'.

Recipient of grant: Mr. R. W. Hume.

Grant assistance of £107 given towards: Cost of materials for miscellaneous minor repairs to roof and windows carried out between 1975 and 1983.

Work carried out using own labour.

52 Toberwine Street, Glenarm.

A three-bay, two-storey rendered house with dormered, slated roof and various window types.

Recipient of grant: Mrs. K. McAllister.

Grant assistance of £68 given towards: Replacement sash windows in original style.

Approximate cost of work: £92. Carried out in 1980.

Contractor: Albert Crooks, Glenarm.

5 Academy Street, Gracehill, Ballymena.

A four-bay, two-storey roughcast building with slated roof and parapet gables. The building was formerly the Girl's Academy and was built about 1790.

Recipient of grant: Major T. S. Cameron.

Grant assistance of £408 given towards: Repairs to chimneys. Re-slating using natural slate. Forming new pitched roof over bathroom. Repairs to rainwater goods. Repairs to external render. Treatment of wood rot. Redecoration of remedial items.

Further financial assistance received from: Northern Ireland Housing Executive.

Approximate cost of work: £6,224.

Carried out in 1981.

Contractor: Andrew W. Kirk, Ballymena.

15 Fenaghy Road, Gracehill.

One of a pair of one-and-a-half-storey houses with gabled dormers to first floor. The walls are roughcast with label mouldings to ground floor windows and doors.

Recipient of grant: Mrs. J. Printer.

Grant assistance of £20 given towards: Replacement entrance door in original style.

Approximate cost of work: £73. Carried out in 1979.

Contractor: Willart Joinery, Kells.

10 and 12 Cennick Road, Gracehill.

Two two-storey houses with slated gabled roofs and rendered walls.

Recipient of grant: Mr. J. E. McKernan.

Grant assistance of £2,163 given towards: Re-slating using natural slate. Replacement metal rainwater goods. External re-rendering. Replacement sash windows in original style. Replacement external doors in original style. Internal re-plastering. Installation of damp-proof solid floors.

Further financial assistance received from: Northern Ireland Housing Executive.

Approximate cost of work: £22,498. Carried out in 1980 and 1981.

Agent: Joseph E. McKernan, Ballymena.

Work carried out using direct labour.

Child's Corner, 2 Aghalee Road, Lower Ballinderry, Lisburn.

Part of a group of two-storey harled buildings with slated roofs, built before 1832.

Recipient of grant: Mr. W. A. Patterson.

Grant assistance of £1,009 given towards: Rebuilding of chimneys. Re-slating using natural slate. Replacement metal rainwater goods. External re-rendering. Replacement sash windows in original style. Replacement panelled entrance door.

Further financial assistance received from: Northern Ireland Housing Executive.

Approximate cost of work: £11,527. Carried out in 1981 and 1982.

Contractor: Patterson Hoare Ltd., Lisburn.

Bessvale, 63 Ballinderry Road, Lisburn.

A harled and whitened thatched house reputedly dating from about 1700. The five-bay single-storey frontage has a centrally positioned panelled door set in a shallow segmental arched opening. The rear and return building are of two storeys. Windows have Georgian-glazed sashes.

Recipient of grant: Messrs. W. & S. J. Tuft.

PHASE ONE – REPAIRS

Grant assistance of £44 given towards: Repairs to thatch.

Approximate cost of work: £131. Carried out in 1976.

Work carried out using direct labour.

PHASE TWO – REPAIRS

Grant assistance of £40 given towards: Repairs to garden wall.

Approximate cost of work: £139. Carried out in 1977.

Work carried out using direct labour.

PHASE THREE – REPAIRS

Grant assistance of £90 given towards:

Modest Houses

Bessvale, 63 Ballinderry Road, Lisburn.

Repairs to thatch.

Approximate cost of work: £272. Carried out in 1978.

Work carried out using direct labour.

PHASE FOUR – REPAIRS

Grant assistance of £115 given towards: Treatment of woodworm. Repairs to timber floors.

Approximate cost of work: £345. Carried out in 1979.

Timber treatment by: Timbercare (N.I.), Lisburn.

PHASE FIVE – REPAIRS

Grant assistance of £375 given towards: Rebuilding of chimneys.

Approximate cost of work: £1,229. Carried out in 1981.

Work carried out using direct labour.

PHASE SIX – ROOF

Grant assistance of £3,990 given towards: Re-thatching.

Approximate cost of work: £5,320. Carried out in 1982 and 1983.

Thatching by: Gerald Agnew, Ahoghill.

20 Riverside, Antrim.

A two-storey, Gothic Revival style, mid-terrace cottage. Original features, such as Georgian-glazed sash windows and panelled entrance door, have been restored.

Recipient of grant: Miss M. McCavana.

Grant assistance of £500 given towards: Repairs to chimney. Re-slating using natural slate. Replacement metal rainwater goods. Repairs to external render. Replacement sash windows in original style. Replacement panelled entrance door. Redecoration of remedial items. Repairs to internal plasterwork. Installation of damp-proof solid floors.

Further financial assistance received from: Northern Ireland Housing Executive.

Approximate cost of work: £6,730. Carried out in 1979 and 1980.

Contractor: G. Graffin, Ballymena.

Hollowville, 125 Belfast Road, Muckamore.

A three-bay, two-storey, early-19th century house with metal lozenge-paned casement windows.

PHASE ONE – REPAIRS

Recipient of grant: Mr. T. Smyth.

Grant assistance of £858 given towards: Re-slating using asbestos-cement slate. Repairs to rainwater goods. Repairs to external render. Redecoration of remedial items. Treatment of woodworm. Repairs to internal plasterwork.

Approximate cost of work: £3,139. Carried out in 1977.

Contractors: Mairs Bros., Ballyclare.

Timber treatment by: Timbertreat Services Ltd., Belfast.

Painting by: William Burns, Doagh.

PHASE TWO – REPAIRS

Recipient of grant: Mr. C. McAlindon.

Grant assistance of £366 given towards: Repairs to chimneys. Repairs to external render.

Approximate cost of work: £1,100. Carried out in 1979.

Contractor: Eamonn Kelly, Ballyclare.

884 Antrim Road, Templepatrick.

A two-storey terrace house with slated roof and roughcast walls built before 1832.

Recipient of grant: Miss W. Guiney.

Grant assistance of £235 given towards: Re-slating. Replacement sash windows in original style. Replacement entrance door in original style.

Further financial assistance received from: Northern Ireland Housing Executive.

Approximate cost of work: £3,430. Carried out in 1979.

Contractor: Allan Moore, Ballyclare.

119 Moyallen Road, Portadown.

A two-storey, probably late-18th century house. The roof is slated and gabled with decorative brick chimneys. Walls are roughcast with a jumble of sash windows some of which are tripartite. A gabled timber porch projects.

Recipient of grant: J. G. Richardson Trustees.

Grant assistance of £284 given towards: Roof repairs. Repairs to leadwork. Repairs to windows. Treatment of woodworm. Installation of silicone injection damp-proof course.

Further financial assistance received from: Northern Ireland Housing Executive.

Approximate cost of work: £10,785. Carried out from 1977 to 1979.

Architects: Houston & Beaumont & Partners, Lurgan and Belfast.

Contractor: T. W. Sergeant, Portadown.

Timber treatment and damp-proof course by: Alexander Greer Ltd., Lurgan.

117 Moyallen Road, Portadown.

A lower two-storey building abutting number 119. The roof is half-hipped and slated with a decorative brick chimney, windows have Georgian-glazed sashes and the panelled entrance is half-glazed.

Recipient of grant: J. G. Richardson Trustees.

Grant assistance of £862 given towards: Repairs to chimneys. Roof repairs. Replacement metal rainwater goods. Replacement sash windows in original style. Replacement panelled entrance door. Repairs to internal plasterwork. Installation of damp-proof solid floors. Professional fees.

Further financial assistance received from: Northern Ireland Housing Executive.

Approximate cost of work: £10,226. Carried out in 1981.

Architects: Caldwell, Deane Partnership, Lurgan, Belfast and Portadown.

Contractor: E. & B. Derby, Lurgan.

98 Dromore Road, Waringstown.

An exceptional two-storey thatched yeoman planter's house dating from about 1680. Walls are harled and limewashed and windows have Georgian-glazed sashes. There is a single-storey slated extension to the north-west and a vernacular porch with sheeted door.

Recipient of grant: Mr. J. Gregson.

Grant assistance of £1,374 given towards: Repairs to thatch. Re-slating of extension.

Approximate cost of work: £3,431. Carried out in 1978 and 1979.

Contractor: J. Morrow, Donacloney.

Thatching by: Gerald Agnew, Ahoghill.

8 Dobbin Street, Armagh.

Part of a two-storey curved terrace

98 Dromore, Road, Waringstown.

believed to have been built to designs by Francis Johnston in 1811. The roof is slated and walls are of roughly squared limestone.

Recipient of grant: Mrs. R. Wilson.

Grant assistance of £28 given towards: Rebuilding of chimney. Re-slating using natural slate. Replacement metal rainwater goods. Repairs to panelled entrance door.

Further financial assistance received from: Northern Ireland Housing Executive.

Approximate cost of work: £1,585. Carried out in 1980.

Contractor: Burns Construction, Armagh.

10 Dobbin Street, Armagh.

Part of a two-storey curved terrace believed to have been built to designs by Francis Johnston in 1811. The roof is slated and walls are of roughly squared limestone.

Recipient of grant: Mr. P. J. Lynch.

Grant assistance of £1,157 given towards: Repairs to chimney. Re-slating using natural slate. Replacement metal rainwater goods. Replacement sash windows in original style. Replacement panelled entrance door. Internal re-plastering. Replacement timber floors. Installation of damp-proof solid floors.

Further financial assistance received from: Northern Ireland Housing Executive.

Approximate cost of work: £16,800. Carried out in 1982.

Contractor: James J. Rice, Markethill.

30 Dobbin Street, Armagh.

Part of a two-storey curved terrace believed to have been built to designs by Francis Johnston in 1811. The roof is slated and walls are of roughly squared limestone.

Recipient of grant: Mr. B. P. Murtagh.

PHASE ONE

Grant assistance of £1,950 given towards: Replacement sash windows in original style.

Approximate cost of work: £1,950. Carried out in 1979.

Contractors: Mallon Bros., Armagh.

PHASE TWO

Grant assistance of £1,900 given towards: Repairs to roof structure, Re-slating using natural slate. Replacement leadwork. Replacement metal rainwater goods.

Approximate cost of work: £5,735. Carried out in 1982.

Contractor: Milford Extensions and Alterations, Milford.

Modest Houses

36 Dobbin Street, Armagh.

Part of a two-storey curved terrace believed to have been built to designs by Francis Johnston in 1811. The roof is slated, walls are of roughly squared limestone, the first floor sash window is tripartite and the panelled entrance door flanked by Doric columns is set under an elliptical fanlight.

Recipient of grant: Mr. J. Campbell.

Grant assistance of £240 given towards: Repairs to windows. Replacement panelled entrance door and encasement.

Approximate cost of work: £856. Carried out in 1980.

Contractors: Mallon Bros., Armagh.

42 Dobbin Street, Armagh.

Part of a two-storey curved terrace believed to have been built to designs by Francis Johnston in 1811. The roof is slated, walls are of roughly squared limestone and windows have plain sashes with a tripartite first floor window. The panelled entrance door with narrow rectangular fanlight is deeply recessed.

Recipient of grant: Mr. E. Gribben.

Grant assistance of £908 given towards: Repairs to roof structure. Re-slating using natural slate. Replacement metal rainwater goods. Repairs to windows. Replacement panelled entrance door and encasement. Repairs to internal plasterwork. Installation of damp-proof solid floors. Repairs to staircase.

Further financial assistance received from: Northern Ireland Housing Executive.

Approximate cost of work: £7,319. Carried out in 1980 and 1981.

Contractor: Armagh Construction Ltd., Armagh.

20 Ogle Street, Armagh.

A small, two-storey mid-terrace house built about 1770. The roof is slated and the frontage is of roughly squared limestone. The single first floor window is tripartite and both it and the ground floor window have Georgian-glazed sashes. The entrance door has a narrow rectangular fanlight.

Recipient of grant: Mr. T. Grimes.

Grant assistance of £1,280 given towards: Repairs to chimney. Replacement metal rainwater goods. Replacement sash windows in original style. Replacement panelled entrance door. Repairs to internal plasterwork.

Further financial assistance received from: Northern Ireland Housing Executive.

Approximate cost of work: £9,482. Carried out in 1980 and 1981.

Contractor: Mallon Bros., Armagh.

25 Charlemont Square West, Bessbrook.

A two-bay, two-storey mid-19th century terrace house. The roof is slated and walls are of stone with brick dressings.

Recipient of grant: Mrs. E. Andrews.

Grant assistance of £203 given towards: Replacement sash windows in original style.

Further financial assistance received from: Northern Ireland Housing Executive.

Approximate cost of work: £9,338. Carried out in 1981.

Work carried out using direct labour.

5 Fountain Street, Bessbrook.

A mid-19th century schoolhouse and master's house now sub-divided to form two dwellings. The building has one-and-a-half storeys, symmetrically planned, with gabled end bays breaking slightly forward and a central gabled dormer. The roof is slated, with decorative barge boards, walls are smooth rendered and windows have plain sashes.

Recipient of grant: Mrs. M. Magowan.

Grant assistance of £900 given towards: Repairs to chimney. Re-slating using asbestos-cement slate. Repairs to rainwater goods. Repairs to windows. Internal re-plastering. Installation of damp-proof solid floors. Redecoration of remedial items.

Further financial assistance received from: Northern Ireland Housing Executive.

Approximate cost of work: £11,500. Carried out in 1981.

Work carried out using direct labour.

Roof work by: Hurst Building Contractors, Newry.

6 Fountain Street, Bessbrook.

A mid-19th century schoolhouse and master's house now sub-divided to form two dwellings. The building has one-and-a-half storeys, symmetrically planned, with gabled end bays breaking slightly forward and a central gabled dormer. The roof is slated, with decorative barge boards, walls are smooth rendered and windows have plain sashes.

Recipient of grant: Mr. W. Hanna.

Grant assistance of £1,533 given towards: Rebuilding of chimney. Re-slating using asbestos-cement slate. Repairs to rainwater goods. Replacement sash windows in original style. Internal re-plastering. Installation of damp-proof solid floors. Redecoration of remedial items. Provision of pitched roof to new extension.

Further financial assistance received from: Northern Ireland Housing Executive.

Approximate cost of work: £11,106. Carried out in 1982.

Work carried out using direct labour.

Roof work by: Hurst Building Contractors, Newry.

17 College Square West, Bessbrook.

A two-storey, late-19th century, terrace house with slated roof and stone walls with brick dressings.

Recipient of grant: Mr. R. J. Stewart.

Grant assistance of £28 given towards. Replacement back door in original sheeted form.

Further financial assistance received from: Northern Ireland Housing Executive.

Approximate cost of work: £1,340. Carried out in 1982.

Contractor: William G. Brown, Bessbrook.

6 and 8 Newry Street, Kilkeel.

A six-bay, three-storey building dated 1790. The roof is slated, the facade is of coursed granite, the windows have Georgian-glazed sashes and two shop fronts occupy the ground floor.

Recipient of grant: Mrs. M. McErlane.

Grant assistance of £2,729 given towards: Repairs to chimneys. Repairs to roof structure. Re-slating using natural slate. Replacement metal rainwater goods. Repairs to external render. Replacement sash windows in original style. Replacement panelled entrance door.

Further financial assistance received from: Northern Ireland Housing Executive.

Approximate cost of work: £7,638. Carried out in 1983.

Contractor: J. McMullan & Son (Kilkeel) Ltd., Kilkeel.

The Willows, Horner's Lane, Rostrevor.

A one-and-a-half-storey, late-19th century, Gothic style house. The roof has bands of fish-scale slating, tall narrow dormer windows and decorative chimneys and barge boards. The walls are of variegated brickwork and the entrance is contained in a decorative gabled and columned porch.

Recipient of grant: Mr. P. M. Bell.

Grant assistance of £3,225 given towards: Re-slating using natural slate. Replacement leadwork. Repairs to rainwater goods. Re-pointing of brickwork. Repairs to windows. Repairs to panelled entrance door. Repairs to internal plasterwork. Redecoration of remedial items. Professional fees.

Approximate cost of work: £11,427. Carried out in 1982.

Agent: Seamus Collins, Warrenpoint.

Contractor: Tom Morgan, Rostrevor, and work carried out using direct labour.

Trevor Lodge, 12 Warrenpoint Road, Rostrevor.

One of two, asymmetrically planned, two-storey houses built in 1815. The roof is slated with gabled dormers, walls are partly smooth rendered and partly roughcast, windows have small-paned casements and the entrance is contained in a two-storey gabled porch with a small conservatory to one side.

Recipient of grant: Mr. J. G. Hyslop.

Grant assistance of £4,775 given towards: Repairs to chimneys. Repairs to roof structure. Re-slating using natural slate. Replacement metal rainwater goods. Repairs to external render. Repairs to windows. Treatment of wood rot. Repairs to internal plasterwork. Repairs to timber floors. Installation of damp-proof solid floors.

Approximate cost of work: £19,590. Carried out from 1980 to 1982.

Contractor: W. A. Coulter, Kilkeel.

Roof work by: W. Fallon, Newry.

Timber treatment by: Rentokil Ltd., Belfast.

16 Victoria Square, Rostrevor.

A three-bay, two-storey house with slated roof and hipped dormer attics. Panelled door with plain sidelights and fanlight is set within an elliptical arched opening. The entrance is flanked by canted bay windows.

Recipient of grant: Trustees of Christian Renewal Centre.

Grant assistance of £830 given towards: Repairs to chimneys. Roof repairs. Repairs to rainwater goods. Repairs to windows. Replacement external doors in original style.

Approximate cost of work: £2,494. Carried out in 1980.

Contractor: N. & H. McBride, Annalong.

4 Havelock Place, Warrenpoint.

A two-storey, early-19th century terrace house with dormered attic. The frontage is smooth rendered, windows have plain sashes and the entrance has a semi-circular fanlight.

Recipient of grant: Miss R. Woods.

Grant assistance of £103 given towards: Replacement panelled entrance door.

Modest Houses

Approximate cost of work: £308. Carried out in 1983.

Work carried out using direct labour.

42 Seaview, Warrenpoint.

A three-bay, two-storey house with slated roof and two-storey flat roof extension set back to one side. The walls are smooth rendered with moulded details, windows have plain sashes and a square corniced porch projects centrally from the main front.

Recipient of grant: Dr. T. M. W. Redman.

Grant assistance of £1,277 given towards: Rebuilding of chimney. Repairs to roof structure. Re-slating using asbestos-cement slate.

Approximate cost of work: £3,830. Carried out in 1983.

Contractor: McArdle & O'Hare Bros., Warrenpoint.

45 Seaview, Warrenpoint.

A two-storey house with attic contained in a highly varied terrace. The roof is slated with a projecting gabled dormer, walls are rendered with moulded details and windows have plain sashes. A tall, decorative double-light window to the projecting porch is contained within a segmental-headed recess. The porch and verandah have a decorative cast-iron balustrade.

Recipient of grant: Mr. T. Coffey.

Grant assistance of £1,105 given towards: Re-slating using asbestos-cement slate. Repairs to rainwater goods.

Approximate cost of work: £4,976. Carried out in 1981.

Contractor: McArdle & O'Hare Bros., Warrenpoint.

19 and 20 Seaview, Warrenpoint.

A pair of two-storey roughcast and stucco houses with dormered attics above canted bays.

Recipient of grant: Rev. G. B. G. McConnell.

Grant assistance of £4,000 given towards: Repairs to chimneys. Re-slating using natural slate to front slopes. Repairs to rainwater goods. Repairs to external render. Replacement sash windows in original style. Replacement entrance doors. Treatment of wood rot. Installation of damp-proof course.

Further financial assistance received from: Northern Ireland Housing Executive.

Approximate cost of work: £19,727. Carried out in 1980 and 1981.

Architects: O'Neill & Greeves, Dungannon.

Contractor: W. Fallon, Newry.

Timber treatment by: Protim Services, Lisburn.

23 Sandy's Street, Newry.

A two-bay, three-storey, smooth rendered terrace house with plain sash windows and panelled entrance door with narrow rectangular fanlight.

Recipient of grant: Mr. J. W. Moody.

Grant assistance of £713 given towards: Re-slating using natural slate. Repairs to external render. Replacement sash windows in original style. Replacement external doors in original style.

Further financial assistance received from: Northern Ireland Housing Executive.

Approximate cost of work: £11,000. Carried out in 1980.

Work carried out using direct labour.

24 Sandy's Street, Newry.

A three-bay, two-storey, smooth rendered terrace house with plain sash windows and panelled entrance door with narrow rectangular fanlight.

Recipient of grant: Mr. C. Crinion.

Grant assistance of £600 given towards: Re-slating using natural slate to front slope. Replacement metal rainwater goods. Replacement sash windows in original style. Replacement panelled entrance door. Repairs to internal plasterwork.

Further financial assistance received from: Northern Ireland Housing Executive.

Approximate cost of work: £9,843. Carried out in 1980.

Contractor: Felix O'Hare & Co. Ltd., Newry.

26 Sandy's Street, Newry.

A three-storey, smooth rendered terrace house with plain sash windows.

Recipient of grant: Miss E. Pollock.

Grant assistance of £618 given towards: Repairs to chimneys. Re-slating using natural slate. Replacement metal rainwater goods. Repairs to external render. Replacement sash windows in original style. Professional fees.

Further financial assistance received from: Northern Ireland Housing Executive.

Architects: J. Lynam Associates, Newry.

Contractor: McCann Bros., Newry.

2 Ann Street, Gilford.

A two-bay, two-storey, mid-19th century mill house. The roof is half-hipped and slated, the frontage is smooth rendered and windows have plain sashes.

Recipient of grant: Mr. T. Irwin.

Grant assistance of £605 given towards: Repairs to chimney. Re-slating using natural slate. External re-rendering. Replacement sash windows in original style. Replacement panelled entrance door. Installation of damp-proof solid floors.

Further financial assistance received from: Northern Ireland Housing Executive.

Approximate cost of work: £7,890. Carried out in 1982.

Contractor: Alexander Turkington, Gilford.

12 Ann Street, Gilford.

A tiny, two-storey, mid-19th century mill house with slated roof, smooth rendered frontage and horizontally divided sash windows.

Recipient of grant: Mrs. J. Gough.

Grant assistance of £480 given towards: Repairs to chimney. Re-slating using natural slate to front slope. Repairs to rainwater goods. Replacement sash windows in original style. Repairs to panelled entrance door.

Further financial assistance received from: Northern Ireland Housing Executive.

Approximate cost of work: £9,000. Carried out in 1981.

Contractor: Versity Contractors Ltd., Lurgan.

26 Ann Street, Gilford.

A two-storey, mid-19th century end-of-terrace mill house. The roof is slated and gabled and walls are smooth rendered.

Recipient of grant: Mr. W. J. Tomlinson.

Grant assistance of £1,832 given towards: Re-slating using natural slate. External

re-rendering. Replacement sash windows in original style. Replacement panelled entrance door. Installation of damp-proof course. Internal re-plastering. Installation of damp-proof solid floors.

Further financial assistance received from: Northern Ireland Housing Executive.

Approximate cost of work: £14,576. Carried out in 1982 and 1983.

Contractor: J. A. Irwin & Sons Ltd., Portadown.

Moyallan Friends Meeting House, Caretakers House, Moyallan, Banbridge.

A rectangular building with a two-storey caretakers wing to the east built in 1736. The west side has a projecting porch at the north end over which the main roof continues, this is linked by a covered way to a gabled coach way at the south end leading to the east side. The roof is slated and gabled, the walls are smooth rendered with raised quoins and the windows have semi-circular arched heads and Georgian-glazed sashes. A clock is mounted on the wall over the coach way.

Recipient of grant: The Society of Friends.

Grant assistance of £675 given towards: Roof repairs. Repairs to rainwater goods. Repairs to external render, Repairs to internal plasterwork. Professional fees.

Approximate cost of work: £1,465. Carried out in 1982.

Architects: G. P. & R. H. Bell, Lurgan and Belfast.

Contractor: B. Timmins, Richhill.

Riversley, 4 Church Street, Banbridge.

Part of a fine early-19th century terrace of two- and three-storey rendered houses.

Recipient of grant: Mr. R. D. Duke.

Grant assistance of £2,450 given towards: Treatment of extensive dry rot involving rebuilding of wall and roof to part of building followed by reinstatement of finishes.

Approximate cost of work: £7,449. Carried out in 1980.

Contractor: D. Chambers, Banbridge.

Tyrella House, 5 Church Street, Banbridge.

Part of a fine early-19th century terrace of two- and three-storey rendered houses.

Recipient of grant: Mr. G. J. Cahill.

Grant assistance of £375 given towards: Repairs to roof structure at rear of property. Re-slating using asbestos-cement slate.

Approximate cost of work: £1,124. Carried out in 1980.

Contractor: W. B. Drake, Gilford.

91 Lurgan Road, Seapatrick, Banbridge.

Part of a late-19th century terrace of two-storey houses with slated roof and smooth rendered frontage with moulded details.

Recipient of grant: Mr. D. Gamble.

Grant assistance of £1,000 given towards: Replacement of inappropriate entrance door and windows installed under a N.I.H.E. grant assisted improvement and repairs scheme.

Approximate cost of work: £1,323.

Carried out in 1982 and 1983.

Contractor: Aubrey Davidson, Banbridge.

93 Lurgan Road, Seapatrick, Banbridge.

Part of a late-19th century terrace of two storey houses with slated roof and smooth rendered frontage with moulded details.

Recipient of grant: Mr. & Mrs. E. W. Shannon.

Grant assistance of £833 given towards: Roof repairs. Repairs to rainwater goods. Repairs to windows.

Further financial assistance received from: Northern Ireland Housing Executive.

Approximate cost of work: £9,375. Carried out in 1980.

Contractor: J. R. Smyth, Tandragee.

Percy Lodge, Church Street, Dromore.

Built to the designs of Thomas Turner in 1859, the house was originally known as Dromore Cottage but was re-named after Bishop Percy who is buried in Dromore Cathedral. It is a one-and-a-half-storey building with 'T'-shaped plan. The gabled roof is slated, with moulded chimneys and decorative barge boards. The walls are in hand-made local brick with stone dressings. Windows are mainly plain sashed in square- or round-headed openings.

Recipient of grant: Mr. J. D. Carlisle.

Grant assistance of £895 given towards: Roof repairs. Repairs to fascia and barge boards. Replacement metal rainwater goods. Re-pointing of brickwork. Treatment of wood rot and subsequent reinstatement.

Approximate cost of work: £2,690. Carried out in 1980.

Contractor: William S. Pyper, Dromore.

Timber treatment by: Timbercare (N.I.), Lisburn.

80 Main Street, Saintfield.

A two-bay, two-storey terrace property. The roof is slated, walls are smooth rendered with moulded details and windows have plain sashes.

Recipient of grant: Mr. & Mrs. E. Mullan.

Grant assistance of £300 given towards: Repairs to chimney. Roof repairs. Repairs to windows. Installation of electro-osmotic damp-proof course. Repairs to internal plasterwork. Installation of damp-proof solid floors.

Further financial assistance received from: Northern Ireland Housing Executive.

Approximate cost of work: £9,500. Carried out in 1982 and 1983.

Work carried out using direct labour.

Damp-proof course by: Radication Ltd., Dunmurry.

11 High Street, Killyleagh.

An early-19th century two-storey terrace house. The roof is slated, walls are smooth rendered, the unusually wide windows have Georgian-glazed sashes and a large three-part window on the ground floor. A stone dressed coach arch leads to the rear and the panelled entrance door with semi-circular fanlight has a dressed stone surround with applique urns. The building has been restored from a totally derelict condition.

Recipient of grant: Miss A. G. McAllister.

Grant assistance of £1,500 given towards: Rebuilding of chimneys. Roof repairs. Replacement metal rainwater goods. Repairs to external render. Replacement sash windows in original style. Installation of damp-proof solid floors. Repairs to staircase.

Further financial assistance received from: Northern Ireland Housing Executive.

Approximate cost of work: £20,551. Carried out in 1981 and 1982.

Contractor: Building Construction & Design Co. Ltd., Crossgar.

7 and 8 Plantation Street, Killyleagh.

Two pre-1834, two-storey, terrace houses with slated roofs, blackstone frontage and Georgian-glazed sash windows. The two properties have been combined to form one dwelling.

Recipient of grant: Miss M. C. Matheson.

Grant assistance of £3,307 given towards: Repairs to chimney. Roof repairs. Repairs to rainwater goods. Re-pointing of stonework. Replacement sash windows in original style. Treatment of wood rot. Installation of damp-proof solid floors.

Further financial assistance received from: Northern Ireland Housing Executive.

Approximate cost of work: £42,966. Carried out in 1979 and 1980.

Contractor: Killyleagh Building Co., Killyleagh.

9 and 10 Plantation Street, Killyleagh.

Two pre-1834, two-storey, terrace houses with slated roofs, blackstone frontage and Georgian-glazed sash windows. The two houses have been combined to form one dwelling.

Recipient of grant: Mr. H. Fitzsimons.

Grant assistance of £940 given towards: Re-slating using natural slate. Replacement metal rainwater goods. Repairs to stonework. Re-pointing of stonework. Replacement sash windows in original style. Installation of damp-proof solid floors.

Further financial assistance received from: Northern Ireland Housing Executive.

Approximate cost of work: £10,000. Carried out in 1979.

Contractor: C. G. Bassett, Downpatrick.

6 and 8 Castle Street, Strangford.

Two, two-storey, rendered, early-19th century terrace houses which have been combined to form one dwelling.

Recipient of grant: Mrs. E. A. McAfee.

Grant assistance of £1,730 given towards: Repairs to chimneys. Re-slating using natural slate. Repairs to rainwater goods. External re-rendering. Replacement sash windows in original style. Replacement external doors in original style. Internal re-plastering. Repairs to timber floors. Installation of damp-proof solid floors.

Further financial assistance received from: Northern Ireland Housing Executive.

Approximate cost of work: £15,220. Carried out in 1981.

Contractors: Harry Price, Portaferry and K. Hynds, Strangford.

1, 5 and 7 Downpatrick Road, Strangford.

Part of a pleasant mid-19th century two-storey terrace. Walls are of random rubble stonework with brick dressings, number seven has a pleasing

shop front.

Recipient of grant: Strangford Credit Union Ltd.

Grant assistance of £215 given towards: Repairs to chimneys. Roof repairs. Replacement metal rainwater goods. Replacement external doors in original style.

Approximate cost of work: £661. Carried out in 1979.

Contractor: J. J. Kerr, Strangford.

2 The Crescent, Ardglass.

A two-storey, semi-detached house forming part of an important composition built by William Ogilvie in 1820, consisting of a curving line of eleven one-, two- and three-storey houses. The roof is slated and gabled, walls are smooth rendered, two-canted ground floor bay windows project from the front and the entrance is at the side.

Recipient of grant: Mr. H. J. Bell.

Grant assistance of £983 given towards: Repairs to chimney. Re-slating using natural slate. Replacement metal rainwater goods. External re-rendering. Replacement sash windows in original style. Reconstruction of bay windows. Replacement panelled entrance door. Installation of damp-proof course. Internal re-plastering. Installation of damp-proof solid floors.

Further financial assistance received from: Northern Ireland Housing Executive.

Approximate cost of work: £8,450. Carried out in 1981 and 1982.

Contractor: Gracey Bros., Bishopscourt, Downpatrick.

9 The Crescent, Ardglass.

A two-storey, end-of-terrace house

with basement built in 1820 by William Ogilvie as part of a curving line of one-, two- and three-storey houses. The roof is gabled and slated, walls are smooth rendered with moulded details, windows have Georgian-glazed sashes and the entrance door is set in the side of a square, crenellated, porch.

The house has been well restored.

Recipient of grant: Mr. T. Doherty.

Grant assistance of £4,080 given towards: Repairs to roof structure. Re-slating using natural slate. Repairs to windows. Replacement external doors in original style. External redecoration. Treatment of wood rot. Repairs to internal plasterwork. Repairs to timber floors.

Approximate cost of work: £13,052. Carried out in 1979 and 1980.

Contractor: D. M. Murray, Downpatrick.

39 Castle Street, Killough.

A wide, two-storey, pre-1833 roadside house. The roof is slated and gabled, walls are smooth rendered and lined, windows have plain sashes and the central panelled entrance door has a narrow, lattice-paned, rectangular fanlight.

Recipient of grant: Mr. G. A. Laird.

Grant assistance of £2,566 given towards: Rebuilding of chimneys. Re-roofing. Replacement metal rainwater goods. External re-rendering. Replacement sash windows in original style. Replacement external doors in original style. Internal re-plastering. Replacement of internal joinery work.

Further financial assistance received from: Northern Ireland Housing Executive.

Modest Houses

Approximate cost of work: £14,000. Carried out in 1981.

Contractor: Denis Magee & Sons, Downpatrick.

Parochial House, 22 Castle Street, Killough.

A fine, three-bay, two-storey Georgian-style house built about 1840. Two parapeted, single-storey wings each contain a panelled door with Ionic half-pilasters set in a segmentally-headed recess. One wing has stone urns.

Recipient of grant: Rev. J. F. Glavin.

Grant assistance of £3,500 given towards: Roof repairs. Replacement metal rainwater goods. Repairs to external render. Repairs to windows. Replacement French casement windows in original style. Replacement external doors in original style. Repairs to internal plasterwork. Repairs to timber floors.

Approximate cost of work: £22,416. Carried out in 1981 and 1982.

Quantity Surveyors: MacFarlane & Partners, Belfast.

Contractor: Milligan Bros., Killough.

83 and 85 Main Street, Dundrum.

Two pre-1834 two-storey roughcast houses which have been combined to form one dwelling.

Recipient of grant: Mrs. M. McShane.

Grant assistance of £2,280 given towards: Rebuilding of chimneys. Re-slating using natural slate. Replacement metal rainwater goods. Replacement sash windows in original style. Replacement panelled entrance door. Repairs to internal plasterwork.

Approximate cost of work: £8,720. Carried out in 1981.

Contractor: Kelly, McEvoy & Brown, Dundrum.

123 to 127 Main Street, Dundrum.

Three, two-storey, houses of about 1835. The roof is slated and gabled, walls are smooth rendered and windows have plain sashes.

Recipient of grant: Mr. M. Redmond.

Grant assistance of £3,224 given towards: Repairs to chimneys. Re-slating using asbestos-cement slate. Replacement metal rainwater goods. Replacement sash windows in original style. Replacement entrance doors in original style. Treatment of wood rot. Internal re-plastering. Replacement timber floors. Installation of damp-proof solid floors.

Further financial assistance received from: Northern Ireland Housing Executive.

Approximate cost of work: £30,200. Carried out between 1981 and 1983.

Contractor: Denis Magee & Sons, Downpatrick.

3 Red Row, Drumaness.

Part of a terrace of two-storey, red brick houses built about 1860.

Recipient of grant: Mr. P. Gartland.

Grant assistance of £662 given towards: Repairs to chimney. Re-slating using natural slate. Replacement metal rainwater goods. Replacement sash windows in original style. Replacement panelled entrance door.

Further financial assistance received from: Northern Ireland Housing Executive.

Approximate cost of work: £6,375. Carried out in 1982.

Architect: C. J. McCauley, Belfast.

Contractor: A. & L. Rea, Ballynahinch.

28 English Street, Downpatrick.

A four-bay, two-storey, later-18th century house. The entrance door has a stone surround with a simple cornice supported on wide rudimentary console brackets.

Recipient of grant: Mr. & Mrs. A. B. Ray.

Grant assistance of £9,120 given towards: Rebuilding of chimney. Re-roofing using natural slate. Replacement metal rainwater goods. Replacement sash windows in original style. Repairs to panelled entrance door and encasement. Repairs to internal plasterwork. Replacement timber floors. Replacement of internal panelled doors. Repairs to staircase. Professional fees.

Approximate cost of work: £33,806. Carried out in 1982.

Architect: J. Desmond Gray, Downpatrick.

Quantity Surveyor: James Anderson, Ballynahinch.

Contractor: P. Wilson, Saintfield.

5 Main Street, Hillsborough.

A low, two-storey brick, end-of-terrace house with slated roof, wide Georgian-paned sash windows, panelled door with simple rectangular fanlight and elliptical coach arch.

Recipient of grant: Mr. A. D. Forsyth.

Grant assistance of £4,100 given towards: Re-slating of return roof using asbestos-cement slate. Replacement metal rainwater goods. Replacement sash windows in original style. Repairs to panelled entrance door. Replacement back door. Repairs to internal plasterwork. Repairs to timber floors. Damp-proofing of basement.

Modest Houses

Approximate cost of work: £25,000.
Carried out in 1979 and 1980.
Work carried out using own and direct labour.

11 Main Street, Hillsborough.

A two-storey terrace house with basement. The roof is slated, walls are rendered and windows have Victorian sashes. The panelled entrance door has decorative sidelights and a wide elliptical fanlight. Railings protect the basement.

Recipient of grant: Mr. B. W. Hunter.

Grant assistance of £1,595 given towards: Repairs to chimneys. Roof repairs. Repairs to rainwater goods. Repairs to windows. Repairs to internal plasterwork. Installation of damp-proof solid floors. External redecoration.

Further financial assistance received from: Northern Ireland Housing Executive.

Approximate cost of work: £12,250. Carried out in 1980 and 1981.

Contractor: M. McCready, Dundonald.

Painting by: Down Decorators, Hillsborough.

14 Main Street, Hillsborough.

A pre-1833 two-storey terrace house with basement. The roof is slated, walls are roughcast, windows have Georgian-paned sashes and the panelled entrance door is set under a semi-circular fanlight. The basement is enclosed by decorative iron railings. The house has been converted to include a photographers studio.

PHASE ONE – REPAIRS

Recipient of Grant: Mr. C. A. B. Cross.

Grant assistance of £120 given towards: Replacement panelled entrance door. Repairs to railings.

Approximate cost of work: £361.
Carried out in 1977.
Contractor: Antrim Street Building Works, Hillsborough.

PHASE TWO

Recipient of grant: Mr. D. Graham.

Grant assistance of £1,685 given towards: Replacement metal rainwater goods. Repairs to external render. Replacement sash windows in original style. Redecoration of remedial items. Repairs to internal plasterwork. Repairs to staircase.

Approximate cost of work: £9,279. Carried out in 1982.

Architects: McKee & Kirk Partnership, Lisburn.

Contractor: William Hawthorne, Hillsborough.

Painting by: Down Decorators, Hillsborough.

22 Main Street, Hillsborough.

A two-bay, three-storey terrace house built before 1833. The roof is slated and gabled, walls are roughcast and windows have plain sashes.

Recipient of grant: Mr. J. E. Sinnerton.

Grant assistance of £2,090 given towards: Rebuilding of chimney. Repairs to roof structure. Re-slating using natural slate. Replacement metal rainwater goods. External re-rendering. Provision of new lintels over structural openings. Replacement sash windows in original style.

Further financial assistance received from: Northern Ireland Housing Executive.

Approximate cost of work: £11,779. Carried out in 1981.

Contractor: Trevor Lilley, Dromore, Co. Down.

27 Main Street, Hillsborough.

A two-bay, two-storey end-of-terrace property with slated gabled roof, blackstone walls with brick dressings, shop front at ground floor and Georgian-glazed sash windows at first floor. The entrance door is panelled and half-glazed with a simple rectangular fanlight over. The house has been rescued from a dangerous state of dereliction and has been successfully restored.

Recipient of grant: Mrs. M. Tinsley.

Grant assistance of £3,800 given towards: Rebuilding of chimney. Re-roofing using natural slate. Replacement metal rainwater goods. Reconstruction of front wall in replica. Replacement sash windows in original style. Treatment of wood rot. Internal re-plastering. Replacement timber floors. Installation of damp-proof solid floors. Replacement staircase.

Further financial assistance received from: Northern Ireland Housing Executive.

Approximate cost of work: £21,700. Carried out in 1982.

Contractor: Stanfield (N.I.) Ltd., Hillsborough.

29 Main Street, Hillsborough.

A two-storey terrace house with slated roof and blackstone frontage with brick dressings. The windows have Georgian-glazed sashes.

Recipient of grant: Mr. P. B. McCollam.

Grant assistance of £1,243 given towards: Re-slating using natural slate. Replacement metal rainwater goods. Re-pointing of stonework. Replacement sash windows in original style. Replacement panelled entrance door.

Treatment of wood rot. Installation of damp-proof course. Internal re-plastering. Repairs to timber floors. Installation of damp-proof solid floors.

Further financial assistance received from: Northern Ireland Housing Executive.

Approximate cost of work: £17,500. Carried out in 1981.

Work carried out using own and direct labour.

31 Main Street, Hillsborough.

A two-storey terrace house with slated roof and blackstone frontage with brick dressings. The windows have Georgian-glazed sashes.

Recipient of grant: Mr. T. McBride.

Grant assistance of £898 given towards: Rebuilding of chimney. Re-slating using natural slate. Replacement metal rainwater goods. Re-pointing of stonework. Replacement sash windows in original style. Replacement panelled entrance door.

Further financial assistance received from: Northern Ireland Housing Executive.

Approximate cost of work: £6,694. Carried out in 1983.

Contractor: Trevor Lilley, Dromore, Co. Down.

33 Main Street, Hillsborough.

A two-storey terrace house with slated roof and blackstone frontage with brick dressings. The windows have Georgian-glazed sashes.

Recipient of grant: Mr. H. Connery.

Grant assistance of £2,000 given towards: Repairs to chimney. Re-slating using natural slate. Replacement back door in original style.

Approximate cost of work: £2,000. Carried out in 1980.

Contractor: M. K. Weir, Lurgan.

29 Main Street, Hillsborough.

Modest Houses

1 The Square, Hillsborough.

A two-bay, three-storey mid-19th century terrace house. The roof is slated and half-gabled, walls are smooth rendered, windows have Georgian-glazed sashes and the panelled door with simple rectangular fanlight shares a common mullion with the shop front.

Recipient of grant: Mrs. J. V. Stoupe.

Grant assistance of £137 given towards: Repairs to chimney. Re-slating using natural slate.

Approximate cost of work: £459. Carried out in 1976.

Roof work by: Thomas S. Dixon & Co. Ltd., Belfast.

2 The Square, Hillsborough.

A three-bay, two-storey mid-19th century terrace house. The roof is slated and abuts the gable of the adjoining property, walls are smooth rendered, windows have Georgian-glazed sashes and the half-glazed entrance door has a margined fanlight over.

PHASE ONE – REPAIRS

Recipient of grant: Mr. T. D. A. Veitch.

Grant assistance of £180 given towards: Re-slating using natural slate.

Approximate cost of work: £637. Carried out in 1976.

Roof work by: Thomas S. Dixon & Co. Ltd., Belfast.

PHASE TWO

Recipient of grant: Mrs. E. M. Holmes.

Grant assistance of £4,420 given towards: Roof repairs. Repairs to external render. Replacement sash windows in original style. Repairs to internal plasterwork. Repairs to timber floors.

Installation of damp-proof solid floors. Replacement of internal panelled doors. Professional fees.

Further financial assistance received from: Northern Ireland Housing Executive.

Approximate cost of work: £18,011. Carried out in 1980.

Quantity Surveyors: Macfarlane & Partners, Belfast.

Contractor: Hugh Lavery, Belfast.

102 Seacliff Road, Bangor.

A two-storey, brick and stone-faced end-of-terrace house built about 1890.

Recipient of grant: Mr. J. D. B. Hamilton.

Grant assistance of £250 given towards: Repairs to chimneys. Re-slating using natural slate. Repairs to brick dressings. Re-pointing of stonework. Repairs to windows.

Further financial assistance received from: Northern Ireland Housing Executive.

Approximate cost of work: not known. Carried out in 1978.

Work carried out using direct labour.

106 Seacliff Road, Bangor.

A late-19th century two-storey terrace house with slated roof, sandstone rubble walls with brick dressings and simply divided sash windows. The panelled door with fanlight is flanked by plain pilasters with decorative corbels supporting a projecting canopy.

PHASE ONE – REPAIRS

Recipient of grant: Mr. B. Bultitude.

Grant assistance of £320 given towards: Roof repairs. Repairs to leadwork. Repairs to panelled entrance door. Installation of silicone injection damp-proof course.

Approximate cost of work: £13,955. Carried out in 1977 and 1978.

Architects: H. A. Patten & Partners, Bangor.

Contractor: R. Gillespie & Sons, Bangor.

PHASE TWO – REPAIRS

Recipient of grant: Rev. W. E. Davison

Grant assistance of £855 given towards: Rebuilding of bay window. Replacement of brick dressings to openings. Replacement stone entrance steps. External re-rendering. Replacement rear door in original sheeted style. Treatment of woodworm.

Approximate cost of work: £2,266. Carried out in 1982.

Contractor: R. Gillespie & Sons, Bangor.

Timber treatment by: Timbertreat Services Ltd., Belfast.

116 and 118 Seacliff Road, Bangor.

Part of a terrace of two-storey houses with basements, possibly built in the late-19th century. The roof is slated and gabled and has bracketted eaves. Walls are smooth rendered, windows have plain sashes and the entrance doors with simple segmentally-headed fanlights have flanking panelled pilasters with bracketted cornice hoods. The entrances are approached by steps with protective railings to the basements.

Recipient of grant: Mrs. G. M. Bailie and executors of Frances Thompson deceased.

Grant assistance of £250 given towards. Rebuilding of chimney.

Further financial assistance received from: Insurance Company.

Modest Houses

Approximate cost of work: £1,134.
Carried out in 1982.
Contractor: James R. Smith, Bangor.

55 Queen's Parade, Bangor.

A three-storey terrace house built about 1880. The roof is slated and hipped over a full height canted bay. Walls are smooth rendered with moulded details; windows are in square-headed openings to the ground and first floors and semi-circular-headed to the second floor, all have plain sashes. The entrance door has a rectangular fanlight and flat canopy supported on brackets.

Recipient of grant: Mr. J. J. Donohue.

Grant assistance of £4,050 given towards: Rebuilding of chimneys. Roof repairs. Repairs to rainwater goods. Re-roofing of bay. Repairs to external render. Repairs to balustrading at front of house. Repairs to windows. Repairs to internal plasterwork.

Approximate cost of work: £5,399.
Carried out in 1981 and 1982.

Contractor: Coey & Johnston Ltd., Bangor.

57 Queen's Parade, Bangor.

One of a pair of three-storey terrace houses built in 1883. The roof is slated and a two-storey bay window rises on the frontage which is roughcast. The windows have plain sashes.

Recipient of grant: Mr. J. Kane.

Grant assistance of £65 given towards: Rebuilding of gable parapet.

Approximate cost of work: £275. Carried out in 1982.

Contractor: Nelson & Sons, Bangor.

58 Queen's Parade, Bangor.

One of a pair of three-storey terrace houses built in 1883. The roof is slated and a two-storey bay window rises on the frontage which is roughcast. The windows have plain sashes.

Recipient of grant: Mrs. M. G. Ainsworth.

Grant assistance of £115 given towards: Repairs to chimney. Roof repairs. Repairs to external render.

Further financial assistance received from: Insurance company.

Approximate cost of work: £780. Carried out in 1982.

Contractor: Nelson & Sons, Bangor.

Marino Villa, Old Quay Road, Marino, Holywood.

A two-storey semi-detached house with cloistered arcade at front, built about 1820. Roof is slated and gabled and walls are rendered and lined.

Recipient of grant: Mr. J. G. S. Adamson.

Grant assistance of £250 given towards: Repairs to chimneys.

Approximate cost of work: £750. Carried out in 1981.

Contractors: J. & R. Property Repairs, Bangor.

Windrush, Old Quay Road, Marino, Holywood.

A two-storey classically styled house with bowed and columned front. The roof is hipped and slated with an eaves cornice and frieze, walls are smooth rendered with moulded quoins and details, windows have horizontally divided sashes and have segmental heads to the ground floor. The entrance porch is set to one side of the house.

Recipient of grant: Mr. T. G. Egan.

Grant assistance of £715 given towards: External re-rendering. External redecoration.

Approximate cost of work: £3,033.
Carried out in 1980.

Work carried out using own and direct labour.

4 High Street, Holywood.

A three-bay, three-storey end-of-terrace house. The roof is gabled and slated, walls are smooth rendered and windows have Georgian-glazed sashes. The panelled entrance doors with small rectangular fanlight is flanked by columns supporting a flat overdoor.

Recipient of grant: Mr. S. J. King.

Grant assistance of £690 given towards: Repairs to chimney. Roof repairs. Replacement metal rainwater goods. Repairs to external render. Repairs to timber floors. Installation of damp-proof solid floors.

Approximate cost of work: £4,553.
Carried out in 1980.

Work carried out using direct labour.

148 High Street, Holywood.

A three-storey terrace house with ground floor bay window.

Recipient of grant: Mr. & Mrs. L. Donaghey.

Grant assistance of £405 given towards: Replacement metal rainwater goods. Re-pointing of brickwork. Replacement French casement windows.

Approximate cost of work: £1,212.
Carried out in 1981.

Modest Houses

Contractor: R. V. Donaldson, Belfast.

Purpose-made rainwater goods by: Mid Ulster Engineering (Craigavon) Ltd., Lurgan.

3 Tudor Park, Holywood.

A mid-19th century, two-storey, semi-detached house with attics. The roof is slated with gabled dormer windows and walls are rendered and lined with moulded quoins.

Recipient of grant: Mrs. N. V. Kerr.

Grant assistance of £815 given towards: Roof repairs. Treatment of wood rot. Repairs to internal plasterwork.

Approximate cost of work: £6,521. Carried out in 1976 and 1977.

Roof work by: Carnduff & Logan Ltd., Belfast.

Timber treatment by: Timbertreat Services Ltd., Belfast.

Plastering by: William Smyth, Belfast.

5 Tudor Park, Holywood.

A mid-19th century, two-storey, semi-detached house. The roof is hipped and slated and walls are of brick with rendered and stone dressings. Windows have horizontally divided sashes. The panelled entrance door is set in a porch at the side of the house. The porch has an entablature and panelled, pilaster quoins.

Recipient of grant: Mr. M. G. Shankey.

PHASE ONE − REPAIRS

Grant assistance of £190 given towards: Roof repairs. Repairs to leadwork. Repairs to rainwater goods.

Approximate cost of work: £740. Carried out in 1978.

Contractor: Combined Building & Joinery Works, Dunmurry.

PHASE TWO − REPAIRS

Grant assistance of £65 given towards: Repairs to brick facings.

Approximate cost of work: £195. Carried out in 1978.

Contractor: H. S. Warwick Ltd., Holywood.

PHASE THREE − REPAIRS

Grant assistance of £590 given towards: Replacement leadwork.

Approximate cost of work: £1,841. Carried out in 1981.

Contractor: H. S. Warwick Ltd., Holywood.

6 Tudor Park, Holywood.

A mid-19th century, two-storey, semi-detached house. The roof is hipped and slated and walls are of brick with rendered and stone dressings. Windows have horizontally divided sashes. The panelled entrance door is set in a porch at the side of the house. The porch has an entablature and panelled pilaster quoins.

Recipient of grant: Mr. W. N. Morton.

PHASE ONE − REPAIRS

Grant assistance of £415 given towards: Repairs to chimney. Roof repairs. Repairs to leadwork.

Approximate cost of work: £1,245. Carried out in 1977.

Contractor: Maypole Building and Roofspace Conversions, Holywood.

PHASE TWO

Grant assistance of £4,381 given towards: Roof repairs. Replacement rainwater goods in purpose-made moulded glass-reinforced plastic. Treatment of wood rot. Repairs to internal plasterwork. Professional fees.

Approximate cost of work: £5,705. Carried out in 1981 and 1982.

Architects: Long, Morrison & Associates, Holywood.

Contractors: Maypole Building and Roofspace Conversions, Holywood.

Timber treatment by: Radication Ltd., Dunmurry, Belfast.

1 Stewart's Place, Holywood.

A mid-19th century, three-storey corner property. The roof is slated, the rounded corner between the two fronts is recessed and the walls are smooth rendered with moulded details. The windows have margin-paned sashes and the entrance is contained in an offset gabled porch.

Recipient of grant: Mr. R. King.

Grant assistance of £1,580 given towards: Replacement metal rainwater goods. Repairs to external render. Replacement lintel to window opening. Repairs to windows. Replacement external door.

Approximate cost of work: £4,743. Carried out in 1980.

Contractor: R. V. Donaldson, Belfast.

1 The Crescent, Holywood.

A two-storey end-of-terrace house built about 1850. The roof is slated, the frontage is of red brick with yellow brick dressings, windows have horizontally divided sashes and the panelled entrance door has sidelights and fanlight.

Recipient of grant: Mr. & Mrs. C. Megarry.

PHASE ONE − REPAIRS

Grant assistance of £223 given towards: Rebuilding of chimney.

Modest Houses

Approximate cost of work: £669. Carried out in 1977.

Contractors: H. S. Warwick Ltd., Holywood.

PHASE TWO − REPAIRS

Grant assistance of £222 given towards: Replacement panelled entrance door.

Approximate cost of work: £667 carried out in 1981.

Contractor: H. S. Warwick Ltd., Holywood.

PHASE THREE − REPAIRS

Grant assistance of £500 given towards: Roof repairs. Repairs to leadwork. Repairs to rainwater goods. Repairs to external render. Repairs to internal plasterwork.

Approximate cost of work: £1,729. Carried out in 1983.

Contractor: R. Finlay, Holywood.

Roof work by: Pentagon (Renovation) Ltd., Darkley, Armagh.

2 Martello Terrace, Victoria Road, Holywood.

A two-storey, double-fronted house with dormered attic. The roof is slated, the main wall of the frontage is of red brick with rendered ground floor canted bay windows and doorcase and first floor aedicule to a central semi-circular-headed window. All windows have horizontally divided sashes.

Recipient of grant: Mr. A. G. McClure.

PHASE ONE

Grant assistance of £560 given towards: Repairs to roof structure. Rebuilding of bay. Treatment of wood rot. Repairs to internal plasterwork.

Approximate cost of work: £1,697. Carried out in 1982.

Work carried out using direct labour.

Timber treatment by: Radication Ltd., Dunmurry, Belfast.

PHASE TWO

Grant assistance of £1,360 given towards: Repairs to roof structure. Reconstruction of dormer windows. Replacement metal rainwater goods. Treatment of wood rot.

Approximate cost of work: £4,324. Carried out in 1983.

Contractor: Ogborn Building Enterprises, Holywood.

1 Ardmore Terrace, Victoria Road, Holywood.

A three-bay, two-storey end-of-terrace house with attic and ground floor bays. The roof is slated and walls are rendered with moulded dressings.

Recipient of grant: Mr. R. Lamrock.

Grant assistance of £146 given towards: Repairs to decorative plasterwork.

Approximate cost of work: £441. Carried out in 1982.

Plastering by: Nicholl Plaster Mouldings, Belfast.

3 Ardmore Terrace, Victoria Road, Holywood.

A three-bay, two-storey terrace house with slated roof and rendered walls with moulded dressings.

Recipient of grant: Mr. C. J. Maginnes.

Grant assistance of £80 given towards: Repairs to rainwater goods. Repairs to external render. Repairs to windows. Repairs to panelled entrance door.

Approximate cost of work: £360. Carried out in 1981.

Painting by: James Jamison, Bangor.

Crofton, 93 Victoria Road, Holywood.

One half of a symmetrically planned group of two, two-storey, houses. The slated roof has projecting exposed rafter eaves, a central gabled feature and forward projecting gabled end wings. The entrance porches are also gabled and all gables have decorative barge boards. The forward projecting end wings contain two-storey flat-roofed canted bay windows. Walls are smooth rendered with raised quoins and label mouldings over windows and door.

Recipient of grant: Mrs. I. Harkness.

PHASE ONE − REPAIRS

Grant assistance of £640 given towards: Repairs to bay window roof. Repairs to external render. Repairs to internal plasterwork.

Approximate cost of work: £858. Carried out in 1979.

Contractor: H. S. Warwick Ltd., Holywood.

PHASE TWO − REPAIRS

Grant assistance of £6,611 given towards: Repairs to chimneys. Rebuilding of chimney. Re-slating using natural slate. Replacement leadwork. Repairs to rainwater goods. Repairs to external render. Repairs to windows. Treatment of wood rot. External redecoration. Repairs to internal plasterwork.

Approximate cost of work: £8,813. Carried out in 1979 and 1980.

Contractor: R. V. Donaldson, Holywood.

Timber treatment by: Rentokil Ltd., Belfast.

Modest Houses

28 Ferry Street, Portaferry.

A five-bay, two-storey pre-1834 property. The roof has been re-slated, walls are smooth rendered and windows have Georgian-glazed sashes. The house has been extensively refurbished.

Recipient of grant: Mr. & Mrs. P. J. Weston.

Grant assistance of £4,333 given towards: Repairs to chimneys. Re-roofing using natural slate. External re-rendering. Replacement metal rainwater goods. Replacement sash windows in original style. Internal re-plastering. Replacement timber floors. Installation of damp-proof solid floors.

Further financial assistance received from: Northern Ireland Housing Executive.

Approximate cost of work: £19,241. Carried out in 1981 and 1982.

Architect: Paddy Byrne Architect, Belfast.

Contractor: J. Kennedy & Co. (Contractors) Ltd., Coleraine.

4 and 6 Main Street, Greyabbey.

Two, two-storey properties which have been combined to form one dwelling. The roof is slated and gabled, walls are smooth rendered, windows have Georgian-glazed sashes and the entrance door has a semi-circular fanlight and moulded surround.

Recipient of grant: Mr. N. Willis.

Grant assistance of £1,976 given towards: Rebuilding of chimneys. Repairs to roof structure. Re-slating using natural slate. Replacement metal rainwater goods. External re-rendering. Replacement sash windows in original style. Repairs to panelled entrance

door. Restoration of fanlight.

Approximate cost of work: £5,989. Carried out in 1981 and 1982.

Contractor: Bailie & Donkin, Greyabbey.

35 New Road, Donaghadee.

An attractive one-and-a-half-storey Victorian semi-detached house built about 1860. The roof is slated with decorative barge boards, walls are rendered with moulded dressings and a gabled end wing, projecting slightly beyond the main facade, has a single storey canted bay window.

PHASE ONE

Recipient of grant: Mr. & Mrs. J. Esplin.

Grant assistance of £399 given towards: Provision of new carved barge boards to match existing. Repairs to rainwater goods.

Approximate cost of work: £399. Carried out in 1976.

Work carried out using own and direct labour

PHASE TWO

Recipient of grant: Mr. T. Dickson.

Grant assistance of £113 given towards: Replacement metal rainwater goods.

Approximate cost of work: £339. Carried out in 1978.

Contractor: Braemar Construction, Bangor.

24 Killaughey Road, Donaghadee.

A good one-and-a-half-storey, five-bay, stone farmhouse built about 1830. The roof has dormers with decorative barge boards, windows have Georgian-glazed sashes and the central panelled entrance door has a rectangular fanlight with margined

panes.

Recipient of grant: Mr. & Mrs. R. Dalzell.

Grant assistance of £600 given towards: Repairs to chimneys. Re-slating. Repairs to external render. Replacement sash windows in original style. Replacement panelled entrance door. Treatment of wood rot. Installation of silicone injection damp-proof course. Repairs to internal plasterwork. Installation of damp-proof solid floors.

Further financial assistance received from: Northern Ireland Housing Executive.

Approximate cost of work: £7,970. Carried out in 1979 and 1980.

Contractor: Robert A. McCurdy, Donaghadee, and work carried out using direct labour.

14 The Square, Comber.

A two-storey, late-19th century house. The roof is tiled, walls are rendered, with Corinthian pilasters at each end of the frontage, and the windows have Georgian-glazed sashes. The central panelled entrance door with sidelights and fanlight is flanked by pilasters with a cornice hood over.

Recipient of grant: Mr. M. N. H. Erskine.

Grant assistance of £530 given towards: Replacement panelled entrance door. External redecoration.

Approximate cost of work: £1,990. Carried out in 1981.

Contractor: F. H. Crockard, Comber.

Painting by: Fisher & Lindsay, Belfast.

191 Killinchy Road, Lisbane.

A group of one- and two-storey buildings built before 1834. The higher building has a slated roof while the

14 The Square, Comber.

single-storey part is thatched. Part of the roughcast walls are smothered in creeper. The windows mainly have Georgian-glazed sashes.

Recipient of grant: Miss A. Morrison.

Grant assistance of £1,220 given towards: Repairs to chimneys. Re-thatching.

Approximate cost of work: £3,664. Carried out in 1980.

Contractor: Savage Bros., Comber.

Thatching by: Irish Thatchers Ltd., Dungannon.

83 Main Street, Lisnaskea.

A pre-1834 two-storey rendered terrace house with slated roof and Georgian-glazed sash windows. The entrance door with rectangular fanlight over is approached by a flight of stone steps.

Recipient of grant: Mr. P. McCarroll.

Grant assistance of £2,447 given towards: Rebuilding of chimney. Re-roofing using natural slate. Replacement metal rainwater goods. Repairs to external render. Replacement sash windows in original style. Replacement panelled entrance door. Installation of damp-proof course. Repairs to internal plasterwork. Repairs to timber floors. Installation of damp-proof solid floors.

Further financial assistance received from: Northern Ireland Housing Executive.

Approximate cost of work: £21,139. Carried out in 1983.

Contractor: Philip Martin, Lisbellaw.

53 Main Street, Lisnaskea.

A pre-1834 two-storey terrace house with slated roof, limestone walls with sandstone dressings. Georgian-glazed sash windows and entrance door with

191 Killinchy Road, Lisbane.

rectangular fanlight approached by steps.

Recipient of grant: Mr. R. Kernaghan.

Grant assistance of £1,130 given towards: Re-slating using natural slate. Replacement metal rainwater goods. Replacement sash windows in original style. Replacement external doors in original style.

Further financial assistance received from: Northern Ireland Housing Executive.

Approximate cost of work: £15,675. Carried out in 1982.

Contractor: B. Ingram, Lisnaskea.

Tullykenneye, 371 Belfast Road, Fivemiletown.

A three-bay, one-and-a-half-storey estate farmhouse with a slated gabled roof and gabled dormer over entrance. Walls are rendered with moulded dressings. Windows are Georgian-glazed sashes and the panelled entrance door is flanked by sidelights with a rectangular fanlight over.

Recipient of grant: Mr. W. H. Montgomery.

Grant assistance of £1,162 given towards: Repairs to chimney. Roof repairs. Repairs to rainwater goods. External re-rendering. Replacement sash windows in original style. Replacement external doors in original style.

Further financial assistance received from: Northern Ireland Housing Executive.

Approximate cost of work: £4,987. Carried out in 1981.

Contractor: William Adams, Fivemiletown.

Modest Houses

Brookemount, Main Street, Brookeborough.

A two-storey rendered house with stone dressings and chimneys and a gablet over the entrance.

Recipient of grant: Mr. J. Brown.

Grant assistance of £1,800 given towards: Sandblasting of chimneys. Roof repairs. Repairs to windows. Repairs to internal plasterwork.

Approximate cost of work: £6,000. Carried out in 1980.

Contractor: William Adams & George Graham, Brookeborough.

Old School House, 21 Moate Road, Cornashee, Lisnaskea.

A pre-1834, two-storey, 'T'-shaped building with Tudor detailing and overhanging hipped roof. Now a dwelling.

Recipient of grant: Mr. H. E. Wilson.

Grant assistance of £105 given towards: Roof repairs. Repairs to rainwater goods. External re-rendering. Replacement entrance door. Cleaning of stone plinth and dressings.

Further financial assistance received from: Northern Ireland Housing Executive.

Approximate cost of work: £7,000. Carried out in 1980.

Contractor: W. H. Fawcett & Sons, Lisnaskea.

Old Railway Station, Belcoo.

A single-storey station house with decorative barge boards.

Recipient of grant: Miss O. O'Dolan.

Grant assistance of £7,535 given towards: Re-roofing using natural slate. Replacement of decorative barge boards. Replacement metal rainwater goods. Replacement windows in original style. Sandblasting and re-pointing of stonework. Internal re-plastering. Undergrounding of electricity supply. Professional fees.

Further financial assistance received from: Northern Ireland Housing Executive.

Approximate cost of work: £21,652. Carried out in 1981.

Agent: E. P. Flanagan & Associates, Enniskillen.

Contractor: J. Gallagher & Sons, Belcoo.

Stone repair by: Ulster Cleanstone Co., Dungannon.

7 Crevenish Road, Kesh.

A three-bay, two-storey mid-Georgian house with slated gabled roof and stone walls.

Recipient of grant: Rev. J. H. F. Keys.

Grant assistance of £1,500 given towards: Repairs to chimneys. Repairs to roof structure. Re-slating using natural slate. Replacement metal rainwater goods. Replacement sash windows in original style. Replacement panelled entrance door. Repairs to internal plasterwork. Installation of damp-proof solid floors.

Further financial assistance received from: Northern Ireland Housing Executive.

Approximate cost of work: £9,155. Carried out in 1960 and 1981.

Contractor: Trevor S. T. Wilson, Kesh.

Letterkeen House, Kesh.

Before conversion to use as a dwelling the building was a schoolhouse and master's dwelling and prior to that was a church. It consists of a single double-height schoolroom having a steeply pitched slated roof and Gothic style windows and, at right angles, the residential block. Walls are of rubble stone throughout.

Recipient of grant: Mrs. C. Irvine.

Grant assistance of £90 given towards: Repairs to chimneys. Roof repairs. Repairs to rainwater goods. Repairs to external render. Repairs to windows. Cleaning of brickwork. Re-pointing of stonework. Repairs to internal plasterwork. Installation of damp-proof solid floors.

Further financial assistance received from: Northern Ireland Housing Executive.

Approximate cost of work: £8,765. Carried out in 1981.

Contractor: William Wilson, Castlederg.

26 The Brooke, Enniskillen.

One of four pre-1834, three-storey houses with slated roofs, smooth rendered walls, sash windows with single vertical divisions, panelled entrance door flanked by fluted columns under an elliptical fanlight and a coach arch to rear.

Recipient of grant: Mrs. A. O'Reilly.

Grant assistance of £1,850 given towards: Rebuilding of chimneys. External re-rendering. Replacement sash windows in original style. Replacement panelled entrance door. Replacement columns flanking front door.

Approximate cost of work: £5,599. Carried out in 1981.

Contractor: Patrick A. Corrigan, Bellaneleck.

2 Willoughby Place, Enniskillen.

A three-bay, two-storey house built about 1840. Rendered with stone cornice and moulding. The central doorway has a diamond-paned fanlight.

Recipient of grant: Mr. K. A. Betty.

Grant assistance of £3,000 given towards: Rebuilding of chimneys. Roof repairs. External re-rendering. Replacement sash windows in original style. Replacement panelled entrance door.

Approximate cost of work: £7,187. Carried out in 1980.

Contractor: Irvine Bros., Enniskillen.

Dunbar House, Magheradunbar, Enniskillen.

A small three-bay, two-storey square house with overhanging eaves built for the Dunbar family in the mid-18th century. The roof was originally thatched. The central panelled door is flanked by Ionic columns and set under an elliptical fanlight.

Recipient of grant: Mrs. G. Moore.

Grant assistance of £430 given towards: Re-slating of central roof well using asbestos-cement slate. Replacement leadwork.

Approximate cost of work: £1,350. Carried out in 1980.

Contractor: Jim Irvine, Lisbellaw.

9 Aberfoyle Terrace, Strand Road, Londonderry.

A two-storey terrace house with half dormer. Walls are red brick with yellow brick dressings. A single-storey yellow brick, canted bay projects at the front. Built around 1902 to a design by W. A. Barker.

Recipient of grant: Miss M. L. Conway.

Grant assistance of £282 given towards: Repairs to chimney. Roof repairs. Re-pointing of brickwork. Repairs to external render. Repairs to windows.

Repairs to internal plasterwork.

Further financial assistance received from: Northern Ireland Housing Executive.

Approximate cost of work: £12,221. Carried out in 1982.

Contractor: Bernard McCorriston, Moville, Co. Donegal.

33 Aberfoyle Terrace, Strand Road, Londonderry.

A two-storey terrace house with half dormer. Walls are red brick with yellow brick dressings. A single-storey, yellow brick, canted bay projects at the front. Built around 1902 to a design by W. A. Barker.

Recipient of grant: Mr. & Mrs. C. Irvine.

Grant assistance of £266 given towards: Repairs to chimney. Re-slating using natural slate. Replacement metal rainwater goods. Re-pointing of brickwork. Repairs to windows. Replacement panelled entrance door. Repairs to internal plasterwork. Installation of damp-proof solid floors.

Further financial assistance received from: Northern Ireland Housing Executive.

Approximate cost of work: £9,300. Carried out in 1982.

Contractor: Village Builders, Londonderry.

7 De Burgh Terrace, Academy Street, Londonderry.

A two-and-a-half-storey, mid-terrace, house set behind a long narrow garden. A single-storey canted bay projects at ground floor level. Windows have simply divided sashes, square-headed at ground floor, segmented at first and round-headed at second. The panelled entrance door has

a narrow, segmented, fanlight.

Recipient of grant: Mr. & Mrs. C. O'Somachain.

Grant assistance of £210 given towards: Repairs to chimney. Roof repairs. Repairs to external render. Repairs to windows. Repairs to panelled entrance door. Treatment of wood rot. Repairs to internal plasterwork.

Further financial assistance received from: Northern Ireland Housing Executive.

Approximate cost of work: £6,200. Carried out in 1981 and 1982.

Contractor: Ivan Parke, Londonderry.

9 De Burgh Terrace, Academy Street, Londonderry.

A two-and-a-half-storey, mid-terrace, house set behind a long narrow garden. A single-storey canted bay projects at ground floor level. Windows have simply divided sashes, square-headed at ground floor, segmented at first and round-headed at second. The panelled entrance door has a narrow, segmented, fanlight.

Recipient of grant: Mr. C. A. Gillespie.

Grant assistance of £1,170 given towards: Roof repairs including repair of ornamental eaves brackets. Repairs to leadwork. Replacement metal rainwater goods. Repairs to external render. Repairs to windows. Repairs to panelled entrance door. External redecoration. Treatment of wood rot. Installation of silicone injection damp-proof course.

Further financial assistance received from: Northern Ireland Housing Executive.

Approximate cost of work: £12,012. Carried out in 1982.

Contractor: Moss Construction, Londonderry.

Modest Houses

7 College Terrace, Londonderry.

A handsome little two-and-a-half-storey mid-terrace house on a steeply sloping street. The frontage is of red brick with dark blue brick details. The windows are simply divided. The panelled entrance door is flanked by narrow architrave margins with tiny console brackets and a semi-circular fanlight over. The attic is gabled with a round-headed window.

Recipient of grant: Mr. & Mrs. J. Gallagher.

Grant assistance of £391 given towards: Repairs to chimney. Roof repairs. Replacement rainwater goods. Re-pointing of brickwork. Repairs to windows. Repairs to panelled entrance door. Repairs to internal plasterwork. Redecoration of remedial items.

Further financial assistance received from: Northern Ireland Housing Executive.

Approximate cost of work: £4,756. Carried out in 1982.

Contractor: Edward Harkin, Londonderry.

9 The Diamond, Portstewart.

One of a series of two-storey 19th century buildings forming the enclosure of the Diamond.

Recipient of grant: Mr. J. G. McClean.

Grant assistance of £751 given towards: Re-slating using natural slate.

Approximate cost of work: £1,382. Carried out in 1978.

Roof work by: H. Hayes & Son, Portstewart.

70 Dunedin Terrace, Lodge Road, Coleraine.

One of seven two-storey houses with attics built about 1880 to designs by J.

& W. Kirkpatrick. The house has a canted bay window and dormers protrude from the fish-scale tiled mansard roof.

Recipient of grant: Mr. B. J. Mullan.

Grant assistance of £1,506 given towards: Roof repairs. Repairs to chimney. Repairs to rainwater goods. Repairs to external render. Repairs to windows. Repairs to internal plasterwork. Installation of damp-proof solid floors.

Further financial assistance received from: Northern Ireland Housing Executive.

Approximate cost of work: £12,336. Carried out in 1981.

Contractor: M. McColgan, Coleraine.

31 Millburn Road, Coleraine.

Built about 1865. One half of a good Victorian rogue-Gothic two-storey rendered villa with an angled entrance porch.

Recipient of grant: Mr. J. Morton.

Grant assistance of £185 given towards: Rebuilding of chimney. Repairs to leadwork.

Approximate cost of work: £560. Carried out in 1982.

Contractor: M. McColgan, Coleraine.

8 and 10 High Street, Draperstown.

One of a two-storey terrace of partly stone houses built about 1830 to the designs of W. J. Booth, the Drapers' Company's London surveyor.

Recipient of grant: Mr. H. Kelly.

Grant assistance of £90 given towards: Replacement sash windows in original style.

Approximate cost of work: £271. Carried out in 1979.

Work carried out using direct labour.

6 Stonard Street, Moneymore.

An early-19th century two-storey building combining a shop and dwelling.

Recipient of grant: Mrs. R. McCutcheon.

Grant assistance of £1,975 given towards: Re-slating using natural slate. Replacement metal rainwater goods. Replacement sash windows in original style. Repairs to doors. Treatment of woodworm.

Further financial assistance received from: Northern Ireland Housing Executive.

Approximate cost of work: £10,924. Carried out in 1981.

Contractors: Lyle & McGarvey, Cookstown.

15 Main Street, Beragh.

A former police barracks with stone walls, a pitched main roof with gabled dormers and porch in cottage style.

Recipient of grant: Mr. P. J. McClean.

Grant assistance of £2,560 given towards: Rebuilding of chimneys. Re-slating using natural slate. Replacement metal rainwater goods. Re-pointing of stonework. Repairs to windows. Treatment of wood rot. Installation of damp-proof course. Repairs to internal plasterwork.

Further financial assistance received from: Northern Ireland Housing Executive.

Approximate cost of work: £16,299. Carried out in 1981.

Contractors: Frank McClean & Sons, Beragh.

New Market House, 3 to 7 High Street, Moneymore.

Built in 1839 to the design of W. J.

Modest Houses

Bank Terrace and Estate Terrace, Caledon.

Modest Houses

Booth, the Drapers' Company's surveyor, the building has an impressive eleven-bay, three-storey frontage faced with finely dressed sandstone. The central three bays project and have a tall carriage arch flanked by square-headed pedestrian passages and surmounted by a large pediment.

Recipient of grant: Mr. T. Campbell.

Grant assistance of £1,250 given towards: Re-roofing using natural slate. Replacement metal rainwater goods. Replacement external doors in original style.

Further financial assistance received from: Northern Ireland Housing Executive.

Approximate cost of work: £6,185. Carried out in 1979.

Architect: Rooney & McConville, Cookstown.

Contractor: S. McGeehan, Coagh.

1 to 3 and 5 Bank Terrace, and 3 and 4 Estate Terrace, Caledon.

Picturesque two-storey terrace houses with slated roofs, limestone walls, Georgian-glazed exposed case sash windows and flush panelled doors with narrow rectangular fanlight over.

Recipient of grant: Caledon Estates Company.

Grant assistance of £440 given towards: Replacement metal rainwater goods. Replacement sash windows in original style.

Further financial assistance received from: Northern Ireland Housing Executive.

Approximate cost of work: £7,980. Carried out in 1980.

Agent: Associated Architectural Consultants, Omagh.

Contractor: A. C. Simpson & Partners Ltd., Armagh.

Tully House, 4 Tullycullion Road, Donaghmore, Dungannon.

A two-storey Georgian house in terrace built before 1833. Slated roof and roughcast walls. Panelled door with sidelights and fanlight set in an elliptical arched opening.

Recipient of grant: Mr. & Mrs. I. M. Reid.

Grant assistance of £1,700 given towards: Re-slating using natural slate. Replacement metal rainwater goods. Repairs to external render. Replacement sash windows in original style. Repairs to panelled entrance door. Treatment of wood rot. Repairs to internal plasterwork. Repairs to timber floors.

Further financial assistance received from: Northern Ireland Housing Executive.

Approximate cost of work: £13,400. Carried out in 1981.

Contractor: Ivor Moore, Dungannon.

36 Northland Row, Dungannon.

A single-fronted two-storey Gothic terrace with attic. There is a canted bay window to one side of the elaborate entrance doorway. The roof has fish-scale slating and decorative ridge tiles. The front elevation is of finely worked ashlar.

Recipient of grant: Mr. D. Rafferty.

Grant assistance of £1,040 given towards: Repairs to leadwork. Replacement metal rainwater goods. Re-pointing of stonework. Treatment of extensive dry rot. Repairs to internal plasterwork. Repairs to timber floors.

Further financial assistance received from: Northern Ireland Housing Executive.

Approximate cost of work: £10,500. Carried out in 1983.

Contractor; McGahan Bros., Drumhorrick, Dungannon.

Residential
Large Houses

Summer Hill, Mount Pleasant,
Stranmillis Road, Belfast.

Huntley, Dunmurry Lane, Belfast.

A two-storey, mid-19th century, house. The roof is slated, walls are smooth rendered and windows have Georgian-glazed sashes. The entrance with eared architraves and keystone is contained in a square projecting pilastered porch.

Recipient of grant: Mr. J. B. Bryson.

PHASE ONE – REPAIRS

Grant assistance of £560 given towards: Re-leading of porch roof. Treatment of wood rot. Repairs to internal plasterwork. Repairs to decorative plasterwork. Redecoration of remedial items.

Approximate cost of work: £2,200. Carried out in 1977.

Contractor: Timbercare (N.I.), Lisburn.

Painting by: J. Magee, Belfast.

PHASE TWO – REPAIRS

Grant assistance of £790 given towards: Repairs to chimneys. Roof repairs. Repairs to rainwater goods. Repairs to rear door. Redecoration of remedial items.

Approximate cost of work: £2,380. Carried out in 1980.

Contractor: H. S. Warwick Ltd., Holywood.

PHASE THREE

Grant assistance of £713 given towards: External redecoration.

Approximate cost of work: £2,298. Carried out in 1982.

Painting by: Fisher & Lindsay Ltd., Belfast.

2 Mount Pleasant, Stranmillis Road, Belfast.

A fine two-storey, double-fronted, red brick terrace house built in 1863. The entrance door with pedimented aedicule is flanked by two canted bay windows. The windows have horizontally divided sashes.

Recipient of grant: Mrs. V. E. Breene.

Grant assistance of £2,950 given towards: Roof repairs. Repairs to external render. Repairs to one and rebuilding of other bay window. Repairs to French casement windows. Repairs to entrance steps.

Approximate cost of work: £8,855. Carried out in 1980.

Contractor: Crawford & Laird, Belfast.

6 Mount Pleasant, Stranmillis Road, Belfast.

A fine two-storey, double-fronted, red-brick terrace house built in 1863. The entrance door with pedimented aedicule is flanked by two canted bay windows. The windows have horizontally divided sashes.

Recipient of grant: Mr. S. Q. A. M. A. Hossain.

PHASE ONE

Grant assistance of £230 given towards: Reducing ground levels and improving drainage.

Approximate cost of work: £684. Carried out in 1979.

Contractor: J. P. Cleary, Belfast.

PHASE TWO

Grant assistance of £575 given towards: Re-slating using natural slate.

Approximate cost of work: £1,725. Carried out in 1980.

Roof work by: Thomas Flynn, Belfast.

PHASE THREE

Grant assistance of £53 given towards:

Repairs to roofs of bay windows.
Approximate cost of work: £160. Carried out in 1980.
Roof work by: Feltway Roofing Contractors, Belfast.

PHASE FOUR
Grant assistance of £510 given towards: Treatment of wood rot and subsequent reinstatement.
Approximate cost of work: £1,615. Carried out in 1983.
Timber treatment by: Timbertreat Services Ltd., Belfast.

9 Mount Pleasant, Stranmillis Road, Belfast.

A fine two-storey, double-fronted, red-brick end-of-terrace house built in 1863. The entrance door with pedimented aedicule is flanked by two single-storey canted bay windows. The windows have horizontally divided sashes.
Recipient of grant: Mr. J. W. Wilson.
Grant assistance of £310 given towards: Replacement of timber beams over bay window openings.
Approximate cost of work: £924. Carried out in 1979.
Contractor: Rentokil Ltd., Belfast.

Summer Hill, Mount Pleasant, Stranmillis Road, Belfast.

A pleasant five-bay, two-storey house built about 1855. The roof is slated and gabled, walls are of red brick and windows have Georgian-glazed sashes. The panelled entrance door is set in a good doorcase with semi-circular-headed sidelights and shallow elliptical decorative fanlight.
Recipient of grant: Mrs. C. Kennedy.

Grant assistance of £6,260 given towards: Repairs to chimneys. Re-slating using natural slate. Repairs to leadwork. Repairs to rainwater goods. Re-pointing of brickwork. Repairs to windows. External redecoration. Treatment of wood rot and subsequent reinstatement. Installation of damp-proof course. Repairs to internal plasterwork. Installation of damp-proof solid floors. Professional fees.
Approximate cost of work: £61,486. Carried out in 1982 and 1983.
Architects: Robert McKinstry & Melvyn Brown, Belfast.
Contractor: Sloan Bros. (C) Ltd., Belfast.
Timber treatment by: Radication Ltd., Dunmurry, Belfast.
Painting by: John Hamilton (Decorators) Ltd., Newtownabbey.

100 Malone Road, Belfast.

A five-bay, two-storey house built in the early-19th century. The roof is slated and gabled, walls are smooth rendered with moulded details and windows have plain sashes. A square, columned portico projects on the main front.
Recipient of grant: Prof. E. E. Evans.
Grant assistance of £130 given towards: Replacement metal rainwater goods. Re-pointing of brickwork.
Approximate cost of work: £391. Carried out in 1980.
Contractor: James McMahon, Belfast.

10 Lower Crescent, Belfast.

Part of an imposing but mutilated terrace of twelve properties built in 1852 by James Corry. The house and

its neighbour form a unified six-bay, three-storey composition. The frontage is of smooth render, rusticated at ground floor with flat two-storey high Corinthian pilasters supporting a plain frieze and modillioned cornice below the attic windows. The roof is concealed behind a decorative parapet. The entrance is recessed in a square-headed porch.
Recipient of grant: Hawksdale Ltd.
Grant assistance of £1,160 given towards: Repairs to chimneys. Repairs to parapet gutter. Repairs to external render. Repairs to windows.
Approximate cost of work: £3,950. Carried out in 1981.
Contractor: Tower Heating Co. Ltd., Belfast.

11 and 12 Lower Crescent, Belfast.

Number 11 is described with number 10 in the previous entry. Number 12 is a plain three-bay, three-storey building added to the terrace in 1878. The roof is slated. with an eaves cornice, the frontage is smooth rendered with moulded details and windows have plain sashes and are square-headed on the lower floors and segmentally-headed on the second floor.
Recipient of grant: Alexandra Properties Ltd.,
Grant assistance of £2,270 given towards: Repairs to chimney. Roof repairs. Repairs to leadwork. Repairs to external render. Repairs to windows. External redecoration. Treatment of wood rot. Installation of silicone injection damp-proof course. Repairs to internal plasterwork. Repairs to staircase.
Approximate cost of work: £7,111.

Large Houses

Carried out in 1979 and 1980.

Contractor: M. & V. Building Co., Downpatrick.

Timber treatment by: Timbercare (N.I.), Lisburn.

31 Rugby Road, Belfast.

Part of an impressive and reasonably well preserved three-storey terrace built in the later-19th century. The roof is slated, with a strong eaves cornice, the frontage is of crisply detailed red and yellow brick, and the plain-sash windows have segmental heads to the ground and second floors and semi-circular heads to the first floor. The half-glazed panelled entrance door has a semi-circular fanlight.

Recipient of grant: Mr. D. S. Cooke.

Grant assistance of £2,600 given towards: Repairs to windows. Treatment of extensive dry rot. Repairs to internal plasterwork. Repairs to timber floors. Professional fees.

Approximate cost of work: £8,621. Carried out in 1981 and 1982.

Architects: Robert McKinstry & Melvyn Brown, Belfast.

Contractor: Crawford & Laird, Belfast.

Timber treatment by: Radication Ltd., Dunmurry, Belfast.

Painting by: Castle Decorators Ltd., Belfast.

39 Rugby Road, Belfast.

Part of an impressive and reasonably well preserved three-storey terrace built in th later-19th century. The roof is slated, with a strong eaves cornice, the frontage is of crisply detailed red and yellow brick and the plain sash windows have square heads to the ground floor, semi-circular heads to

the first floor and segmental heads to the second floor. The half-glazed panelled door has a semi-circular fanlight.

Recipient of grant: Mr. L. Kennedy.

Grant assistance of £700 given towards: Replacement metal rainwater goods. Re-pointing of brickwork. Treatment of extensive dry rot. Installation of damp-proof course. Removal of wall panelling and restoration after treatment of rot. Repairs to internal plasterwork. Replacement timber floors.

Approximate cost of work: £2,192. Carried out in 1982.

Contractor: M. P. Building Services, Belfast.

Timber treatment by: Lacey Timbertreatments Ltd., Belfast.

53 Rugby Road, Belfast.

Part of an impressive and reasonably well preserved three-storey terrace built in the later-19th century. The roof is slated, with a strong eaves cornice, the frontage is of crisply detailed red and yellow brick and the plain sash windows have square heads to the ground floor, semi-circular heads to the first floor and segmental heads to the second floor. The half-glazed panelled door has a semi-circular fanlight.

Recipient of grant: Dr. R. R. Eccleshall.

Grant assistance of £220 given towards: Repairs to windows and redecoration. Installation of damp-proof solid floors.

Approximate cost of work: £742. Carried out in 1983.

Contractor: Andersonstown Building Works, Belfast.

Painting by: J. Henry, Belfast.

37 University Road, Belfast.

Part of an imposing three-storey terrace of five houses built in 1848 now fully rebuilt following severe bomb damage. The roof is slated, walls are smooth rendered with moulded details including a dentilled cornice, pedimented aedicules to the first floor windows and rusticated ground floor. The windows have plain sashes, and the entrance is set in a Doric pilastered porch.

Recipient of grant: Mr. J. A. G. Whyte.

Grant assistance of £2,870 given towards: Repairs to roof structure. Re-slating using natural slate. Repairs to external render. Restoration of porch in original style. Replacement sash windows in original style. Treatment of wood rot. Repairs to internal plasterwork.

Approximate cost of work: £11,200. Carried out in 1980.

Contractor: Joe Wright, Lisburn.

10 Wellington Park, Belfast.

One of two central houses in a handsome Victorian terrace of four three-storey houses built about 1855. The houses at either end break forward slightly, the roof is hipped and slated, the frontage is of brick with moulded details and the windows have margined pane sashes to the ground and first floors and Georgian-pane sashes to the second floor. The half-glazed panelled entrance door is contained in a square-columned porch.

Recipient of grant: Mr. & Mrs. C. H. Knight.

Grant assistance of £3,941 given towards: Repairs to chimney. Roof repairs. Repairs to domelight. Repairs to rainwater goods. Re-pointing of brickwork. Repairs to external render. Repairs to windows. Repairs to panelled entrance door. Treatment of wood rot. Installation of damp-proof course. Repairs to timber floors. Installation of damp-proof solid floors. Repairs to internal plasterwork.

Further financial assistance received from: Northern Ireland Housing Executive.

Approximate cost of work: £26,226. Carried out in 1980 and 1981.

Contractor: Robert Irvine, Belfast.

Timber treatment and damp-course by: Protim Services, Lisburn.

Beardiville House, Ballyhome Road, Coleraine.

A five-bay, two-storey house with four-bay single-storey extension to the north frontage. The house appears to have been re-built in the mid-18th century although a house has stood on the site since the 17th century. Walls are rendered, roof hipped and slated and windows are narrow being only two panes wide. The central bay of the main front projects slightly and contains a porchway with semi-engaged Tuscan columns with a heraldic plaque dated 1713 over the doorway. The gate lodge consists of two small single-storey buildings with half-hipped roofs and rubble basalt walls on either side of a central, pedimented archway.

Recipient of grant: Mr. J. L. Baxter.

PHASE ONE — REPAIRS

Grant assistance of £150 given towards: Provision of flat roof over central roof valley.

Approximate cost of work: £446. Carried out in 1979.

Roof work by: Haire Bros., Coleraine.

PHASE TWO — SECURING GATE LODGES

Grant assistance of £105 given towards: Blocking up windows and door openings.

Approximate cost of work: £351. Carried out in 1981.

Contractor: S. Watton, Coleraine.

PHASE THREE — FENCE REPAIRS

Grant assistance of £80 given towards: Repairs to driveway fencing.

Approximate cost of work: £241. Carried out in 1981.

Contractor: S. Watton, Coleraine.

PHASE FOUR — DECORATION OF MAIN HOUSE

Grant assistance of £390 given towards: External redecoration.

Approximate cost of work: £1,272. Carried out in 1982.

Painting by: T. Millar, Coleraine.

30 Kerr Street, Portrush.

A three-storey, late-19th century, smooth rendered terrace house with projecting first floor canted bay. Windows are plain-sashed with moulded surrounds.

Recipient of grant: Mr. M. Maen.

Grant assistance of £1,658 given towards: Roof repairs. Repairs to windows. Repairs to panelled entrance door. Redecoration of remedial items.

Approximate cost of work: £4,279. Carried out in 1979.

Contractor: J. Elliott, Portrush.

31 Kerr Street, Portrush.

A three-storey, late-19th century, smooth rendered terrace house with projecting first floor canted bay. Windows are plain-sashed with moulded architraves.

Recipient of grant: Miss P. Murphy.

Grant assistance of £1,680 given towards: Roof repairs. Repairs to windows. Repairs to panelled entrance door. Redecoration of remedial items.

Approximate cost of work: £3,353. Carried out in 1979.

Contractor: J. Elliott, Portrush.

O'Harabrook, Enagh Road Ballymoney.

An unusual house in that it has been reorientated since its original construction in the mid-18th century. The south gable of the original two-storey house now forms a central four-bay projection with four-bay, two-storey wings having been added to the east and west. The house is roughcast. The appearance of the south front has been somewhat marred by the addition of an inappropriate porch and conservatory within the last century.

Recipient of grant: Col. A. J. H. Cramsie.

Grant assistance of £10,000 given towards: Repairs to roof structure. Re-slating using natural slate with asbestos-cement slates to inner slopes.

Approximate cost of work: £34,027. Carried out in 1979.

Roof work by: T. Shaw & Son, Ballymoney.

Moore Lodge, 166 Vow Road, Kilrea.

A beautifully located three-bay, two-storey, roughcast house built about 1759 probably by Sampson Moore. Tripartite windows set in shallow segmental bows flank a central

Large Houses

timber porch. A service wing projects to the rear. The house has been well restored.

Recipient of grant: Mr. A. Boyd.

RESTORATION PROJECT

Grant assistance of £24,600 given towards: Repairs to chimneys. Roof repairs. Replacement leadwork. Replacement metal rainwater goods. Repairs to external render. Replacement sash windows in original style. Repairs to panelled entrance door. Rebuilding of defective structural walls. Treatment of wood rot. Repairs to internal plasterwork. Installation of damp-proof solid floors. Redecoration of remedial items. Repairs to stone garden wall. Professional fees.

Approximate cost of work: £121,645.

Contractor: Thomas Shaw & Son, Ballymoney.

Ballymoney Rectory, Queen's Street, Ballymoney.

A two-storey red brick house with hipped roof and pilastered porch. Built in the mid-19th century and restored in 1960.

Recipient of grant: Select Vestry, St Patrick's Parish Church.

PHASE ONE — REPAIRS

Grant assistance of £70 given towards: Replacement sash window in original style.

Approximate cost of work: £220. Carried out in 1979.

Work carried out using direct labour.

PHASE TWO — REPAIRS

Grant assistance of £125 given towards: Replacement doors to out-buildings in original style.

Approximate cost of work: £375. Carried out in 1981.

Contractor: J. S. Dunlop, Ballymoney.

17 Mill Street, Cushendall.

A two-bay, three-storey mid-19th century rendered house with moulded quoins and Georgian-glazed sash windows.

Recipient of grant: Mr. P. J. McCollam.

Grant assistance of £2,793 given towards: Repairs to chimney. Rebuilding of chimney. Repairs to rainwater goods. Repairs to external render. Replacement sash windows in original style. Replacement panelled entrance door. Repairs to internal plasterwork. Repairs to timber floors. Installation of damp-proof solid floors. Repairs to staircase. Redecoration of remedial items.

Further financial assistance received from: Northern Ireland Housing Executive.

Approximate cost of work: £21,220. Carried out in 1981 and 1982.

Contractor: Martin Jamieson, Ballycastle.

The Rectory, 3 Coast Road, Cushendall.

A three-bay, two-storey building with dormered attic, built about 1830. The Georgian-glazed windows have rather ungainly pedimented aedicules. A square, flat-roofed, porch projects from the front elevation.

Recipient of grant: Mrs. M. Lynn.

Grant assistance of £1,030 given towards: Rebuilding of chimney. Repair of porch roof. Repairs to leadwork. Repairs to external render.

Approximate cost of work: £3,110. Carried out in 1981.

Contractor: Martin Jamieson, Ballycastle.

Glendun Lodge, Cushendun.

A four-bay, two-storey roughcast house with slated roof and unusually wide sixteen-pane sash windows. Built about 1810. The house has been carefully restored after having been gutted by fire in 1979.

Recipient of grant: Mrs. P. M. S. English.

Grant assistance of £4,000 given towards: Balance of cost of restoration not covered by insurance.

Approximate cost of work: £40,300. Carried out in 1981 and 1982.

Contractor: Murray & Partners, Glenariff.

Old Rectory, Billy, Bushmills.

An unusually large glebe house of three-storeys built about 1810. The front has a full height projecting bow.

Recipient of grant: Mrs. M. E. A. Page.

Grant assistance of £6,580 given towards: Repairs to chimneys. Re-slating using natural slates. Replacement metal rainwater goods. External re-rendering. Replacement sash windows in original style. Replacement panelled entrance door. Treatment of wood rot. Repairs to internal plasterwork. Repairs to timber floors. Repairs to staircase. Redecoration of remedial items.

Further financial assistance received from: Northern Ireland Housing Executive.

Approximate cost of work: £35,980. Carried out from 1981 to 1983.

Contractor: Hugh Taggart & Sons Ltd., Ballymoney.

Large Houses

Old Rectory, Billy, Bushmills.

Drumnagesson House, Bushmills.

A late-18th century three-bay, two-storey house with attic and basement. The central pedimented bay projects slightly and has a square, flat-roofed porch approached by steps. Walls are rendered and windows Georgian-glazed. The house was altered in the 19th century.

Recipient of grant: Mr. D. Kane.

Grant assistance of £2,695 given towards: Re-slating using asbestos-cement slate. Replacement metal rainwater goods. Replacement sash windows in original style. Replacement panelled entrance doors.

Further financial assistance received from: Northern Ireland Housing Executive.

Approximate cost of work: £15,610.

Carried out in 1979.

Contractor: Boyd McIntyre, Bushmills.

The Agent's House, 27 to 29 Altmore Street, Glenarm.

A series of early-19th century rendered buildings gabled and dormered.

Recipient of grant: Mr. E. Lammey.

Grant assistance of £650 given towards: Repairs to roof structure. Re-slating using natural slate. Repairs to rainwater goods.

Work carried out using direct labour.

Crannie, 33 Lower Cairncastle Road, Larne.

A five-bay, two-storey rendered house with a square porch, built about 1850.

Recipient of grant: Mr. J. Gault.

Grant assistance of £3,000 given towards: Repairs to chimneys. Repairs to rainwater goods. Repairs to external render. Repairs to windows. Installation of electro-osmotic damp-proof course. Repairs to internal plasterwork. Installation of damp-proof solid floors.

Approximate cost of work: £17,000. Carried out from 1980 to 1983.

Work carried out using own and direct labour.

Underwood, 74 Hillmount Road, Cullybackey.

A one-and-a-half storey house built about 1850. The facade is of blackstone with brick dressings and, Georgian-paned sash windows.

Recipient of grant: Mr. T. A. Fisher.

Grant assistance of £886 given towards: Repairs to chimney. Roof repairs. Replacement metal rainwater goods.

Replacement sash windows in original style. Repairs to internal plasterwork. Repairs to timber floors.

Further financial assistance received from: Northern Ireland Housing Executive.

Approximate cost of work: £5,932. Carried out in 1981.

Contractor: W. M. McMaster, Cullybackey.

Hazel Bank, 85 Hillmount Road, Craigs, Cullybackey.

A pre-1857 three-bay two-storey rendered house with hipped, slated roof. Georgian-glazed sash windows with an early Victorian trifora over the entrance.

Recipient of grant: Mr. and Mrs. R. P. Margrain.

Grant assistance of £143 given towards: Repairs to rainwater goods. Repairs to external render.

Approximate cost of work: £430. Carried out in 1980.

Contractor: Samuel Graham, Ahoghill.

Springmount, 49 Springmount Road, Glarryford, Ballymena.

A five-bay, two-storey rendered house with hipped slated roof, Georgian-glazed sash windows with moulded architraves and central elliptically arched doorway. The main block is flanked by two two-storey hipped roof wings of reduced height.

Recipient of grant: Mr. J. H. Ross.

Grant assistance of £425 given towards: Repairs to rainwater goods. Repairs to windows. Replacement entrance door in original style. External redecoration.

Approximate cost of work: £1,283. Carried out in 1982.

Large Houses

Contractor: A. Cusick (Contractors) Ltd., Armoy, and work carried out using direct labour.

Painting by: P. J. Boyle, Ballycastle.

Tullymore Schools, 1 Carnlough Road, Broughshane.

Formerly a school now converted for use as a dwelling. The building consists of a central three-bay, one-and-a-half-storey block with closely spaced gabled dormers with decorative barge boards and a recessed ground floor behind a colonade of slender Ionic columns. The central block is flanked by two-bay, single-storey wings. Windows have Georgian-glazed sashes.

Recipient of grant: Mr. W. Wylie.

Grant assistance of £2,010 given towards: Re-slating using natural slate. Replacement windows in original style. Treatment of wood rot. Redecoration of remedial items.

Further financial assistance received from: Northern Ireland Housing Executive.

Approximate cost of work: £12,575. Carried out in 1979.

Agent: Joseph E. McKernan, Ballymena.

Contractor: Charles Johnson, Cullybackey.

Painting by: D. E. Brown & Co., Ballymena.

The Rectory, 37 Raceview Road, Broughshane.

A two-storey, rogue Gothic Victorian rectory with three intricately detailed bay windows and a three-storey crenellated tower with traceried window. The roof is gabled and slated and walls are of stone with brick

The Rectory, 37 Raceview Road, Broughshane.

dressings. Built about 1870.

Recipient of grant: The Select Vestry, St. Patrick's Church.

Grant assistance of £1,125 given towards: Roof repairs. Repairs to chimneys. Repairs to rainwater goods. Re-pointing of stonework. Repairs to windows and door. External redecoration.

Approximate cost of work: £4,937. Carried out in 1978 and 1979.

Contractor: John Surgenor & Son, Ballymena.

90 Ballygarvey Road, Ballymena.

Part of a later-19th century asymmetrically planned ten-bay, two-storey gabled and pedimented terrace. The central pediment contains a clock above a semi-circular-headed window, and coach arch. Other windows are square-headed with margined sashes. The entrance doors have lean-to porches.

Recipient of grant: Miss J. Hannon.

Grant assistance of £112 given towards: External re-rendering.

Approximate cost of work: £225. Carried out in 1982.

Contractor: Andrew W. Kirk, Ballymena.

Cleggan Lodge, 162 Carnlough Road, Aghafatten, Broughshane.

A multi-gabled two- and three-storey house built before 1777 as a rather eccentric thatched shooting lodge for the O'Neills of Shanes Castle. It was restored and enlarged in 1927 in the

Cleggan Lodge, Broughshane.

process loosing many of its unusual features. The walls are roughcast.

Recipient of grant: Mr. H. O'Neill.

Grant assistance of £10,000 given towards: Provision of a flat roof in place of a central valley. Re-slating using existing hexagonal slates to front areas. Replacement sash windows in original style. Treatment of wood rot.

Approximate cost of work: £29,775. Carried out in 1978 and 1979.

Architects: Robert McKinstry & Melvyn Brown, Belfast.

Quantity Surveyors: W. H. Stephens & Sons, Belfast.

Structural Engineers: Martin & Hamilton Ltd., Ballymena.

Greenfield House, Kells.

A five-bay, two-storey rendered house with segmental arched entrance. The house was originally owned by the Arthur family of the nearby linen mill. It was restored in 1914 by the Dinsmore family.

Recipient of grant: Mr. P. V. Hutchinson.

Grant assistance of £2,050 given towards: Treatment of extensive dry rot. Repairs to chimneys. Roof repairs. Repairs to internal plasterwork. Repairs to decorative plasterwork.

Approximate cost of work: £6,150. Carried out in 1981.

Contractor: Alistair Caldwell, Kells.

Timber treatment by: Timbercare (N.I.), Lisburn.

New Lodge, Shankbridge, Ballymena.

A three-bay, two-storey rendered house with an elliptically arched

entrance containing cable moulded columns.

Recipient of grant: Mr. R. Witherspoon.

Grant assistance of £5,800 given towards: Repairs to chimneys. Repairs to roof structure. Re-slating using natural slate. Replacement metal rainwater goods. Replacement sash windows in original style. Repairs to entrance screen. Treatment of wood rot. Repairs to internal plasterwork. Repairs to timber floors. Redecoration of remedial items.

Approximate cost of work: £24,200. Carried out in 1979.

Contractor: McCavana Contracts, Randalstown.

141 Moneygran Road, Portglenone.

A mid-19th century, three-bay, two-storey house with blackstone walls and cross-paned windows.

Recipient of grant: Mr. & Mrs. J. M. McCloskey.

Grant assistance of £2,084 given towards: Rebuilding of chimneys. Repairs to roof structure. Re-slating using natural slate. Replacement barge boards. Replacement metal rainwater goods.

Further financial assistance received from: Northern Ireland Housing Executive.

Approximate cost of work: £8,445. Carried out in 1982 and 1983.

Contractor: Paddy Madden, Kilrea.

Legatirriff House, Legatirriff, Ballinderry.

A two-storey, 18th century, thatched house with four moulded and rendered chimneys. Walls have a modern roughcast finish and the windows have Georgian-glazed sashes set in unrecessed cases. The panelled entrance

door with plain fanlight is asymmetrically positioned. A single-storey extension extends to the south.

Recipient of grant: Dr. D. R. Hadden.

PHASE ONE—ROOF

Grant assistance of £473 given towards: Re-thatching.

Approximate cost of work: £1,892. Carried out in 1975 and 1976.

Thatching by: R. Douglas, Ballygowan.

PHASE TWO – REPAIRS

Grant assistance of £57 given towards: Replacement panelled entrance door.

Approximate cost of work: £227. Carried out in 1976.

Contractor: Fred Scandrett, Aghalee.

PHASE THREE – REPAIRS

Grant assistance of £300 given towards: Treatment of wood rot and subsequent reinstatement.

Approximate cost of work: £1,149. Carried out in 1979.

Timber treatment by: Rentokil Ltd., Belfast.

PHASE FOUR – REPAIRS

Grant assistance of £270 given towards: Repairs to thatch.

Approximate cost of work: £822. Carried out in 1980.

Thatching by: Irish Thatchers Ltd., Annaghmore, Dungannon.

PHASE FIVE – REPAIRS

Grant assistance of £70 given towards: Repairs to thatch.

Approximate cost of work: £212. Carried out in 1981.

Thatching by: Irish Thatchers Ltd., Annaghmore, Dungannon.

Large Houses

The Glebe, Upper Ballinderry, Lisburn.

A fine three-bay, two-storey, double-pile house with contiguous outbuildings, in the manner of Charles Lanyon. The roof is hipped and slated, with modillioned eaves, walls are smooth rendered, with moulded details, windows have Georgian-glazed sashes in square-headed openings and a square rusticated porch with semi-circular-headed openings projects from the entrance front.

Recipient of grant: Mr. T. C. Lilburn.

Grant assistance of £15,000 given towards: Repairs to roof structure. Re-slating using natural slate. Treatment of extensive dry rot. Installation of silicone injection damp-proof course. Repairs to timber floors. Repairs to internal plasterwork.

Approximate cost of work: £45,507. Carried out in 1980.

Timber treatment by: Timbercare (N.I.), Lisburn.

Springfield, Brookemount, Lisburn.

A large two-storey house built about 1850 by the Richardson family. The roof is hipped and slated with moulded chimneys and decorative chimney pots and projecting eaves supported on paired brackets. The walls are smooth rendered with moulded surrounds to windows which have segmental heads to the first floor and plain sashes. The panelled entrance door is set in an engaged portico with entablature supported on console brackets.

Recipient of grant: Mr. T. H. Caldwell.

Grant assistance of £8,250 given towards: Repairs to chimneys. Treatment of extensive dry rot. Repairs to roof

structure. Re-slating part of roof using asbestos-cement slates. Replacement leadwork. Repairs to internal plasterwork. Treatment of damp in basement.

Approximate cost of work: £25,650. Carried out in 1978.

Timber treatment by: Ulster Woodcare Specialists, Belfast.

Lagan Lodge, 27 Church Hill, Lambeg.

Part of what was originally a Hugenot farmhouse built about 1730. The roofs are gabled and slated, walls are of rubble stonework and windows have Georgian-glazed sashes.

Recipient of grant: Mr. J. E. Watson.

Grant assistance of £5,105 given towards: Rebuilding of chimneys. Repairs to roof structure. Re-slating using natural slate. Provision of new lintels over window openings. External re-rendering. Replacement sash windows in original style. Replacement external doors in original style. Installation of damp-proof course. Repairs to internal plasterwork. Repairs to timber floors. Professional fees.

Further financial assistance received from: Northern Ireland Housing Executive.

Approximate cost of work: £23,863. Carried out in 1981.

Architects: H. A. Patton & Partners, Bangor.

Contractor: Davis & Cochrane Ltd., Dunmurry, Belfast.

Farmhill House, Black's Road, Dunmurry.

A three-bay, two-storey house possibly designed by Lanyon or

Turner. The roof is hipped and slated, walls are of brick with stone dressings, windows have plain sashes and single-storey bays project at the sides of the building.

Recipient of grant: Dr. T. G. Milliken.

Grant assistance of £122 given towards: Roof repairs. Repairs to flat roof over bay window. Repairs to rainwater goods. Repairs to internal plasterwork.

Approximate cost of work: £367. Carried out in 1976.

Contractor: Crawford & Laird, Belfast.

Roof work by: Prentice Bros., Finaghy, Belfast.

Hermitage, 7 Ahoghill Road, Randalstown.

A sprawling, single-storey house with hipped slated roof, roughcast walls and Georgian-glazed sash windows.

Recipient of grant: Mr. J. W. Wallace.

Grant assistance of £1,345 given towards: Roof repairs. Repairs to rainwater goods. Repairs to windows. Treatment of woodworm. Repairs to internal plasterwork. Repairs to timber floors.

Approximate cost of work: £4,047. Carried out in 1980 and 1981.

Contractor: James Rainey & Sons, Randalstown.

Timber treatment by: Rentokil Ltd., Belfast.

Antrim House, 11 Riverside, Town Parks, Antrim.

A five-bay, three-storey early-19th century house with a two-storey lean-to extension to the south gable and a single-storey extension to the front. The roof is hipped and slated, walls are rendered, windows have Georgian-glazed sashes and the

Large Houses

panelled entrance door with decorative sidelights and fanlights are recessed in an elliptically-arched opening.

Recipient of grant: Trustees of St John's Free Presbyterian Church.

PHASE ONE – REPAIRS

Grant assistance of £132 given towards: Repairs to chimneys. Roof repairs.

Approximate cost of work: £336. Carried out in 1976.

Contractor: Wilson Partners, Antrim.

PHASE TWO

Grant assistance of £350 given towards: Roof repairs. Repairs to rainwater goods.

Approximate cost of work: £1,058. Carried out in 1980.

Contractor: John McG. Johnston, Bangor.

Ballybrophy House, 26 New Lodge Road, Muckamore.

A five-bay, two-storey, pre-1780 house with attics. The roof is half-hipped and slated, walls are rendered, windows have Georgian-glazed sashes and the attractive entrance doorway is flanked by Tuscan columns. The spacious stone-built coach yard is entered through a coach arch surmounted by a pediment and flanked by two-storey houses, originally for staff.

Recipient of grant: Mr. S. Hood.

Grant assistance of £790 given towards: Repairs to rainwater goods. External re-rendering. Repairs to windows.

Approximate cost of work: £2,440. Carried out from 1977 to 1979.

Contractor: C. Penny, Ballyclare.

Islandreagh, 2 Islandreagh Road, Muckamore.

A three-bay, two-storey, pre-1780 house. The roof is slated and gabled, walls are roughcast, windows have Georgian-glazed sashes and the panelled entrance door has an elaborate fanlight. Recent extensions, single-storey to the west and two-storey to the east, have been carefully designed in keeping with the original house which has also been refurbished.

Recipient of grant: Mr. S. D. Logan.

Grant assistance of £195 given towards: Replacement panelled entrance door.

Approximate cost of work: £586. Carried out in 1981.

Architects: Isherwood & Ellis, Belfast and Ballymena.

Contractor: Window-Glaze, Belfast.

Dunadry House, 42 Ballybentragh Road, Antrim.

A five-bay, two-storey house with attics and a two-storey return and single-storey extension to the east. The roof is slated and gabled and windows have Georgian-glazed sashes.

Recipient of grant: Mr. P. Dennison.

Grant assistance of £7,010 given towards: Rebuilding of chimneys. Repairs to roof structure. Re-slating using natural slate. External re-rendering. Replacement sash windows in original style. Replacement panelled entrance door. Redecoration of remedial items. Installation of damp-proof course. Internal re-plastering. Replacement timber floors. Installation of damp-proof solid floors. Professional fees.

Approximate cost of work: £20,334.

(Value of grant-aided work only). Carried out in 1979 and 1980.

Architects: Isherwood & Ellis, Belfast and Ballymena.

Work carried out using direct labour.

The Old Rectory, 40 Oldstone Road, Muckamore.

A one-and-a-half-storey, 'T'-shaped, mid-19th century house. The roof is slated and gabled, with bracketted projecting eaves and barges, walls are smooth rendered with moulded details and windows to the main block are Venetian in style with plain sashes, the remainder having Georgian-glazed sashes. The entrance is to one side of a central projecting gabled porch.

Recipient of grant: Mr. S. J. Allen.

Grant assistance of £100 given towards: Treatment of woodworm.

Approximate cost of work: £291. Carried out in 1978.

Timber treatment by: Rentokil Ltd., Belfast.

Glenhurst, 20 Oldstone Road, Muckamore.

An attractive Regency Gothic house with a five-bay, two-storey, main block and two-bay, single-storey wing. The roofs are slated and gabled, walls are smooth rendered and windows have decorative margined sashes set in Gothic pointed openings and Tudor drip mouldings, at ground floor. The half-glazed panelled entrance door with decorative fanlight is flanked by plain pilasters supporting a broken pediment.

Recipient of grant: Mr. D. Steele.

Grant assistance of £1,000 given towards: Re-slating using natural slate.

Large Houses

Replacement timber floors.
Approximate cost of work: £1,482. Carried out in 1979.
Contractor: David Wilson, Dunadry, Co. Antrim.

Crookedstone House, 1 Ballyarnott Road, Aldergrove, Crumlin.

A five-bay, two-storey harled and thatched house with porch built about 1700, and with more recent additions to the north.
Recipient of grant: Mrs. A. J. C. Cunningham.
Grant assistance of £230 given towards: Emergency repairs to thatching.
Approximate cost of work: £318. Carried out in 1982.
Architects: Ferguson & McIlveen. Belfast.
Thatching by: Gerald Agnew, Ahoghill.

Ben-Neagh, Seacash, 11 Crumlin Road, Crumlin.

A large pre-1833 five-bay, two-storey house with hipped slated roof, roughcast walls, Georgian-glazed sash windows (unusually tall on the ground floor) and a metal framed conservatory/porch which somewhat detracts from the appearance of the property.

Recipient of grant: Mr. A. S. F. Peel.

Grant assistance of £1,580 given towards: Roof repairs. Repairs to leadwork. Replacement metal rainwater goods. Treatment of wood rot. Repairs to internal plasterwork. Repairs to decorative plasterwork.

Approximate cost of work: £4,740. Carried out in 1979.

Roof work by: Pentagon (Renovation) Ltd., Darkley, Co. Armagh.

Timber treatment by: Rentokil Ltd., Belfast.
Plastering by: Alexander Law, (N.I.), Ltd., Belfast.

Lakeview, 99 Lurgan Road, Pigeontown, Ballyvollen, Glenavy.

A two-storey, 'U'-shaped rendered house with Georgian-glazed sash windows and entrance, set in an elliptically-arched opening.
Recipient of grant: Mrs. M. Boyd.
Grant assistance of £2,130 given towards: Repairs to chimneys. Re-slating using natural slate. Repairs to leadwork. Replacement metal rainwater goods. Repairs to windows. Installation of damp-proof solid floors.
Further financial assistance received from: Northern Ireland Housing Executive.
Approximate cost of work: £8,150. Carried out in 1979 and 1980.
Contractor: Beckett & Mullholland, Craigavon.

Glynn Park, Taylors Avenue, Carrickfergus.

A tall, three-bay, three-storey house built in 1776 with a two-storey crenellated bay at the front and a long two-storey extension wing to the west. The house shows 'a confusing mixture of classical determination and gothic fancy'. UAHS. Carrickfergus.
Recipient of grant: Mr. R. Huffam.
Grant assistance of £163 given towards: Repairs to leadwork.
Approximate cost of work: £520. Carried out in 1978 and 1979.
Contractor: L. Hamill & Sons, Ballyclare.

Crookedstone House, 1 Ballyarnott Road, Crumlin.

Large Houses

Ennismore House, Maghery, The Birches, Portadown.

A single-storey slated and rendered house with mid-to-late-Georgian detailing.

Recipient of grant: Dr. W. A. Norris.

Grant assistance of £4,430 given towards: Repairs to roof structure. Re-slating using natural slate to main roof. Re-slating using asbestos-cement slate to kitchen roof. Repairs to leadwork. Repairs to internal plasterwork.

Approximate cost of work: £13,766. Carried out in 1980.

Contractor: William Mulholland, Lurgan.

The Firs, Mahon Road, Portadown.

A three-bay, two-storey house built about 1830. The roof is slated and gabled, walls are smooth rendered with moulded details and lining to the ground floor, windows have Georgian-glazed sashes and a central flat-roofed porch projects.

Recipient of grant: Mr. S. McClelland.

Grant assistance of £4,730 given towards: Repairs to chimneys. Re-slating using natural slate. Repairs to leadwork. Replacement metal rainwater goods. Replacement sash windows in original style. Treatment of woodworm. Repairs to internal plasterwork. Repairs to timber floors. Installation of damp-proof solid floors. Professional fees.

Approximate cost of work: £17,839. Carried out in 1982 and 1983.

Architect: Clive Henning, Portadown.

Contractor: R. Uprichard & Sons, Portadown.

The Rectory, Ardmore, Derryadd, Lurgan.

A fine three-bay, two-storey late Georgian house in a secluded lough-shore setting. Venetian sash windows flank the central doorway. Roof is hipped and slated walls are roughcast and colour washed.

Recipient of grant: Select Vestry, Ardmore Church.

Grant assistance of £713 given towards: Rebuilding of chimneys. Re-slating using natural slate. Replacement leadwork. Replacement metal rainwater goods. External re-rendering. Replacement sash windows in original style. Replacement panelled entrance door.

Further financial assistance received from: Northern Ireland Housing Executive.

Approximate cost of work: £7,386. Carried out in 1981.

Contractor: Stevenson Bros., Derryadd, Lurgan.

Old Drumlyn House, 115 Moyallen Road, Portadown.

A two-storey, probably late-18th century, house. Roof is slated and gabled with a decorative brick chimney. Walls are roughcast with Georgian-glazed sash windows.

Recipient of grant: J. G. Richardson Trustees.

Grant assistance of £1,352 given towards: Repairs to chimneys. Roof repairs. Replacement metal rainwater goods. Replacement sash windows in original style. Replacement external doors in original style. Restoration of porch. Installation of damp-proof course. Repairs to internal plasterwork. Installation of damp-proof solid floors. Professional fees.

Further financial assistance received from: Northern Ireland Housing Executive.

Approximate cost of work: £13,172. Carried out in 1981.

Architects: Caldwell Deane Partnership, Lurgan, Belfast and Portadown.

Contractor: E. & B. Derby, Lurgan.

Springfield House, 15 Springfield Road, Magheralin.

A five-bay, two-storey house with hipped roof, rendered walls and central, flat-roofed square porch. The first floor is smooth rendered with moulded architraves to the windows, the ground floor is lined and has vermiculated dressings to quoins and windows. Windows have horizontally divided sashes. The house was remodelled in the mid-19th century and has a large return. It has been extensively restored.

Recipient of grant: Mr. T. Clarke.

Grant assistance of £4,800 given towards: Repairs to chimneys. Re-slating using natural slate. Replacement metal rainwater goods. Repairs to external render. Replacement sash windows in original style. Replacement panelled entrance door. Repairs to internal plasterwork. Installation of damp-proof solid floors. Repairs to timber floors. Undergrounding of electricity cables.

Approximate cost of work: £37,000. Carried out from 1979 to 1982.

Architect: Ian Donaldson, Armagh.

Contractor: George McCullagh, Portadown.

Newforge House, Magheralin, Lurgan.

A three-storey, symmetrical dwelling

Large Houses

Newforge House, Magheralin, Lurgan.

house with basement built about 1790. The roof is slated, walls are harled and the entrance door is contained within a crudely pedimented Adamesque doorcase. An earlier house survives as outbuildings at the rear.

Recipient of grant: Mr. R. H. Mathers.

Grant assistance of £4,600 given towards: Repairs to chimneys. Repairs to roof structure. Re-slating using natural slate. Repairs to rainwater goods. Repairs to internal plasterwork.

Approximate cost of work: £11,598. Carried out in 1979 and 1980.

Contractor: Rowley Construction Co., Belfast.

Tallbridge House, Cranagill, Portadown.

The present house was built about 1850 on the site of an earlier house. It is five-bays and two-storeys with an attic and a slated and gabled roof. Walls are rendered and lined. Windows have moulded surrounds and Georgian-glazing. The central panelled entrance door and decorative fanlight is set within a semi-circular archivolt and flanking pilasters.

Recipient of grant: Mrs. S. J. Hamilton.

Grant assistance of £290 given towards: Repairs to entrance gates. Repairs to decorative plasterwork,

Approximate cost of work: £864. Carried out in 1979 and 1980.

Contractor: James Wilson & Sons, Hamilton's Bawn.

Plastering by: Greenhill Mills Ltd., Loughgall.

Metalwork by: G. Elliott, Richhill.

Crannagael, Cranagill, Portadown.

A three-bay, two-storey Georgian house with slated gabled roof and rendered walls with applied mouldings. Windows have Georgian-glazed sashes. A square porch, with parapeted roof and side door, projects centrally.

Recipient of grant: Mr. J. Nicholson.

Grant assistance of £3,050 given towards: Repairs to chimneys. Replacement metal rainwater goods. External re-rendering. Restoration of missing cornice and mouldings on porch. Repairs to windows. Redecoration of remedial items.

Approximate cost of work: £9,150. Carried out in 1982.

Contractor: George Roleston, Dungannon.

Marlacoo House, 146 Marlacoo Road, Portadown.

A three-bay, two-storey house with late-Georgian detailing.

Recipient of grant: Mr. E. B. Wilson.

PHASE ONE

Grant assistance of £2,000 given towards: Re-slating using asbestos-cement slate of two-storey outbuilding. Making good after demolition of out-of-keeping return building. Repairs to windows. Repairs to internal plasterwork. Installation of damp-proof solid floors.

Approximate cost of work: £6,061. Carried out in 1976.

Architects: Fersuson & McIlveen, Belfast.

Contractor: Sloan Bros. (C) Ltd., Belfast.

PHASE TWO

Grant assistance of £5,980 given towards: Repairs to roof structure. Re-slating using natural slate. Replacement leadwork. Repairs to rainwater goods. Repairs to internal plasterwork. Professional fees.

Approximate cost of work: £16,634. Carried out in 1982.

Architects: Ferguson & McIlveen, Belfast.

Contractor: Ron Forbes, Portadown.

Timber treatment by: Radication Ltd., Dunmurry, Belfast.

Willowbank, Armagh Road, Keady.

A three-bay, two-storey late Georgian country house. The roof is hipped and slated with corbelled eaves, walls are roughcast, windows have Georgian-glazed sashes and the panelled entrance door with elliptical fanlight is flanked by Ionic columns.

Recipient of grant: Dr. E. S. Dorman.

Grant assistance of £1,680 given towards: Roof repairs. Replacement metal rainwater goods.

Approximate cost of work: £5,100. Carried out in 1979.

Contractor: McMurray Bros., Keady.

Course Lodge, 38 and 40 Annagreagh Road, Richhill.

A two-storey farmhouse with hipped and slated roof and two-bay windows to the front. Walls are roughcast with stone dressings, windows have Georgian-glazed sashes and the panelled entrance door is set under a semi-circular fanlight.

REPAIRS TO NO 38 ANNAGREAGH ROAD

Recipient of grant: Mr. J. G. McNally.

Grant assistance of £150 given towards: Re-slating using natural slate. Replacement metal rainwater goods. Repairs to external render. Replacement sash windows in original style.

REPAIRS TO NO 40 ANNAGREAGH ROAD

Recipient of grant: Mrs. A. E. Wilson.

Grant assistance of £165 given towards: Re-slating using natural slate. Replacement metal rainwater goods. Repairs to external render. Replacement sash windows in original style.

Further financial assistance received from: Northern Ireland Housing Executive.

Approximate cost of work: £11,330. Carried out in 1978.

Agent: William J. Cornett, Armagh.

Contractor: A. A. Quinn (Builders) Ltd., Tandragee.

Fruitfield House, 38 Ballyleny Road, Richhill.

A three-bay, two-storey, early-19th century farmhouse with hipped slated roof, rendered walls, Georgian-glazed sash windows and panelled entrance door set in a projecting hip-roofed porch.

Recipient of grant: Mrs. O. M. Hall.

Grant assistance of £1,450 given towards: External re-rendering. Repairs to windows. External redecoration.

Approximate cost of work: £5,442. Carried out in 1981.

Architects: G. P. & R. H. Bell, Belfast.

Contractor: S. Coulter, Portadown.

Painting by: F. McGurgan, Portadown.

Belview, Drumorgan.

A five-bay, two-storey, early-19th century vernacular farmhouse with gabled and slated roof, roughcast walls, marginal sash windows and entrance door set in a recessed arch in a projecting gabled porch.

Recipient of grant: Messrs. M. & G. McHugh.

Grant assistance of £730 given towards: Rebuilding of chimneys. Replacement sash windows in original style. Replacement external doors in original style. Repairs to internal plasterwork. Installation of damp-proof solid floors.

Approximate cost of work: £2,191. Carried out in 1982.

Work carried out using direct labour.

Beechill House, Keady Road, Ballyards.

A three-bay, two-storey, early-19th century, simply detailed, classical house with basement and return building.

Recipient of grant: Mr. W. J. Gray.

Grant assistance of £3,080 given towards: Roof repairs. Repairs to rainwater goods. Re-pointing of stonework. Repairs to windows. Replacement external doors in original style. Treatment of wood rot. Internal re-plastering. Repairs to decorative plasterwork.

Approximate cost of work: £20,000. Carried out in 1979.

Architect: Ian Donaldson, Armagh.

Work carried out using direct labour.

Large Houses

Woodford House, Newry Road, Armagh.

A two-storey Tudoresque farmhouse. Some of the stonework may have been re-used from an earlier building.

Recipient of grant: Mr. J. G. Kelly.

Grant assistance of £2,600 given towards: Repairs to chimneys. Re-slating using natural slate. Replacement leadwork. Replacement metal rainwater goods. Replacement windows in original style. Treatment of wood rot. Repairs to internal plasterwork. Restoration of garden wall balustrading.

Approximate cost of work: £7,832. Carried out in 1980 and 1981.

Contractor: McArdle Bros., Armagh.

Plastering by: John McNally, Armagh.

2 Beresford Row, The Mall, Armagh.

A three-bay, three-storey, early-19th century house, possibly designed by Francis Johnston. The roof is gabled and slated, walls are of roughly dressed limestone; windows have Georgian-glazed sashes and the panelled entrance door with semi-circular fanlight is set in a Gibbsian surround.

Recipient of grant: Mr. W. Mann.

Grant assistance of £315 given towards: Replacement metal rainwater goods. Treatment of wood rot. Repairs to timber floors.

Approximate cost of work: £948. Carried out in 1981.

Contractor: McArdle Bros., Armagh.

10 Beresford Row, The Mall, Armagh.

A two-bay, three-storey early-19th century house, possibly designed by Francis Johnston. The roof is slated, walls are of ashlar limestone and windows have Georgian-glazed sashes with a tripartite window to the ground floor. The panelled entrance door with plain sidelights and fanlight is set in an elliptically-arched opening. The doorcase forms part of a symmetrical composition which also includes a central coach arch and the entrance to adjacent house.

Recipient of grant: Mr. F. W. McKeown.

Grant assistance of £535 given towards: Re-slating using natural slate. Repairs to rainwater goods.

Approximate cost of work: £1,750. Carried out in 1979.

Roof work by: J. Robinson, Craigavon.

1 St. Marks Place, The Mall, Armagh.

A three-storey early-19th century end-of-terrace house, possibly designed by Francis Johnston. The roof is gabled and slated, walls are of a warm coloured random rubble with brick dressings and limestone quoins; windows have Georgian-glazed sashes and the panelled entrance door is set under a semi-circular decorative fanlight.

Recipient of grant: Mr. J. C. Butler.

Grant assistance of £3,210 given towards: Roof repairs. Repairs to rainwater goods. Re-pointing of brickwork. Replacement sash windows in original style. Repairs to panelled entrance door. Replacement external doors in original style. Treatment of wood rot. Installation of silicone injection damp-proof course. Repairs to internal plasterwork. Repairs to timber floors.

Installation of damp-proof solid floors. Repairs to staircase. Professional fees.

Approximate cost of work: £14,983. Carried out from 1979 to 1981.

Quantity Surveyors: J. B. Kingston & Partners, Armagh.

Work carried out using direct labour.

Timber treatment and damp-proof course by: Timbercare (N.I.), Lisburn.

2 St. Mark's Place, The Mall, Armagh.

A three-storey early-19th century mid-terrace house, possibly designed by Francis Johnston. The roof is slated and walls are of a warm coloured, random rubble with brick dressings. The windows have Georgian-glazed sashes and a recent, hip-roofed bay projects at ground floor level. The panelled entrance door is set under a semi-circular decorative fanlight.

Recipient of grant: Mr. W. G. Harrison.

Grant assistance of £340 given towards: Repairs to windows. Treatment of dry rot and subsequent reinstatement. Redecoration of remedial items.

Approximate cost of work: £1,079. Carried out in 1981.

Contractor: P. B. McCabe, Armagh.

Timber treatment by: Timbercare (N.I.), Lisburn.

4 Mallview Terrace, The Mall West, Armagh.

A two-bay, three-storey, mid-19th century mid-terrace house. The roof is slated and gabled where it drops to its two-storey neighbour, walls are of snecked limestone random rubble, windows have plain sashes set in exposed flush cases and the sheeted entrance door is set under a narrow rectangular fanlight.

Recipient of grant: Mrs. F. H. Cardew.

Grant assistance of £125 given towards: Replacement panelled entrance door.

Approximate cost of work: £365. Carried out in 1982.

Contractor: S. G. Graham, Portadown.

1 Hartford Place, The Mall, Armagh.

A three-storey, end-of-terrace house. The roof is slated, walls are of red brick with stone quoins and windows have plain sashes.

Recipient of grant: Mr. J. E. Lamb.

Grant assistance of £1,262 given towards: Roof repairs including re-slating of return roof. Re-pointing of brickwork.

Approximate cost of work: £7,967. Carried out in 1980.

Architect: Ian Donaldson, Armagh.

Contractor: Burns Construction, Armagh.

36 Victoria Street, Armagh.

A three-storey red brick Victorian house with yellow brick dressings and plain sash window.

Recipient of grant: Mr. C. P. McNabb.

Grant assistance of £970 given towards: Repairs to chimneys. Roof repairs. Repairs to rainwater goods. Repairs to bay window including replacement of leaded roof.

Approximate cost of work: £2,980. Carried out in 1981.

Contractor: John Lavery, Armagh.

Coolmere, Greencastle Street, Kilkeel.

A three-bay, two-storey house of

about 1860. The roof is hipped, walls are rendered with granite dressings, the sash windows have a single vertical division and there is a semi-circular fanlight over the entrance door.

Recipient of grant: Mr. F. M. Chambers.

Grant assistance of £2,090 given towards: Rebuilding of chimney. Repairs to roof structure. Re-slating using natural slate. Replacement leadwork.

Approximate cost of work: £6,337. Carried out in 1981.

Contractor: J. Graham & Sons (Kilkeel) Ltd., Kilkeel.

The Vicarage, Kilbroney Road, Rostrevor.

A three-bay, two-storey house with basement and lower two-bay, two-storey extension to the east. The central bay of the garden front is bowed with a gabled half dormer to the first floor and a pedimented porch projects to the north. The roof is hipped and slated, walls are roughcast and some windows have Georgian-glazed sashes. Built about 1850.

Recipient of grant: Select Vestry, Kilbroney Parish.

Grant assistance of £1,030 given towards: Roof repairs. Repairs to rainwater goods. Repairs to stonework. Repairs to windows. Repairs to panelled entrance door. Treatment of wood rot. Redecoration of remedial items.

Approximate cost of work: £3,683. Carried out from 1979 to 1981.

Contractor: Wylie & Cunningham, Newry.

Timber treatment by: Timbercare (N.I.), Lisburn.

Painting by: E. & J. McSherry, Rostrevor.

Kilbroney House, 83 Kilbroney Road, Rostrevor.

A two-storey, multi-gabled house in the manner of Thomas Duff built in the early-19th century. The roof is slated, with tall ornate chimneys and decorative barge boards, walls are roughcast and windows are mainly paired double-hung Georgian-glazed sashes. The house has been restored.

Recipient of grant: Mr. & Mrs. W. A. J. McDonald.

Grant assistance of £12,500 given towards: Repairs to chimneys. Re-slating using natural slate. Replacement leadwork. Repairs to rainwater goods. Repairs to verandah. Repairs to windows. Repairs to internal plasterwork. Repairs to timber floors. Installation of damp-proof solid floors. Redecoration of remedial items.

Approximate cost of work: £63,173. Carried out in 1982 and 1983.

Architects: Smith & Fay, Newry.

Contractor: John B. Haughian & Son, Rostrevor.

The Manse, 16 Main Street, Hilltown.

A three-bay, two-storey mid-19th century house. The roof is slated and gabled, walls are roughcast, windows have plain sashes and the entrance has a semi-circular radial fanlight.

Recipient of grant: Hilltown Presbyterian Church.

Grant assistance of £770 given towards: Roof repairs. Replacement metal rainwater goods. Repairs to external render. Replacement sash windows in

Kilbroney House, 83 Kilbroney Road, Rostrevor.

original style. Replacement panelled entrance door. Repairs to internal plasterwork. Repairs to timber floors. *Further financial assistance received from:* Northern Ireland Housing Executive. *Approximate cost of work:* £13,018. Carried out in 1980 and 1981.

Agent: W. Boyd, Warrenpoint.
Contractor: D. & E. Cromie, Hilltown.

Mount Pleasant, 38 Gilford Road, Gilford.

A five-bay, two-storey, late-18th century house with semi-basement.

The walls are smooth rendered with moulded details, windows have Georgian-glazed sashes and tripartite windows flank the panelled entrance door which has Ionic columns, decorative frieze and an elliptical spider's-web fanlight.

Recipient of grant: Mr. R. A. Buller.

Grant assistance of £170 given towards: Repairs to decorative plasterwork in drawing room.

Approximate cost of work: £504. Carried out in 1978.

Plastering by: Alexander Law, Belfast.

Stramore House, 82 Stramore Road, Gilford.

A seven-bay, three-storey house. The roof is hipped and slated, walls are roughcast with moulded dressings and windows have Georgian-glazed sashes to the upper floors and plain sashes to the ground floor. The entrance is contained in a square, projecting, central porch.

Recipient of grant: Mr. I. V. W. Watson.

Grant assistance of £1,050 given towards: Roof repairs. Replacement metal rainwater goods. Replacement of Georgian-glazed screen. Repairs to internal plasterwork. Repairs to timber floors.

Approximate cost of work: £3,327. Carried out in 1980 and 1981.

Contractor: Thomas McClimond, Scarva.

Milltown House, Lenaderg, Banbridge.

A two-storey, five-bay house built about 1825. The roof is hipped and slated with bracketted eaves, the facade is smooth rendered and lined and windows have Georgian-glazed sashes. The entrance is set in an Ionic columned portico. A decorative cast-iron balcony supported on slender columns projects on one side.

Recipient of grant: Mrs. S. Gilchrist.

Grant assistance of £780 given towards: Roof repairs. Repairs to rainwater goods. External redecorating including gates and railings.

Approximate cost of work: £2,498. Carried out in 1980.

Contractor: I. Turkington, Waringstown.

Painting by: Jim Walsh, Banbridge.

Banford House, Banbridge.

A five-bay, three-storey house with semi-basement. Hipped roof with moulded eaves cornice. Walls are roughcast. The entrance is recessed in a segmental-arched opening with decorative sidelights within an engaged Ionic-plastered portico with enriched frieze. A tripartite window above, follows a similar arrangement.

Recipient of grant: Mr. & Mrs. R. Boyd.

Grant assistance of £25,000 given towards: Repairs to chimneys. Roof repairs. Repairs to rainwater goods. Repairs to external render. Repairs to windows. Repairs to entrance steps and railings. Treatment of extensive dry rot and subsequent reinstatement.

Approximate cost of work: £61,700. Carried out in 1980 and 1981.

Architects: M. H. Ferguson, Banbridge.

Contractor: Kerr Bros., Banbridge.

Timber treatment by: Timbertreat Services Ltd., Belfast.

Scarva House, Scarva.

The original house, probably dating from the mid-18th century, was extensively remodelled in a Jacobean style between 1833–61. As it stands today the house consists of a central two-storey main block with hipped roof, and forward projecting side wings forming a forecourt. The walls are roughcast.

Recipient of grant: A. W. Buller.

Grant assistance of £13,200 given towards: Roof repairs. Repairs to roof structure. Re-slating inner slopes of roof in asbestos-cement slate. Replacement of pitched roof over two-storey entrance porch. Repairs to external render. Replacement sash windows in original style. Treatment of wood rot. Repairs to internal plasterwork. Replacement timber floors. Installation of damp-proof solid floors.

Approximate cost of work: £43,790. Carried out in 1981.

Architects: Ferguson & McIlveen, Belfast.

Contractor: Aubrey Davidson, Banbridge.

Timber treatment by: Radication Ltd., Dunmurry, Belfast.

28 Ballymore Road, Fourtowns, Loughbrickland.

A three-bay, two-storey harled and whitened late-18th century house with graded slate roof. The doorway is set in an elliptical arched opening and the windows are Georgian-glazed.

Recipient of grant: Mr. L. Malone.

Grant assistance of £230 given towards: Repairs to chimney. Repairs to rainwater goods. Repairs to external render.

Approximate cost of work: £1,025. Carried out in 1978.

Contractor: McDonald Bros., Newry.

Huntly House, 107 Huntly Road, Banbridge.

A fine five-bay, two-storey mid-19th

century house with tetrastyle Ionic portico and lower two-storey wing extending to one side. The roofs are hipped and slated with modillioned eaves cornice, walls are smooth rendered with moulded details and windows have Georgian-glazed sashes. The interior is elaborately detailed. The house has been well restored.

Recipient of grant: Mr. B. Magee.

Grant assistance of £1,485 given towards: Repairs to chimneys. Re-slating using natural slate. Repairs to rainwater goods.

Approximate cost of work: £4,450. Carried out in 1980.

Contractor: McParland & Gordon Ltd., Banbridge.

Avonmore House, 15 Church Square, Banbridge.

A very fine three-storey rendered house with basement built in 1791. The ground floor is rusticated and the highly decorative doorcase is approached by a flight of steps with railings. The ground floor windows are set in arched recesses, with dentils and festoons above the triple lights.

Recipient of grant: Banbridge District Council.

Grant assistance of £200 given towards: External redecoration.

Approximate cost of work: £596. Carried out in 1979.

Painting by: Ivan J. Gault, Banbridge.

Slate Quarry House, Dromara.

A three-bay, two-storey, early-19th century, rendered house with quoins and heavy moulded architraves to Georgian-glazed sash windows. The panelled entrance door is set in a

segmental arched opening with decorative sidelights and fanlight.

Recipient of grant: Mr. M. J. O'Reilly.

Grant assistance of £977 given towards: Re-slating using natural slate. Replacement metal rainwater goods. Repairs to external render. Replacement sash windows in original style. External redecoration. Repairs to internal plasterwork. Repairs to timber floors. Installation of damp-proof solid floors.

Approximate cost of work: £3,288. Carried out in 1976.

Contractor: Joseph McClune & Son, Dundrum, and work carried out using direct labour.

Marybrook, Kinallen, Dromara.

A five-bay, one-and-a-half storey rendered house with gabled feature above the elliptical-arched entrance. Formerly a manse. The house has been well restored.

Recipient of grant: Mr. A. S. Pepper.

Grant assistance of £1,600 given towards: Repairs to chimneys. Roof repairs. Repairs to rainwater goods. Replacement sash windows in original style. Repairs to panelled entrance door and screen. Installation of damp-proof course. Internal re-plastering. Repairs to timber floors. Installation of damp-proof solid floors. Repairs to internal panelled doors. Repairs to staircase. Redecoration of remedial items.

Further financial assistance received from: Northern Ireland Housing Executive.

Approximate cost of work: £16,000.

Architects: H. A. Patton & Partners, Belfast.

Contractor: W. J. Law & Co., Lisburn.

Balleevy House, 11 Balleevy Road, Banbridge.

A five-bay, three-storey, harled stone building with semi-basement built for the mill owners, the Crawford family, who lived at Balleevy from 1769 to 1919. The hipped roof is slated above a moulded eaves cornice. Windows are Georgian-glazed. The panelled entrance door with its semi-circular looped fanlight is flanked by acanthus-topped columns rising to an open pediment.

Recipient of grant: Dr. W. H. Crowe.

Grant assistance of £6,800 given towards: Repairs to chimneys. Re-slating using natural slate to outer slopes and asbestos-cement to inner slopes. Repairs to rainwater goods. Treatment of wood rot and subsequent reinstatement. Installation of damp-proof course. Internal re-plastering. Redecoration of remedial items.

Approximate cost of work: £13,670. Carried out in 1978 and 1979.

Contractor: Timbercare (N.I.), Lisburn.

Parkmount, Corbet, Banbridge.

A two-storey, mid-19th century house with full-height bows flanking a porch with two Corinthian columns. The roof is gabled and slated and at the front is concealed behind a dentilled cornice and parapet blocking course. The frontage is smooth rendered with moulded details and the windows have plain sashes.

Recipient of grant: Mr. E. McEvoy.

Grant assistance of £3,210 given towards: Repairs to chimneys. Repairs to roof structure. Re-slating using natural slate. Replacement leadwork. Repairs to rainwater goods.

Large Houses

Approximate cost of work: £9,635. Carried out in 1980

Contractor: Shandor Construction Co., Ltd., Katesbridge.

Magherally Rectory, 46 Kilmacrew Road, Banbridge.

Built in 1780, the rectory is an 'L'-shaped five-bay, three-storey building with basement. The roof is hipped and slated with chimneys rising from the gables. The walls are rendered and the main front is symmetrical with a gablet over a semi-circular arched doorway with radial fanlight.

Recipient of grant: Select Vestry, Magherally Parish.

Grant assistance of £733 given towards: Repairs to roof structure. Re-slating using natural slate. Replacement sash windows in original style. Repairs to internal plasterwork. Redecoration of remedial items.

Further financial assistance received from: Northern Ireland Housing Executive.

Approximate cost of work: £7,300. Carried out in 1980.

Contractor: Victor Greer & Son, Dromore.

Edenordinary, 98 Halfway Road, Banbridge.

A three-bay, two-storey, rendered house built in the mid-19th century adjoining a former hem stitching factory, part of which remains. Windows are Georgian-glazed and the entrance is set in an elliptical arched opening.

Recipient of grant: Mr. H. J. Mitchell.

Grant assistance of £1,000 given towards: Re-slating using natural slate. Repairs

to windows. Repairs to rainwater goods. Repairs to panelled entrance door and screen.

Approximate cost of work: £3,099. Carried out in 1979.

Contractor: J. McKinney, Dromore, Co. Down.

Kinallen Manse, Tulliniskey Road, Dromara.

A five-bay, two-storey house with canted bays and square porch built in 1858. The roof is hipped and slated, walls are smooth rendered with moulded details and windows have Georgian-paned sashes.

Recipient of grant: First Dromara Presbyterian Church.

Grant assistance of £790 given towards: Repairs to external render, including strings and quoins. Provision of lintels over structural openings. External redecoration.

Approximate cost of work: £2,392. Carried out in 1980 and 1981.

Contractor: James Cairns & Son, Dromore, Co. Down.

Painting by: James H. Elliott, Dromara.

The Manse, Church Street, Dromore.

A three-bay, two-storey house with canted bay windows and bracketed lean-to canopy over the entrance. The roof is hipped and slated with tall decorative brick chimneys and a central gablet on the entrance front. Walls are of red brick and windows have plain sashes set mainly in segmental-headed openings on the ground floor and square-headed openings on the first floor.

Recipient of grant: Dromore Non-subscribing Presbyterian Church.

Grant assistance of £6,750 given towards: Rebuilding of defective gable wall following settlement of foundations. Reinstatement of roof, windows, doors and brick detailing. Professional fees.

Approximate cost of work: £16,169. Carried out in 1981.

Architects: James M. McCormick & Co., Lurgan.

Structural Engineers: Dr. I. G. Doran & Partners, Belfast.

Contractor: Finlay & Shaw Ltd., Dromore, Co. Down.

Saintfield House, 71 Old Belfast Road, Saintfield.

Built by Francis Price about 1750, the house, although considerably altered, retains much of its original charm. The main entrance front is of three bays and two storeys with basement, the central doorcase has simple cut stone pilasters. The walls are rendered but with stone quoins and eaves course. The main block is flanked by three-bay, single-storey ranges.

Recipient of grant: Col. M. C. Perceval-Price.

Grant assistance of £1,350 given towards: Repairs to leadwork. Treatment of wood rot. Repairs to internal plasterwork.

Approximate cost of work: £4,059. Carried out in 1981.

Architects: Hobart & Heron, Belfast.

Contractor: Timbercare (N.I.), Lisburn.

Maymore House, 97 Comber Road, Toye, Downpatrick.

A fine three-bay, two-storey house built about 1840 by Lord Dufferin for the Harper family. The roof is slated and gabled, walls are of rubble stone with brick dressings, windows have Georgian-glazed sashes and the panelled entrance door with flanking Doric columns and sidelights is set under a decorative elliptical fanlight.

Recipient of grant: Mr. C. G. Gotto.

Grant assistance of £370 given towards: Removal of recent metal frame windows and replacement with traditional casement door and sliding sash windows as original.

Approximate cost of work: £1,102. Carried out in 1979.

Contractor: John Shields, Killyleagh.

Goshen Lodge, 9 Comber Road, Killyleagh.

A pre-1834 three-bay, two-storey Regency house. The square porch is

flanked by ground floor canted bays and on the left hand gable a large semi-circular bay projects. The roof is hipped and slated with projecting eaves and decorative fascia boards. The walls are smooth rendered.

Recipient of grant: Mrs. A. M. Smyth.

Grant assistance of £1,975 given towards: Re-slating using natural slate. Repairs to leadwork. Repairs to rainwater goods. Repairs to eaves soffit. Repairs to panelled entrance door.

Approximate cost of work: £5,925. Carried out in 1981 and 1982.

Contractor: John Shields, Killyleagh.

Echo Hall, Spa Road, Ballynahinch.

A good quality five-bay, two-storey

late-Georgian house with single-bay wings. The roof is hipped and slated with crudely modillioned eaves to the wings; walls are of rubble stonework and windows have Georgian-glazed sashes with a Venetian window over the entrance doorway.

Recipient of grant: Mr. R. H. Dicker.

Grant assistance of £3,365 given towards: Rebuilding of chimneys. Roof repairs using natural slate to both main house and stable block. Repairs to rainwater goods. Repairs to external doors. Treatment of wood rot and subsequent reinstatement. Installation of damp-proof solid floors.

Approximate cost of work: £10,936. Carried out in 1982.

Echo Hall, Spa Road, Ballynahinch.

Large Houses

Contractor: R. E. Crompton, Ballynahinch.

15 Castle Street, Strangford.

A large three-bay, three-storey merchant's house. Walls are rendered, windows generally have Georgian-glazed sashes and the entrance doorcase and fanlight is of good quality.

Recipient of grant: Mr. J. J. Kerr.

Grant assistance of £380 given towards: Roof repairs. Repairs to external render. Replacement sash windows in original style. Repairs to internal plasterwork. Repairs to timber floors. Installation of damp-proof solid floors.

Further financial assistance received from: Northern Ireland Housing Executive.

Approximate cost of work: £6,000. Carried out in 1979.

Work carried out using direct labour.

Harbour House, 1 Quay Road, Strangford.

A large, gable-fronted, three-storey corner house on a raised basement, inset to the side of a fine three-storey stone warehouse. The roof is slated, walls are roughcast and windows have Georgian-glazed sashes with tripartite units to the side elevation. The eliptically-arched entrance doorcase is approached by stone steps and the front garden is attractively walled.

Recipient of grant: Miss M. McKibbin.

Grant assistance of £590 given towards: Replacement leadwork. Repairs to external render. Repairs to windows.

Approximate cost of work: £1,775. Carried out in 1982 and 1983.

Contractor: B. McPolin, Rathfriland.

3 and 5 Kildare Street, Ardglass.

3 and 5 Kildare Street, Ardglass.

A three-bay, two-storey house formerly the Temperance Hotel. The roof is slated and gabled, walls are smooth rendered with raised quoins and windows have Georgian-glazed sashes. Sadly a valuable late-Georgian shop front has been removed. The entrance door is panelled and has a narrow rectangular fanlight.

Recipient of grant: Mr. S. Milligan.

Grant assistance of £9,300 given towards: Rebuilding of chimneys. Re-slating using natural slate. Replacement metal rainwater goods. Replacement sash windows in original style. Replacement panelled entrance door. Treatment of wood rot. Repairs to internal plasterwork. Repairs to timber floors. Installation of damp-proof solid floors.

Approximate cost of work: £39,000. Carried out in 1981.

Contractor: W. P. Taggart & Sons, Downpatrick.

8 The Crescent, Ardglass.

A fine three-bay, three-storey house flanked by lower two-storey properties on either side and built by William Ogilvie in 1820 as part of a curving line of eleven one-, two- and three-storey houses. The roof is gabled and slated, walls are roughcast and windows have Georgian-glazed sashes. An earlier gabled porch has been removed and the semi-circular-headed doorcase has been restored.

Recipient of grant: Mr. P. Milligan.

Grant assistance of £5,390 given towards: Repairs to chimneys. Repairs to roof structure. Re-slating using natural slate. Repairs to rainwater goods. External re-rendering. Replacement sash windows in original style. Replacement external doors in original style. Repairs to railings. Internal re-plastering.

Further financial assistance received from: Northern Ireland Housing Executive.

Approximate cost of work: £33,583. Carried out in 1980.

Architect: E. A. J. McKibben, Downpatrick.

Contractor: W. P. Taggart, Downpatrick.

Ballyhossett House, Downpatrick.

A five-bay, two-storey, pre-1833 double-pile house with later additions. The roofs are gabled and slated, walls are smooth rendered with moulded quoins and windows have Georgian-glazed sashes. A square porch with fluted Ionic pilasters projects centrally from the main elevation.

Recipient of grant: Sir John Anderson.

Grant assistance of £90 given towards:

Roof repairs.

Approximate cost of work: £297. Carried out in 1979.

Architects: Houston & Beaumont, Belfast.

Contractor: W. P. Taggart, Downpatrick.

8 Main Street, Dundrum.

Part of a six-bay, three-storey building which was formerly the Downshire Arms Hotel built in 1825. The roof is hipped and slated, walls rendered with moulded dressings and windows have Georgian-glazed sashes. There is an excellent porch with free-standing Doric columns to one end of the frontage.

Recipient of grant: Mrs. L. E. McKinney.

Grant assistance of £900 given towards: Roof repairs. Partial re-slating of main roof using natural slate. Re-slating of returns using asbestos-cement slate. Repairs to leadwork.

Approximate cost of work: £2,745. Carried out in 1981.

Contractor: Peter O'Hare, Ballynahinch.

76 Trassey Road, Newcastle.

A two-storey early-19th century traditional farmhouse. The roof is slated and gabled, walls are of whitewashed rubble stonework, windows have vertically divided sashes set in exposed cases and a gabled porch projects from the frontage.

Recipient of grant: Mr. S. Morrison.

Grant assistance of £834 given towards: Main house – Rebuilding of chimneys. Re-slating using natural slate. Replacement metal rainwater goods. External re-rendering. Repairs to

internal plasterwork. Repairs to timber floors. Barn – Rebuilding of chimney. Re-slating using natural slate. Replacement metal rainwater goods.

Further financial assistance received from: Northern Ireland Housing Executive.

Approximate cost of work: £6,503. Carried out in 1982.

Contractor: Cromie & Bradshaw, Rathfriland.

Ballywillwill House, 25 Clonvaraghan Road, Castlewellan.

A large five-bay, two-storey classically detailed house built in 1816. The roof is hipped and slated, walls are roughcast with granite dressings and the windows, some of which are tripartite, have Georgian-glazed sashes. The panelled entrance door with semi-circular fanlight is flanked by semi-circular-headed windows, all intricately glazed. A wide Doric columned porch, spanning the central three bays, is surmounted by an impressive reclining lion and four urns.

Recipient of grant: Mr. E. Wright.

Grant assistance of £585 given towards: Roof repairs. Repairs to windows.

Approximate cost of work: £1,765. Carried out in 1978.

Contractor: Joseph McClune & Son, Dundrum.

Greenwood, Farranfad Road, Seaforde.

A five-bay, two-storey house built before 1834. The roof is gabled and slated with a small central gable over a first floor Venetian window. The walls are smooth rendered and the panelled entrance door is flanked by sidelights

Large Houses

76 Trassey Road, Newcastle.

and set under a decorative elliptical fanlight. The house has been extensively restored.

Recipient of grant: Mr. M. D. Watt.

Grant assistance of £300 given towards: Roof repairs.

Approximate cost of work: £390. Carried out from 1980 to 1982.

Contractor: Austin Killen, Seaforde.

Highlands, 37 Farranfad Road, Seaforde.

An irregularly planned, two-storey, multi-gabled house possibly built in the mid-19th century. The roofs are slated, walls are rendered, with moulded quoins, and windows are Georgian-glazed with casements to the ground floor and double-hung sashes to the first. A canted oriel window projects at first floor level above the heavily moulded rectangular entrance.

Recipient of grant: Lady Lucy Faulkner.

Grant assistance of £95 given towards:

Repairs to leadwork. Repairs to internal plasterwork.

Approximate cost of work: £292. Carried out in 1980.

Contractor: Alex. Kennedy, Seaforde.

Ardilea House, Clough.

A two-storey house with single-storey extensions built about 1748 but much altered. The slated roofs are hipped and gabled. A full height canted bay is positioned on the south-east front and a gabled porch with decorative barge boards is positioned on the south-west front. Windows have mainly Georgian glazing.

Recipient of grant: Mr. P. Fitzpatrick.

Grant assistance of £500 given towards: Installation of silicone injection damp-proof course.

Approximate cost of work: £1,500. Carried out in 1982.

Damp-proof course by: Doulton Wallguard (N.I.) Ltd., Belfast.

Finnebrogue House, Downpatrick.

A two-storey Georgian house with attic and basement built in the late 17th century, restored in 1795 and further altered in 1936. The north front has a five-bay central block and two-bay projecting wings. The roof is hipped and slated with moulded and dentilled eaves, walls are roughcast, windows have Georgian-glazed sashes and the fine central entrance doorway is set in the recessed bays of the north front.

Recipient of grant: Trustees of Major J. R. Perceval Maxwell.

Grant assistance of £330 given towards: Repairs to chimneys. Roof repairs. Repairs to internal plasterwork.

Approximate cost of work: £825. Carried out in 1977.

Contractor: Alex. Kennedy, Seaforde.

110 Irish Street, Downpatrick.

A large four-bay, three-storey terrace town house with basement. The roof is slated and walls are smooth rendered. The panelled entrance door with semi-circular fanlight is set in a pilastered doorcase with broken pediment overdoor; the door is approached by stone steps.

Recipient of grant: Miss B. V. Rice.

Grant assistance of £90 given towards: Treatment of wood rot.

Approximate cost of work: £280. Carried out in 1981.

Timber treatment by: Timbertreat Services Ltd., Belfast.

25 English Street, Downpatrick.

One of two, two-storey, town houses with attic and basement, Regency in appearance but built about 1840. The two houses form a five-bay symmetrical composition consisting of a flat central bay containing a tall semi-circular-headed coach arch flanked by single-bay, full height, segmental bows and with the entrances contained in flat single-bay outer sections. The slated roof is concealed behind a high parapet containing the attic windows. The walls of the upper floors are smooth rendered, the ground floor is of channelled ashlar sandstone and the basement is of squared and coursed granite. Windows have Georgian-glazing with semicircular heads to the first floor. The panelled entrance doors with semi-circular fanlights are set in doorcases with extraordinary Doric pilasters and are approached by stone steps.

Recipient of grant: Mrs. L. M. Dickson.

Grant assistance of £1,670 given towards: Repairs to external render. Repairs to windows. Replacement panelled entrance door. Replacement railings to match number 27.

Approximate cost of work: £3,545. Carried out in 1979.

Architects: Shanks, Leighton, Kennedy & Fitzgerald, Belfast.

Contractor: J. J. Kerr, Strangford.

27 English Street, Downpatrick.

One of two, two-storey, town houses with attic and basement, Regency in appearance but built about 1840. The two houses form a five-bay symmetrical composition consisting of a flat central bay containing a tall semi-circular-headed coach arch flanked by single-bay, full height, segmental bows and with the entrances contained in flat single-bay outer sections. The slated roof is concealed behind a high parapet containing the attic windows. The walls of the upper floors are smooth rendered, the ground floor is of channelled ashlar sandstone and the basement is of squared and coursed granite. Windows have Georgian-glazing with semi-circular heads to the first floor. The panelled entrance doors with semi-circular fanlights are set in doorcases with extraordinary Doric pilasters and are approached by stone steps.

Recipient of grant: Dr. & Mrs. A. Clint

Grant assistance of £770 given towards: Repairs to chimney. Re-slating using natural slate. Repairs to leadwork. Repairs to external render. Repairs to windows.

27, 29 English Street, Downpatrick.

Further financial assistance received from: Northern Ireland Housing Executive.

Approximate cost of work: not known. Carried out in 1979.

Work carried out using direct labour.

Ballydugan House, Ballydugan.

A five-bay, three-storey Georgian house with basement built by Captain Henry Webb in 1781 and remodelled and extended about 1815. The central panelled entrance door with semi-circular fanlight is flanked by attached Doric columns with a broken pediment over and approached by steps. The house has been extensively restored.

Recipient of grant: Mr. S. Mackie.

Grant assistance of £2,700 given towards: Re-roofing using natural slate. Making good after removal of cantilevered Victorian passageway at rear of house.

Approximate cost of work: £27,633. Carried out in 1980.

Architects: Houston & Beaumont & Partners, Belfast.

Contractor: W. G. Cochrane & Sons, Crossgar.

Wellington Lodge, 67 Lisburn Road, Hillsborough.

A three-bay, two-storey house formerly a mid-17th century coaching inn but altered to its present appearance about 1790. The roof is gabled and slated, walls are rendered with raised mouldings and sash windows are tripartite to outer bays. The central panelled door with sidelights is set under an elliptically-arched fanlight.

Recipient of grant: Mr. J. H. Bryson.

PHASE ONE – REPAIRS

Grant assistance of £460 given towards: Replacement sash windows in original style. Redecoration of remedial items.

Approximate cost of work: £1,379. Carried out in 1978.

Contractor: D. J. Dickson, Crossgar.

PHASE TWO – REPAIRS

Grant assistance of £1,900 given towards: Rebuilding of chimneys. Roof repairs. Replacement rainwater goods. Repairs to windows. Repairs to external doors. Treatment of woodworm. Internal re-plastering. Repairs to timber floors.

Approximate cost of work: £6,512. Carried out in 1981.

Contractor: D. J. Dickson, Crossgar.

9 Main Street, Hillsborough.

A four-bay, two-storey, mid-terrace house with basement. The roof is slated, walls are rendered, windows have Georgian-glazed sashes and the panelled entrance door with decorative sidelights and an elliptical fanlight is approached by a steep flight of steps. Railings protect the basement and a square coach arch penetrates to the rear.

Recipient of grant: Mr. R. Graham.

Grant assistance of £500 given towards: Re-slating using natural slate. Replacement metal rainwater goods.

Further financial assistance received from: Northern Ireland Housing Executive.

Approximate cost of work: £2,714. Carried out in 1980.

Roofwork by: McMahon (Roofing) & Co., Belfast.

Hill House, 35 Main Street, Hillsborough.

A three-bay, three-storey house with attic built before 1833. The entrance is set in a single-storey extension at the rear of the gable of the main house. The roof is gabled and slated, walls are of red brick to the upper floors and smooth rendered to the ground floor. The windows have Georgian-glazed sashes and the panelled entrance door with sidelights is set under a segmental fanlight.

Recipient of grant: Mr. M. Ewart.

Grant assistance of £573 given towards: Roof repairs. Re-pointing of brickwork. Silicone treatment of brickwork. External redecoration.

Approximate cost of work: £1,878. Carried out in 1981.

Contractor: Trevor Lilley, Dromore, Co. Down, and work carried out using own labour.

11 The Square, Hillsborough.

A four-bay, three-storey, late-18th century end-of-terrace house. The roof is slated and gabled, the frontage is of brick with brick eaves course, windows have Georgian-glazed sashes and the panelled entrance door with semi-circular fanlight is approached by

stone steps. The house has been carefully restored.

Recipient of grant: Mr. A. N. Castle.

Grant assistance of £3,000 given towards: Repairs to chimneys. Repairs to roof structure. Re-slating using natural slate. Replacement metal rainwater goods. Replacement sash windows in original style. Replacement panelled entrance door, and removal of rectangular fanlight over door and remodelling to provide semi-circular fanlight to match adjoining properties. Treatment of wood rot. Installation of silicone injection damp-proof course. Repairs to internal plasterwork. Professional fees.

Further financial assistance received from: Northern Ireland Housing Executive.

Approximate cost of work: £46,000. Carried out in 1980.

Architects: Robert McKinstry & Melvyn Brown, Belfast.

Contractor: E. Wilkinson & Sons, Hillsborough.

Timber treatment by: Timbercare (N.I.), Lisburn.

Blundell House, 12 The Square, Hillsborough.

A three-bay, three-storey, late-18th century Georgian house with basement. The roof is of slate, frontage is of brick, windows have Georgian-glazed sashes and the panelled entrance door with semi-circular fanlight is approached by a broad flight of stone steps. The basement is protected by railings.

Recipient of grant: Mr. J. R. Eyre-Maunsell.

PHASE ONE − REPAIRS

Grant assistance of £138 given towards:

Silicone treatment of brickwork to eliminate penetrating dampness.

Approximate cost of work: £414. Carried out in 1979.

Contractor: Radication Ltd., Dunmurry, Belfast.

PHASE TWO − REPAIRS

Grant assistance of £990 given towards: Repairs to chimneys. Roof repairs. Repairs to leadwork. Repairs to rainwater goods.

Approximate cost of work: £3,944. Carried out in 1979.

Contractor: W. C. Hodgen Ltd., Belfast.

PHASE THREE − REPAIRS

Grant assistance of £100 given towards: Repairs to internal plasterwork.

Approximate cost of work: £3,944. Carried out in 1982.

Contractor: T. Montgomery, Baillie's Mills, Lisburn.

13 The Square, Hillsborough.

A three-bay, three-storey, late 18th century Georgian house with basement. The roof is slated, frontage is of brick, windows have been restored to the original Georgian-glazed sashes and the panelled entrance door with semi-circular fanlight is approached by a broad flight of stone steps. The basement is protected by railings.

Recipient of grant: Mr. and Mrs. J. P. L. Stevenson.

PHASE ONE − RESTORATION

Grant assistance of £76 given towards: Repairs to windows including restoration of astragals.

Approximate cost of work: £190. Carried out in 1976.

Large Houses

Contractor: Francis McKeown, Hillsborough.

PHASE TWO – REPAIRS

Grant assistance of £190 given towards: Roof repairs. Repairs to rainwater goods. Replacement window to dormer.

Approximate cost of work: £485. Carried out in 1979.

Contractor: Antrim Street Building Works, Lisburn.

PHASE THREE – REPAIRS

Grant assistance of £45 given towards: Roof repairs. Repairs to external render. Repairs to dormer window. Repairs to railings.

Approximate cost of work: £113. Carried out in 1980.

Contractor: Antrim Street Building Works, Lisburn.

PHASE FOUR – REPAIRS

Grant assistance of £96 given towards: Re-rendering and re-slating of east gable wall.

Approximate cost of work: £237. Carried out in 1981.

Contractor: Trevor Lilley, Dromore, Co. Down.

PHASE FIVE – REPAIRS

Grant assistance of £75 given towards: Roof repairs. Repairs to external render. Repairs to entrance steps.

Approximate cost of work: £186. Carried out in 1982.

Contractor: Trevor Lilley, Dromore, Co. Down.

Blessington House, 18 Ballynahinch Street, Hillsborough.

A four-bay, two-storey house

13 The Square, Hillsborough.

comprising part of a sixteen-bay terrace originally built about 1780 as two houses for Lord Downshire's agent and sub-agent. The roof is slated, frontage is smooth rendered with moulded architraves to windows and the entrance has a projecting portico with paired Doric columns. The house has good decorative cast-iron railings.

Recipient of grant: Mr. M. McCrory.

PHASE ONE – RESTORATION OF HOUSE

Grant assistance of £7,800 given towards: Repairs to chimneys. Re-slating using natural slate. Repairs to rainwater goods. Repairs to windows. Repairs to panelled entrance door. External redecoration. Treatment of wood rot. Installation of silicone injection damp-proof course. Repairs to internal plasterwork. Installation of damp-proof solid floors. Replica replacement of internal joinery.

Professional fees.

Further financial assistance received from: Northern Ireland Housing Executive.

Approximate cost of work: £24,952. Carried out from 1980 to 1982.

Architect: Alexander Burns, Newtownabbey.

Contractor: Timbercare (N.I.), Lisburn.

PHASE TWO – RESTORATION OF COBBLED YARD

Grant assistance of £150 given towards: Provision of drainage.

Approximate cost of work: £1,355. Carried out in 1983.

Work carried out using direct labour.

Fairford House (formerly Harty House), 25 Ballynahinch Street, Hillsborough.

A four-bay, two-storey house built before 1833, the home of Sir Hamilton Harty (1879–1941). The roof is slated and gabled, walls are smooth rendered with moulded details, windows have Georgian-glazed sashes and the door encasement contains a panelled door with plain semi-circular fanlight over.

PHASE ONE – REPAIRS

Recipient of grant: Mr. V. Loughlin.

Grant assistance of £283 given towards: Repairs to chimneys. External re-rendering. Repairs to windows.

Approximate cost of work: £1,580. Carried out in 1976.

Contractor: James Walsh Builders (N.I.) Ltd., Lisburn.

PHASE TWO – RESTORATION

Recipient of grant: Mr. P. H. S. Newel.

Grant assistance of £3,900 given towards: Repairs to chimneys. Re-slating using

natural slate to front slope and asbestos-cement to other slopes. Replacement metal rainwater goods. External re-rendering. Repairs to windows. Repairs to panelled entrance door. Treatment of wood rot. Installation of silicone injection damp-proof course. Installation of damp-proof solid floors. Repairs to internal panelled doors.

Approximate cost of work: £12,774. Carried out in 1980.

Architect: George W. S. Scott, Belfast.

Contractor: D. Curran, Belfast.

Roden House, 1 Park Street, Hillsborough.

A pleasant five-bay, two-storey house built by the Downshire family. The roof is slated and gabled, walls are smooth rendered, window sashes have single vertical divisions and the panelled entrance door with sidelights and fanlight is set in an elliptically-arched opening.

Recipient of grant: Mr. H. C. Boyd.

Grant assistance of £485 given towards: Paving to front and side of house.

Approximate cost of work: £1,458. Carried out in 1979.

Contractor: Walker, Dempster & Co. Ltd., Dromore, Co. Down.

Kilwarlin House, 129 Moira Road, Hillsborough.

A five-bay, two-storey house possibly built in the later-19th century. The roof is hipped and slated, walls are of brick and windows have horizontally divided sashes. The elliptically-arched doorway contains a panelled door with plain sidelights and fanlight.

Recipient of grant: Mr. J. Kilpatrick.

Grant assistance of £848 given towards: Repairs to chimneys. Rebuilding of chimney. Repairs to rainwater goods. Re-pointing of brickwork. Installation of electro-osmotic damp-proof course. Replacement timber floors.

Further financial assistance received from: Northern Ireland Housing Executive.

Approximate cost of work: £7,938. Carried out in 1982.

Contractor: Francis McKeown, Hillsborough.

Timber treatment by: Rentikil Ltd., Belfast.

Chrome Hill, Lambeg.

A two-storey 'T'-shaped house with an extension to the east and curved bay to the west built in the 17th century and remodelled in 1750. The roof is slated, walls are roughcast with stone dressings and windows have Georgian-glazed sashes. The flush-panelled entrance door is set in a moulded stone surround with a pediment containing a coat-of-arms.

Recipient of grant: Mr. R. J. McKinstry.

Grant assistance of £1,487 given towards: Partial re-slating of roof using natural slate. Remodelling of dormer window. Replacement of lead to bow window roof. Repairs to leaded lights. Treatment of rising damp. Repairs to internal plasterwork. Repairs to timber floors.

Approximate cost of work: £4,538. Carried out in 1975 and 1976.

Architects: Robert McKinstry & Partner, Belfast.

Contractor: Thomas T. Gray, Belfast.

Roof work by: Hubert Shellard & Sons Ltd., Lisburn.

Leadwork by: R. B. Wilson Ltd.,

Large Houses

Belfast.
Repairs to leaded lights by: Joseph McManus Ltd., Belfast.

Fairmount, 34 Old Kilmore Road, Moira.

A three-bay, two-storey farmhouse built in 1880. The roof is hipped and slated, walls are roughcast and windows have plain sashes. The entrance is contained in a segmentally-arched opening.
Recipient of grant: Mr. R. Brown.
Grant assistance of £1,710 given towards: Rebuilding of chimneys. Re-slating using natural slate. Repairs to rainwater goods. Repairs to windows. Repairs to internal plasterwork.
Further financial assistance received from: Northern Ireland Housing Executive.
Approximate cost of work: £10,127.
Carried out in 1980 and 1981.
Contractor: David McFarland, Crumlin.

Seaview, 31 Farnham Road, Bangor.

A two-storey house with single-storey wings, built in 1845. The roof is hipped and slated, walls are rendered and lined and windows have plain sashes. The panelled entrance door and decorative fanlight is set under a moulded segmental archivolt with keystone and is flanked by pilasters.
Recipient of grant: Mr. M. G. Foley.
Grant assistance of £4,700 given towards: Repairs to chimneys. Roof repairs. Repairs to rainwater goods. Repairs to external render. Repairs to windows. Repairs to panelled entrance door. External redecoration. Professional fees.
Approximate cost of work: £14,515.

Carried out in 1979.
Architects: The Robinson Patterson Partnership, Bangor.
Work carried out using direct labour.

Princeton Villa, 66 Princetown Road, Bangor.

A double-fronted, two-storey house with dormered attics, possibly built in the late-19th century. The roof is slated and gabled with bracketted eaves. Two-storey canted bay windows rise on either side of the entrance and are surmounted by balustraded parapets. Walls are smooth rendered with moulded details and windows have plain sashes, segmental heads to the ground and first floors and semi-circular heads to the dormered attic windows. The entrance is contained in a square columned portico.
Recipient of grant: Miss M. E. Lyttle.
Grant assistance of £825 given towards: Roof repairs. Repairs to barge boards. Repairs to rainwater goods. Repairs to external render. Repairs to windows. External redecoration.
Approximate cost of work: £1,100.
Carried out in 1980.
Contractor: G. H. Grant, Bangor.

Bridge House, Killaire Avenue, Carnalea.

A two-storey house built in 1870 and formerly owned by Joseph Jaffe the only Jewish Lord Mayor of Belfast. The roof is hipped with a corbelled eaves frieze, walls are rendered and lined and the windows have plain sashes and moulded architraves at first floor. The panelled entrance door is contained in a central square projecting

porch with pilasters, entablature and balustraded parapet.
Recipient of grant: Prof. W. S. B. Lowry.
Grant assistance of £1,147 given towards: Roof repairs. Repairs to leadwork. Extensive repairs to corbelled eaves. Repairs to rainwater goods. Repairs to balustrading of porch.
Approximate cost of work: £7,505.
Carried out in 1978 and 1979.
Contractor: Andrew H. Stothers Ltd., Holywood.

Greenmount, 205 Belfast Road, Craigavad.

A late-19th century Scottish baronial style two-storey house. The roof is slated and has crow-stepped gables to the main front. A circular, conical roofed, turret rises to one side of the main front and a two-storey crenellated canted bay to the other. The entrance is set in a two storey crenellated feature with a bracketted cast-iron balustrade at first floor level. Walls are smooth rendered and windows have plain sashes.
Recipient of grant: Judge R. J. Babington.

PHASE ONE
Grant assistance of £1,840 given towards: Roof repairs including securing of slates to turret roof. Repairs to leadwork.
Approximate cost of work: £5,529.
Carried out in 1979 and 1980.
Contractor: H. S. Warwick Ltd., Holywood.

PHASE TWO – REPAIRS
Grant assistance of £455 given towards: Main house – External redecoration.

Yard area – Repairs to rainwater goods. Repairs to stonework. Re-pointing of stonework. Repairs to external doors.

Approximate cost of work: £1,015. Carried out in 1982.

Work carried out using direct labour.

Painting by: W. Robinson, Newtownards.

140 High Street, Holywood.

A three-storey, end-of-terrace house with ground floor bay window. Roof is slated and gabled, ground floor and gable walls are smooth rendered and upper floors have brick facing.

Recipient of grant: The Abbeyfield, Holywood & District Society Ltd.

Grant assistance of £1,986 given towards: Repairs to chimney. Repair of main roof. Re-slating of return roof using asbestos-cement slate. Repairs to rainwater goods. Repairs to external render. Repairs to windows. Professional fees.

Approximate cost of work: £6,854. Carried out in 1980 and 1981.

Architects: D. W. Boyd & Co., Belfast.

Contractor: John Boyd (Carryduff) Ltd., Carryduff.

80 Church Road, Holywood.

A three-storey, end-of-terrace house, built in the later-19th century. The roof is slated, with projecting bracketted eaves, and the frontage is of red brick with a flat-roofed two-storey square rendered bay to one side of the entrance. The windows are set in square openings with moulded architraves and have plain sashes.

Recipient of grant: Mr. H. Scammell.

Grant assistance of £1,360 given towards: Rebuilding of chimney. Repairs to rainwater goods. Repairs to windows.

Approximate cost of work: £4,206. Carried out in 1980.

Contractor: H. S. Warwick Ltd., Holywood.

4 The Crescent, Holywood.

A three-bay, two-storey terrace house built about 1850. The roof is slated, the frontage is of red brick with yellow brick dressings, windows have horizontally divided sashes and the panelled entrance door has sidelights and fanlight.

Recipient of grant: Lt. Col. D. C. McCormack.

Grant assistance of £300 given towards: Roof repairs. Installation of damp-proof course.

Approximate cost of work: £957. Carried out in 1981.

Roof work by: Pentagon (Renovation) Ltd., Darkley, Armagh.

Damp-proof course by: Doulton Wallguard (N.I.) Ltd., Belfast.

7 The Crescent, Holywood.

A three-bay, three-storey terrace house built about 1850. The roof is slated, the frontage is of smooth render and single-storey canted bay windows with parapeted roofs flank the central doorcase. The windows have horizontally divided sashes on the ground floor and Georgian-glazing to the upper floors.

Recipient of grant: Mr. T. E. Burrows.

PHASE ONE – REPAIRS

Grant assistance of £312 given towards: Repairs to external render.

Approximate cost of work: £936. Carried out in 1982.

Contractor: H. S. Warwick Ltd., Holywood.

PHASE TWO – REPAIRS

Grant assistance of £215 given towards: Repair of fractured roof purlin. Professional fees.

Approximate cost of work: £573. Carried out in 1982.

Structural Engineers: Kirk, McClure & Morton, Belfast.

Contractor: H. S. Warwick Ltd., Holywood.

8 Ferry Street, Portaferry.

A very fine, three-bay, three-storey house in a sloping terrace, built about 1810. The roof is slated and walls are smooth rendered with moulded dressings. The sash windows have a variety of glazing arrangements and the central panelled entrance door with sidelights and fanlight is set in a doorcase with a dentilled cornice hood supported by decorative brackets over panelled pilasters.

Recipient of grant: Mr. P. J. McHenry.

Grant assistance of £1,240 given towards: Roof repairs. Repairs to external render.

Approximate cost of work: £3,734. Carried out in 1983.

Contractor: Joseph McClune & Son, Dundrum.

Roof work by: Pentagon (Renovation) Ltd., Darkley, Armagh.

18 and 20 Ferry Street, Portaferry.

A fine 18th century six-bay, two-storey combined dwelling and warehouse, now converted into flats.

The walls are rendered with decorative mouldings and the entrance is set in a pedimented and pilastered stone portico.

Recipient of grant: Mr. R. P. Brown.

Grant assistance of £440 given towards: Repairs to roof structure. Re-slating using natural slate. Repairs to rainwater goods. Repairs to roof parapet. Repairs to windows. Repairs to entrance steps. Replacement panelled entrance door. Repairs to internal plasterwork.

Approximate cost of work: £5,945. Carried out in 1978 and 1979.

Contractor: McGreevy Bros., Shrigley, Killyleagh.

The Rectory, 8 Cloghy Road, Portaferry.

A pleasant two-storey house built in 1818 with a more recent three-storey extension to the rear. The roof is slated and gabled, walls are roughcast with vermiculated quoins, windows have Georgian-glazed sashes. A good quality door and fanlight is unfortunately obscured by a Victorian porch.

Recipient of grant: Ballyphilip and Ardquin Parish.

Grant assistance of £272 given towards: Re-slating using natural slate.

Approximate cost of work: £815. Carried out in 1979.

Contractor: R. Mullan, Portaferry.

Mourne View, 1 Manse Road, Carrowdore.

A six-bay, two-storey house built before 1834. The roof is gabled and slated, walls are rendered and windows have Georgian-glazed sashes. An inappropriate gabled porch projects.

Recipient of grant: Mr. A. Muckle.

Grant assistance of £440 given towards: Replacement timber floors.

Approximate cost of work: £1,384. Carried out from 1981 to 1983.

Contractor: Ray Graham (Ards) Ltd., Newtownards.

Rosebank, 8 Millisle Road, Donaghadee.

A five-bay, two-storey house with lean-to wings at each end built about 1770. The walls are roughcast, windows are Georgian-glazed and the central panelled entrance door is flanked by attached Doric columns with frieze and cornice over. The house has been restored from dereliction and almost certain loss by the present owner.

Recipient of grant: Mr. M. Reid.

Grant assistance of £9,750 given towards: Repairs to chimneys. Re-slating using natural slate. Repairs to rainwater goods. Repairs to external render. Replacement sash windows in original style. Treatment of wood rot. Repairs to timber floors. Repairs to staircase.

Further financial assistance received from: Northern Ireland Housing Executive.

Approximate cost of work: £70,000. Carried out from 1979 to 1982.

Architect: Neill Kenmuir, Donaghadee.

Work carried out using direct labour.

Timber treatment by: Radication Ltd., Dunmurry, Belfast.

Ballyvester House, 84 Ballyvester Road, Donaghadee.

A fine, five-bay, two-storey early-18th century farmhouse with attics. The roof is slated and gabled, walls are limewashed random rubble, windows have Georgian-glazed sashes and the panelled entrance door with semi-circular fanlight is set in a cut-stone surround. Three of the windows on the entrance front are in fact painted dummys so placed as to maintain the symmetry of the facade.

Recipient of grant: Mr. A. M. Macnaghten.

PHASE ONE – REPAIRS

Grant assistance of £50 given towards: Repairs to rainwater goods.

Approximate cost of work: £183. Carried out in 1978.

Work carried out using direct labour.

PHASE TWO – REPAIRS

Grant assistance of £393 given towards: Repairs to chimneys. Roof repairs. Repairs to rainwater goods. Repairs to windows.

Approximate cost of work: £1,608. Carried out in 1980.

Contractor: Harold Baillie, Greyabbey.

PHASE THREE – REPAIRS

Grant assistance of £50 given towards: Repairs to chimney.

Approximate cost of work: £150. Carried out in 1980.

Contractor: Harold Baillie, Greyabbey.

PHASE FOUR – REPAIRS

Grant assistance of £50 given towards: Repairs to internal plasterwork.

Approximate cost of work: £127. Carried out in 1982.

Plastering by: W. & J. & S. Moore, Donaghadee.

Large Houses

Swiss Cottage, 23 Ballyblack Road, Newtownards.

An unusual one-and-a-half-storey Victorian, cottage-orné style, house. The roof is steeply pitched, slated and gabled with, over the entrance, a gabled feature containing a double window. The frontage is of red brick with yellow brick and smooth rendered dressings. Windows have plain sashes set in pointed openings and the panelled entrance door with sidelights is set under a triple pointed fanlight. The house has been restored to a high standard.

Recipient of grant: Mr. & Mrs. T. J. Monson.

Grant assistance of £2,585 given towards: Repairs to chimneys. Roof repairs. Repairs to leadwork. Repairs to barge boards. Replacement metal rainwater goods. External re-rendering. Re-pointing of brickwork. Replacement sash windows in original style. Treatment of wood rot. Installation of electro-osmotic damp-proof course. Installation of damp-proof solid floors.

Approximate cost of work: £6,737. Carried out in 1980 and 1981.

Contractor: Cordner and Bailie, Boardmills, and work done using direct labour.

Timber treatment by: Rentokil Ltd., Belfast.

Ardara, 11 Ballygowan Road, Comber.

A large two-storey house built in 1872 with later additions including curved and square bay windows. The roof is hipped and slated with projecting eaves, walls are smooth rendered with moulded details and the windows have plain sashes. The three-bay entrance front has a central projecting square porch flanked on either side by paired semi-circular-headed windows.

Recipient of grant: Mr. T. M. Andrews.

Grant assistance of £200 given towards: Repairs to chimneys. Repairs to leadwork. External redecoration.

Approximate cost of work: £582. Carried out in 1980.

Work carried out using direct labour.

Hill Farm, 29 Whiterock Road, Killinchy.

A three-bay, two-storey, mid-19th century farmhouse with slated gabled roof, harled rubble walls, and Georgian-glazed windows.

Recipient of grant: Mr. R. A. Magowan.

Grant assistance of £900 given towards: Re-slating using natural slate. Replacement metal rainwater goods. External re-rendering. Replacement sash windows in original style. Installation of damp-proof solid floors.

Further financial assistance received from: Northern Ireland Housing Executive.

Approximate cost of work: £5,693. Carried out in 1980.

Contractor: N. P. McGowan, Killinchy.

Newton Lodge, 86 Beechill Road, Belfast.

A single-storey Georgian house with attic. The roof is hipped and slated, walls are roughcast and the windows have Georgian-glazed sashes. The panelled entrance door is flanked by four Ionic columns and sidelights with a decorative fanlight over, all set in a deep elliptically-arched opening with moulded archivolt.

Recipient of grant: Dr. O. Hunter.

PHASE ONE – REPAIRS

Grant assistance of £230 given towards: Roof repairs. Repairs to leadwork. Repairs to rainwater goods. Treatment of wood rot and subsequent reinstatement.

Approximate cost of work: £683. Carried out in 1979.

Contractor: V. R. Wilson, Belfast.

Timber treatment by: Timbertreat Services Ltd., Belfast.

PHASE TWO – REPAIRS

Grant assistance of £2,180 given towards: Installation of new lintels over structural openings. Repairs to panelled entrance door. External redecoration. Installation of silicone injection damp-proof course. Repairs to internal plasterwork. Installation of damp-proof solid floors. Restoration of internal joinery work. Repairs to fireplace.

Approximate cost of work: £7,036. Carried out from 1980 to 1982.

Contractor: William Mitchell (Shopfitting) Ltd., Belfast.

Damp-proof course by: Danlor Services, Belfast.

Hollybrook House, 28 Ballagh Road, Lisnaskea.

A three-bay, two-storey, pre-1834 house with attic and basement. The roof is hipped and slated, walls are roughcast with smooth dressings, windows have Georgian-glazing and the panelled entrance door is set under a segmental fanlight. The house has been restored following fire damage.

Recipient of grant: Mr. J. Hall.

Grant assistance of £5,900 given towards:

Rebuilding of chimneys. Re-roofing using natural slate. Replacement metal rainwater goods. External re-rendering. Replacement sash windows in original style. Internal re-plastering. Replacement timber floors. Repairs to internal joinery. Installation of damp-proof solid floors.

Further financial assistance received from: Northern Ireland Housing Executive.

Approximate cost of work: £32,390. Carried out in 1982 and 1983.

Contractor: McKenzie & Hunter, Ballinamallard, and work carried out using direct labour.

Ashbrooke House, Lurgan Bane, Brookeborough.

Built in 1830 as a dower house by Sir Henry Brooke probably to designs by William Farrell. The five-bay, two-storey front has large sash windows with a tripartite window over the central projecting solid porch with Tuscan columns. The main shallow pitched roof has overhanging eaves supported on mutules. A long wing extends to the rear.

Recipient of grant: The Lord Brookeborough.

Grant assistance of £700 given towards: Repairs to chimneys. Roof repairs. Replacement metal rainwater goods. Re-pointing of stonework.

Approximate cost of work: £5,365. Carried out in 1981 and 1982.

Architects: John Storie & Partners, Enniskillen.

Contractor: M. Armstrong & Sons, Tempo, and H. Pierce & Sons Ltd., Enniskillen and work carried out using direct labour.

Ashbrooke House, Brookeborough.

Large Houses

Greenhill House, Brookeborough.

A three-bay, two-storey, mid-18th century classical house with basement, of Gibbsian detail and composition. Walls are roughcast with stone dressings. A central gable projects on the east front with a carved coat-of-arms contained within the pediment. The entrance contained within a moulded and blocked architrave is approached by steps.

Recipient of grant: Mr. & Mrs. P. M. Hicks.

Grant assistance of £1,000 given towards: Re-slating using natural slate. Repairs to external render. Replacement sash windows in original style. Replacement external doors in original style. Repairs to internal plasterwork. Repairs to timber floors. Repairs to staircase. Repairs to railings to entrance steps. Professional fees.

Further financial assistance received from: Northern Ireland Housing Executive.

Approximate cost of work: £13,645. Carried out from 1979 to 1981.

Agent: F. A. Sweeny & Partners, Enniskillen.

Contractor: Andrew Farry, Tempo.

Hallcraig, Springfield, Enniskillen.

A plain, three-storey, double-pile stone built farmhouse built about 1721. It retains an early entrance doorcase with an open scroll pediment.

Recipient of grant: Mr. K. Scott.

Grant assistance of £962 given towards: Re-slating inner slopes of roof in natural slate. Replacement leadwork. Repairs to rainwater goods. External re-rendering. Repairs to windows.

Further financial assistance received from: Northern Ireland Housing Executive.

Approximate cost of work: £7,580. Carried out in 1981.

Contractor: Kenneth Slevin, Enniskillen.

Rossfad House, Rossfad, Ballinamallard.

A tall three-storey house with basement, built about 1780. The front is three-bays wide and the side four-bays. The Georgian-glazed windows diminish in size on each floor.

Recipient of grant: Dr. J. R. Williams.

Grant assistance of £2,615 given towards: Repairs to chimneys. Re-slating using natural slate. Replacement leadwork. Replacement metal rainwater goods. Professional fees.

Approximate cost of work: £7,467. Carried out in 1981.

Architect: Richard H. Pierce, Enniskillen.

Work carried out using direct labour.

30 Willoughby Place, Enniskillen.

The end house in a three-storey mid-19th century terrace. Walls are rendered and the panelled door with fanlight over is set under an elliptical arch and approached by stone steps.

Recipient of grant: Rev. & Mrs. T. E. B. Benson.

Grant assistance of £124 given towards: Roof repairs. Treatment of woodworm.

Approximate cost of work: £1,004. Carried out in 1976.

Contractor: Wilson & Ward, Enniskillen.

Timber treatment by: Rentokil Ltd., Belfast.

38 Willoughby Place, Enniskillen.

A three-bay, two-storey rendered house with basement.

Recipient of grant: Mr. B. O'Connor.

Grant assistance of £2,385 given towards: Re-slating using natural slate. Repairs to rainwater goods. Repairs to windows. Treatment of wood rot. Repairs to internal plasterwork. Installation of damp-proof solid floors in basement. Repairs to internal panelled doors.

Further financial assistance received from: Northern Ireland Housing Executive.

Approximate cost of work: £12,000. Carried out in 1982 and 1983.

Contractor: Hugh Hackett, Beragh and work carried out using direct labour.

40 Willoughby Place, Enniskillen.

A three-bay, two-storey rendered terrace house with basement.

Recipient of grant: Mr. B. Corrigan.

Grant assistance of £85 given towards: Repair of entrance doorway and railings. External redecoration.

Approximate cost of work: £450. Carried out in 1980.

Painting by: H. G. McDermott, Enniskillen.

Willoughby House, 46 Willoughby Place, Enniskillen.

A three-bay, two-storey early Victorian villa. The right-hand bay, containing the entrance, is set back from the remainder of the frontage.

Recipient of grant: Mr. J. E. Richardson.

Grant assistance of £160 given towards: Roof repairs. Repairs to rainwater goods. Repairs to internal plasterwork.

Large Houses

Approximate cost of work: £516. Carried out in 1979.

Contractor: A. J. Humphreys, Enniskillen.

Straidarran House, Clagan Road, Claudy.

A five-bay, one-and-a-half-storey house with basement, built in the mid-18th century. The roof is half-hipped and the walls are rendered. The panelled entrance door with sidelights and decorative fanlight are set in an elliptically-arched opening and approached by a double perron. A long, five-bay castellated wing of stone construction was added to the west about 1830.

Recipient of grant: Mr. & Mrs. R. Hart.

Grant assistance of £515 given towards: Repairs to rainwater goods. Repairs to external render. Repairs to fanlight. Redecoration of remedial items. Treatment of woodworm.

Approximate cost of work: £1,585. Carried out in 1980.

Work carried out using direct labour.

Timber treatment by: Rentokil Ltd., Belfast.

Tamnagh Lodge, Park.

A two- and three-storey hunting lodge dramatically sited high on the side of the river valley. The roofs are slated and gabled, walls are smooth rendered and windows have Georgian-glazed sashes. The house has been energetically, if not absolutely correctly, restored from a derelict condition.

Recipient of grant: Mr. H. Logue.

Grant assistance of £8,500 given towards: Repairs to chimneys. Re-roofing using

Tamnagh Lodge, Park.

natural slate. Replacement metal rainwater goods. Repairs to external render. Restoration of circular windows and arched doorway discovered when wall plaster was removed. Replacement sash windows in original style. Repairs to timber floors. Repairs to staircase.

Further financial assistance received from: Northern Ireland Housing Executive.

Approximate cost of work: £45,500. Carried out from 1979.

Architects: F. M. Corr & Associates, Belfast and Londonderry (part service).

Agents: Mulheron & Nash, Londonderry.

The Oaks, 227 Glenshane Road.

A two-storey house with three-bay entrance front with an Ionic columned porch and five-bay garden front with central pediment. Built for the Lyle family and remodelled in 1867 for Acheson Lyle to the designs of John McCurdy.

Recipient of grant: Mr. A. M. Allen.

Grant assistance of £10,020 given towards: Re-slating using natural slate to outer slopes and asbestos-cement slate to inner slopes. Repairs to roof domes. Repairs to leadwork. Treatment of woodworm. Installation of electro-osmotic damp-proof course.

Large Houses

Repairs to internal plasterwork. Repairs to decorative plasterwork. Installation of damp-proof solid floors in basement. Redecoration of remedial items.

Approximate cost of work: £26,405. Carried out in 1980 and 1981.

Contractor: Robert Simpson, Goshaden, Co. Londonderry.

Timber treatment by: Timbercare (N.I.), Lisburn.

Foyle Park, Eglinton.

A large four-bay, two-storey Georgian house occupying a magnificent site overlooking the Foyle estuary. The house was built about 1800 and in 1829 was opened as an agricultural school for the education of the sons of local farmers. It reverted to private occupation when the school eventually closed. Walls are roughcast with brick dressings. The panelled entrance door with sidelights and the decorative fanlight is set in a segmental arched opening. The house has been restored from a dilapidated condition and converted into flats.

Recipient of grant: Lt.-Col. K. B. L. Davidson.

Grant assistance of £2,525 given towards: Roof repairs. Rebuilding of chimneys. Repairs to leadwork. External re-rendering. Repairs to windows. Treatment of wood rot. Internal re-plastering. Re-laying of stone paving.

Further financial assistance received from: Northern Ireland Housing Executive.

Approximate cost of work: £15,981. Carried out in 1978 and 1979.

Architect: Caroline Dickson, Londonderry.

Contractor: Martin Dolan, Eglinton.

Roof work by: Conservobond, Dun Laoghaire.

Timber treatment by: Timbershield, Lisburn.

Woodbury, Main Street, Eglinton.

The former Eglinton police barracks is a three-bay, two-storey building with gabled slated roof and central projecting gabled and rendered porch. The front is of stone with rendered dressings to windows the upper sashes of which are Georgian-glazed.

Recipient of grant: Mrs. M. K. Turner.

Grant assistance of £3,088 given towards: Repairs to leadwork. Replacement metal rainwater goods. External re-rendering. Replacement window.

Approximate cost of work: £3,272. Carried out in 1982.

Contractor: Jim Boyle Construction, Eglinton.

Beech Hill, 32 Ardmore Road, Londonderry.

The third house on the site by the Skipton family. The present two- and three-storey house dates from 1729. It was enlarged in the mid-19th century and again at the end of the century when a massive and elaborate two-storey porte-cochère was added. Walls are rendered. Retains window types and interior detail from the various building periods. Described by Alistair Rowan as 'a complex and very curious jumble'.

Recipient of grant: Mr. J. M. A. Nicholson.

Grant assistance of £11,000 given towards: Repairs to chimneys. Minor roof repairs. Repairs to rainwater goods.

Repairs to windows. Treatment of wood rot. Installation of damp-proof course. Repairs to internal plasterwork. Repairs to staircase.

Further financial assistance received from: Northern Ireland Housing Executive and Department of Health and Social Services.

Approximate cost of work: £55,371. Carried out in 1978 and 1979.

Architect: Caroline Dickson, Londonderry. (part service)

Agent: Ian N. Foster, Londonderry. (part service)

Quantity Surveyors: Thomas Earl Associates, Coleraine.

Contractor: Charles A. Forbes, Ltd., Londonderry and also work carried out using direct labour.

Glenkeen House, 80 Ardmore Road, Londonderry.

A four-bay, two-storey house with basement. The middle two bays on both fronts are bowed. Central Tuscan columned entrance with entablature. Georgian-glazed sash windows. Built about 1790.

Recipient of grant: Mr. J. M. A. Nicholson.

Grant assistance of £150 given towards: Treatment of wood rot and subsequent reinstatement.

Further financial assistance received from: Department of Health and Social Services.

Approximate cost of work: £1,288. Carried out in 1977.

Architect: Caroline Dickson, Londonderry.

Contractor: Charles A. Forbes, Ltd., Londonderry.

Large Houses

Timber treatment by: Protim Services, Lisburn.

68 Ballougry Road, Mullennan.

An early-19th century three-bay, two-storey rendered house with radial fanlight and Georgian glazing.

Recipient of grant: Mr. E. W. Black.

Grant assistance of £3,000 given towards: Rebuilding of chimneys. Replacement sash windows in original style. Replacement panelled entrance door. Treatment of wood rot. Repairs to timber floors.

Approximate cost of work: £10,870. Carried out in 1981.

Contractor: Brown & Harkin, Cloughfin.

Timber treatment by: Rentokil Ltd., Belfast.

5 St. Columb's Court, Londonderry.

One of a terrace of three-storey plain red brick houses forming a unified design with symmetrical gabled dormers over two of the houses. Built before 1900 to a design by J. Ballantine.

Recipient of grant: Trustees of St. Columb's Court.

Grant assistance of £567 given towards: Repairs to chimney. Minor roof repairs. Replacement metal rainwater goods. Repairs to windows. Repairs to internal plasterwork. Installation of damp-proof solid floors.

Further financial assistance received from: Northern Ireland Housing Executive.

Approximate cost of work: £10,576. Carried out in 1981 and 1982.

Contractor: Robert Logue & Son, Londonderry.

8 Clarendon Street, Londonderry.

A fine, three-storey, mid-19th century red brick terrace house with Georgian-glazed sash windows and panelled entrance door with flanking columns and fanlight set in an elliptically-arched opening.

Recipient of grant: Mr. L. M. McDaid.

Grant assistance of £1,520 given towards: Repairs to chimneys. Roof repairs. Re-pointing of brickwork. Repairs to windows. Replacement panelled entrance door. Treatment of wood rot. Repairs to internal plasterwork. Redecoration of remedial items.

Approximate cost of work: £5,986. Carried out in 1981.

Architect: Charles Hegarty, Londonderry.

Contractor: McCloskey & Co., Londonderry.

9 Clarendon Street, Londonderry.

A large two-bay, brown-brick terrace house post-1845 but Georgian in character. 'Fine, but never intended to be very good' (Alistair Rowan).

Recipient of grant: Mrs. J. O'Doherty.

Grant assistance of £700 given towards: Demolition of unsafe bay window following service of a public health order and subsequent reinstatement of facade to match remainder of terrace.

Approximate cost of work: £1,768. Carried out in 1982.

Contractor: Moss Construction, Londonderry.

42 Clarendon Street, Londonderry.

A three-storey, mid-19th century, mid-terrace house with vertically divided sash windows and panelled

door with flanking columns and fanlight over.

Recipient of grant: Mr. B. De Glin.

Grant assistance of £318 given towards: Repairs to windows. Installation of damp-proof solid floors.

Approximate cost of work: £954. Carried out in 1982.

Contractor: Brown & Carlin, Londonderry.

47 Clarendon Street, Londonderry.

A mid-19th century, three-storey, red brick terrace house with dormered attic. Windows have plain sashes and the panelled entrance door with fanlight is set in an elliptically-arched opening.

Recipient of grant: Mr. D. F. McKenna.

Grant assistance of £300 given towards: Silicone treatment of brickwork. Treatment of wood rot and subsequent reinstatement.

Approximate cost of work: not known. Carried out in 1980.

Work carried out using direct labour.

55 Clarendon Street, Londonderry.

A three-bay, three-storey, end-of-terrace house with attic. The ground floor and gable are smooth rendered and the upper floors are of red brick. Windows are deeply recessed with round-headed plain sashes on the ground floor, square-headed at the first floor and segmentally-headed at second floor.

Recipient of grant: Mrs. L. O'Boyle.

Grant assistance of £717 given towards: Repairs to chimney. Roof repairs. Repairs to external render. Repairs to windows. Repairs to internal plasterwork.

Large Houses

Further financial assistance received from: Northern Ireland Housing Executive.
Approximate cost of work: £8,956. Carried out in 1979 and 1980.
Contractor: Samuel Anthony & Sons Ltd., Londonderry.

65 Clarendon Street, Londonderry.

A mid-19th century, three-storey rendered terrace house with plain sashed windows with moulded surrounds and double panelled entrance doors set under a semi-circular fanlight.
Recipient of grant: Mr. R. L. Christie.
Grant assistance of £520 given towards: Repairs to chimney. Roof repairs. Repairs to rainwater goods. Repairs to windows. Treatment of wood rot. Repairs to internal plasterwork.
Further financial assistance received from: Northern Ireland Housing Executive.
Approximate cost of work: £5,318. Carried out in 1981.
Work carried out using direct labour.

69 Clarendon Street, Londonderry.

A fine mid-19th century three-storey terrace house with dormered attic. The facade is of red brick with yellow brick dressings. Windows have Georgian-glazed sashes and the panelled entrance door is set under a squashed, segmental fanlight.
Recipient of grant: Mr. & Mrs. D. Mullan.
Grant assistance of £710 given towards: Restoration of brick facade involving stripping of paint, re-pointing and application of silicone treatment. External redecoration.
Approximate cost of work: £2,147. Carried out in 1982 and 1983.

Work carried out using direct labour.
Painting by: Noel Gallagher, Londonderry.

11 Crawford Square, Londonderry.

A fine three-storey rendered terrace house built before 1871 to the designs of Robert Collins. A two-storey bay projects at the front.
Recipient of grant: Mr. P. L. Thrower.
Grant assistance of £620 given towards: Repairs to roof structure. Re-slating using asbestos-cement slate. Repairs to leadwork. Repairs to rainwater goods.
Approximate cost of work: £1984. Carried out in 1979.
Contractor: James M. Jefferson & Sons, Londonderry.
Grant assistance of £50 given towards: Repairs to external render.
Approximate cost of work: £150. Carried out in 1981.
Plastering by: J. Phelan, Londonderry.

13 Crawford Square, Londonderry.

A fine three-storey rendered terrace house built before 1871 to the designs of Robert Collins. A two-storey bay projects at the front.
Recipient of grant: Mr. B. J. Toal.
Grant assistance of £140 given towards: External redecoration.
Approximate cost of work: £420. Carried out in 1982.
Painting by: Noel Gallagher, Londonderry.

8 Clarence Avenue, Londonderry.

Part of a fine terrace of three-storey early-20th century, red brick houses built on a steeply sloping avenue. A canted bay window at ground and first floor becomes a square half-timbered gabled dormer at second floor level. Windows have coloured glass upper panes and the entrance has double, three-panel doors.
Recipient of grant: Mr. & Mrs. D. Simpson.
Grant assistance of £800 given towards: Roof repairs. Repairs to rainwater goods. Repairs to external render. Repairs to windows. Replacement panelled entrance door. Repairs to internal plasterwork. Repairs to timber floors. Redecoration of remedial items.
Further financial assistance received from: Northern Ireland Housing Executive.
Approximate cost of work: £8,150. Carried out in 1980 and 1981.
Work carried out using direct labour.

18 Northland Road, Londonderry.

A tall, three-storey, rendered, mid-terrace house with attics built in 1890 to designs by W. A. Barker. A canted bay window projects at ground level, windows have plain sashes with segmented heads and the double-panelled entrance doors are set under a plain segmented fanlight.
Recipient of grant: Mr. D. L. Bell.
Grant assistance of £1800 given towards: Repairs to chimney. Roof repairs. Repairs to rainwater goods. Repairs to external render. Repairs to windows. Installation of silicone injection damp-proof course. Repairs to internal plasterwork. Replacement of defective timber beams. Repairs to timber floors. Redecoration of remedial items.
Approximate cost of work: £6,748. Carried out in 1981.

Large Houses

Contractor: Colman Callan, Londonderry.

Damp-proof course by: Protim Services, Lisburn.

16 Northland Road, Londonderry.

A tall, three-storey, rendered, mid-terrace house with attics built in 1890 to designs by W. A. Barker. A canted bay window projects at ground floor level, windows have plain sashes with segmented heads and the double-panelled entrance doors are set under a plain segmented fanlight.

Recipient of grant: Mr. M. McGinley.

Grant assistance of £610 given towards: Repairs to rainwater goods. Repairs to external render. Cleaning of brickwork.

Approximate cost of work: £1,936. Carried out in 1981.

Contractor: Colman Callan, Londonderry.

Hampstead Hall, 40 Culmore Road, Londonderry.

A five-bay, two-storey Georgian style house with rendered walls and hipped slated roof. The entrance door is set in an elliptically-arched opening.

Recipient of grant: Mr. W. J. Greene.

Grant assistance of £1,300 given towards: Repairs to chimneys. Roof repairs. Repairs to external render. Repairs to windows. Repairs to original internal joinery work. Repairs to internal plasterwork.

Approximate cost of work: £4,015. Carried out between 1979 and 1981.

Work carried out using direct labour.

Troy Hall, 9 and 9a Troy Park, Culmore Road, Londonderry.

A large two-storey brick house with a jumble of bays, gables, turrets and balconies. Built before 1835.

Recipient of grant: Mr. G. K. Ward and Mr. P. A. O'Donnell.

PHASE ONE

Grant assistance of £865 given towards: Roof repairs. Replacement leadwork. Repairs to rainwater goods.

Approximate cost of work: £2,636. Carried out in 1979 and 1980.

Contractor: George Cregan & Sons Ltd., Londonderry.

PHASE TWO

Grant assistance of £700 given towards: Repairs to defective bay window roofs. Treatment of wood rot. Repairs to internal plasterwork. Repairs to timber floors.

Approximate cost of work: £2,115. Carried out in 1981.

Contractor: Pedersen & Richardson, Londonderry.

PHASE THREE

Grant assistance of £325 given towards: Roof repairs. Repairs to internal joinery work.

Approximate cost of work: £982. Carried out in 1983.

Contractor: Trygve Pedersen, Londonderry.

48 Glenedra Road, Fincairn, Feeny.

A five-bay, two-storey roughcast house built about 1860 with slated and gabled roof, yellow bricked chimneys, panelled entrance door with plain rectangular fanlight over and sash windows with margined panes.

Recipient of grant: Mrs. M. K. McCullagh.

Grant assistance of £2,700 given towards: Repairs to chimneys. Re-slating using natural slate. Replacement metal rainwater goods. External re-rendering. Replacement sash windows in original style. Replacement panelled entrance door. Repairs to internal plasterwork. Installation of damp-proof solid floors.

Further financial assistance received from: Northern Ireland Housing Executive.

Approximate cost of work: £19,257. Carried out in 1982 and 1983.

Work carried out using direct labour.

Bovevagh Old Rectory, 30 Camnish Road, Dungiven.

A two-storey Georgian style house with attic built in 1772. Walls are rendered. The panelled and glazed entrance door is flanked by rusticated pilasters with moulded caps all under a semi-circular fanlight.

Recipient of grant: Select Vestry of Bovevagh Parish.

Grant assistance of £275 given towards: Rebuilding of chimney. Roof repairs. Replacement metal rainwater goods. Repairs to external render.

Approximate cost of work: £903. Carried out between 1975 and 1982.

Contractor: W. J. Quigley & Son, Dungiven.

Walworth, Ballykelly, Limavady.

This five-bay, two-storey house was built around 1730 standing on the site originally occupied by the north-east tower of the Fishmonger's bawn of 1613–19 of which the other three towers and linking walls remain in varying degrees of preservation and now forming a courtyard to the house. The house has a late-18th century Georgian appearance with roughcast walls and stone dressings.

Recipient of grant: Mr. E. G. C. Brown.

PHASE ONE – MAIN HOUSE

Grant assistance of £1,200 given towards: Roof repairs. Repairs to external render. External redecoration.

Approximate cost of work: £3,742. Carried out in 1980.

Contractor: Roe Ulster Limited, Limavady.

PHASE TWO – RESTORATION OF FLANKER TOWERS

Grant assistance of £4,732 given towards: Rebuilding of north-west flanker tower. Re-roofing using natural slate. Repairs to stonework and re-pointing. Replacement doors and windows in original style. Replacement floors.

Approximate cost of work: £12,867. Carried out in 1982 and 1983.

Architects: Smyth & McMurtry, Limavady.

Contractor: McCloskey & O'Kane Ltd., Eglinton.

The Manse, Clooney Road, Ballykelly.

A fine example of a Victorian villa built around 1850. The walls are rendered with sandstone dressings. A porch is contained in the angle of the 'T' plan. Sash windows have narrow margined panes.

Recipient of grant: Ballykelly Presbyterian Church.

Grant assistance of £400 given towards:

Re-roofing using natural slate. Replacement side door in original style.

Further financial assistance received from: Northern Ireland Housing Executive.

Approximate cost of work: £3,070. Carried out in 1979.

Contractor: McArthur & Young, Largy, Limavady.

Church Hill, Ballykelly.

A three-bay, two-storey house built in ashlar sandstone with a hipped slated roof and overhanging eaves. A small stone-built flat-roofed porch projects from the central bay. The house is linked by high rubble stone walls to single-storey hip-roofed pavilions, each with a single round-headed window in a relieving arch, the whole forming a symmetrical composition. The group was built in 1824 by the Fishmonger's Company as a model farm.

Recipient of grant: Mr. M. S. Fulton.

Grant assistance of £650 given towards: Roof repairs. Replacement leadwork.

Approximate cost of work: £1,999. Carried out in 1981.

Contractor: O. Martin, Limavady.

Roof work by: Pentagon (Restoration) Ltd., Darkley.

Clover Hill, Burnally, Limavady.

A three-bay, two-storey, red-brick, mid-Georgian house with half-hipped roof. The double-panelled entrance doors are set under a semi-circular fanlight.

Recipient of grant: Mr. G. Gilfillan.

Grant assistance of £1,450 given towards: Repairs to chimneys. Roof repairs. Replacement metal rainwater goods.

Re-pointing of brickwork. Repairs to external render. Replacement sash windows in original style. Replacement external doors in original style. Repair of fanlight. Treatment of wood rot. Repairs to internal plasterwork.

Further financial assistance received from: Northern Ireland Housing Executive.

Approximate cost of work: £12,440. Carried out in 1979.

Contractor: William Douglas, Limavady.

Aghanloo House, Limavady.

A two-storey rendered house with attics and square porch. Built about 1789.

Recipient of grant: Miss M. Young.

Grant assistance of £2,900 given towards: Repairs to chimneys. Roof repairs. Repairs to rainwater goods. Repairs to windows. Treatment of wood rot. Repairs to timber floors. Professional fees.

Further financial assistance received from: Northern Ireland Housing Executive.

Approximate cost of work: £16,174. Carried out in 1978.

Architects: Albert Wallace & Partners, Londonderry and Strabane.

Contractor: John Hegarty & Sons Ltd., Limavady.

Timber treatment by: Protim Services Ltd., Lisburn.

36 and 38 Catherine Street, Limavady.

A four-bay, three-storey block of two Georgian brick-faced terrace houses.

Recipient of grant: Mr. & Mrs. G. Loughrey.

Large Houses

Grant assistance of £1,552 given towards: Re-slating using natural slate. Repairs to rainwater goods. Re-pointing of brickwork. Repairs to external render. Repairs to windows. Repairs to internal plasterwork. Repairs to timber floors.

Further financial assistance received from: Northern Ireland Housing Executive.

Approximate cost of work: £22,486. Carried out in 1981.

Architect: Gerard Loughrey, Limavady.

Contractor: Blair & Feeney Joinery Works, Limavady.

Movanagher School, Ballyaghanea.

A single-storey school built by the Mercer's Company about 1840. The building forms a symmetrical composition with projecting gabled wings with attics and central twin-gabled porch. Walls are of blackstone with red brick dressings. Windows are Georgian-paned sashes.

Recipient of grant: Mr. T. Brizzell.

Grant assistance of £610 given towards: Repairs to decorative barge boards. Repairs to rainwater goods. Re-pointing of stonework. Replacement sash windows in original style.

Further financial assistance received from: Northern Ireland Housing Executive.

Approximate cost of work: £11,434. Carried out in 1979.

Contractor: James McMullan, Rasharkin.

Camus House, 27 Curragh Road, Macosquin, Coleraine.

A late Georgian five-bay, two-storey, double-pile roughcast house with slated gabled roof. The panelled entrance door with sidelights and fanlights are contained within an elliptical arched opening.

Recipient of grant: Mrs. J. King.

Grant assistance of £400 given towards: Replacement sash windows in original style.

Approximate cost of work: £1,232. Carried out in 1982.

Contractor: Bristow Engineering (N.I.) Ltd., Portglenone.

St. Margaret's Rectory, Aghadowey.

A two-storey Regency house of irregular plan. Built around 1840 and named after the daughter of William Orr, linen merchant. Walls are rendered, roof slated and windows traceried. A square bay projects on the south gable and a canted bay on the east. Described by Alistair Rowan as 'curiously pretty'.

Recipient of grant: Mr. R. McMaster.

Grant assistance of £6,360 given towards: Roof repairs. Reinstatement after demolition of out-of-keeping extension. Repairs to windows and doors. Treatment of wood rot. Redecoration of remedial items.

Approximate cost of work: £20,375. Carried out between 1977 and 1979.

Architects: W. & M. Given, Coleraine.

Contractor: A. & F. O'Loughlin, Lisgorgan, Upperlands.

Timber treatment by: Rentokil Ltd., Belfast.

Gortin House, 65 Ballygawley Road, Aghadowey.

Built about 1830. Described by Alistair Rowan as 'a neat crisp brick house with a high hipped roof that overhangs the eaves, and double chimneystacks'.

Recipient of grant: Mr. W. J. Clyde.

Grant assistance of £3,980 given towards: Re-slating using asbestos-cement slate. Repairs to rainwater goods. Re-pointing of brickwork. Repairs to windows.

Approximate cost of work: £15,000. Carried out between 1979 and 1982.

Architect: R. Robinson & Sons, Ballymoney.

Work carried out using direct labour.

Landmore House, Aghadowey.

Built by Alick Orr, a linen merchant, in 1788. Landmore House is a double-pile, five-bay, Georgian brick house with attics and basement. The panelled door with decorative sidelights and fanlight is contained within a segmental arched opening with flanking pilasters and moulded archivolt.

Recipient of grant: Mr. S. Hazlett.

Grant assistance of £3,496 given towards: Repairs to roof structure. Re-slating using natural slate to outer slopes and asbestos-cement to inner slopes. Repairs to windows.

Approximate cost of work: £10,226. Carried out in 1977.

Architect: R. Robinson & Sons, Ballymoney.

Contractor: M. Moody, Garvagh.

Rushbrook House, 15 Craigmore Road, Blackhill, Coleraine.

A two-storey, double-pile, roughcast house built about 1803. The

Landmore House, Aghadowey, Co. Londonderry.

semi-circular-headed entrance doorcase is contained within a two-storey projecting bow on the south gable. The garden front has five bays with Georgian-glazed sash windows.

Recipient of grant: Mr. E. Hegarty.

Grant assistance of £1,480 given towards: Roof repairs. Replacement sash windows in original style. Repairs to panelled entrance door. Redecoration of remedial items.

Approximate cost of work: £5,016. Carried out in 1980.

Contractor: M. Moody, Garvagh.

Ballintemple House, 40 Churchtown Road, Garvagh.

A five-bay, two-storey, double-pile house with single- and two-storey returns. The single-storey return may represent the original lodge which was built about 1770. Walls are roughcast, windows are Georgian-paned sliding sashes and the panelled entrance door with decorative sidelights and fanlight is set in an elliptical arched opening.

Recipient of grant: Mrs. A. Lee.

PHASE ONE

Grant assistance of £2,800 given towards: Roof repairs. Rebuilding of defective gable wall. External re-rendering. Repairs to windows. Treatment of wood rot. Installation of silicone injection damp-proof course. Repairs to internal plaster work. Installation of damp-proof solid floors.

Approximate cost of work: £9,512. Carried out in 1977 and 1978.

Contractor: Dickie & Hamilton, Coleraine.

Timber treatment and damp-proof course by: Timbercare (N.I.) Ltd., Lisburn.

PHASE TWO

Grant assistance of £250 given towards: Repairs to leadwork. Repairs to internal plasterwork.

Approximate cost of work: £745. Carried out in 1981.

Contractor: Dickie & Hamilton, Coleraine.

Rock Ryan House, 2 Promenade, Castlerock.

Built in 1862 as a public bath house. It is one-and-a-half-storeys, constructed of coursed basalt which was derived from the tunnelling for the railway. Before conversion to a dwelling in 1906 it was used as a church by the Church of Ireland.

Recipient of grant: Mr. & Mrs. M. E. Dark.

Grant assistance of £5,000 given towards: Repairs to roof structure. Re-slating using natural slate. Replacement leadwork. Replacement dormers in original style. Repairs to decorative barge boards. Repairs to windows. Replacement panelled entrance door. Redecoration of remedial items. Professional fees.

Approximate cost of work: £16,790. Carried out in 1979.

Architects: Dalzell & Campbell, Coleraine/Portrush/Belfast/Londonderry.

Contractor: John Rainey & Co., Portrush.

Mount Pleasant, 23 Mountsandel Road, Coleraine.

Built in 1879. 'A pleasing Victorian cottage orné, stuccoed, with Tudor-style drip mouldings, and a spectacular view across the river.' (Coleraine and Portstewart, U.A.H.S. 1972).

Recipient of grant: Professor A. Macfadyen.

Grant assistance of £565 given towards: Rebuilding of chimney. Restoration of decorative ridge tiles. Repairs to boundary wall.

Approximate cost of work: £1,696. Carried out in 1978.

Contractor: M. McColgan, Coleraine.

Salem Lodge, 33 Millburn Road, Coleraine.

A finely detailed Victorian rogue-Gothic, two-storey rendered villa with steeply pitched gables either side of an arcaded timber entrance porch. Ground floor windows are plain sashed and paned in square bays with hipped roofs whilst first floor windows

Salem Lodge, Millburn Road, Coleraine.

are tripartite set in segmental pointed openings with hood moulds. Built about 1865.

Recipient of grant: Mr. R. A. Robinson.

Grant assistance of £770 given towards: Roof repairs. Repairs to fascia and barge boards. Repairs to external render. Repairs to windows.

Approximate cost of work: £2,600. Carried out in 1977.

Contractor: S. D. Thompson, Coleraine.

Ampertain House, Upperlands.

A two-storey rendered house built about 1840 with a hipped slated roof and shallow porch. A wing was added in 1915.

Recipient of grant: Mr. A. A. M. Clark.

Grant assistance of £1,070 given towards: Roof repairs. Repairs to leadwork. Repairs to rainwater goods. Treatment of wood rot.

Further financial assistance received from: Northern Ireland Housing Executive.

Approximate cost of work: £8,692. Carried out between 1976 and 1980.

Work carried out using direct labour.

Timber treatment by: Rentokil Ltd., Belfast and Timbershield Ltd., Lisburn.

The Rectory, Maghera.

A gaunt square four-bay, three-storey glebe house built in 1825. Walls are roughcast and roof is hipped with overhanging eaves and chimneys grouped in the centre.

Recipient of grant: Select Vestry, Clonmore Parish.

Grant assistance of £70 given towards: Repairs to windows.

Approximate cost of work: £217. Carried out in 1979.

Work carried out using own labour.

Termoneeny House, Ballymacpeake, Portglenone.

A three-bay, two-storey roughcast house with basement and attics.

Recipient of grant: Mr. H. H. Convery.

Grant assistance of £440 given towards: Removal of existing corrugated iron roof over scullery and replacing with natural slate. Repairs to external render. Repairs to windows. Replacement external doors in original style. Repairs to staircase. Redecoration of remedial items.

Approximate cost of work: £1,947. Carried out in 1978 and 1979.

Work carried out using direct labour.

Fortwilliam, 20 Fortwilliam Road, Tobermore, Magherafelt.

A five-bay, two-storey harled and whitened house with hipped slated roof built about 1790. The entrance is recessed in a Gibbsian surround with a decorated rectangular fanlight. Windows are Georgian-glazed sashes.

Recipient of grant: Mr. H. Bradley.

Grant assistance of £838 given towards: Replacement sash windows in original style. Replacement panelled entrance door. Treatment of damp in basement.

Approximate cost of work: £2,500. Carried out in 1977.

Contractor: S. G. McKeown, Cookstown.

Aughrim House, 97 Aughrim Road, Magherafelt.

A three-storey harled roadside house built about 1840.

Recipient of grant: Mr. A. R. Hogg.

Grant assistance of £431 given towards: Repairs to roof structure. Re-slating using natural slate. Repairs to leadwork. Repairs to external render. Repairs to windows.

Further financial assistance received from: Northern Ireland Housing Executive.

Approximate cost of work: £6,295. Carried out in 1980 and 1981.

Contractor: Gregg & Lees, Magherafelt.

24 and 26 High Street, Moneymore.

A late-19th century three-bay, two-storey rendered building with rusticated ground floor containing a shop front and half-glazed entrance door with glazed fanlight over. Windows have plain sashes.

Recipient of grant: Mr. R. Chambers.

Grant assistance of £520 given towards: Repairs to chimneys. Roof repairs. Repairs to rainwater goods. Repairs to external render. External redecoration.

Approximate cost of work: £1,580. Carried out in 1979.

Contractor: R. S. Kells, Moneymore.

Painting by: John C. Eastwood, Cookstown.

The Rectory, Moneymore.

A two-storey sandstone building with basement. Hipped roof over modillioned eaves. Entrance is set within an engaged Doric portico approached by steps. Windows have Georgian-glazed sashes.

Recipient of grant: Select Vestry, Desertlyn Church.

Large Houses

PHASE ONE

Grant assistance of £650 given towards:
Roof repairs. Replacement rainwater goods. Repairs to entrance steps.
Approximate cost of work: £2,801. Carried out in 1979.
Contractor: J. Derby, Magherafelt.

PHASE TWO

Grant assistance of £360 given towards:
Replacement leadwork.
Approximate cost of work: £920. Carried out in 1982.
Contractor: J. & P. McArdle Bros., Armagh.

20 Ballygillen Road, Coagh.

A pre-1832 two-storey Georgian farmhouse with gabled slated roof, blackstone rubble walls with brick lintels. Georgian-paned sash windows with exposed cases and panelled entrance door with narrow decorative rectangular fanlight.
Recipient of grant: Mr. R. J. Brown.
Grant assistance of £1,580 given towards:
Repairs to chimneys. Re-roofing using natural slate. Repairs to rainwater goods. Repairs to external render. Re-pointing of stonework and brickwork. Replacement sash windows in original style. Repairs to panelled entrance door. Repairs to internal plasterwork. Installation of damp-proof solid floors. Professional fees.
Further financial assistance received from: Northern Ireland Housing Executive.
Approximate cost of work: £15,400. Carried out in 1981.
Agent: Uel Henry, Cookstown.
Contractor: Ian Clarke, Cookstown.

Ballyronan House, Ballyronan, Magherafelt.

A two-storey 'T'-shaped, roughcast house with gabled slated roof and Georgian-paned sash windows including tripartite gable windows.
Recipient of grant: Mr. J. A. McLean.
Grant assistance of £4,403 given towards:
Repairs to roof structure. Re-slating using both asbestos-cement and natural slate. Replacement leadwork. Replacement metal rainwater goods. External re-rendering. Replacement sash windows in original style. Replacement panelled entrance door. Treatment of extensive dry rot. Repairs to internal plasterwork. Internal re-plastering. Installation of damp-proof solid floors.
Further financial assistance received from: Northern Ireland Housing Executive.
Approximate cost of work: £25,014. Carried out from 1980 to 1982.
Work carried out using direct labour.

Kildress Rectory, Corhoney, Cookstown.

A two-storey, 'L'-shaped house with harled walls built in 1791. A segmented bow with conical slated roof three windows wide, projects on the front elevation and contains the entrance in a square, moulded surround. On either side of the bow are tripartite windows to the ground floor.
Recipient of grant: Select Vestry, Kildress Parish Church.
Grant assistance of £3,932 given towards:
Repairs to roof structure. Re-slating using natural slate. External re-rendering. Repairs to windows and doors. Repairs to entrance steps.

Approximate cost of work: £12,590. Carried out in 1978 and 1979.
Contractor: Malcolm Thom, Cookstown.

Killycolp House, Cookstown.

A two-storey, double-pile house in an early 19th century style. The roof is hipped on the front block. Windows are Georgian-glazed sashes with margins to the ground floor.
Recipient of grant: Mr. J. H. Hamilton.
Grant assistance of £2,495 given towards:
Repairs to chimneys. Re-slating using natural slate. Repairs to rainwater goods. Replacement external doors in original style. Treatment of woodworm. Repairs to internal joinery. Internal re-plastering. Repairs to timber floors. Installation of damp-proof solid floors.
Further financial assistance received from: Northern Ireland Housing Executive.
Approximate cost of work: £14,087. Carried out in 1979 and 1980.
Contractor: Ferson Bros., Killycurragh, Cookstown.
Timber treatment by: Protim Services, Lisburn.

Loy House, 80 Chapel Street, Cookstown.

Part of the Stewart family dower house possibly designed by John Nash now sub-divided into two dwellings. The house incorporates the central segmental bow front and the more grand of the two entrances with its fluted Doric columns supporting a flat plinth. The walls are roughcast and the windows Georgian-glazed.
Recipient of grant: Mr. G. Conway.

Grant assistance of £410 given towards: Repairs to leadwork. Repairs to rainwater goods. Replacement of skirting boards in original style. Redecoration of remedial items.
Approximate cost of work: £1,230. Carried out in 1978.
Contractor: Anthony Nugent, Cookstown.

Loy House, 82 Chapel Street, Cookstown.

Part of the Stewart family dower house possibly designed by John Nash now sub-divided into two dwellings.
Recipient of grant: Mr. J. McGahan.
Grant assistance of £450 given towards: Roof repairs. Repairs to leadwork. Repairs to rainwater goods. Repairs to external render. Repairs to windows. Repairs to internal plasterwork. Replacement floors. Redecoration of remedial items.
Approximate cost of work: £1,587. Carried out in 1977.
Contractor: B. B. McDevitt, Newtownstewart.

Errington, 82 Relagh Road, Trillick.

A two-storey gabled house with basement and wings, built about 1800 with late-19th century modifications. The walls are rendered and lined with heavy sandstone dressings.
Recipient of grant: Major A. Gibbon.
Grant assistance of £2,800 given towards: Roof repairs. Replacement metal rainwater goods. Repairs to external render. Replacement sash windows in original style. Repairs to internal plasterwork. Repairs to timber floors.
Further financial assistance received from:

Northern Ireland Housing Executive.
Approximate cost of work: £16,773. Carried out in 1979.
Architects: Stone & Lynch, Enniskillen.
Contractor: Andy Boyle, Enniskillen.

Old Mountjoy, 205 Gortin Road, Omagh.

A large, rambling, two- and three-storey house, with crenellated stone walls, tower and turrets.
Recipient of grant: Dr. D. Pollock.

PHASE ONE – ROOF
Grant assistance of £7,982 given towards: Repairs to roof structure. Re-slating using natural slate. Repairs to leadwork.
Approximate cost of work: £18,917. Carried out in 1981 and 1982.
Agent: K. Collins, Omagh.
Contractor: McCabe Bros., Omagh.

PHASE TWO – DUCKBOARDS
Grant assistance of £100 given towards: Provision of duck boards to roof.
Approximate cost of work: £119. Carried out in 1982.
Work carried out using direct labour.

PHASE THREE – PARAPET
Grant assistance of £2,460 given towards: Repairs to roof parapets. Treatment of wood rot. Repairs to internal plasterwork. Repairs to timber floors.
Approximate cost of work: £6,158. Carried out in 1982 and 1983.
Work carried out using direct labour.

Corick House, Clogher.

The original house of 1697 was virtually rebuilt in an Italianate style by Lanyon, Lynn and Lanyon in 1863. It is a large-scale two-storey rendered

house with basement with a three-storey tower set in the angle of the 'L'-shaped plan.
Recipient of grant: Mrs. J. E. B. Maclagan.
Grant assistance of £1,630 given towards: Re-slating of belvedere tower using natural slate. Replacement metal rainwater goods. Professional fees.
Approximate cost of work: £4,435. Carried out in 1982.
Architect: William Dent, Omagh.
Contractor: McCallan Bros., Clare, Carrickmore.

Fernshaw, 28 Old Moy Road, Dungannon.

A two-storey 'L'-shaped house with attic and extension to rear. The roof is slated and gabled, walls are roughcast and windows are Georgian-glazed sashes. The property has been extensively restored.
Recipient of grant: Mr. J. D. Hazelton.
Grant assistance of £5,560 given towards: Rebuilding of chimneys including replacement in replica of octagonal pots. Re-roofing using natural slate. Replacement metal rainwater goods. External re-rendering. Replacement sash windows in original style. Porch replacement in replica. Replacement external doors in original style. Internal re-plastering. Installation of damp-proof solid floors. Professional fees.
Further financial assistance received from: Northern Ireland Housing Executive.
Approximate cost of work: £21,468. Carried out in 1980 and 1981.
Architect: F. M. W. Schofield, Dungannon.
Work carried out using direct labour.

Large Houses

Laurelvale, Broughadowey Road, Dungannon.

A long, two-storey, roughcast house, basically Georgian with many alterations.

Recipient of grant: Mr. R. G. Boston.

Grant assistance of £1,450 given towards: Repair to chimneys. Re-slating using natural slate. Replacement metal rainwater goods. Rebuilding of unsound walls. Repairs to external render. Replacement sash windows in original style. Repairs to internal plasterwork. Repairs to timber floors. Repairs to staircase.

Further financial assistance received from: Northern Ireland Housing Executive.

Approximate cost of work: £26,470. Carried out in 1980.

Contractor: P. F. McKearney, Dungannon.

Grange Park, 35 Grange Road, Moy.

A five-bay, two-storey house with attics built about 1800. Large tripartite windows flank the entrance door.

Recipient of grant: Mr. J. T. Ward.

Grant assistance of £1,400 given towards: Repairs to chimney. Roof repairs. Replacement sash windows in original style. Replacement external doors in original style. Repairs to internal plasterwork.

Approximate cost of work: £4,210. Carried out in 1981 and 1982.

Work carried out using direct labour.

Lisbeg House, Ballygawley.

Built to replace an earlier house in a two-storey symmetrical design in cut stone simply detailed in the Venetian style. Contiguous farm buildings are approached through a cut stone archway with water storage in the tower over.

Recipient of grant: Mr. W. R. Cooper.

Grant assistance of £1,500 given towards: Roof repairs. Repairs to rainwater goods. Repairs to external render. Rebuilding of bay windows. Replacement sash windows in original style. Replacement panelled entrance door. Treatment of extensive dry rot. Installation of damp-proof course. Repairs to internal plasterwork. Repairs to timber floors. Professional fees.

Further financial assistance received from: Northern Ireland Housing Executive.

Approximate cost of work: £11,224. Carried out in 1981 and 1982.

Agent: Edwards Building Advisory Service, Ballygawley.

Contractor: W. Anderson, Fivemiletown.

Timber treatment by: Timbershield Ltd., Lisburn

Annagh House, 6 Glencrew Road, Aughnacloy.

A simple Georgian classically detailed house, it's unusual plan may derive from an earlier, less formal, structure.

Recipient of grant: Mrs. I. Montgomery.

Grant assistance of £1,537 given towards: Repairs to chimneys. Re-slating using natural slate. External re-rendering. Replacement sash windows in original style. Repairs to panelled entrance door. Repairs to internal plasterwork.

Further financial assistance received from: Northern Ireland Housing Executive.

Approximate cost of work: £13,490. Carried out in 1982.

Contractor: Pat Monaghan, Fivemiletown.

26 Northland Row, Dungannon.

A distinguished three-bay, three-storey Georgian terrace house with basement. Window sash boxes are exposed and the panelled entrance door with rectangular fanlight over is set in a Gibbsian surround. The stables are dated 1762.

Recipient of grant: Mr. J. J. Little.

Grant assistance of £100 given towards: Treatment of woodworm.

Approximate cost of work: £115. Carried out in 1980.

Timber treatment by: Timbertreat Services Ltd., Belfast.

4 Northland Place, Dungannon.

Originally a three-bay, two-storey house, symmetrically planned with a central flat-roofed porch. The addition of an extra bay to the right-hand-side of the frontage creates the present rather unbalanced appearance. The roof is gabled and slated, walls are smooth rendered with moulded quoins and windows have Georgian-glazed sashes with exposed cases. The house was built about 1790.

Recipient of grant: Mr. J. K. Adams.

Grant assistance of £1,766 given towards: Repairs to roof structure. Re-slating using natural slate. Repairs to rainwater goods.

Approximate cost of work: £5,298. Carried out in 1981.

Contractor: McAleer & Teague, Dromore, Co. Tyrone.

Residential
Mansions and Castles

Interior: The Argory, Moy.

Lismachan House, 378 Belmont Road, Belfast.

A two-storey house with single-storey east wing, designed by Thomas Jackson in 1870. Both roofs are hipped and slated, with modillioned eaves cornices, walls are smooth rendered with heavily moulded details and the windows are grouped and have plain sashes with segmental heads to the first floor and semi-circular heads to the ground floor. The panelled entrance door with plain semi-circular fanlight is set in a forward projecting three-storey square tower centrally positioned on the main block. The house has been converted for use as flats.

Recipient of grant: John Yeats Estates Ltd.

Grant assistance of £2,080 given towards: Treatment of extensive dry rot and subsequent reinstatement.

Approximate cost of work: £6,025. Carried out in 1980 and 1981.

Architects: Brian Emerson Associates, Hillsborough.

Contractor: E. Huey, Belfast.

Timber treatment by: Rentokil Ltd., Belfast.

Painting by: J. R. McKee & Son, Belfast.

Benvarden House, Dervock, Ballymoney.

The house was bought by the Montgomerys in 1798 who have been responsible for many alterations to the original hunting lodge including the addition of the east and west wings with their canted bays and higher ground floor ceilings.

Recipient of grant: Mr. H. J. Montgomery.

PHASE ONE — MAIN HOUSE REPAIRS

Grant assistance of £1,838 given towards: Repairs to lean-to roofs at front of house. Repairs to main roof. Repairs to chimneys. Repairs to leadwork. Replacement metal rainwater goods. Repairs to windows. Repairs to internal plasterwork.

Approximate cost of work: £4,235. Carried out in 1976 and 1977.

Work carried out using direct labour.

PHASE TWO — GARDEN WALLS

Grant assistance of £410 given towards: Provision of buttresses to garden wall.

Approximate cost of work: £2,064. Carried out in 1978 and 1979.

Work carried out using own labour.

PHASE THREE — MAIN HOUSE AND BRIDGE REPAIRS

Grant assistance of £1,180 given towards: Repairs to chimneys. External redecoration of main house and Victorian bridge.

Approximate cost of work: £3,435. Carried out in 1979.

Work carried out using direct labour.

Painting by: B. Patton, Portballintrae and Eric Fulton, Coleraine.

PHASE FOUR — MAIN HOUSE REPAIRS

Grant assistance of £256 given towards: Roof repairs. Repairs to roof parapet. Making good of courtyard wall after demolition of extension.

Approximate cost of work: £780. Carried out in 1981.

Contractor: W. & R. Adams, Ballymoney.

PHASE FIVE — REPAIRS TO COTTAGE, NO. 30 BENVARDEN ROAD

Grant assistance of £323 given towards: Re-slating using natural slate. Replacement metal rainwater goods.

Mansions and Castles

Replacement sash windows in original style. Replacement external doors in original style.

Further financial assistance received from: Northern Ireland Housing Executive.

Approximate cost of work: £4,269. Carried out in 1982.

Work carried out using own labour.

PHASE SIX – MAIN HOUSE AND BOUNDARY WALL REPAIRS

Grant assistance of £509 given towards: Roof repairs. Repairs to rainwater goods. Repairs to external render. Repairs to estate boundary wall.

Approximate cost of work: £1,207. Carried out in 1982.

Contractor: W. & R. Adams, Ballymoney. (Main house).

Work carried out using own labour. (Boundary wall).

PHASE SEVEN – RESTORATION OF COURTYARD BUILDINGS

Grant assistance of £4,860 given towards: Re-slating using natural slate. Repairs to windows. Replacement external doors in original style. Repairs to brick archway. Repairs to cupola. Repairs to weathervane.

Approximate cost of work: £14,839. Carried out from 1982 onwards.

Contractor: R. Taggart, Ballymoney, and work carried out using own labour.

Leslie Hill, Ballymoney.

An imposing, double-pile, rendered, Georgian house with three storeys and basement. Built by James Leslie about 1758. The entrance front is seven bays wide of which the middle three project and are surmounted by a pediment containing a half-oculus. The central

doorway approached by a flight of steps, consists of a panelled door flanked by Doric columns rising to a broken pediment. The symmetrical wings and pavilions to either side were demolished in the 1950's.

Recipient of grant: Mr. J. F. Leslie.

Grant assistance of £2,012 given towards: Repairs to chimneys. Re-slating using natural slate. Repairs to leadwork. Replacement metal rainwater goods.

Approximate cost of work: £5,030. Carried out in 1975.

Contractor: J. S. Dunlop, Ballymoney.

Dundarave House, Whitepark Road, Bushmills.

A fine restrained Italianate palazzo style house after the fashion of the Reform Club in London, in a magnificent setting of parkland overlooking the north Antrim coastline. Designed in 1847 by Charles Lanyon, the main house is six bays by four and two storeys high. A lower services wing extends to the north-east. The three main fronts are each treated differently with the entrance front having a large three-bay porch with Corinthian pilasters and columns and a heavy balustrade. On the main garden front the two central bays recede and have a handsome ground floor projecting bow window. All three fronts are surmounted by a balustrade of typical Lanyon detail. The building is rendered with dressed sandstone details. The interior is of superb quality.

Recipient of grant: Sir Patrick Macnaghten.

Grant assistance of £4,500 given towards: Restoration of external decorative features in reconstructed stone

including eaves corbel brackets and dentils and window aedicules. Repairs to lead lined parapet gutter.

Approximate cost of work: £33,882. Carried out in 1983.

Architects: R. Robinson & Sons, Ballymoney.

Contractor: J. S. Dunlop, Ballymoney.

Redhall, Ballycarry.

Formerly an O'Neill castle it was remodelled and partially rebuilt when in the possession of the Edmondstone family (1609–1780). The wings were added by the Ker family about 1798 when the entrance hall assumed its present position. The tower is thought to have been added after 1869 by the McAuley family from Crumlin who were also responsible for the external plaster and the red, painted finish. The building is three storeys high with tower and basement; the wings are single-storey.

Recipient of grant: Mr. J. McClintock.

Grant assistance of £3,907 given towards: Restoration of single-storey south wing following a severe dry rot outbreak. Repairs to roof structure. Re-slating using natural slate. Repairs to internal plasterwork. Repairs to decorative plasterwork. Repairs to external render. Repairs to windows.

Approximate cost of work: £9,768. Carried out in 1976 and 1977.

Contractor: Timbercare (N.I.), Lisburn.

Galgorm Castle, Galgorm, Ballymena.

The house appears to have been built around 1645 to a double-pile plan, the front being five bays wide and three storeys high. It was extensively remodelled around 1830 when it was given its large sash windows in brick surrounds and curious central Flemish gable and semi-circular-headed battlements. Later still, some detail alterations were the responsibility of Sir Charles Lanyon. Of the earlier period interior, only the oak staircase survives.

Recipient of grant: The Hon. Christopher Brooke.

Grant assistance of £10,640 given towards: Repairs to chimneys. Repairs to roof structure. Re-slating using natural slate. Replacement of lead valleys. Repairs to internal plasterwork. Professional fees.

Approximate cost of work: £43,200. Carried out in 1983.

Architects: John Storie & Partners, Enniskillen.

Contractor: D. Herbison, Cullybackey.

Timber treatment by: Timbertreat (N.I.), Lisburn.

Castle Upton, Templepatrick.

Castle Upton has a complex history dating from the late-16th century. Originally a plantation castle it was extensively remodelled by Robert Adam in 1783 and 1788 to become an impressive mass with three great crenellated towers, capped by high conical roofs, with embattled parapets linking them. It was again drastically altered to virtually its present, rather less interesting, appearance by Edward Blore in 1837 and much of Adam's contribution has been lost.

Recipient of grant: Sir Robin Kinahan.

PHASE ONE – BALLROOM

Grant assistance of £550 given towards: Roof repairs.

Approximate cost of work: £1,065. Carried out in 1977.

Roof work by: Edward McMahon & Sons, Belfast.

PHASE TWO – BALLROOM

Grant assistance of £23 given towards: Roof repairs.

Approximate cost of work: £47. Carried out in 1978.

Architects: Isherwood & Ellis. Belfast and Ballymena.

Roof work by: Edward McMahon & Sons, Belfast.

PHASE THREE – BALLROOM

Grant assistance of £60 given towards: Provision of access to roof to facilitate inspection.

Approximate cost of work: £127. Carried out in 1980.

Architects: Isherwood & Ellis, Belfast and Ballymena.

Contractor: Timbercare (N.I.), Lisburn.

PHASE FOUR – REPAIRS

Grant assistance of £4,580 given towards: Provision of new flat roofing to ballroom. Provision of cast-iron rainwater goods to ballroom roof. Repairs to chimney. Repairs to porch roof. Professional fees.

Approximate cost of work: £9,193. Carried out in 1980 and 1981.

Architects: Isherwood & Ellis, Belfast and Ballymena.

Contractor: F. B. McKee & Co. Ltd., Belfast.

Castle Dobbs, Carrickfergus.

Castle Dobbs is a remarkable example of the surviving co-existence of two distinct architectural styles. The house was built in the mid-18th century and was based on designs found in James Gibbs' pattern book 'A Book of Architecture'. However, in the mid-19th century a programme of alterations and improvements was instigated in an Italianate style almost certainly under the direction of Sir Charles Lanyon but these were for some unaccountable reason abandoned before completion. The house today therefore has a relatively plain parapeted mid-Georgian central block of two storeys on a raised basement with the original Georgian glazing while the two storey east and west wings with forward projecting pavilions have been fully subjected to Lanyon's Italianate treatment. Much of the original Georgian interior also survives. The house is at present the subject of a major conservation scheme.

Recipient of grant: Captain R. A. F. Dobbs.

Grant assistance of £150 given towards: Taking down of ceilings in west wing to allow examination of roof structure.

Approximate cost of work: £396. Carried out in 1981.

Architects: Isherwood & Ellis, Belfast and Ballymena.

Work carried out using own labour.

Waringstown House, Waringstown.

Built in 1667 by William Waring the house was one of the first unfortified houses built in Ireland. It was of two storeys and probably thatched. Incredibly, an almost complete oak butt-purlin roof timbering system has survived the 18th century addition of an extra storey. The walls are largely of stone and mud construction and are

Mansions and Castles

Waringstown House, Waringstown.

harled. The south-east tower has been saved from virtual collapse but the remainder of this important building continues to be in a perilous condition.

Recipient of grant: Mr.
M. H. St. C. Harnett.

Grant assistance of £9,625 given towards: Careful demolition and rebuilding of south-east tower while roof remained propped in position. Restoration of original floors and windows. Repairs to chimney on main house. Repairs to main house walls. Repairs to drawing room floor. Professional fees.

Approximate cost of work: £32,802. Carried out in 1983.

Architect: J. G. O'Neill, Lurgan.

Quantity Surveyors: Terry Doherty, Belfast.

Contractor: The Rocks, Dromore, Co. Down.

The Argory, Moy.

The Argory is a 295 acre estate with an 1820 neo-classical house and associated outbuildings. The demesne was given to the National Trust in 1979 by Mr. W. A. M. MacGeough Bond and the Ulster Land Fund provided an endowment of £828,500. The house was originally designed by A. & J. Williamson of Dublin as a single massive, two-storey, ashlar faced block; this, however, has been added to on the north side on a number of occasions. The present two-storey north wing culminates at its west end in an octagon and this in turn is linked to the main house by a full height passageway. In the mid-19th century the main entrance was switched from the west front to a rather mean, square porch on the east front.

Recipient of grant: The National Trust.

Grant assistance of £240,000 given towards: Restoration of the main house. Conversion in North wing to provide custodian's accommodation. Restoration of the Land Stewarts house. Restoration of gate lodge. Conversion of outbuildings to provide tea and reception rooms. Restoration of grounds. Restorations of pathways and drives.

Approximate cost of work: £270,683. Carried out from 1980 to 1982.

Architects: Robert McKinstry & Melvyn Brown, Belfast. (Custodians flat.)

Contractors: Philip Hobson & Co., Moy. (Main house, gate lodge, tea rooms and grounds) and A. C. Simpson & Partners Ltd., Armagh. (Main house, custodians flat.)

Timber treatment by: Radication Ltd., Dunmurry. (Gate lodge.)

Mansions and Castles

Painting by: James Greer, Ballynahinch. (Main house.)

Gosford Castle, Markethill.

A three- and four-storey castle designed in the Norman Romanesque revival style on a grand scale completed in 1839 to designs by Thomas Hopper. Roofs are slated with lead flats. Walls are of ashlar granite with crenellated and corbelled parapets and battered dark rubble base. The entrance tower and west end of the garden front were added in the mid-19th century. The castle has found a new use as a hotel and is undergoing a process of conversion and restoration.

Recipient of grant: O'Neill & Smyth Enterprises Ltd.

PHASE ONE

Grant assistance of £17,500 given towards: Roof repairs. Treatment of wood rot. Repairs to internal plasterwork. Repairs to floors.

Approximate cost of work: £67,000. Carried out in 1982 and 1983.

Architect: M. D. Architects, Belfast.

Quantity Surveyors: Donald A. MacNiven & Partners, Belfast.

Work carried out using direct labour.

Timber treatment by: Lacey Timbertreatments, Belfast.

Rich Hill House, Rich Hill.

A two-storey mansion with attics built about 1870. Dutch-gabled side wings project forward to form an entrance courtyard. The oak butt purlin roof is slated and has Dutch-gabled dormers and decorative moulded chimneys, walls are roughcast, the square-headed windows have vertically divided sashes

Narrow Water Castle, Warrenpoint.

165

and the double panelled entrance doors are flanked by Doric columns with freize and pediment cover.

Grant assistance of £2,790 given towards: Repairs to rainwater goods. Repairs to external render. External redecoration.

Approximate cost of work: £6,982. Carried out in 1981 and 1982.

Work carried out using own labour.

Narrow Water Castle, Warrenpoint.

A fine, irregularly planned, Tudor Gothic style house built in 1837 to designs by Thomas Duff. The roofs are slated and have tall, decorative chimney stacks. The multi-panelled ashlar granite south and east fronts have square and canted bay windows and a plain parapet surmounted by gablets. The bulk of the house is of two storeys with basements and attics, to the west rises a four-storey crenellated tower with an engaged circular stair turret and to the north-east, the entrance is contained in a turreted and balustraded gatehouse feature. The castle and its outbuildings are being progressively restored.

Recipient of grant: Mr. R. Hall.

PHASE ONE

Grant assistance of £3,160 given towards: Repairs to chimneys. Re-pointing of towers. Restoration of missing stone cornice. Repairs to external render.

Approximate cost of work: £6,324. Carried out in 1978.

Contractor: Heatley Bros. & Morgan, Warrenpoint. (Leadwork).

Stone repair by: John McPolin, Newry.

PHASE TWO

Grant assistance of £3,900 given towards:

Repairs to chimneys. Replacement metal rainwater goods. Repairs to external render. Re-pointing of stonework. Restoration of library doors (including casting of new parliament hinges).

Approximate cost of work: £8,325. Carried out in 1979.

Contractor: John McPolin, Newry.

Library doors by: Greenbank Timber & Metal Ltd., Warrenpoint.

Parliament hinges by: James Mackie & Sons Ltd., Belfast.

PHASE THREE

Grant assistance of £2,580 given towards: Repairs to chimneys. Replacement metal rainwater goods. Re-pointing of stonework.

Approximate cost of work: £5,529. Carried out in 1980.

Contractor: John McPolin, Newry.

Gilford Castle, Castle Street, Gilford.

A late-19th century two- and three-storey house designed in the Elizabethan Revival style by Belfast architects Young & Mackenzie. The roof is slated and multi-gabled and walls are of stone with projecting bay windows. A round tower with conical roof is contained at the junction of one wing and the main front and the entrance is approached through an open, square portico and balustrade and corner knops.

Recipient of grant: Wing Commander M. Wright.

Grant assistance of £450 given towards: External redecoration.

Approximate cost of work: £1,375. Carried out in 1981.

Painting by: Noel Foy, Portadown.

Moyallan House, Stramore Road, Moyallan.

A two-storey classically styled rendered house. The main block with parapeted roof was built before 1833 and the hip-roofed extensions and verandah were added in the later-19th century. The house has a fine group of outbuildings with hipped roofs and rendered walls with stone dressings. The property has been extensively restored.

Recipient of grant: Trustees of T. W. Richardson.

PHASE ONE – MAIN HOUSE, STABLES, AND GROUNDS

Grant assistance of £10,000 given towards: Restoration of grounds. Main house – Treatment of wood rot. Restoration of verandah. Stables – Repairs to roof structure. Re-slating using natural slate. Replacement metal rainwater goods. Repairs to external render. Repairs to windows. Repairs to doors. Repairs to timber floors.

Approximate cost of work: £44,948. Carried out in 1979 and 1980.

Architect: William C. Callaghan, Portadown.

Contractor: T. W. Sergeant, Rich Hill.

Timber treatment by: Timbercare (N.I.), Lisburn.

Repairs to verandah: Moodage Engineering, Gilford.

PHASE TWO – MAIN HOUSE

Grant assistance of £2,700 given towards: External redecoration. Treatment of wood rot and subsequent reinstatement.

Approximate cost of work: £8,478. Carried out in 1981 and 1982.

Architect: William C. Callaghan, Portadown.

Mansions and Castles

Painting by: Frank Lappin & Son Ltd., Portadown.

PHASE THREE – MAIN HOUSE

Grant assistance of £3,250 given towards: Repairs to roof structure. Roof repairs. Replacement metal rainwater goods. Treatment of extensive dry rot. Repairs to internal plasterwork.

Approximate cost of work: £120,000. Carried out from 1982 to 1983.

Architect: William C. Callaghan. Portadown.

Work carried out using direct labour.

Timber treatment by: Lacey Timbertreatment, Belfast.

Killyleagh Castle, Killyleagh.

The original castle built by John de Courcy in the late-12th century was rebuilt, in a Scottish style in 1610 and was partially destroyed in the Cromwellian siege of 1649. The castle was rebuilt again in 1666 but fell into decay until 1847 when it was extensively remodelled to its present appearance by Charles Lanyon. Although lavish in his Tudor style treatment of the building, Lanyon respected the original character to a remarkable extent. The blackstone gatehouse screen at the opposite end of the bawn also dates from mid-19th century. Without doubt the castle is one of the most exciting and romantic buildings in the north of Ireland.

Recipient of grant: Lt. Col. D. A. Rowan-Hamilton.

PHASE ONE – MAIN HOUSE

Grant assistance of £7,027 given towards: Repairs to chimney. Re-slating of five roof pitches using natural slate to outer slopes. Repairs to leadwork. Repairs to rainwater goods. Re-pointing of

stonework to roof of oriel window. Repairs to internal plasterwork.

Approximate cost of work: £12,570. Carried out from 1979 to 1981.

Contractor: J. M. Beers, Killyleagh.

PHASE TWO – GATEHOUSES

Grant assistance of £1,780 given towards: Replacement of defective flat roof over gatehouse. Replacement of turret roof. Re-glazing of windows.

Approximate cost of work: £2,967. Carried out in 1980.

Contractor: J. M. Beers, Killyleagh.

Montalto House, Ballynahinch.

Of the original two-storey Montalto House built by Sir John Rawdon in the later-18th century, only the Lady's sitting-room with its fine plasterwork by Dublin craftsmen, survives unaltered. The house was enlarged to its present austere three-storey appearance in 1837 by the Ker family who adopted the unusual measure of reducing ground level around the building and creating a new ground floor in the original basement area. The main front is seven bays wide

Montalto House, Ballynahinch.

Mansions and Castles

with full-height canted bays running at each end and in the centre. The roof is hipped and slated behind a parapet, the walls are partly of well-matched render, windows have Georgian-glazed sashes with square heads and moulded surrounds to the upper floors and semi-circular heads with plain surrounds to the ground floor, the entrance is set in an insignificant Doric porch.

PHASE ONE
Recipient of grant: The Earl of Clanwilliam.

PHASE ONE – DRAWING ROOM
Grant assistance of £19,000 given towards: Repairs to roof structure. Re-slating using asbestos-cement slate. Treatment of extensive dry rot. Internal re-plastering. Repairs to decorative plasterwork. Professional fees.
Approximate cost of work: £37,211. Carried out in 1978.
Architects: Ferguson & McIlveen, Belfast.
Roof work by: Down Building Services, Holywood.
Timber treatment by: Radication Ltd., Dunmurry, Belfast.
Specialist plasterwork by: Alexander Law, Belfast.

PHASES TWO AND THREE
Recipient of grant: Montalto Estates Ltd.,

PHASE TWO – LADY'S SITTING ROOM
Grant assistance of £190 given towards: Restoration of lady's sitting room.
Approximate cost of work: £479. Carried out in 1981.
Painting by: William Dobbin, Ballynahinch.

PHASE THREE – DRY ROT REINSTATEMENT
Grant assistance of £27,000 given towards: Re-roofing of south-west corner of building using natural slate. Replacement of structural supports over openings. External re-rendering. Replacement sash windows in original style. Treatment of extensive dry rot. Internal re-plastering. Professional fees.
Approximate cost of work: £68,109. Carried out in 1982 and 1983.
Architects: Hobart & Heron, Belfast.
Contractor: Fairley Bros., Ballynahinch.

King's Castle, Hill Street, Ardglass.

An early-19th century three- and four-storey castellated building on an elevated site. The walls are of blackstone linking two towers, one square and the other octagonal. The building is undergoing a process of gradual restoration following severe fire damage in 1980.
Recipient of grant: Mr. & Mrs. C. Ward.
Grant assistance of £5,000 given towards: Repairs to chimneys. Repairs to roof structure. Re-slating using natural slate. Replacement leadwork, including tower roof. Replacement metal rainwater goods. Re-pointing of stonework. Repairs to external render. Replacement windows in original style. Professional fees.
Approximate cost of work: £60,000. Carried out in 1983.
Architect: C. J. McCauley, Belfast.
Contractor: Ward Builders, Killough.

Clandeboye House, Clandeboye, Bangor.

A two-storey later-Georgian house designed by Robert Woodgate (Sir John Soane's assistant), informally planned with the main fronts being placed at right angles to each other. The roof is hipped and slated with a parapet gutter behind a low blocking course. Walls are smooth rendered with moulded stalls. Windows have Georgian-glazed sashes. The south entrance front has a four columned, flat roofed portico, a pediment above the three central first floor windows and a canted ground floor bay window to the east side. The east front has a full-height segmental three-bay bow.
Recipient of grant: Clandeboye Estate Co. Ltd.
Grant assistance of £3,800 given towards: Repairs to chimneys. Preliminary investigative contract involving stripping and re-slating one section of roof.
Approximate cost of work: £15,000. Carried out in 1981 and 1982.
Architects: Caldwell Deane Partnership, Belfast.
Quantity Surveyors: Ian Kirkpatrick, Bell & Partners, Bangor.
Contractor: D. J. Dickson Ltd., Crossgar.

Portaferry House, Portaferry.

Located in beautiful parkland overlooking Strangford Lough, the house, built in 1821 to designs by William Farrell comprises a five-bay, three-storey central block with slightly projecting canted two-storey end bays of the same height. The entrance is contained in a curious projecting porch faced with six Ionic columns. The roof is slated and hipped over the end bays, walls are smooth rendered with moulded dressings and the windows, tripartite above the central porch, have

168

Georgian-glazed sashes. The house is unoccupied.

Recipient of grant: Trustees of Nugent Estate.

PHASE ONE

Grant assistance of £10,400 given towards: Treatment of extensive dry rot. Repairs to chimneys.

Approximate cost of work: £26,011. Carried out in 1981.

Contractor: Orion Construction Ltd., Greyabbey.

Timber Treatment by: Timbercare (N.I.), Lisburn.

PHASE TWO

Grant assistance of £3,950 given towards: Repairs to leadwork.

Approximate cost of work: £9,973. Carried out in 1982.

Contractor: Timbercare (N.I.), Lisburn.

Ballywalter Park, Ballywalter.

A superb Italianate, three-storey mansion, six bays by four with single-storey balustraded wings bowed at their west ends, designed by Charles Lanyon and built about 1845. The roof is slated and hipped, with tall moulded chimneys and deep, bracketted, eaves. Walls are smooth rendered with moulded enrichments to quoins and windows. A grand balustraded and columned portico, three bays wide, projects on the east front. A single-storey sandstone conservatory wing, with cast-iron framed glass dome, extends to the north-west.

Recipient of grant: The Lord Dunleath.

PHASE ONE

Grant assistance of £79,480 given towards:

Conservatory, Ballywalter Park, Ballywalter.

Repairs to chimneys. Roof repairs. Replacement leadwork. Lining of stone perimeter eaves gutters with glass-reinforced plastic. Repairs to external render including moulded details. Treatment of extensive dry rot and subsequent reinstatement. Restoration of library ceiling. Repairs to conservatory including re-glazing with curved glass. External redecoration. Professional fees.

Approximate cost of work: £226,445. Carried out from 1980 to 1982.

Architects: Robert McKinstry & Melvyn Brown, Belfast.

Quantity Surveyors: Hastings & Baird, Belfast.

Contractor: Crawford & Laird, Belfast.

Timber treatment by: Radication Ltd., Dunmurry, Belfast.

Plastering by: Nichol Plaster Mouldings, Belfast.

Painting by: John Hamilton (Decorators) Ltd., Newtownabbey.

Glazing by: Robert Wilson, Ballymena.

PHASE TWO

Grant assistance of £5,000 given towards: Repairs to chimneys. Repairs to leadwork. Replacement metal rainwater goods. Repairs to external render. Treatment of wood rot and subsequent reinstatement. Minor repairs to stable roof.

Approximate cost of work: £17,584. Carried out in 1982 and 1983.

Architects: Robert McKinstry & Melvyn Brown, Belfast.

Quantity Surveyors: Hastings & Baird, Belfast.

Contractor: D. R. Martin & Son Ltd., Newtownabbey.

Mount Stewart House, Greyabbey.

An impressive two-storey, Renaissance-style house built from 1840–1850 on the site of an earlier, 18th century house. The slated roof is concealed behind a balustraded parapet and the walls are of dark stone rubble with Scrabo stone dressings. The entrance front has a central two storey pedimented portico with Ionic columns and the end bays, with tripartite windows, are surmounted with pedimented features. The central three bays of the garden front project and are also surmounted by a pediment containing a coat-of-arms in the tympanum. This front is terminated at both ends by full height bows.

Recipient of grant: The National Trust.

Grant assistance of £20,000 given towards: Treatment of extensive dry rot in roof of main house.

Approximate cost of work: £28,175. Carried out in 1981.

Work carried out using direct labour.

Timber treatment by: Radication Ltd., Dunmurry, Belfast.

Colebrook House, Brookeborough.

A large unsophisticated two-storey classical house built around an earlier three-storey house to designs by William Farell. The walls, which were intended to be rendered, are rubble with fine ashlar dressings. The entrance front is a nine-bay, two-storey composition with a Greek Ionic portico.

Recipient of grant: The Hon. Alan Brooke.

Grant assistance of £4,022 given towards: Repairs to entrance portico. Repairs to sash windows. Professional fees.

Approximate cost of work: £10,921. Carried out from 1980 to 1982.

Architects: Storie & Lynch, Enniskillen.

Work carried out using direct labour.

Castle Coole, Enniskillen.

Built between 1790 and 1797 for the first Earl of Belmore, Castle Coole is James Wyatt's finest building. The design is carefully balanced, consisting of a nine-bay, two-storey central block linked to single-storey pavilions by colonnaded wings. The construction is of finely worked smooth ashlar Portland stone. The central block is nine bays wide by two storeys high, the window openings are plain, a four columned Ionic portico projects on the entrance front and on the park side of the house this is answered by a segmental bow with fluted giant columns. The high slated roof can be clearly seen behind the balustrading. The wings are colonnaded on the entrance front and have plain, five-bay walls on the park side. The pavilions each have a large tripartite window sub-divided by Doric columns on the entrance front and Venetian windows to the park front. Much of the fine ashlar stonework has spalled and deteriorated as a result of the rusting of the iron cramps used in the original construction. The stonework is currently being painstakingly restored to its former glory by a team of stone masons specially assembled to carry out the work using Portland stone quarried from the Weston S Quarry in Dorset.

Recipient of grant: The National Trust.

PHASES ONE TO FOUR

Grant assistance of £255,000 given towards: Roof repairs. Cutting out and

Castle Coole, Enniskillen.

replacement of defective stonework. Repairs to windows. Professional fees.

Approximate cost of work: £340,251. Carried out from 1979 to 1982.

Architects: John Storie & Partners, Enniskillen.

Quantity Surveyors: V. B. Evans & Co., Belfast.

Stone repair by: Stone Craft, Annalong.

PHASES FIVE AND SIX

Grant assistance of £10,000 given towards: Roof repairs. Cutting out and replacement of defective stonework. Repairs to windows. Professional fees.

Approximate cost of work: £193,660. Carried out in 1983.

Architects: John Storie & Partners, Enniskillen.

Quantity Surveyors: V. B. Evans & Co., Belfast.

Contractor: H. & J. Martin Ltd., Belfast.

Bellarena, Limavady.

A complex, much altered house possibly dating from the late-17th century. While not presenting a unified appearance, it is a building with many attractive features. The main front is a five-bay, two-storey block of coursed basalt, galleted, and with sandstone dressings. An ungainly Venetian window at first floor level protrudes into the pediment above. At ground floor level the semi-circular sandstone porch was added by Lanyon to accommodate a double return staircase as part of his generally inappropriate remodelling of the interior. Other elevations are equally curious. Bellarena possesses one of the most complete sets of 19th century farm buildings. The house has been gradually restored from near abandonment.

Recipient of grant: Mr. R. J. G. Heygate.

Grant assistance of £316 given towards: Repairs to leadwork.

Approximate cost of work: £633. Carried out in 1975.

Contractor: D. Mullan, Limavady.

Grant assistance of £3,993 given towards: Repairs to chimneys. Roof repairs. Repairs to staircase. Repairs to windows. Treatment of woodworm. Replacement of drawing room ceiling. Structural repairs to outbuildings. Replacement external doors in original style in courtyard.

Approximate cost of work: £7,187. Carried out in 1977.

Contractor: Dickie & Hamilton, Coleraine, and work carried out using direct labour.

Timber treatment by: Rentokil Ltd., Belfast.

Grant assistance of £1,753 given towards: Replacement leadwork including dormers to rear courtyard. Repairs to rainwater goods. Redecoration of drawing room.

Approximate cost of work: £7,641. Carried out in 1978.

Interior design: David Mlinaric Ltd., London.

Bellarena, Limavady.

Contractor: Dickie & Hamilton, Coleraine.
Painting by: Hargan & Tosh, Coleraine.

Drenagh, 17 Dowland Road, Limavady.

Charles Lanyon's first large country house commission. Built in 1836 on the site of an earlier house dating from the 1730's. The house is neo classical two storeys of finely detailed ashlar sandstone with three different main elevational treatments. A balustraded parapet conceals the roof. The interior is planned around a large central hall, lit by a circular flat leaded light.

Recipient of grant: Mrs. P. M. Walsh.

PHASE ONE
Grant assistance of £263 given towards: Repairs to leadwork.
Approximate cost of work: £640. Carried out in 1976.
Contractor: Dickie & Hamilton, Coleraine.

PHASE TWO
Grant assistance of £1,400 given towards: Repairs to chimneys. Roof repairs. Repairs to rainwater goods. Stonework repairs. Redecoration of remedial items.
Approximate cost of work: £2,868. Carried out in 1978.
Contractor: Dickie & Hamilton, Coleraine.

PHASE THREE
Grant assistance of £250 given towards: Repairs to leadwork including clock tower.
Approximate cost of work: £513. Carried out in 1980.
Contractor: Dickie & Hamilton, Coleraine.

PHASE FOUR
Grant assistance of £680 given towards: Treatment of wood rot and subsequent reinstatement.
Approximate cost of work: £1,363. Carried out in 1980.
Contractor: Dickie & Hamilton, Coleraine.

PHASE FIVE
Grant assistance of £3,800 given towards: Repairs to leadwork. Treatment of extensive dry rot. Repairs to internal plasterwork.
Approximate cost of work: £7,615. Carried out in 1981.
Contractor: William Douglas, Limavady.
Timber treatment by: Rentokil Ltd., Belfast.

Bellaghy Castle, Deerpark Road, Bellaghy.

A long two-storey, seven-bay house with rendered front and harled and whitened rear. The castle was originally built by the Vintners' Company and was reconstructed by the Earl Bishop of Derry in 1791 after having been destroyed by fire in 1642. Of the original building, the south-east tower and look-out tower survive. The entrance door with decorative fanlight and sidelights is contained within a porch.

Mansions and Castles

Recipient of grant: Dr. F. De V. Thomas.
Grant assistance of £126 given towards: Repairs to windows.
Approximate cost of work: £334. Carried out in 1978.
Work carried out using direct labour.

Lissan House, Cookstown.

The original house which was built about 1690 was enlarged in 1800 when the single-storey octagonal drawing room was added and again in 1870 when the staircase hall was remodelled and the massive porte cochère and round clock tower were added. The main nine-bay, three-storey front is rendered, with a variety of window types.
Recipient of grant: Lady V. L. Staples.
Grant assistance of £1,430 given towards: Repairs to leadwork. Repairs to rainwater goods. Replacement casement windows.
Approximate cost of work: £4,089. Carried out in 1980 and 1981.
Contractor: Benson Bros. (Cookstown) Ltd., Cookstown.

Killymoon Castle, Cookstown.

On the north bank of the Ballinderry River, Killymoon is one of John Nash's earliest and best country houses in the picturesque style. The house was built in 1803 on the site of an earlier house which was destroyed by fire. Nash used a variety of features to create his house including a two-storey porte cochère flanked by octagonal turrets, various crenellated towers and a six-light window of Norman interface arcading. The large vaulted entrance hall is dramatically approached by a narrow staircase. The house is being progressively restored.
Recipient of grant: Mr. T. J. Coulter.
Grant assistance of £3,940 given towards: Roof repairs. Repairs to windows. Repairs to doors and internal joinery work. Repairs to internal plasterwork. (Cost of materials only, grant aided).
Approximate cost of work: not known. Carried out from 1976 to 1982.
Work carried out using direct and own labour.

Baronscourt House, Newtownstewart.

The house built about 1780 to designs by George Stewart has been remodelled on a number of occasions in the course of its history, by Sir John Soane and his assistant Robert Woodgate, by William Vitruvius Morrison and finally, in 1947, by Sir Albert Richardson. The house is one of the grandest neo-classical compositions in Ireland. The north front has a central Ionic tetrastyle and is terminated by two-storey projecting pavilions. The seven-bay, two-storey south front has a shallow central pediment with urn finials and four-bay flanking wings with cornice hoods to ground floor windows and lugged architraves to the first floor windows. The sumptuous interior is almost entirely as designed by Morrison.
Recipient of grant: Abercorn Estates.

PHASE ONE – SOUTH FRONT
Grant assistance of £1,515 given towards: Replacement of defective sandstone dressings to south front windows.
Approximate cost of work: £3,029. Carried out in 1977.
Quantity Surveyors: Ogilby & McCutcheon, Belfast.

Contractor: Jack Lynch, Castlederg.

PHASE TWO – ROOF AND LIBRARY
Grant assistance of £9,620 given towards: Repairs to part of roof structure, slates and leadwork. Repairs to Brown Library ceiling subsequent to dry rot outbreak.
Approximate cost of work: £19,868. Carried out in 1979.
Architects: Building Design Partnership, Belfast.
Contractor: Jack Lynch, Castlederg.
Timber treatment by: Protim Services, Lisburn.
Plastering by: Alexander Law, Belfast.

PHASE THREE – MAIN STAIRCASE
Grant assistance of £1,340 given towards: Repairs to cornice subsequent to treatment of dry rot in main staircase.
Approximate cost of work: £2,685. Carried out in 1978.
Timber treatment by: Rentokil Ltd., Belfast.
Plastering by: Alexander Law, Belfast.

PHASE FOUR – PORTICO
Grant assistance of £1,700 given towards: Repairs to portico.
Approximate cost of work: £3,400. Carried out in 1980.
Contractor: Jack Lynch, Castlederg.

PHASE FIVE – EAST WING
Grant assistance of £2,910 given towards: Repairs to roof. Reinstatement subsequent to treatment of dry rot.
Approximate cost of work: £5,824. Carried out in 1982.
Contractor: Jack Lynch & Sons (Contracts) Ltd., Castlederg.
Timber treatment by: J. P. Timber Services Ltd., Belfast.

Bridges, Boundaries and Estate Buildings

Holy Trinity Church, Main Street, Portrush.

The boundary wall railings and gates to the church which dates from 1841.

Recipient of grant: The Church of Ireland, Ballywillan Parish.

Grant assistance of £1,169 given towards: Re-rendering of walls. Provision of new copings. Provision of new gates and railings to match original.

Approximate cost of work: £3,507. Carried out in 1981 and 1982.

Contractor: Smyth Steel Ltd., Blackhill, Coleraine.

Dr. Adam Clarke Memorial Methodist Church, Causeway Street, Portrush.

The boundary wall, gates and railings to the church which was built in 1887.

Recipient of grant: Portrush Methodist Church.

Grant assistance of £2,000 given towards: Removal of deteriorated sandstone plinth wall and replacement with pre-cast concrete replica. Removal of railings and replacement in replicas.

Approximate cost of work: £6,000. Carried out in 1980 and 1981.

Contractor: A. Cusick (Contractors) Ltd., Armoy.

Replacement railings by: General Engineers, Kilrea.

Coach House, Glenarm Castle, Glenarm.

Recipient of grant: Antrim Estates Co.

Grant assistance of £5,100 given towards: The taking down and re-construction of the rear wall of the coach house which had become unstable.

Approximate cost of work: £17,616. Carried out in 1980 and 1981.

Structural Engineers: Stephen R. Farrell, Ballymena, Belfast and Londonderry.

Contractor: David Patton & Sons (N.I.) Ltd., Ballymena.

Brocklamont House, 2 Old Galgorm Road, Ballymena.

Boundary wall to house.

Recipient of grant: Mr. L. Glynn.

Grant assistance of £1,360 given towards: Re-building of stone boundary wall.

Approximate cost of work: £4,079. Carried out in 1982.

Contractor: Antrim Construction Co. Ltd., Antrim.

Terrace and Camelia House, Shane's Castle, Randalstown.

The terrace, some walls and Camelia House were all that had been completed when work was brought to an abrupt halt when the 1780 O'Neill castle was destroyed by fire in 1816 during the execution of a grandiose remodelling designed by John Nash. The Camelia House has an arcade of thirteen semi-circular-headed windows with a castellated parapet and small square terminal towers.

Recipient of grant: The Lord O'Neill.

PHASE ONE – REPAIRS TO TERRACE

Grant assistance of £2,312 given towards: Re-pointing and capping of terrace wall.

Approximate cost of work: £4,625. Carried out in 1975.

Contractor: J. Rainey & Co., Belfast.

PHASE TWO – REPAIRS TO CONSERVATORY AND TOWER

Grant assistance of £2,931 given towards: Conservatory – Repairs to roof

Clock Tower, The Stables, Castle Upton, Templepatrick.

175

structure. Replacement metal rainwater goods. Repairs to windows. External redecoration. Repairs to internal plasterwork. Tower – Replacement timber floors. Provision of staircase.

Approximate cost of work: £5,735. Carried out in 1975 and 1976.

Contractor: Derek A. Weir, Randalstown.

Mill at Newmill, Hollybank Road, Ballywee, Doagh, Ballyclare.

A derelict water powered mill complex.

Recipient of grant: Mr. J. A. Murphy.

Grant assistance of £375 given towards: Repairs to mill race walls.

Approximate cost of work: £375. Carried out in 1980.

Work carried out using own labour.

Gateway and walling of Quaker graveyard, Muckamore.

A rubble blackstone boundary wall and inscribed arched gateway to a Quaker graveyard founded about 1670 and referred to in Alexander Irvine's 'My Lady of the Chimney Corner'.

Recipient of grant: Mr. L. Reford.

Grant assistance of £400 given towards: Repairs to wall and archway. Re-painting of gates.

Approximate cost of work: £1,200. Carried out in 1980.

Contractor: Bruce Contractors, Lisburn.

The Stables, Castle Upton, Templepatrick.

The stables at Castle Upton built in 1788–9 for Viscount Templeton are the finest surviving example of Robert

Adam's castle style applied to office buildings. The main yard is entered through an impressive battlemented archway flanked by four bold turrets; opposite is a towered archway leading to the second yard. Each corner has an irregular octagonal tower. The walls are of coarse basalt and a unique feature is the use of specially moulded brick to reproduce in miniature Adam's distinctive machiolated cornice on the corner and archway towers.

Recipient of grant: Sir Robin Kinahan.

PHASE ONE – RESTORATION OF CLOCK TOWER

Grant assistance of £5,179 given towards: Repairs to weathervane. Replacement metal rainwater goods. Repairs to stonework. Repairs to windows. Repairs to internal plasterwork. Repairs to internal joinery. Repairs to timber floors. Professional fees.

Approximate cost of work: £10,266. Carried out in 1976 and 1977.

Architects: Isherwood & Ellis, Belfast and Ballymena.

Quantity Surveyors: V. B. Evans & Co., Belfast and Coleraine.

Contractor: W. J. Hynds & Son Ltd., Belfast.

PHASE TWO – ADAM HOUSE

Grant assistance of £1,537 given towards: Roof repairs. Repairs to windows. Repairs to internal plasterwork. Repairs to timber floors. Professional fees.

Approximate cost of work: £7,682. Carried out in 1977 and 1978.

Architects: Isherwood & Ellis, Belfast and Ballymena.

Contractor: T. J. Hanna, Antrim.

Roof work by: McMahon (Roofing) & Co., Belfast.

PHASE THREE – ADAM HOUSE

Grant assistance of £580 given towards: Roof repairs.

Approximate cost of work: £1,169. Carried out in 1981.

Contractor: F. B. McKee & Co. Ltd., Belfast.

Tassagh Viaduct.

A disused railway viaduct over the valley of the Callan River. It is about 176 metres long and of a minimum height of 20 metres. There are 11 brick arches on tall battered concrete piers. The parapet and dressings are in sandstone.

Recipient of grant: Northern Ireland Transport Holding Co.

Grant assistance of £289 given towards: Essential structural re-pointing.

Approximate cost of work: £1,157. Carried out in 1976.

Contractor: S. & G. Lester, Armagh.

Ballyroney Presbyterian Church, Ballyroney.

Boundary gates and railings.

Recipient of grant: Ballyroney Presbyterian Church.

Grant assistance of £92 given towards: Preparation and re-painting of gates and railings. (Materials only).

Approximate cost of work: £92. Carried out in 1981.

Work carried out using own labour.

Silcock's Mill, Marybrook House, Raleagh Road, Crossgar.

An early-19th century flax and corn mill complex.

Recipient of grant: Mr. J. Lewis-Crosby.

Bridges, Boundaries and Estate Buildings

Silcock's Mill, Marybrook House, Crossgar.

Grant assistance of £2,200 given towards: Restoration of mill complex and machinery including kiln, eel trap, weir, sluices, mill pond, scutch mill and corn mill. Roof repairs. Replacement floors. Replacement metal rainwater goods. External re-rendering. Replacement sash windows in original style. Repairs to internal plasterwork.

Approximate cost of work: £10,980. Carried out between 1977 and 1980.

Work carried out using direct labour and International Voluntary Service Labour.

Ballee House, Downpatrick.

A range of one- and two-storey stone outbuildings with slated roofs.

Recipient of grant: Mrs. J. C. Maxwell.

Grant assistance of £2,430 given towards: Re-roofing using natural slate subsequent to fire damage.

177

Approximate cost of work: £13,798. Carried out in 1983.

Contractor: Milligan Bros., Killough.

5 Palatine Square, Killough.

The outbuildings to a fine late-18th or early-19th century rectory.

Recipient of grant: Mr. & Mrs. P. J. Conway.

Grant assistance of £340 given towards: Construction of a new garage in place of the original outbuilding with a sympathetic treatment of the new frontage and including the repair of the gable and quoins of the main house.

Approximate cost of work: £3,144. Carried out in 1979.

Contractor: Milligan Bros., Killough.

Railway Station Tower, Railway Station, Newcastle.

A squat square tower centrally positioned on the frontage of the former railway station built in 1905 probably to designs by W. H. Morris, the railway company's assistant engineer and now much mutilated. The tower is of glazed red brick with a blank upper storey with four large clock faces above, bartizans on the corners and an octagonal copper spire with a weathervane.

Recipient of grant: Mr. W. F. Wilson.

Grant assistance of £250 given towards: Roof repairs. Treatment of wood rot and subsequent reinstatement.

Approximate cost of work: £803. Carried out in 1978.

Contractor: Joseph McClune & Son, Dundrum.

Timber treatment by: Timbertreat Services Ltd., Belfast.

Entrance Gates, Portaferry House, Church Street, Portaferry.

A gatescreen comprising cast-iron railings and gates and two square rusticated stone piers with fluted frieze, projecting cornice and surmounted by knops.

Recipient of grant: Ards Borough Council.

Grant assistance of £1,650 given towards: Repairs to stonework involving glass-reinforced plastic surface application. Repairs to fence and gates. Professional fees.

Approximate cost of work: £6,971. Carried out in 1982.

Architects: McAdam Design, Newtownards.

Stone repair by: H. L. Stuart-Cox & Co. Ltd.

Ornamental bridges, Ballywalter Park, Ballywalter.

Two bridges with classically detailed balustraded parapets.

Recipient of grant: Dunleath Estates.

Grant assistance of £400 given towards: Manufacture of ornamental balustrades for bridges.

Approximate cost of work: £1,300. Carried out in 1980.

Architects: Robert McKinstry & Melvyn Brown, Belfast.

Contractor: Nicholl Plaster Mouldings, Belfast.

Stables, Jamestown House, (Magheracros House), Ballinamallard.

A pleasant early-19th century house on the Ballinamallard River. The stables

Ornamental Bridge, Ballywalter Park, Ballywalter.

Bridges, Boundaries and Estate Buildings

Sphinx at Gate Lodge, Caledon House, Caledon.

were built in 1837 and comprise two-storey stone outbuildings with pedimented central archway around a courtyard.

Recipient of grant: Col. J. C. O'Dwyer.

Grant assistance of £1,200 given towards: Roof repairs. Repairs to stonework. Repairs to windows. Replacement external doors in original style including doors to carriage arch. Redecoration of remedial items. Re-location of overhead cables.

Approximate cost of work: £4,936. Carried out in 1978 and 1979.

Contractor: Elliott Construction, Enniskillen.

Ballylaggan Reformed Presbyterian Church, Aghadowey.

Stone boundary wall.

Recipient of grant: Ballylaggan Reformed Presbyterian Church.

Grant assistance of £860 given towards: Re-pointing of perimeter stone wall.

Approximate cost of work: £2,597. Carried out in 1981.

Contractor: S. J. Linton, Garvagh.

Ringsend Presbyterian Church, Aghadowey.

The boundary wall to the church built in 1897.

Recipient of grant: Ringsend Presbyterian Church.

Grant assistance of £425 given towards: Re-pointing of stonework.

Approximate cost of work: £1,265. Carried out in 1980.

Contractor: W. J. McIntyre, Coleraine.

White Bridge, Baronscourt Estate, Newtownstewart.

Recipient of grant: Abercorn Estates.

Grant assistance of £1,050 given towards: Repairs to bridge.

Approximate cost of work: £3,170. Carried out in 1980.

Contractor: Jack Lynch, Castlederg.

Sphinx at Gate Lodge, Caledon House, Caledon.

One of two Coade stone sphinxes sitting on large, flat panelled piers to the estate entrance gates.

Recipient of grant: Caledon Estates Co.

Grant assistance of £70 given towards: In-situ repair of sphinx.

Approximate cost of work: £199. Carried out in 1980.

Contractor: A. C. Simpson & Partners Ltd., Armagh.

Stables, Caledon House, Caledon.

Built in the late-18th century probably to designs by Thomas Cooley who was also responsible for the design of the core of the main house. The stables consist of a spacious cobbled courtyard enclosed by a range of outbuildings. The central three bays of the nine-bay south-facing entrance front project and contain a tall arched carriageway with a pediment and bell cupola over. Six arcaded coach houses face the entrance across the courtyard. Walls are of coursed rubble with ashlar quoins and architraves.

Recipient of grant: Caledon Estates Co.

Grant assistance of £503 given towards: Repairs to louvres of cupola. Re-pointing of stonework. Replacement leadwork.

Approximate cost of work: £1,509. Carried out in 1979.

Contractor: A. C. Simpson & Partners Ltd., Armagh.

Conservation Areas

Grant-aid to unlisted buildings in Conservation Areas

The Department of the Environment, through its Historic Monuments and Buildings Branch is not only empowered to list individual buildings but can also, where a whole street, village or urban area has a visual integrity of architectural importance, declare a Conservation Area. Inevitably, there are listed buildings within Conservation Areas, and grant-aid is allocated to them in the normal way but there are also grants available to unlisted buildings within these areas where such buildings though modest, help to maintain the visual continuity of the streetscape.

It is relatively straightforward to encourage an owner to take pride in maintaining an attractive individual listed building, but it is much more difficult to engender a collective pride amongst all the inhabitants of a Conservation Area. A Conservation Area works best when there is local awareness of and support for, those qualities which have made it worthy of such a designation. If these do not exist then not only are individual local developers less aware of the necessity to maintain the visual integrity of the area, because of lack of local discussion, but the more unscrupulous amongst them will not feel any social pressure to conform. Further, if local residents feel that their Conservation Area is imposed by outsiders they may even feel antagonistic towards the idea. Sometimes in such cases a Conservation Area is seen as an impediment to competitive commercial development – such development being envisaged as bright and modern, and conservation being imagined as its antithesis. Present legislation permits tight control of development in these areas, but until a positive attitude towards conservation is fostered in the population by education through the media, and an awareness of the value of our traditional streetscape and the success of conservation in other countries has grown, some statutory Conservation Areas will continue to be controversial and difficult to maintain.

Conservation Areas are not museums; they all form part of living communities, growing, developing and evolving. Change is inevitable. Buildings are renovated or demolished and rebuilt. The difficulty then arises of deciding what style is appropriate to the new or renovated property. There is a whole spectrum of ideas on what is an appropriate appearance for new work in a Conservation Area, from a fully researched reproduction of the exterior of the building as it was one hundred or so years ago, to the use of 'Olde Englishe' plastic lettering on an illuminated sign. Moreover, the degree of care taken in

Portaferry Conservation Area.

181

Conservation Areas

designing the work varies a great deal. A few owners are prepared to invest the time, interest and effort necessary to create work of taste and sensitivity; most are not. It is significant to note that only one in seven grant-aided schemes of non-listed buildings in Conservation Areas had the benefit of a chartered architect. Not all schemes were large enough to require such advice but most would have benefited significantly as a result. Most new work in Conservation Areas, particularly to shopfronts, is an amalgam of plate glass, aluminium and ill-proportioned plastic signs, together with pebble-dash and flat roofs.

In spite of these problems there are now 22 Conservation Areas in Northern Ireland, some very successful, with much local support and interest, and one or two losing the battle against the Philistines.

Conservation Areas designated

Gracehill	26 March 1975	Draperstown	26 October 1979
Cushendall	6 October 1975	Cushendun	13 June 1980
Hillsborough	25 June 1976	Moneymore	12 September 1980
Londonderry		Carnlough	30 January 1981
(Central)	25 February 1977	Killough	27 March 1982
Sion Mills	25 March 1977	Armagh	1 July 1981
Carrickfergus	10 June 1977	Portaferry	11 March 1983
Antrim (Riverside)	30 September 1977	Newry	20 May 1983
Londonderry		Bessbrook	14 October 1983
(Clarendon Street)	10 February 1978	Moira	9 December 1983
Glenarm	12 May 1978	Moy	24 May 1984
Rostrevor	9 February 1979	Caledon	24 May 1984

Grant-aid has been paid to just under 100 schemes involving individual unlisted buildings in Conservation Areas. In almost all cases the grant-aid is for 'extra-over' costs where a particular shape, material or style required to render the work sympathetic to the streetscape, is more expensive than might otherwise be the case.

For instance, where natural slate is used instead of asbestos or concrete tiles or where a pitched roof is used instead of a flat one or where vertical sliding sash windows are used instead of the casement or night-vent type.

Again, a written description of all of these schemes appears but, as in the preceding section on grant-aid to listed buildings it has not been possible to photograph all schemes. Because of the higher proportion of this type of scheme in Hillsborough, Killough and Antrim (Riverside) these three areas are reviewed in depth.

Conservation Areas

21 Joymount, Carrickfergus.

Two-storey end-of-terrace dwelling.

Recipient of grant: Mr. James R. Beattie.

Grant assistance of £360 given towards: Repairs to external render. Repairs to decorative plasterwork. Repairs to rainwater goods. Repairs to chimney. Replacement external doors in original style.

Approximate cost of work: £1,090. Carried out in 1980.

Contractor: Kearney Builders, Newtownabbey.

22 Joymount, Carrickfergus.

Recipient of grant: Mr. Robert Harpur.

Grant assistance of £280 given towards: Repairs to decorative plasterwork. Repairs to rainwater goods. Repairs to windows. Repairs to panelled entrance door. Redecoration of remedial items. Treatment of woodworm. Treatment of wood rot.

Approximate cost of work: £846. Carried out in 1980.

Contractor: Kearney Builders, Newtownabbey.

19 High Street, Carrickfergus.

Three-storey terrace property.

Recipient of grant: Reid Partnership Ltd.

Grant assistance of £5,500 given towards: Re-roofing using natural slate. Rebuilding of chimneys. Replacement sash windows in original style.

Total cost of grant-eligible items: £9,193. Carried out in 1980 and 1981.

Agent: Reid Partnership Ltd., Carrickfergus.

Contractor: Reid Partnership Ltd., Carrickfergus.

21 West Street, Carrickfergus.

Three-storey commercial terrace property.

Recipient of grant: Mr. Robert McFadden.

Grant assistance of £450 given towards: New shopfront.

Approximate cost of work: £1,577. Carried out in 1983.

Agent: J. Gilbert, Carrickfergus.

Contractor's name not recorded.

Carrickfergus Conservation Area.

Conservation Areas

The Cedars, Riverside, Antrim.

Two-storey early 19th century detached residence.

Recipient of grant: Mr. James John Bailie.

Grant assistance of £3,070 given towards: Replacement sash windows in original style.

Approximate cost of work: £3,239. Carried out in 1980 and 1981.

Contractor: David Wilson, Dunadry.

Joinery by: Samuel Overend, Magherafelt.

8 Riverside, Antrim.

Two-storey terrace dwelling.

Recipient of grant: Mr. Bernard Totten.

Grant assistance of £360 given towards: Sympathetic treatment of street elevation as part of general improvement scheme.

Further financial assistance received from: Northern Ireland Housing Executive.

Approximate cost of work: £6,077. Carried out in 1980 and 1981.

Work carried out using direct labour.

Plastering by: Johnston & McCann, Randalstown.

Joinery by: Antrim Joinery Works, Antrim.

14 Riverside, Antrim.

Two-storey terrace dwelling.

Recipient of grant: Mr. P. Cummings.

Grant assistance of £500 given towards: Sympathetic treatment of street elevation as part of general improvement scheme.

Further financial assistance received from: Northern Ireland Housing Executive.

Approximate cost of work: £8,429.

Carried out in 1983.

Contractor: T & R Builders, Ballymena.

17 Riverside, Antrim.

A pre-1857 five-bay, two-storey house pebble-dashed and set back from the street.

Recipient of grant: Mr. Henry J. Gribben.

Grant assistance of £5,677 given towards: Sympathetic treatment of external appearance of conversion of large house into five flats.

Further financial assistance received from: Northern Ireland Housing Executive.

Approximate cost of work: £55,540. Carried out in 1982 and 1983.

Agent: Grace K. O'Neill, Magherafelt.

Work carried out using direct labour.

Antrim (Riverside) Conservation Area – 'Riverside House'.

31 Riverside, Antrim.

Two-storey terrace dwelling.

Recipient of grant: Mr. Roger Mankelow.

Grant assistance of £276 given towards: Sympathetic treatment of street elevation as part of general improvement scheme.

Further financial assistance received from: Northern Ireland Housing Executive.

Approximate cost of work: £8,650. Carried out in 1981.

Agent: Stanley Rankin, Randalstown.

Contractor: Douglas Milligan, address unknown.

33 Riverside, Antrim.

A two-storey terrace dwelling.

Recipient of grant: Mr. Thomas McMillan.

Grant assistance of £1,150 given towards: Sympathetic treatment of street elevation as part of general improvement scheme.

Further financial assistance received from: Northern Ireland Housing Executive.

Approximate cost of work: £10,210. Carried out in 1980 and 1981.

Work carried out using own labour.

35 Riverside, Antrim.

Two-storey terrace dwelling.

Recipient of grant: Mr. Albert Anderson.

Grant assistance of £650 given towards: Sympathetic treatment of street elevation as part of general improvement scheme.

Further financial assistance received from: Northern Ireland Housing Executive.

33 Riverside, Antrim.

Approximate cost of work: £11,000. Carried out in 1982.

36 Riverside, Antrim.

Two-storey terrace dwelling.

Recipient of grant: Mr. John Blair.

Grant assistance of £1,016 given towards: Sympathetic treatment of street elevation as part of general improvement scheme.

Further financial assistance received from: Northern Ireland Housing Executive.

Approximate cost of work: £8,500. Carried out in 1980 and 1981.

Architect: Mairs & Wray, Crumlin.

Contractor: Beeline Timber Engineering, Lisburn.

43/45 Riverside, Antrim.

Two-storey terrace dwelling.

Recipient of grant: Mr. Richard Shannon.

Grant assistance of £105 given towards: Replacement panelled entrance door.

Approximate cost of work: £318. Carried out in 1982.

Contractor: W. J. Hogg, Doagh.

69 Riverside, Antrim.

Two-storey terrace dwelling.

Recipient of grant: Mr. James Loughlin.

Grant assistance of £352 given towards: Sympathetic treatment of street elevation as part of general improvement scheme.

Further financial assistance received from: Northern Ireland Housing Executive.

Approximate cost of work: £9,144. Carried out in 1980 and 1981.

Contractor: Alan Hogg & Son, Antrim.

72/74 Riverside, Antrim.

Two-storey terrace dwelling.

Recipient of grant: Mr. Thomas Moore.

Grant assistance of £838 given towards: Sympathetic treatment of street elevation as part of general improvement scheme.

Further financial assistance received from: Northern Ireland Housing Executive.

Approximate cost of work: £11,015. Carried out in 1982 and 1983.

Contractor: Sam Jackson, Newtownabbey.

88 Riverside, Antrim.

Two-storey terrace dwelling.

Recipient of grant: Mr. & Mrs. Ernest Bates.

Grant assistance of £667 given towards: Sympathetic treatment of street elevation as part of general improvement scheme.

Further financial assistance received from: Northern Ireland Housing Executive.

Approximate cost of work: £10,000. Carried out in 1982.

Agent: Jackie Milliken, Ballymena.

Contractor: McCaughey & Kearney, Ballymena.

90 Riverside, Antrim.

Two-storey terrace dwelling.

Recipient of grant: Mr. Paul Lowry.

Grant assistance of £366 given towards: Sympathetic treatment of street elevation as part of general improvement scheme.

Further financial assistance received from: Northern Ireland Housing Executive.

Approximate cost of work: £8,990. Carried out in 1981.

Contractor: Beare Enterprises, Newtownabbey.

4 Barrack Court, Hillsborough.

Two-storey mews dwelling.

Recipient of grant: Mr. E. C. B. Gilman.

Grant assistance of £2,205 given towards: Sympathetic treatment of street elevation as part of general improvement scheme.

Further financial assistance received from: Northern Ireland Housing Executive.

Approximate cost of work: £22,269. Carried out in 1982.

Hillsborough Conservation Area: Lisburn Street.

Architect: Raymond C. Leith, Belfast.

Contractor: A. Cusick Ltd., Armoy.

24 Ballynahinch Street, Hillsborough.

Two-storey mews dwelling.

Recipient of grant: Mrs. May Law.

Grant assistance of £437 given towards: Sympathetic treatment of street elevation as part of general improvement scheme.

Further financial assistance received from: Northern Ireland Housing Executive.

Approximate cost of work: £4,096. Carried out in 1983.

Contractor: W. Hogg, Hillsborough.

Painting by: R. J. Nicholson, Broomhedge.

2 Park Street, Hillsborough.

Three-bay, single-storey terrace dwelling.

Recipient of grant: Mr. Alan Murphy.

Grant assistance of £1,200 given towards: Sympathetic treatment of street elevation as part of general improvement scheme.

Further financial assistance received from: Northern Ireland Housing Executive.

Approximate cost of work: £15,700. Carried out in 1983.

Agent: P. B. McCollam, Hillsborough.

Contractor: Ernest McLaughlin.

9 Lisburn Street, Hillsborough.

Terrace dwelling.

12–14 Lisburn Street, Hillsborough.

Recipient of grant: Mrs. Joyce Green.

Grant assistance of £380 given towards: Sympathetic treatment of street elevation as part of general improvement scheme.

Further financial assistance received from: Northern Ireland Housing Executive.

Approximate cost of work: £3,789. Carried out in 1982.

Contractor: James Walsh, Lisburn.

Painting by: Down Decorators, Hillsborough.

11 Lisburn Street, Hillsborough.

Two-storey terrace property.

Recipient of grant: Sermet (N.I.) Ltd.

Grant assistance of £680 given towards: Sympathetic treatment of street elevation of commercial premises as part of general repairs scheme.

Approximate cost of work: £2,442. Carried out in 1983.

Contractor: James Walsh Builders (N.I.) Ltd., Lisburn.

Painting by: Down Decorators, Hillsborough.

12–14 Lisburn Street, Hillsborough.

Two-storey terrace property.

Recipient of grant: Mr. Verus Reaney.

Grant assistance of £1,375 given towards: Replacement shopfront.

Approximate cost of work: £19,790. Carried out in 1979.

Architects: McKee & Kirk Partnership, Lisburn.

Contractor: Antrim Street Building Works, Lisburn.

37 Lisburn Street, Hillsborough.

Three-bay, two-storey terrace dwelling.

Recipient of grant: Mr. Paul Sinte.

Grant assistance of £1,850 given towards: Treatment of woodworm. Roof repairs. Repairs to chimneys. Repairs to leadwork. Repairs to external render. Replacement sash windows in original style. Replacement external doors in original style. Redecoration of remedial items.

Approximate cost of work: £5,557. Carried out in 1982 and 1983.

Contractor: R. E. Crompton, Ballynahinch.

Painting by: Down Decorators, Hillsborough.

42 Lisburn Street, Hillsborough.

Two-storey terrace dwelling.

Recipient of grant: Mr. A. P. Hunter.

Grant assistance of £670 given towards: Sympathetic treatment of street elevation as part of general improvement scheme.

Further financial assistance received from: Northern Ireland Housing Executive.

Approximate cost of work: £7,012. Carried out in 1980.

Contractor: Lesmar Developments, Hillsborough.

43 Lisburn Street, Hillsborough.

Two-storey, three-bay terrace dwelling.

Recipient of grant: Mr. Thomas Baxter.

Grant assistance of £1,603 given towards: Sympathetic treatment of street elevation as part of general improvement scheme.

Further financial assistance received from: Northern Ireland Housing Executive.

Approximate cost of work: £19,608. Carried out in 1982.

Agent: T. H. Haskins, Lisburn.

Contractor: Alcon Construction, Dromore, Co. Down.

46 Lisburn Street, Hillsborough.

Two-storey terrace dwelling.

Recipient of grant: Mr. William Dewart.

Grant assistance of £380 given towards: Re-slating using natural slate. Replacement metal rainwater goods. External re-rendering.

Approximate cost of work: £1,143. Carried out in 1981.

Contractor: Lesmar Developments Ltd., Hillsborough.

47 Lisburn Street, Hillsborough.

Three-bay, two-storey terrace dwelling.

Recipient of grant: Mrs. Vanessa Walsh.

Grant assistance of £785 given towards: Sympathetic treatment of street elevation as part of general improvement scheme. External redecoration.

Further financial assistance received from: Northern Ireland Housing Executive.

Approximate cost of work: £7,437. Carried out in 1979–1980.

Architect: Mabel Martin, Maze, Lisburn.

Contractor: The Belleisle Building Co. Ltd., Dromore, Co. Down.

Painting by: Down Decorators, Hillsborough.

188   *43 Lisburn Street, Hillsborough.*

7 High Street, Cushendall.

Three-storey terrace dwelling.

Recipient of grant: Mr. Paul McAlister.

Grant assistance of £1,220 given towards: Sympathetic treatment of roof, front elevation and rear extension as part of general improvement scheme to dwelling.

Further financial assistance received from: Northern Ireland Housing Executive.

Approximate cost of work: £13,994. Carried out in 1981 and 1982.

Architects: McCutcheon & Wilkinson, Ballymena.

Contractor: Vincent Hughes, Newtowncrommelin.

22–26 Shipquay Street, Londonderry.

Three-storey terrace commercial property.

Recipient of grant: Northern Counties Properties Ltd.

Grant assistance of £175 given towards: Replacement sash windows in original style.

Approximate cost of work: £1,100. Carried out in 1979.

Architects: Albert Wallace & Partners, Londonderry.

Contractor: E. Doherty & Sons Ltd., Londonderry.

15 Fountain Street, Londonderry.

Three-storey terrace dwelling.

Recipient of grant: Mr. George Wray.

Grant assistance of £240 given towards: Re-slating using natural slate. Replacement metal rainwater goods. Replacement sash windows in original style. Replacement external doors in

Cushendall Conservation Area.

189

original style. Replacement of external finish.

Further financial assistance received from: Northern Ireland Housing Executive.

Approximate cost of work: £7,205. Carried out in 1979.

Contractor: Robert Logue & Son, Londonderry.

3 Artillery Street, Londonderry.

Terrace dwelling.

Recipient of grant: Miss Moya Mullen.

Grant assistance of £166 given towards: Sympathetic treatment of street elevation as part of general improvement scheme.

Further financial assistance received from: Northern Ireland Housing Executive.

Approximate cost of work: £5,500. Carried out in 1979

Contractor's name not recorded.

4 Artillery Terrace, Londonderry.

Two-storey terrace dwelling with dormer.

Recipient of grant: Mr. Terence Mellon.

Grant assistance of £250 given towards: Sympathetic treatment of street elevation as part of general improvement scheme.

Further financial assistance received from: Northern Ireland Housing Executive.

Approximate cost of work: £6,317. Carried out in 1980.

Contractor: S. Johnston, Londonderry.

25 Ferryquay Street, Londonderry.

Terrace property.

Recipient of grant: Mother Superior, Convent of Mercy, Londonderry.

Grant assistance of £600 given towards: Roof repairs.

Londonderry (Central) Conservation Area.

Conservation Areas

Approximate cost of work: £1,785.
Carried out in 1980.

Architect: Charles Hegarty,
Londonderry.

Contractor: McCloskey & Co.,
Londonderry.

3 Orchard Street, Londonderry.

Three-storey terrace dwelling.

Recipient of grant: Mr. Patrick O'Kane.

Grant assistance of £705 given towards:
Sympathetic treatment of street
elevation as part of general
improvement scheme. Treatment of
woodworm. Treatment of wood rot.

Further financial assistance received from:
Northern Ireland Housing Executive.

Approximate cost of work: £9,435.
Carried out in 1983.

Contractor: P. Duffy, Londonderry.

The Gatelodge, The Observatory, College Hill, Armagh.

Stone gate pier adjoining 'gothick' gate
lodge.

Recipient of grant: The Guardians &
Governors of Armagh Observatory.

Grant assistance of £30 given towards:
Repairs to gate pier.

Approximate cost of work: £97. Carried
out in 1981.

Architects: G. P. & R. H. Bell, Lurgan.

Contractor: Armagh Construction,
Armagh.

Footbridge at Sion Mills.

Suspension footbridge spanning the
River Mourne some 600 metres east
of Sion Mills. Built 1931, of 60 metres
span, one metre wide, it consists of
two lattice steelwork towers eight
metres high supporting two suspension

cables which carry two lattice girders
and a timber deck. Funds transferred
from Department of Environment,
Historic Monuments and Buildings
Branch to Department of the
Environment, Roads Service.

Grant assistance of £800 given towards:
Restoration of footbridge.

Further financial assistance received from:
The Department of Agriculture,
Drainage Division and Strabane
District Council.

Approximate cost of work: £24,755.
Carried out in 1979 and 1980.

Structural Engineers: The Department of
the Environment (N.I.).

Contractor: Plant and Machinery
Engineering Co. Ltd., Larne.

67 Main Street, Sion Mills.

Single-storey terrace dwelling with
dormer.

Recipient of grant: Mrs. Jean
McGuinness.

Grant assistance of £78 given towards:
Sympathetic treatment of street
elevation as part of general
improvement scheme.

Further financial assistance received from:
Northern Ireland Housing Executive.

Approximate cost of work: £3,000.
Carried out in 1982.

Agent: D. Doherty.

Work carried out using direct labour.

73 Main Street, Sion Mills.

Single-storey terrace dwelling with
dormer.

Recipient of grant: Mr. William Mullin.

Grant assistance of £309 given towards:
Sympathetic treatment of street
elevation as part of general
improvement scheme.

Armagh Conservation Area.

Further financial assistance received from: Northern Ireland Housing Executive.

Approximate cost of work: £12,270. Carried out in 1982.

Agent: W. J. Mullin, Strabane.

Contractor: Mourne Valley Roofing & Construction Co., Sion Mills.

1 Emerson Terrace, Sion Mills.

Two-storey terrace dwelling.

Recipient of grant: Mr. A. Hyndman.

Grant assistance of £298 given towards: Sympathetic treatment of street elevation as part of general improvement scheme.

Further financial assistance received from: Northern Ireland Housing Executive.

Approximate cost of work: £6,429. Carried out in 1981 and 1982.

Agent: W. Loughlin, Strabane.

Contractor: Kee & Robb, Strabane.

Newry Conservation Area.

1 Baggot Street, Newry.

Two-storey terrace dwelling.

Recipient of grant: Mr. Liam Leddy.

Grant assistance of £500 given towards: Sympathetic treatment of street elevation as part of general improvement scheme.

Further financial assistance received from: Northern Ireland Housing Executive.

Approximate cost of work: £11,500. Carried out in 1982.

Agent: John Collins & Co., Camlough.

Work carried out using direct labour.

7 Kildare Street, Newry.

Three-storey terrace commercial property.

Recipient of grant: Mr. J. C. Smith.

Grant assistance of £1,000 given towards: Sympathetic repair to commercial premises following bomb damage.

Approximate cost of work: £13,108. Carried out in 1982 and 1983.

Agent: B. J. Breen, Bessbrook.

Contractor: Colin Meehan, Newry.

34 Bridge Street, Rostrevor.

Two-storey terrace dwelling.

Recipient of grant: Mrs. P. Watts.

Grant assistance of £443 given towards: Sympathetic treatment of street elevation as part of improvement scheme.

Further financial assistance received from: Northern Ireland Housing Executive.

Approximate cost of work: £7,252. Carried out in 1980 and 1981.

Agent: Cole Partnership, Warrenpoint.

Contractor: John Byrne, Warrenpoint.

57 High Street, Draperstown.

Single-storey terrace dwelling with

Rostrevor Conservation Area.

steep gabled dormer shared with adjoining property.

Recipient of grant: Mr. William Eardley.

Grant assistance of £610 given towards: Sympathetic treatment of street elevation as part of general improvement scheme.

Further financial assistance received from: Northern Ireland Housing Executive.

Approximate cost of work: £10,225. Carried out in 1979–1980.

Agent: J. McKinney, Magherafelt.

Contractor: S. Irvine, Magherafelt.

63 Magherafelt Road, Draperstown.

Single-storey terrace dwelling.

Recipient of grant: Mr. Charles O'Hagan.

Grant assistance of £1,097 given towards: Sympathetic treatment of street elevation as part of general improvement scheme.

Further financial assistance received from: Northern Ireland Housing Executive.

Approximate cost of work: £11,780. Carried out in 1981 and 1982.

Contractor: Michael McBride, Draperstown.

Stone repair by: Dominick Kelly, Draperstown.

Thatching by: S. J. Spillane, Tobermore.

49/51 St. Patrick's Street, Draperstown.

Two-storey terrace property.

Recipient of grant: Mr. Bernard McAuley.

Grant assistance of £1,200 given towards: Sympathetic treatment of street elevation of Public House and General Store as part of renovation scheme.

Draperstown Conservation Area.

Approximate cost of work: £20,000. Carried out in 1982 and 1983.
Agent: R. T. McGuckian & Son, Magherafelt.
Contractor: Higgins Bros., Desertmartin.

22 Castle Street, Glenarm.

Two-storey terrace dwelling.
Recipient of grant: Mr. Fergus Leckie.
Grant assistance of £890 given towards:
External re-rendering. Re-slating using natural slate. Rebuilding of chimney. Replacement metal rainwater goods. Replacement sash windows in original style. Replacement of sheeted front door with five-pane fanlight.
Further financial assistance received from: Northern Ireland Housing Executive.
Approximate cost of work: £8,845. Carried out in 1979.
Contractor: F. McCorry, Larne.

11 Altmore Street, Glenarm.

Two-storey terrace dwelling.
Recipient of grant: Mr. Hamilton Moore.
Grant assistance of £1,730 given towards: Sympathetic treatment of street elevation as part of general improvement scheme.
Further financial assistance received from: Northern Ireland Housing Executive.
Approximate cost of work: £14,125. Carried out in 1980.
Agent: English & Drummond, Larne.
Contractor: G. Millar, Ballymena,

34 Toberwine Street, Glenarm.

Two-storey terrace dwelling.
Recipient of grant: Mr. Alexander Clarke.
Grant assistance of £225 given towards: Sympathetic treatment of street elevation as part of general improvement scheme. Treatment of woodworm. Treatment of wood rot.
Further financial assistance received from: Northern Ireland Housing Executive.
Approximate cost of work: £3,775. Carried out in 1982 and 1983.
Contractor: Charley McAuley, Glenarm.
Timber treatment by: Timbertreat Services Ltd., Belfast.

5 The Cloney, Glenarm.

Two-storey detached dwelling.
Recipient of grant: Mr. Laurence McAllister.
Grant assistance of £1,400 given towards: Re-slating using natural slate. Repairs to chimneys. Repairs to leadwork. Repairs to rainwater goods.

Glenarm Conservation Area.

Approximate cost of work: £4,250.
Carried out in 1981.
Contractor: Arthur Agnew, address
unknown.

4 Main Street, Cushendun.

Two-storey terrace dwelling.
Recipient of grant: The National Trust.
Grant assistance of £2,600 given towards:
Sympathetic treatment of street

Cushendun Conservation Area.

elevation as part of general improvement scheme and internal repairs.

Further financial assistance received from: Northern Ireland Housing Executive.

Approximate cost of work: £17,057. Carried out in 1980 and 1981.

Architect: Gordon McKnight, Holywood.

Contractor: McCarthy & Sharpe, Cushendun.

36 Great James Street, Londonderry.

Three-storey mid-19th century terrace dwelling.

Recipient of grant: Mr. Peter Pyne.

Grant assistance of £120 given towards: Repairs to external render. External redecoration.

Further financial assistance received from: Northern Ireland Housing Executive.

Approximate cost of work: £5,000. Carried out in 1978 and 1979.

Contractor: John Davidson, Londonderry.

58 Great James Street, Londonderry.

Two-storey terrace dwelling.

Recipient of grant: Mr. Tony Crowley.

Grant assistance of £397 given towards: Sympathetic treatment of street elevation as part of general improvement scheme.

Further financial assistance received from: Northern Ireland Housing Executive.

Approximate cost of work: £6,375. Carried out in 1982.

Contractor: W. & J. McMonagle Ltd., Londonderry.

196

68 Great James Street, Londonderry.

Three-storey mid-19th century terrace dwelling.

Recipient of grant: Mr. Colm Doherty.

Grant assistance of £1,600 given towards: Roof repairs. Repairs to chimneys. Repairs to windows. Repairs to panelled entrance door. Repairs to external render.

Approximate cost of work: £5,766. Carried out in 1981 and 1982.

Contractor: Dolan & Johnston, Newbuildings.

74 Great James Street, Londonderry.

Three-storey mid-19th century terrace dwelling.

Recipient of grant: Miss Mary Duffy.

Grant assistance of £800 given towards: Roof repairs.

Approximate cost of work: £2,463.

Carried out in 1981.

Contractor: Foncy Condren, Londonderry.

19 Princes Street, Londonderry.

Three-storey terrace house with dormer.

Recipient of grant: Mr. & Mrs. D. Simpson.

Grant assistance of £403 given towards: Sympathetic treatment of street elevation as part of general improvement scheme.

Further financial assistance received from: Northern Ireland Housing Executive.

Approximate cost of work: £6,556. Carried out in 1981.

Contractor: Village Builders, address unknown.

46 Clarendon Street, Londonderry.

Three-storey mid-19th century terrace dwelling.

Londonderry (Clarendon Street) Conservation Area.

Recipient of grant: Mr. Leslie Cunnah.

Grant assistance of £570 given towards: Treatment of woodworm. Repairs to windows. Repairs to doors. Redecoration of remedial items.

Approximate cost of work: £7,040. Carried out in 1982.

Contractor: Foncy Condren, Londonderry.

45 Smith Street, Moneymore.

Two-storey terrace dwelling.

Recipient of grant: Mr. Samuel Wilson.

Grant assistance of £1,940 given towards: Sympathetic treatment of street elevation as part of general improvement scheme.

Further financial assistance received from: Northern Ireland Housing Executive.

Approximate cost of work: £23,197. Carried out in 1982.

Contractor: Colgan & Whyte, Moneymore.

2 Lakeview, Bessbrook, Newry.

Three-storey, three-bay, semi-detached 19th century villa.

Recipient of grant: Mr. R. J. Corkey.

Grant assistance of £830 given towards: Re-slating using natural slate. Replacement leadwork. Replacement metal rainwater goods. Professional fees.

Approximate cost of work: £2,697. Carried out in 1978.

Agent: J. Collins & Co.

Contractor: Keatings Bros., Camlough.

12 College Square West, Bessbrook.

Two-storey terrace dwelling.

Recipient of grant: Mr. A. McMurray.

Moneymore Conservation Area.

Bessbrook Conservation Area.

Grant assistance of £815 given towards: Sympathetic treatment of street elevation as part of general improvement scheme.

Further financial assistance received from: Northern Ireland Housing Executive.

Approximate cost of work: £6,356. Carried out in 1980 and 1981.

Agent: A. H. Kellett, Newry.

Contractor: Wylie & Cunningham, Newry.

25 Shore Road, Portaferry.

Single-storey cottage.

Recipient of grant: Mrs. K. McMullan.

Grant assistance of £973 given towards: Sympathetic treatment of street elevation as part of general improvement scheme.

Further financial assistance received from: Northern Ireland Housing Executive.

Approximate cost of work: £11,419. Carried out in 1982 and 1983.

Agent: Paul Ferguson, Designer, Belfast.

Work carried out using direct labour.

Killough Clinic, Main Street, Killough.

Recipient of grant: Eastern Health and Social Services Board.

Grant assistance of £1,084 given towards: Undergrounding of unsightly electricity cables.

Approximate cost of work: £1,085. Carried out in 1981.

Work carried out by the Northern Ireland Electricity Service.

24 Main Street, Killough.

Single-storey terrace dwelling.

Recipient of grant: Mr. Cyril J. Craig.

Killough Conservation Area.

Grant assistance of £1,390 given towards: Re-slating using natural slate. Replacement metal rainwater goods. Replacement sash windows in original style. Replacement panelled entrance door. Repairs to external render.

Further financial assistance received from: Northern Ireland Housing Executive.

Approximate cost of work: £19,374. Carried out in 1980.

Contractor: Raymond Burke, Ardglass.

28 Main Street, Killough.

Single-storey terrace dwelling with dormers.

Recipient of grant: Mr. John Boyd.

Grant assistance of £1,575 given towards:

Roof repairs. Repairs to dormer windows. Repairs to windows. Repairs to panelled entrance door. Repairs to external plasterwork.

Further financial assistance received from: Northern Ireland Housing Executive.

Approximate cost of work: £6,686. Carried out in 1978–1983.

Roof work by: Raymond Burke, Ardglass.

Plastering by: John Gilchrist, Ardglass.

Joinery by: O'Donnell & McAuley, Downpatrick.

46 Main Street, Killough.

Single-storey, end-of-terrace dwelling.

Recipient of grant: Mrs. L. M. Fitzgerald.

46 Main Street, Killough.

Conservation Areas

Grant assistance of £460 given towards:
Sympathetic treatment of street elevation as part of general improvement scheme.
Further financial assistance received from: Northern Ireland Housing Executive.
Approximate cost of work: £13,908. Carried out in 1982 and 1983.
Architects: Shanks, Leighton, Kennedy & Fitzgerald, Belfast.
Contractor: Hugh O'Boyle Ltd., Downpatrick.

28 Castle Street, Killough.

Single-storey terrace dwelling with dormers.
Recipient of grant: Mr. Paul Brady.
Grant assistance of £843 given towards: Sympathetic treatment of street elevation as part of general improvement scheme.
Further financial assistance received from: Northern Ireland Housing Executive.
Approximate cost of work: £4,888. Carried out in 1981.
Contractor: Raymond Burke, Ardglass.

40 Castle Street, Killough.

Two-storey end-of-terrace dwelling.
Recipient of grant: The Misses Margaret and Olive Rea.
Grant assistance of £410 given towards: Repairs to external render. Repairs to windows. Repairs to chimneys. Treatment of wood rot. Treatment of rising damp.
Approximate cost of work: £1,262. Carried out in 1980.
Contractor: G. McGlurg, Killough.
Timber treatment and damp-proof course by: Protim Services, Belfast.

1 The Square, Killough.

Two-storey townhouse with bay windows.
Recipient of grant: Mr. John McAuley.
Grant assistance of £734 given towards: Sympathetic treatment of street elevation as part of general improvement scheme.
Further financial assistance received from: Northern Ireland Housing Executive.
Approximate cost of work: £7,202. Carried out in 1981.
Contractor: McGrady Bros., Downpatrick.
Timber treatment and damp-proof course by: Timbercare, Lisburn.

2 The Square, Killough.

Two-storey terrace townhouse.
Recipient of grant: Mr. T. Smyth.
Grant assistance of £1,650 given towards: Sympathetic treatment of street elevation as part of general improvement scheme.
Approximate cost of work: £2,100. Carried out in 1981.
Contractor: Oliver Burns, Downpatrick.

1 Chapel Street, Killough.

Two-storey, end-of-terrace dwelling.
Recipient of grant: Mr. William Fagan.
Grant assistance of £668 given towards: Sympathetic treatment of street elevation as part of general improvement scheme.
Further financial assistance received from: Northern Ireland Housing Executive.
Approximate cost of work: £15,880. Carried out in 1981 and 1982.
Agent: G. I. Martin, Belfast.
Contractor: Raymond Burke, Ardglass.

6 Quay Lane, Killough.

Two-storey dwelling.
Recipient of grant: Mrs. A. A. Catherall.
Grant assistance of £600 given towards: Sympathetic treatment of street elevation as part of general improvement scheme.
Further financial assistance received from: Northern Ireland Housing Executive.
Approximate cost of work: £15,200. Carried out in 1982.
Contractor: Hugh O'Prey. Downpatrick.

'Holmcroft', School Road, Killough.

New domestic garage at detached dwelling.
Recipient of grant: Mr. Michael G. Kelly.
Grant assistance of £280 given towards: Sympathetic treatment of roof and window of new domestic garage.
Total cost of work not recorded.
Work carried out using direct labour.

9 Fisherman's Row, Killough.

Single-storey terrace dwelling with dormers.
Recipient of grant: Mrs. Rita Heathwood.
Grant assistance of £1,000 given towards: Sympathetic treatment of street elevation as part of general improvement scheme.
Further financial assistance received from: Northern Ireland Housing Executive.
Approximate cost of work: £14,935. Carried out in 1982.
Contractor: Milligan Bros., Killough.

1 and 2 The Square, Killough.

Conservation Areas

Caledon Conservation Area.

Moira Conservation Area.

Moy Conservation Area.

Gracehill Conservation Area.

Conservation Areas

Carnlough Conservation Area.

14–16 Joy Street, Belfast – Northern Ireland Housing Executive.

Massereene Hospital, Antrim – Northern Health and Social Services Board.

Almshouses, Seaforde, Co. Down – Hearth Housing Association.

The Court House, Enniskillen – Northern Ireland Courts Service.

Funding From Other Government Sources

During the past ten years there have been restoration and repair schemes carried out to listed buildings where, because all the costs were already being borne by government, it was unnecessary to divert grant aid through the Historic Monuments and Buildings Branch of the Department of the Environment; these buildings are often owned by government departments or public bodies wholly or substantially funded by government.

However, most of them have received the benefit of advice and comment from the Department of the Environment and the Historic Buildings Council, and from these buildings four schemes are illustrated.

THE REPAIR AND MAINTENANCE OF HISTORIC BUILDINGS

A Brief Guide for
Owners, Architects and Agents

Written by
Richard Oram

**THE REPAIR AND MAINTENANCE OF
HISTORIC BUILDINGS
A Brief Guide for Owners, Architects and Agents**

1.0 INTRODUCTION

1.1 Sources of Information
(A) Some Useful Organisations
(B) A Selection of Publications

1.2 Consultants and Specialist Technical Advice

2.0 BUILDING ELEMENTS

2.1 Chimneys, Flues and Hearths
2.1.1 Historical Note
2.1.2 Faults and Repair
2.1.3 Notes on the Preparation of Contract
Specifications
2.1.4 Technical References

2.2 Roofs
2.2.1 Historical Note
2.2.2 Faults and Repair
(A) Thatch
(B) Slates and Tiles
(C) Lead, Copper and Zinc
2.2.3 Notes on the Preparation of Contract
Specifications
2.2.4 Technical References

2.3 Roof Drainage
2.3.1 Historical Note
2.3.2 Faults and Repair
2.3.3 Notes on the Preparation of Contract
Specifications
2.3.4 Technical References

2.4 Masonry Walls
2.4.1 Historical Note
2.4.2 Faults and Repair
(A) Ground Settlement
(B) Damp
(C) Ferro-concrete or Reinforced
Concrete
(D) Mud
(E) Stone
(F) Brickwork
(G) Pointing
2.4.3 Notes on the Preparation of Contract
Specifications
2.4.4 Technical References

2.5 Wall Finishes – External
2.5.1 Historical Note
2.5.2 Faults and Repair
2.5.3 Notes on the Preparation of Contract
Specifications
2.5.4 Technical References

A Brief Guide for Owners, Architects and Agents

1.0 INTRODUCTION

In these notes each principal element is examined in turn; an historical introduction is followed by descriptions of the more common faults and suggestions are made for remedial work. References for further technical investigation are included with each section.

When embarking on repairs, the aim should always be to rectify faults in such a manner that as much of the original building fabric is retained as is consistent with reasonable performance standards.

The work of past builders is not without fault. When replacement is the only sensible choice, the original design should be reviewed critically and obvious shortcomings should not be repeated. In the case of 'listed' buildings these changes may require approval – known as 'listed building consent' – from the Department of the Environment for Northern Ireland.

Most of the repair work which becomes necessary on older buildings is the result of neglect. The value of regular inspections cannot be over-emphasised. Small scale systematic maintenance will guarantee a practically infinite life for most building elements and should be the policy of all caring owners of older buildings.

1.1 Sources of Information

Among the sources of information which may be helpful in sorting out the problems of maintaining old buildings are the following:

(A) Some Useful Organisations

- Association of Building Component Manufacturers, 26 Store Street, London WC1E 7BT (01) 637 9083
- British Board of Agrément, PO Box 195, Bucknalls Lane, Garston, Watford, Herts. WD 2 7NG (092 73) 70844
  Publish: Agrément Certificates
- British Standards Institution, Linford Wood, Milton Keynes MK14 6LE
  Publish: British Standards; British Standard Codes of Practice
- Building Centre, 26 Store Street, London WC1E 7BT (01) 637 1022

(Other Centres at Birmingham, Bristol, Cambridge, Coventry, Dublin, Durham, Glasgow, Liverpool, Manchester, Nottingham, Southampton, Stoke-on-Trent)
- Building Conservation Trust, Apartment 39, Hampton Court Palace, East Molesley, Surrey KT8 9BS (01) 943 2277
- Building Research Advisory Service, Garston, Watford WD2 7JR (092 73) 76612, and at Kelvin Road, East Kilbride, Glasgow G75 0RZ (035 52) 33001
  Publish: Digests
- Federation of Building and Civil Engineering Contractors (N.I.) Ltd., 143 Malone Road, Belfast BT9 6SU (0232) 661711
- Her Majesty's Stationery Office, Government Bookshop, 80 Chichester Street, Belfast BT1 4JY
  Publish: Building Regulations (Northern Ireland)
    Department of the Environment (P.S.A.) Advisory Leaflets*
    Historic Buildings and Monuments Commission Research and Technical Advisory Notes
- Industrial Science Division, Department of Economic Development, 17 Antrim Road, Lisburn BT28 3AL (084 62) 5161
- Joint Conservation Laboratory, Queen's University, 13 University Square, Belfast BT7 1NN (0232) 245133
- National Building Agency, N.B.A. House, 7 Arundel Street, London WC2R 3DZ (01) 836 4488
  Publish: 'Easiguides'
- Society for the Protection of Ancient Buildings (S.P.A.B.), 37 Spital Square, London E1 6DY (01) 377 1644.

(B) A Selection of Publications

- ASHURST, J. and DIMES, F. G. 'Stone in Building – its use and Potential Today'. London: The Architectural Press Ltd., 1977.
- BOWER, J. 'Guide to Domestic Building Surveys'. London: The Architectural Press.

*This series is out of print but remains a valuable reference.

- BUILDING DESIGN. 'Easibriefs'. Morgan-Grampian (Construction Press) Ltd., Calderwood Street, London SE18.
- BUILDING REFURBISHMENT AND MAINTENANCE. Periodical published by Morgan-Grampian (Construction Press) Ltd., Calderwood Street, London SE18.
- 'Care and Conservation of Georgian Houses – A Maintenance Manual'. London: The Architectural Press with Edinburgh New Town Conservation Committee, 1980.
- 'Care for your Church – A Manual for Ministers and Fabric Committees'. Edinburgh: The Saint Andrew Press on behalf of The Advisory Committee on Artistic Matters and The Church of Scotland General Trustees, 1983.
- COUNCIL FOR THE CARE OF CHURCHES. 'How to look after your Church'. London: Church Information Office, 1970.
- MARTIN, D. G. 'Maintenance and Repair of Stone Buildings'. London: Council for the Care of Churches, Church Information Office, 1970.
- MITCHELL, G. A. and A. M. 'Building Construction'. London: Batsford, Editions of 1911, 1915, 1919, 1920.
- SEELEY, I. H. 'Building Maintenance'. London: Macmillan Press Ltd., 1976.
- STONE DEVELOPMENTS LTD. 'Natural Stone Directory'. London: Ealing Publications Ltd., 1977–78.

1.2 Consultants and Specialist Technical Advice

A good deal of maintenance and repair work can be carried out perfectly well by a competent and experienced builder. However, there is a need for professional or technical advice, the presentation of specifications and contract supervision.

Such advice is recommended where:

(i) special restoration techniques must be employed beyond the normal scope of a builder – for example, decorative plasterwork; stained or painted glass; historical reconstruction of interior decoration; redesigning unsatisfactory roof constructions and roof drainage systems; structural collapse;

(ii) the cause of building failure is not easily traced so that a programme of dismantling and inspection is necessary before the necessary repair work can be specified;

(iii) the builder will be working on his own, because the owner is absent and not able to make day-to-day decisions on the extent of work, standards of finish, and so on;

(iv) the decision is made to employ a series of specialist contractors, but no general co-ordinating contractor;

(v) an owner simply wants the burden of organising and supervising the work taken on by someone else. For the owner who will not be on the spot this is always a wise decision.

If an owner does not know who to go to, the various professional institutes will usually give guidance. Before finally selecting any firm or individuals it can be useful to visit other work with which they have been involved. If the person chosen is a member of a partnership or an employee of a firm it is possible to insist on that person always dealing with the work by having this condition written into a formal agreement.

A written agreement between building owner and consultant is a precaution against future claims of negligence. Most professional bodies will provide standard forms for such use.

A consultant appointed to take total charge of the work must be prepared and capable of providing the following services:

(1) Inspection of the building and in discussion with the owner to recommend and outline a plan of work. This work will probably be charged by the consultant on a time basis.

(2) On acceptance of a plan, to gather enough technical and specialist information to provide a reasonably accurate estimate of costs. From these costs the consultant can compute his fee for carrying out the rest of the work.

(3) To prepare documentation of the chosen scheme sufficient to obtain all the necessary statutory approvals and a sympathetic response from any organisation which may be willing to offer grant-aid.

(4) On receipt of necessary approvals, to prepare any drawings, bills, specifications or other documentation to permit calculation of a final estimate of cost and be ready to ask for prices from builders.

213

(5) To select builders and specialists capable of the work and of reaching the required standards and asking them to prepare tenders for the work. When tenders are submitted to check that they cover all the specified work.

(6) When the work is in hand to instruct the builder on any unforeseen problems, and to make sufficient visits to ensure that the agreed standards and practices are being followed.

(7) If it becomes apparent that additional work and costs will be involved, to consult with the owner to decide future action.

(8) Where a builder wants interim payments, to be prepared to certifiy that enough work of an acceptable standard has been completed to justify payment and to prepare a list of any defects which up to that point may have come to light.

(9) To carry out an inspection on completion of the work and prepare a list of any defects. A defects liability period, and a retention of some of the contract money, may have been agreed at tender stage requiring a further inspection when this time is up; to arrange for any necessary inspections by organisations' offering grant.

(10) At the end of a commission to give advice on future maintenance, especially if modern synthetic materials have been used; to provide record documentation of the works as completed if they are at variance with the original proposals.

Having discharged his duties the consultant is due his final payment of fees.

These paragraphs describe the full service provided by a consultant but the building owner may want to do some of this work himself. This division of responsibility should be written into the agreement between the owner and his consultant. If only a part service is being given it is extremely important to agree on who will have the responsibility for instructing the builder and approving the completed work. A proportionally smaller fee will in these circumstances be charged.

More differences of opinion (often leading to court cases) occur in this sphere than in any other. When a full service is being paid for, the client must pass all his requests to the consultant, not direct to the builder, otherwise the consultant cannot be expected to take responsibility for the resulting work.

Proposals in drawing form alone will never be enough to establish acceptable standards; written specifications must deal with the materials to be used, methods of work and the final standards to be achieved. If a written description is still inadequate, the contract should include for the builder to provide specific samples of materials or workmanship, or both, to be approved before the work is put in hand.

If grants from the Department of the Environment are involved, it can help to discuss the tender documents with the professional officers of Historic Monuments and Buildings Branch before asking for prices from builders.

2.0 BUILDING ELEMENTS

2.1 Chimneys, Flues and Hearths

2.1.1 *Historical Note*

The chimney is a relative latecomer as a building element. It was only during the 14th century that it became at all common, even for the dwellings of the 'well to do' and very many poorer dwellings remained without any special provision to remove smoke until well into the 19th century. However, the chimney in some form or other will be an essential element of any older building that is in use today.

From the outset, chimneys have always been a prominent characteristic of the building of which they form part, although sometimes their shape has been disguised as an urn or other ornament.

The burning of wood and turf required a wide hearth and flue but coal, which increased in common use during the late 18th into the 19th century, burnt best in more confined grates lifted off the hearth stone. The essential fire in every household was the one used for cooking. The use of coal led to the development of closed ranges which were often set into the opening of the old hearth. Most local stone was difficult to dress to form flues, and instead brick was used, some of very poor quality.

With the use of coal came the need for a more efficient draft leading to patented fittings with registers and other contrivances. At the top of the stack, pots were set to reduce turbulence and improve draft. The use of pots become increasingly common from the middle of the 18th century. Set well down into the stack with only a small projection they were often made of cast-iron. Terra Cotta and faience soon became more popular with the result that in the later 19th century an enormous range of standard pots of all sizes and shapes, some very decorative, were generally available. Because of the increased risk of fire from coal, parliamentary enactments of 1774 and 1834 sought to regulate construction materials and design. The most recent development in flue construction has been the liner. All flues until modern times had at best, been parged with lime plaster as they were built but smooth clay or metal liners have very much increased the efficiency and safety of the flue and make it more easily cleaned.

Until recent times, the stack has also been a symbol of social standing. Hearth, bricks and coal have all been subject to tax at one time. To afford them showed wealth. This social importance can be seen expressed in the building of dummy stacks, a fashion very common in the early 19th century. By contrast the poor man, while he had a hearth, could not afford coal to burn nor bricks to build his chimney.

2.1.2 *Faults and Repair*

(i) Breakdown of the pointing or masonry of the stack:
This may be caused by chemical or local climatic reasons.

Smoke and fumes will escape discolouring the stack or filling the roof space; the stack may lean; mortar and perhaps pieces of masonry may fall; adjacent timbers become charred.

In severe cases the stack must be rebuilt; in less advanced stages the stack may be saved by grouting in a lining to the flue and repointing or rerendering.

(ii) Water gaining entry between the stack and the roof covering:
Chimney breasts will become damp and rot is likely to affect any timber built close to the stack.

Renew the flashings around the stack. If this junction is only flanched with mortar it is advisable to repair using full detailed lead flashings (this does not apply to thatch). After the building is made water-proof cut out any powdered bricks, replace and repoint. Repair or replace the damaged timbers.

(iii) Damp trapped inside unused flues:
This can be the cause of damp patches inside the building and be the source of a general fungal attack. The water can enter at the top of the stack or be driven in through the wall of the flue which may be no thicker than 100 mm.

A ventilating cap should be fitted to the top of the stack which will prevent water driving down but allow a circulation of air. Where fireplaces have been blocked other ventilators should be fitted so that air can travel up the flue and keep it dry.

(iv) Damaged and cracked pots:
Replacement is the only satisfactory answer. There is a wide variety of designs still available and several firms will make 'specials' to order. If the design is unique and a one-off replacement is too costly to consider it may be possible to carry up the fumes using an insert tube and to repair the pot using modern adhesives.

The condition of flues and stacks should be checked every five years.

2.1.3 *Notes on the Preparation of Contract Specifications*

(a) Preparation and Demolition

215

Clearly identify which stacks are to be worked on.

Demolition

If there is to be demolition and rebuilding, a record drawing or photograph may be necessary to obtain a proper match. The builder must be told if he is to set aside any materials from the demolition for reuse. Describe the extent of demolition – state if the builder is to use his discretion.

(b) Reconstruction

Workmanship – describe any special requirements or samples for which the builder should get approval before proceeding further.

Materials

Bricks – state whether they are to be reused after demolition or new. It is increasingly difficult to get new large (2⅞″) bricks so, if these are needed, it is advisable to ensure a supply in advance. If the stack is to be rendered then modern concrete bricks or blocks can be used.

Mortar – if the stack is being patched it may be important that the new pointing matches the old in style and colouring.

Liners – 200 mm diameter vitrified clay sections are most commonly used. Other types should be chosen with specialist advice and may need to be installed by a specialist. The type of fuel burnt will be a factor in the choice.

Pots – old pots can usually be reused but if replacements are necessary then the match will be important and size, colour and manufacturer should be named.

Flashings – lead, code 4, is the most commonly used material for soakers and cover flashings. If it is decided to use a modern synthetic material it should be chosen from those that have been given an independent test by a recognised testing organisation and found to have an expected life span compatible with that of the adjoining roof.

Renders – these will usually be specified to match other existing renders. If there is any doubt about getting a good match a sample panel should be specified.

After the work to the stacks is complete the rainwater system must be checked to be sure that it has not been choked by rubbish from the chimney work.

2.1.4 *Technical References*

British Standards:
B.S. 1181 – Flue Linings in Terminals in Clay.
B.S.C.P. 131 – Flue for Domestic Solid Fuel Appliances.

Building Regulations (N.I.) Part I

D.O.E. Advisory Leaflets No. 30 and 31 – Installation of Solid Fuel Appliances; No. 44 – Smoky Chimneys; No. 50 – Chimneys for Domestic Boilers.

N.B.A. 'Easiguide' to Fire Protection in Houses.

S.P.A.B. 'Chimneys in Old Buildings'.

2.2 Roofs

2.2.1 *Historical Note*

The roof has been an essential element of every habitable building since building began. It is also one of the largest and therefore one of the most costly elements. In all but the most prestigious of buildings, the materials used have been those most easily obtained locally. This principle has only been superseded since the development of modern transport. The available materials locally were thatch, timber shingles and split slate or stone; clay tiles have been made locally but never on a large scale and so the number of tiled buildings in Northern Ireland is small. All these traditional materials require a pitch to be waterproof and so, except where an owner has been wealthy enough to afford large areas of lead, all roofs until the recent advent of manufactured sheet materials have always been pitched, with lead used to waterproof junctions and other difficult areas.

The supporting roof structures are generally timber although there are some 19th century examples of cast-iron. From the period of the Plantation onward native timber became more and more scarce. The size of scantlings reduces until legislation and constructional handbooks codified and standardised timber sizes. The simplest of roofs were the trunks and larger limbs of trees spanning as purlins between supporting cross walls with the lighter members set at right angles to support the roof covering. The fixing of slates required more accuracy than thatch and so sawn timbers had to be used, with battens. Early slates were held by a wooden peg, usually oak, which was simply lodged over the batten. The weight of subsequent slate courses kept each slate in place and the complete roof would be finally wind and weather proofed by plastering (torching) the joints on the inside. Later the general availability of nails led to the use of sarking (boarding) as a bed for the slates. In this way slating material of a variety of sizes could be used together without the problems of gauging and setting the individual battens.

Until the latter end of the 18th century, nails were individually forged from iron which made them relatively expensive. The next development was to cut, shear or cast nails and in modern times the steel wire nail has become almost universal. However, steel nails even when they are protected by a coating of zinc (galvanised) have a much shorter life than the slates which they secure. During the 19th century wrought or cast-iron nails were used, today these are not available and the British Standard lists copper, aluminium or silicon-bronze as being the best choice for a lasting job.

The general availability of iron in the form of nails, belts and straps also revolutionised timber roof frames.

The jointing of timbers was simplified and pegs were completely replaced by the new material. There are rare surviving examples of pegged roof construction and these are of the greatest historical interest and importance. For this reason they should always be repaired rather than replaced by a modern frame. Some late 19th century slating is decorative with banding of different colours and the tails of the slates are sometimes cut to form a pattern.

Raised gables are a strong characteristic of many Ulster roofs. It has the practical advantage of giving the verge of the roof protection against high winds. This is especially valuable in conjunction with thatch or pegged slates. It was developed as a decorative feature and used widely into the early years of the 19th century.

Eaves details in buildings of masonry construction were usually corbelled; here the last course at the head of the wall is set slightly forward of the main wall face to protect the end of the rafters and to give a bed for the tail for the first course of slates. Alternatively the wall was carried up to form a parapet containing a secret gutter behind it. Variations from these two forms made their appearance during the Regency Period when deep overhangs became the fashion and were sometimes beautifully decorated with fretted and carved wooden fascias. The utilitarian boxed-eaves and verges of modern standard construction are not suitable substitutes and can very badly disfigure older buildings. The ridge is also a characteristic detail. Dressed stone or lead rolls and sometimes cast-iron were used until standard earthenware products became generally available. In the late 19th century decorative crestings became the fashion.

2.2.2 Faults and Repair

Neglect of a faulty roof will quickly lead to damage in every other building element.

(A) Thatch:
Faults – the first signs of failure are normally at the junctions to chimneys and gables and along ridges. If not attended to, these faults will gradually get worse often aggravated by birds and vermin.

Symptoms – the early stages are identified from outside; leaks follow with water running down the inner face of the nearest walls often discoloured with material from the scraws which underlie the thatch.

Repair – inspect the roof every year and stitch in new material where faults are beginning to show. With regular maintenance a full topping out may only be necessary twice in a generation. After many such toppings the thatch will get too heavy for the supporting timbers. It will then be necessary to strip back to the scraws and rethatch. If the surface of the thatch is changed the relation to chimneys and protective gables must be checked. Periodically it will be necessary to raise both to provide a weatherproof junction.

(B) Slates and Tiles
Faults – most common is the failure of the nails securing the slates to the battens.

Pegged slates are now very rare. Failure in such roofs often takes the form of large sections of the roof slipping in one mass with slates, battens and torching all moving together. Roofs built without the use of felt sarking, are well ventilated so that while the damp is kept out, decay in the timbers is unusual. Frost will sometimes break up the surface of slates and tiles especially where there are accumulations of mosses and lichens which hold the water. Water will enter roofs because of the failure of flanchings and flashings. This is discussed together with the problems of flat roofs.

Symptoms – slipped slates will not always let in water at first. If they fall clear of the roof they will be obvious enough but they may simply lodge in the guttering or behind chimneys. Regular inspections of older roofs are therefore important. If damp patches are apparent inside they are not necessarily an indication of where the roof failure is located. Water can travel considerable distances before it is seen. Because any water that gets in will run down the inner slopes of the framework it is the rafter feet and the wall plate that are most vulnerable to resulting decay.

Repair – individual slipped slates can be pinned up but if this problem becomes a regular occurrence the only satisfactory repair is to strip and reslate. On a building of historic importance as much of the original material as is possible should be reused. The builder must be told that this is the intention right from the start so that careful stripping and storage can be organised. Before reslating the timber frame must be checked for decay and affected members replaced.

If new timber is to be used, it is advisable to choose material that has been chemically treated against decay. The supplier can provide a certificate confirming that the treatment meets the British Standard. Additional sarking with modern roofing felt is a wise precaution. The slating battens will certainly need to be renewed and should also be pretreated against decay. To give reasonable life expectancy to the new roof the British Standard recommendation in the choice of slating nails must be followed, i.e. use aluminium, copper or silicon-bronze nails not the zinc plated steel nails which most builders will use if not instructed to the contrary. All metal flashings and their supporting structures should also be checked and replaced where decayed. A new roof will not be ventilated in the same way as the old now that sarking felt has been fitted and so it may be necessary to ventilate the roof spaces by other means; for example, by using ventilators on the ridge or by breaking into disused chimney flues the accumulation of stagnant pockets of humid warm air can be avoided and prevent new outbreaks of fungal attack.

There are countless proprietory dressings being advertised to waterproof decaying slate and tiles roofs. Most have a very short life expectancy and render the slates unfit for reuse when eventually stripping is the only option left. They are therefore never recommended by the Department for use on historic buildings.

(C) Lead, Copper and Zinc:
Faults – most failures are for the following reasons:

(1) the sheet has been punctured perhaps by a falling slate;
(2) corrosion by acids either from atmospheric pollution (this may be locally generated from a chimney on the building itself) or from organic growths;
(3) crystallisation (sometimes called metal fatigue) caused by the poor design of fixings or the location and form of joints;
(4) failure of the supporting structure.

Symptoms – in all cases water will get into the building. The place where it shows inside is not a reliable indication of the location of the failure. Inspection of the roof covering will reveal the reason:

(1) the failure will usually be an obvious gash;
(2) the surface will be powdering and discoloured; if a finger is run across the surface an uneven ridged

texture will be apparent. It is quite possible that no holes will be observed;

(3) the surface will be cracked and the sheet may have puckered into a ridge;

(4) there will be apparent ponding away from outlets.

Repair –

(1) replacement sections can be welded over the gash;

(2) the affected area will have to be taken up and replaced. Organic growth can often be prevented by fitting copper strips higher up the roof which will cause a toxic wash. If this is not possible then sacrificial flashings must be fitted; these are additional flashings which will take the full force of the destructive run-off and protect the main flashing below;

(3) the affected section must be taken up and the area redesigned to prevent a similar build up of stresses in the future;

(4) the affected section must be taken up and the supporting structure repaired; it may be possible to reuse the old metal sheeting.

In all repairs do not use solder. It is not a long term repair and welding is much more reliable. Do not reduce the thickness (code) of the sheets unless the frequency of joints is altered to meet the changed thermal movement.

The metal sheet must be free to allow movement. This is facilitated by fitting an isolating membrane. The material used must remain stable and not become sticky in the very high temperatures which build up under the metal sheeting.

It may be decided to replace lead with a modern synthetic sheeting. If this is the case bear in mind that the rest of the roof if in good repair is likely to have a trouble free life span up to 100 years, and so the choice of synthetic sheet should be from those products that have been given independent ageing tests (Agrément Board or similar) and found to have an expected life of at least 20 to 25 years. It is wasteful to use materials like mineral felt which will have to be replaced long before the other adjoining roofing material so causing needless disruption of sound slates, nails and battens.

It is advisable to check the condition of any roof once a year. The inspection could be made to coincide with regular clearing out of the rainwater drainage system.

After any roof repair the rainwater system should always be checked to ensure that it has not been blocked with rubbish from the works.

2.2.3 *Notes on the Preparation of Contract Specifications*

(a) Preparation and Stripping
Areas to be worked on should be identified – a location drawing may be useful both for identification and record purposes.

Stripping – if slates are to be stripped carefully and kept for reuse this must be clearly stated and a place for storage identified.

Condition of timbers – in many roofs it is impossible to be sure of the extent of decay in timbers until the roof covering is stripped. When this stage is reached the consultant or owner should inspect the stripped work and decide in detail what is to be done.

(b) Reconstruction
Straw for thatch – if the thatcher is not providing a complete service, it may be necessary to find straw in advance and buy it in. If the owner is providing materials this should be specified, as should any required attendance by a builder, e.g. for transport or scaffolding.

Slating – any requirement to reuse existing slates or to buy in new or second-hand materials must all be specified. The delivery period for the supply of new slates can be considerable; in such cases advance purchase may be advisable. Any size grading in the new work must be specified. The choices are to place all of one size on each slope or to grade them on every slope from the smallest at the ridge to the largest at the eaves. The decision can depend on the location of the building and whether it stands on its own or is in a group or terrace where matching with its neighbours is important. State if the roof is to be sarked with felt or close boarding or be torched with plaster. The details at gable, eaves and ridge must all be drawn or described in words because the modern equivalents which many builders may use, if not otherwise directed, will seriously erode the historic authenticity of the building. This description should include, where required, the colouring of mortar for setting the ridge so as to tone in with slates. Methods to be used for the ventilation and insulation of roof cavities should be included. Describe the slating nails, the size of battens, the type of preservative treatment and the methods to be employed for repairing structural members. Indicate when the builder must contact the consultant or owner for a decision and when he can use his own discretion.

Flashings and flats – if a modern synthetic material is to be used make sure that the manufacturer's advisory literature is available to the operatives on site. The documents to be referred to should be named in the specification. Where metal is used – the guage of the sheet; the type of the joints, both mechanical and physical (e.g. standing seam and lead weld); the method of fixing; supporting structures; isolating membranes; the minimum fall; the choice of sacrificial flashings or copper strips as protection against acid attack – must all be described. If there are any design failures in the old roof or the form is to be remodelled for practical reasons then a drawing will be necessary. Include a requirement that when the work is finally complete a check is made to ensure that the rainwater discharge system is working and not choked with debris.

2.2.4 *Technical References*

British Standards
B.S. 5534 – Slating and Tiling
B.S.C.P. 143 – Lead, Zinc and Copper
B.S. 690 – Asbestos Slates
B.S. 402 – Clayridge Tiles
B.S.C.P. 153 – Rooflights
B.S. 4471 – Battens for Slating and Tiling
B.S.C.P. 112 – Structural timbers
B.S. 5268 – Chemical Treatment and Fire Protection of Timber
B.S. 5250 – Control of Condensation

Building Regulations (Northern Ireland)
Part C10 – Weather Resistance
Part D12 – Structural Timber

D.O.E. Advisory Leaflet
No. 42 – Woodworm
No. 46 – Leadburning

Lead Development Association – Lead Sheet in Buildings

Building Design 'Easibrief' 'Roof Tile Fixings' 10 September 1982.

Advisory Organisations:
Copper Development Association – Orchard House, Mutton Lane, Potters Bar, Hertfordshire EN6 3AP.
Lead Development Association – 34 Berkeley Square, London W1X 6AJ.
Zinc Development Association – 34 Berkeley Square, London W1X 6AJ.
Timber Research and Redevelopment Association – Stocking Lane, Hughenden Valley, High Wycombe, Buckinghamshire HP14 4NP.
Rubber and Plastics Research Association – Shawbury, Shrewsbury, Shropshire SY4 4NR.
Master Thatchers (National Society of) – 32 Meadow Gardens, Waltham Chase, Southampton, Hampshire SO3 2JN.
The Guild of Thatchers in Ireland – c/o An Foras Forbartha, St. Martin's House, Waterloo Road, Dublin 4.

2.3 Roof Drainage

2.3.1 *Historical Note*
Until the commercial availability of cast-iron in the late

18th century rainwater was either allowed to run off at the eaves to be collected in a gully or other type of drain at ground level or it was collected in lead lined gutters at roof level; these were either secreted behind masonry parapets or more rarely boxed out in timber. The water was then collected into lead hopper heads and discharged down lead pipes. During the first half of the 19th century cast-iron replaced lead for all but the most distinguished of buildings and continued as the most common material for that purpose. Only in modern times has cast-iron been rivalled by plastics and cast and cold formed aluminium. Decoration was a feature of prestigious work during both 18th and 19th centuries. In lead work the hopper heads and pipe brackets were often embellished. Cast-iron was sometimes decorated in a similar way and other details like the gutter support brackets and joints between sections of gutter were also featured. The cast-iron range in the mid-19th century offered many variations from the simple half-round to ogee sections with very complicated mouldings; even secret and valley gutters were being made in cast-iron.

Today the available range is very much less, offering three basic profiles in a variety of sizes.

2.3.2 *Faults and Repair*

The most common fault is poor maintenance. There can be no other building element which suffers more from neglect and where the consequences can be so catastrophic. The misdirection of rainwater can cause rapid decay in almost every component of a building. A badly functioning system is worse than having none at all – simply letting the water run straight off the roof to the ground. Always check that the water is running freely in gutters and pipes before looking for any other cause.

Fault 1: Undersizing of components.
Symptom: Water running over in heavy downpours.
Repair: Redesign the installation – the fitting of additional downpipes and resetting falls may be enough, otherwise a complete new installation may be necessary.
Fault 2: Incorrect setting of the gutter with the inner edge being lower than the outer, or the falls being wrongly directed, or the relation to the edge of the roof covering being wrongly set.
Symptom: Water running over always in specific locations.

Repair: Resetting.
Fault 3: Fractured or decayed components.
Symptom: Damp will be apparent initially inside the building because these faults are most common on the face which lies against the building. The damp will attract vegetable growth and discolouration on the outer face.
Repair: Replace the defective component. Ogee and box gutter sections must be painted thoroughly on all faces before assembly. Downpipes must always be free of the wall surface and never embedded in the plaster.
Fault 4: Poorly designed discharge and ground drainage.
Symptom: Saturated walls, either at ground level or close to the discharge of one roof onto another.
Repair: Discharge all roofs separately and directly to ground level. At ground level fit backinlet gulleys or similar, which provide for rodding. Check underground runs for fracture and provide sufficient manholes and catch pits so that free flow can be checked and drains unblocked when necessary.

The following precautionary measures should always be taken:
 (i) After building work to chimneys or roofs always check that the rainwater installation has not been choked by debris.
 (ii) Fit secret gutters and flat roofs behind parapets with an overflow wherever possible. The overflow should be located so that if it discharges it will be noticed, and the discharge occur before the water rises above the level of the counterflashings.
(iii) Check the whole installation twice every year. Flats and secret gutters should be checked more often during the autumn when they may clog with leaves. Where practical fit snow boards.
(iv) Check the fall of the gutters in relation to the prevailing wind. In exposed areas a gutter falling against the wind can prevent the movement of water causing it to spill over, even though there is no blockage.

To maintain the character of a building it is important that the detail at the eaves is not altered, for example, by fitting a fascia board, where none had existed, simply to mount a gutter.

Some modern substitute materials can be used where eaves gutters are to be totally replaced. Cast-aluminium is very similar in appearance to cast-iron and so are most of the cold formed seamless gutter sections. However, seamless downpipes are flimsy, badly detailed and look quite different from any of the original work. Simple profiles which are no longer available as standard can be fabricated from steel and galvanised.

P.V.C. is now a very popular material, but it is not recommended by the Department of the Environment as a substitute material, because of its general appearance and because:

(i) it is easily damaged by ladders;
(ii) when downpipes become blocked and the gutter is over-loaded the profile may distort and not return to its original shape after the blockage is cleared;
(iii) it has a high thermal movement so that it is difficult to paint successfully and is noisy when it expands and contracts.

2.3.3 *Notes on the Preparation of Contract Specifications*

An initial inspection of the installation will be the basis for deciding whether or not modification is necessary. This inspection may be carried out by the professional consultant or he may instruct the builder to do so.

Check:

(i) for broken or missing sections and leaking joints;
(ii) that all roofs have a separate discharge to the ground;
(iii) that all lengths of gutter and downpipe together with all associated gulleys and underground drainage have a clear flow.

If (i), (ii) and (iii) are satisfactory, but the installation still does not work then, check:

(iv) the sizes of gutters and downpipes against the expected volume of water;
(v) the prevailing wind direction against the design flow direction;
(vi) the relation of the gutter setting to the level of the eaves and angle of the roof;
(vii) that the setting of the gutter is such that the outer edge is below the height of the inner edge and not the reverse;

(viii) the fall on the gutter – a minimum of 1 in 360 is recommended.

After the installation has been checked the necessary work can be specified. Only minor repairs can be completed with the gutter in position. If the gutter has to be dismantled decide whether or not any sections are to be reused. If a new set of gutters and downpipes are required then the material and pattern must be specified together with the type of brackets and mountings to be used. If old sections are to be reused, then while they are on the ground they should be thoroughly cleaned, treated with a rust inhibitor and primed on all faces. (NOTE – for lead lined secret gutters see the section on flat roofs 2.2.; for paint see section 2.9.)

2.3.4 *Technical References*

British Standards
B.S. 460 – Cast Iron
B.S. 2997 – Cast-aluminium
B.S. 1091 – Pressed Steel
B.S. 5493 – Protection of Iron and Steel against corrosion
B.S. 729 – Hot dip galvanizing
B.S. 217 – Red lead
B.S. 6367 – Drainage of roofs and paved areas
B.S.C.P. 3012 – Cleaning of metal surfaces.

Building Regulations (N.I.) Part N. 8 & 9

Building Research Establishment Digests
70 – Painting Iron and Steel
188 ⎫
189 ⎭ – Roof Drainage

D.O.E. Advisory Leaflet No. 11 – Painting Metalwork.
National Building Agency – 'Easiguide' to Drainage Installation in Housing.
Building Design 'Easibrief' – 11 November 1983.

2.4 **Masonry Walls**

2.4.1 *Historical Note*

Mud and fieldstone are the earliest walling materials met with in buildings that remain in use today. Both have continued in use throughout recorded time into the beginning of this century. A limited amount of rubble stonework is still built today and there are a few people living who can give first-hand accounts of building with

best stones would be used to face the work, with the poorer material thrown in with generous supplies of mortar to level up the core. Lintels were either single large stones or a series of timbers. Attempts at arching are very rare in this type of construction because of the way in which the walls are made up. The enlargement of openings or breaking out new openings can be a very hazardous and destructive operation.

Earth burnt to form bricks, is a technique dating from Roman times, but good brickearth is rare in Ulster beyond the confines of the Lagan Valley and the fuel for kilning has been expensive. To add to the problems of cost, bricks themselves were taxed between 1784 and 1833. The use of brick in most areas, was therefore sparse and generally confined to dressing window and door openings or the construction of flues and chimneys. To escape tax the size of bricks gradually increased so that by the mid-19th century the usual depth of a brick course had reached 80 mm. Decorative brickwork is rare until the late 19th century when cheap transport made available a wide variety of imported bricks. In earlier buildings it is unusual to find anything but the most basic English and Flemish bond work.

When coal became widely available brick making was concentrated into industrial centres; previously bricks were made on site from locally dug clay. Because of the difficulties and expense of manufacture a place was found for every brick whatever its faults, the worst unburnt or deformed examples being built into internal partitions. During the 18th century it became accepted practice to bond masonry walls by making use of horizontal timbers built in as the work progressed. Unfortunately these provide free passage for fungal and beetle attack linking every element of the building.

Fully dressed stonework (ashlar) is the 'Rolls Royce' of masonry work. Very few local quarries produced material of a sufficiently consistent grain (freestone) for it to be used in this way with the result that ashlar is relatively rare in the Province. Where it is found the stone used has often been imported.

Stone and brick used for habitable buildings requires mortar. The simplest material was earth but the greater number of buildings that survive in use were built with a mortar using burnt limestone. These mixes of lime with earth or sand were used primarily to form a bedding for the unevenly shaped stones or bricks providing stability

mud. Construction in these materials is necessarily massive and openings are small, giving buildings of these types very high qualities of thermal insulation.

Mud is found in use in three basic forms: monolithic; in courses bonded with straw; and as unbaked bricks. The material is strong and perfectly stable as long as it is kept dry and for this reason it was always lime washed.

Mud was also used as a binder in rubble stone construction, when it was often mixed with lime.

Rubble stonework is found in all regions but shales and sandstones are the most suitable. Both these types of stone can be split along the bedding planes giving shapes that can be knit tightly together. The quality of rubble stonework varies widely. The best has the stones selected in size to form a consistent pattern throughout, with special stones set to bind the corners and other weak points.

However carefully executed though, such stonework was rarely built to be seen. To make buildings weathertight and waterproof, the mortar which was squashed out of the joints as the work proceeded was plastered out over the face and then given a wash of lime or burnt earth. The

and keeping the weather out. Some superior work made use of hydraulic limes which, because of their silica and alumina content formed a set through their entire depth. These are the forerunners of the proprietary cements but most construction work made use of a simple hydrated lime which only carbonate and harden where they are in contact with the air. During the 19th century more complex mixes were developed using crushed furnace ash (so called black mortar) and similar bonding materials having a greater structural strength than pure lime. A revolution in mortar mixes followed the development of Portland Cement about 1830. This material was designed to have a complete chemical setting quality and a structural strength up to five times that of any other known material. It was not long before it was discovered that Portland Cement mixed with a filler like sand or gravel and possibly reinforced with steel rods could be the principal building material, taking the place of both brick and stone, in the form of ferro concrete.

Today there are very few local commercial quarries producing building stone and none of these are suitable for fine ashlar work. Clay bricks are made outside Dungannon but their appearance is quite different from earlier bricks made here so that matching material must be imported. Hydrated lime is still freely available but hydraulic limes have to be imported.

2.4.2 *Faults and Repair*

(A) Ground settlement:

Symptom: Deformation and cracking, generally orientated vertically; sometimes outward leaning walls.

Repair: Most settlement takes place early in the life of a building. If this is the case it may be sufficient to replace any fractured lintels or other structural members and then grout the cracks. Old settlement patterns are unlikely to be the cause of further movement or structural collapse. If the settlement is new or progressive the course must be located – the local water table may have been altered by new building work nearby, or a drain may have been fractured. After dealing with the cause it may be necessary to provide new foundations by underpinning the old foundations with additional structural support.

(B) Damp:

Symptom: Discolouration; paper not staying on the wall; appearance of powdery or crystalline deposits on the wall face; frost damage to brick, stone or mortar.

Repair: The position of the damp will be a good guide to its origin – failures of the roof; rainwater drainage and external plasters are dealt with in other sections. Ground damp can be counteracted in two ways:

(i) Piping water away before it reaches the structure. This will involve a trench around the building, piped to falls together with manholes and catch pits for maintenance, and the excavation backfilled with stones.

(ii) Making the wall itself resistant to damp. If the ground level is high and cannot be reduced then the wall must be 'tanked'. This means that the wall is excavated and protected by a waterproof membrane, which itself is protected from puncture by a second skin of masonry and then backfilled.

If ground levels relate correctly to the walls, i.e. are below the level of the floor and damp is showing at the lower part, then it will be necessary to provide a horizontal barrier within the wall. The most common methods are:

(i) To cut through the thickness of the wall and insert an impervious sheet, usually copper. This method is only suitable for walls with continuous horizontal mortar bed joints, e.g. brick or ashlar stone work.

(ii) To inject the wall with a chemical which prevents water movement. In solid rubble masonry walls the core often contains voids and decayed mortar which will result in an uneven distribution of the chemical. To avoid this the wall should be prepared by washing out the loose material at the base of the wall and then grouting to fill the voids. The grout should be of similar strength to the original mortar. The chemical can then reasonably be expected to form an even and continuous barrier.

(iii) To prevent capillary action in the wall by electro-osmosis. This type of installation is specialist work. The wall is prepared by stripping the plaster to a hight of about 1 m. A continuous metal strip is then fastened to the masonry and the surface made good.

Damp higher up the wall can sometimes be related to flues no longer in use. Flues on external walls reduce the effective thickness of the walls and where there is not protection at the head of the stack considerable amounts of water can drive in, and not dry out because there is no air movement. This problem can often be cured by fitting ventilating caps at the top of the stack which prevent rain entering, but allow air to circulate. Lower down in the flue fit a ventilator so that air can move through the length of the flue.

In walls where weather exposure is severe and a very dense stone or brick has been used, the wind will sometimes force rainwater right through the full thickness of the wall. The simplest cure is to render the outer face but if this is not possible, for appearance reasons, specialist advice is necessary.

(C) Ferro concrete or reinforced concrete: The most frequent cause of failure is corrosion of the reinforcement. Poor compaction when originally placed will cause later decay. Contained chemical impurities, possibly introduced from the sand or aggregate, or added intentionally at the time of construction to increase plasticity in the mix, or to make possible work in frosty weather, are another cause.

(D) Mud: The worst enemy of this material is damp. A relatively constant low level of damp is good for the cohesion of the walling material. Water will be constantly taken up and then given off according to weather conditions; this is called 'breathing''. When the water level reaches saturation this cohesion breaks down. The outer lime shield may have failed, and this will lead to the gradual erosion of the wall face but if quantities of water enter the core from either the head or the foot of the wall then the problem must be treated urgently or a total collapse of that section of wall must eventually be expected.

(E) Stone: Local weather conditions caused repeated wetting and drying, and atmospheric pollution are severe enemies of all stones. The incorrect bedding of sedimentary stonework can result in the total breakdown of individual stones. Iron, built in as ties or cramps, rusts and swells eventually bursting the stonework open. Where the stone itself is extremely durable for example basalt and granite the problems are found at the joints. All these decay patterns are aggravated by frost.

Basic structural damage to stonework often results from impact or explosions. Ill considered structural alterations can provide the initial weakness; for example, the creation of large ground floor shop fronts and clear sales areas cutting lateral stability to a minimum or perhaps the creation of rooms in a roof space causing the essential structural tie members to be severed.

(F) Brickwork: Behaves in a similar way to stone. The bricks themselves can be broken down by chemicals present in the clay at the firing or from adjacent building materials. Poor firing is another problem. When bricks were expensive every brick possible was found a job in the structure often in cross walls and flues where they were not originally seen.

(G) Pointing: The general principle of pointing is that the joint should be weaker than the brick or stone with which it is used. In this way it is the joint which decays and not the masonry face. Consequently it is necessary after a period of time to renew mortar joints. The frequency of renewal will depend very much on the quality of the work and the weather conditions. There are many examples of work upwards of two centuries old which are perfectly sound. It must also be remembered that older buildings do not have specially designed joints to accommodate thermal movements. It is in fact the flexibility of the relatively weak mortar beds which provides the necessary movement, and this must not be inhibited by bad repairs.

Repointing is a job which, if it is to have any life and be at all effective, must be carefully done. The joint must be cut back square to an even depth. It must not be feathered off at the ends into old work. Just before repointing flush out to clear all loose material; this will ensure that the new mortar has a good grip and does not suffer from too much suction. Work must start at the top of the wall, and the new mortar must be well rammed in. The finished joint must not project beyond the face of the adjoining masonry. The strength of the new mortar must always be matched to the original work and it should never be stronger than the stone or brick from which the walls are built. Any mortar used in historic work should be in the range – 1:3 lime to sand, up to 1:1:6 cement to lime to sand, or 1:3 masonry cement to sand. These higher strength mixes are for use only in exposed conditions with dense brick and stonework.

Hydraulic limes will give higher strengths but in most work non hydraulic material is quite sufficient. The process of running the lime to putty will take at least 16 hours. In all mixes the proportion of bonder to filler is in the range of 1:3. The amount of water used must be kept to a practical minimum.

2.4.3 *Notes on the Preparation of Contract Specifications*

Identify the areas to be worked on, and for this photographs can sometimes be as valuable as drawings. Describe the types of work necessary in each area, i.e. repointing; individual stones or bricks to be cut out and replaced; parts of the walling to be taken down and rebuilt; location and size of ties, pins, blockbonding, ring beams, underpinning, etc. What materials from cutting out or demolition should be set aside for reuse and any cleaning or other preparation which must be carried out. Describe replacement materials whether they are to be new or second-hand and in this context it may be necessary to say from where they can be obtained. Limes, cements, sands, aggregates and mortar mixes should be included with descriptions of colouring, sizing, etc. Indicate how these should be stored and protected before use. Describe damp-proofing courses and chemical dressings, and any pinning or other reinforcing techniques to be employed. Describe the required quality and appearance of the finished product, any bonding pattern or finish to the joints that is particularly required and name any

sample areas that must be approved before the general work proceeds.

2.4.4 *Technical References*

British Standards

Damp
C.P. 102 }
B.S. 743 } – Damp-proof Courses
B.S. 3826 – Damp Repellants for Masonry
B.S. 4254 – Polysulphide Sealants
B.S. 5250 – Control of Condensation

Bricks and Blocks
B.S. 187 – Calcium Silicate Bricks
B.S. 3921 – Clay Bricks
B.S. 4729 – Special shaped Bricks
B.S. 6270 – Pt. 1 Stone and Brickwork – Cleaning and Repair

Concrete Blocks
B.S. 6073 – Structural Blocks
B.S. 1217 – Non-structural Blocks and Cast-stone

Cement: Lime
B.S. 12 – Standard Portland Cement
B.S. 5224 – Masonry Cement
B.S. 890 – Lime
B.S. 4721 – Readymix Mortars

Building Regulations Northern Ireland – Part D

Building Research Establishment Digests
27 – Rising Damp
77 – Damp-proof courses
125 – Colourless Treatments for Masonry
139 – Control of Lichens, Moulds and Similar Growths
150 – Concrete Materials
160 – Mortars in Brickwork
177 – Decay and Conservation of Stone Masonry

D.O.E. Publications

Advisory Leaflets
6 – Limes for Building
8 – Bricklaying in Cold Weather
16 – Mortars for Brick and Blockwork
23 – Damp-proof Courses
58 – Inserting a Damp-proof Course

Historic Buildings and Monuments Commission Technical Notes

1 ⎫
2 ⎭ – Control of Organic Growth

10 – Clay Products
11 – Rising Damp
14 – Grouting
15 – Stone Preservation – Brethane

Society for the Preservation of Ancient Buildings

Leaflets ⎰ Cleaning Stone and Brickwork
⎱ – Pointing Stone and Brick Walling
⎱ Outward Leaning Walls

Cement and Concrete Association – Advisory Leaflet

The Repair of Concrete Structures – 47.021

'Concrete' Magazine Jan. 1980 – Aspects of cement based mortars for Brickwork and Blockwork
Ecclesiastical Architects & Surveyors Ass. – Mortars, Plasters and Renders in Conservation
Brick Development Association – Conservation of Brick Buildings
Building Design – Cleaning of Brickwork 'Easibrief' 15 Oct. 1982 and 18 Nov. 1983

Advisory Organisations
Brick Development Association – 3/5 Bedford Row, London WC1R 4BU
Cement & Concrete Association – Wexham Springs, Slough, SL3 6PL and 2 Rutland Square, Edinburgh 1
Council for the Care of Churches, 83 London Wall, London EC2
Department of Economic Development, Industrial Science Division, 17 Antrim Road, Lisburn.

2.5 Wall Finishes – External

2.5.1 *Historical Note*

Throughout history masonry walls have been finished by rendering. At first the residue from the mortared joints was spread out over the wall face. Later an additional application of mortar was daubed or thrown onto the wall face. These plasters were various mixtures of lime, earth, sand and sometimes dung or blood. Their purpose was to improve the weather-proofing of the wall. Thick porous plasters are very good in this respect. Because they are porous they reduce the water run-off and the concentra-

tion of moisture at vulnerable joints. Afterwards they give off water by evaporation.

No early decorative uses of external plaster survive in the Province but by the end of the 18th century it had become common to use external plastering to imitate the details and features of stonework. To achieve these finishes limes or gypsums were mixed with oil and ironed in smooth. The techniques improved with the development of materials. In Northern Ireland the most common form of plaster used up to the mid-19th century was 'Roman Cement'. This was a trade name for a naturally occurring clay and lime mix which produced a very durable hydraulic set. From this time onward mixes based on Portland Cement gradually became predominant. During this whole period the early simple lime mixes continued in use for construction with less architectural pretention. Both lime and Portland Cement are still generally available but the earlier proprietary materials are now out of production.

Tiles and faiences became popular facing materials during the 19th century. If faced with problems relating to these materials very specialist advice will be needed. They are very temperamental and delicate and not in the range of experience of the usual building tradesmen.

2.5.2 *Faults and Repair*

Cracking: This may first be apparent from damp showing inside the building if the cracks are not clearly visible outside. The method of repair will depend on the cause.

(i) New renders will crack because:
- the mix was too strong for the backing;
- accelerated drying out either because the backing was not properly prepared or because the newly rendered face was exposed to wind or sun before the set was complete.

Cracks due to these causes, provided they are not filled with dirt or vegetable growth, can be simply repaired with a resin or latex based filler. If the plaster has lost its adhesion to the backing it must be cut out and replaced. The section cut out must be a clean geometrical shape; ragged edges can be the cause of poor adhesion and result in a messy appearance.

(ii) Older renders will crack because:
- structural movement has occurred;
- There is loss of adhesion due to the backing being saturated or to a build up of soluble salts at the interface of masonry and plaster.

In both cases the initial cause must be investigated before areas are stripped and replastered. Loss of adhesion is almost always the result of damp in the wall behind. This may be because of the failure of another element, e.g. chimneys, roof, gutters or the joint against window frames.

Older lime based plasters and renders made from 'Roman Cement' will crumble rather than crack if kept continuously damp.

The mix for the repair of renders must match the strength of the adjoining work. Colour may also be important and so the choice of sand must be carefully made. In such cases trial mixes should be prepared until a good colour match is achieved. Enough material for the whole job should then be dry mixed together and stored until required.

Renders will also be damaged by impact. In these cases a simple patch repair will usually be sufficient. After repair it may be wise to protect the wall against future similar damage, by using kerbs, bollards or fenders.

A thick porous plaster coating will give the best weather-proofing and durability results on solid masonry walls. To build up a thick finish (over 30 mm), three coat work is advisable. Where more than one coat is applied the strongest coat must be the first with each successive coat becoming weaker.

A proportion of 1:3 binder to aggregate, should be the basis of all mix designs – mixes based on lime rather than Portland Cement will always be closer to the character of the old plaster and be more flexible but they do require more care in preparation. If there are plastered mouldings or other details in the work to be repaired and if these details are sound they can be saved by isolating them using saw cuts before the areas of old plaster are hacked off. All lichens and other vegetable growths in the area of repair must be cleaned off and killed.

A general inspection of plastered surfaces should be made about every ten years. If the plaster is painted then the inspection can be made when redecoration is undertaken. Any creepers must be controlled; Ivy is particularly destructive and should never be allowed to cover buildings. Trees can take root in unlikely places and must be dug out and destroyed as soon as they are noticed. All plant growth should be checked annually.

2.5.3 *Notes on the Preparation of Contract Specifications*

Describe the areas to be repaired or replastered; key drawings or photographs will usually be necessary. Describe mouldings and any other detailed work that must be protected and retained. Detail preparatory procedures – taking records of mouldings ; raking out of joints in the substrate; undercutting adjoining plaster work; killing lichens and other vegetable growth; damping to control suction.

Give guidance on cutting out and detailing of replacement work; methods to be employed; how to deal with day work joints; name materials to be used to fill fine cracks. Describe the materials to be used for main repair work together with the mixes and finishes. Include any required colour matching, pigments to be used, etc. If sample areas are required to achieve an acceptable match before the main work proceeds this must be stated.

Arrange for the protection and spraying of finished

work to prevent cracking while curing. If aggregate is to form part of the final texture remember that crushed aggregates are relative newcomers to the building trade. Today there is very little choice available, so if an exactly matching texture is important then a natural aggregate must be used. If it is decided to use a crushed aggregate get samples and choose one which is squarish in shape and not one made up of long pointed granules.

2.5.4 *Technical References*

British Standards
B.S. 12 – Portland Cement
B.S. 882 – Natural Aggregates
B.S. 890 – Lime
B.S. 5262 – External Renders

Building Research Establishment
Digest 139 – Control of Lichens, Moulds and Similar Growths
Digest 196 – External Renders

Historic Buildings and Monuments Commission
Technical Notes 1 and 2 – Control of Organic Growth
Technical Note 6 – External Renders

Cement and Concrete Association – Appearance matters. 2: External rendering – 47.102
Ecclesiastical Architects & Surveyors Association – Mortars, Plasters and Renders in Conservation

Department of the Environment Advisory Leaflets
 6 – Limes for Building
15 – Sands for Plaster, Mortars and Rendering
27 – Rendering Outside Walls

2.6 **Wall Finishes – Internal**

2.6.1 *Historical Note*
The two materials used throughout until very recent times are lime based plasters and timber in the form of sheeting or panelling. The date of the work can only be ascertained from the form of moulding and other details.

Wall plaster was applied either direct to the masonry or onto a timber framed lining. Usually three coats were used. The preparation coats were bonded with a variety of fibrous materials like hair or vegetable fibres such as flax and a smooth finish was achieved using a pure lime-putty. During the late 18th century the use of gypsum became common for the finishing work and through the 19th cen-

tury gypsum was marketed in more developed forms until today it provides most of the plaster in general use. Run cornices and decorative centre pieces are features in many quite modest farm houses and are very much a part of the character of Ulster's older dwellings. Decorative plastering reached a peak of excellence in the early 19th century and included some very specialised techniques such as Scagliola and Scraffito. In the late 19th century detail was more often cast rather than worked in situ and standards generally declined. Timber work of any age, is quite rare in the Province. Most match board sheeting was a 19th century feature often fitted over older plastered finishes. Full scale panelling is practically unknown except in houses of distinction. Local areas of panelling are more common, for example the panelled encasement of windows complete with shutters and of door reveals where they pass through massive masonry walls. A study of features like this can tell a lot about the age of a house. Some farmhouse kitchens were lined with storage units and presses of all kinds built in the manner of panelling but very few of these have survived changing fashions.

Embossed papers, papermaché and other similar materials have been used since the 16th century. However, in the second half of the 19th century they became very much more popular and are often found used for decorative dados and friezes in buildings of this period.

2.6.2 *Faults and Repair*

(A) Plaster: Old plaster will only fail by reason of faults elsewhere in the structure or by bad usage and impact damage. The two most common causes of failure are structural movement and damp. In both cases the cause must be dealt with before any attempt is made to repair the plaster.

Structural movement will appear as a clear pattern of cracks.

Damp may cause discolouration, the break up of paint, loss of adhesion of papers, build up of woolly looking crystals on the surface and eventually the crumbling of the plaster itself.

In the case of plain plaster it is always best to cut out and replace as soon as the cause of the failure has been attended to. In the case of ceilings it may be a good opportunity to strengthen the structural timbers by fitting bridging or some similar method. External walls should be backed and dubbed out with light weight insulating plaster as a precaution against condensation. It is perfectly safe to use modern plasters for these repairs.

In the case of decorative plaster, where the decoration itself has not suffered, it is usually possible using a saw to cut around and isolate the decorative work from the plain plaster which is to be taken down. The decorative work can then be left in position while the surrounding plaster is replaced. If the decorative work is on the ceiling and the key has broken up leaving the plaster in danger of falling, the floor above should be lifted and the plaster work secured from above. Where the decoration has itself been damaged then sections will have to be cut out and replaced. Straight run mouldings can be repaired in situ using a template cut to the profile of the old work. More intricate work may have to be cast using moulds taken from the remaining good work.

(B) Timber Panelling and Sheeting: Here damp, fungus and boring insects are the enemies. The supporting battens and studding are the most susceptible and all replacement timbers must be factory treated against decay. Where varnishes and stains have been used care must be taken to match the type of timber and the finish on the replacement work. This is work which in most instances should be entrusted to specialists.

(C) Embossed Papers: Work related to these materials should always be placed in specialist hands.

Before beginning the repair of any decorative work it is a wise precaution to make a comprehensive photographic record.

2.6.3 *Notes on the Preparation of Contract Specifications*

(A) Plaster Work: Describe the extent and location of stripping and replastering; patching or other in situ repairs; the recording of existing work (i.e. preparation for replacement castings or photographic or drawn records to be made if alternative replacements are proposed). Specify the precautions to be taken to protect existing decorative work for retention. Specify the repair work and modification (i.e. any ventilation or treatment against beetle or fungal attack) for the supporting structures. Specify any new methods for supporting the old plaster work. Specify work to prepare surfaces for plastering and the number and type of coatings to be used in the repair. Describe the techniques to be used for the repair of decorative work.

(B) Timber: Properly and adequately record any areas and details which must be replaced to ensure the replacements are a proper match of the old. Identify the areas for replacement. Specify temporary and long-term protective treatments for areas to remain. Specify species and samples of timber for replacements, and methods for fixing.

(C) Decorative Papers: Identify areas for protection and specify the removal, treatment and reinstatement of sections which can be salvaged. Replacement material is almost certainly going to be a matter for a specialist. Redecoration should never be hurried, especially onto new plaster or areas which have been previously saturated. These should all be left until thoroughly dried out.

2.6.4 *Technical References*

British Standards
B.S. 890 – Building Limes
B.S. 1191 – Gypsum Building Plaster

B.S. 1369 – Expanded Metal Lath
B.S. 3452 ⎫
B.S. 3453 ⎬ – Preservatives for Timbers
B.S. 4072 ⎪
B.S. 5056 ⎭
B.S. 3826 – Damp Repellents for Masonry
B.S. 5250 – Control of Condensation
B.S. 5492 – Internal Plaster

Building Research Establishment
Digest 213 – Choosing Specifications for Plastering

Department of the Environment Advisory Leaflets
 2 – Gypsum Plaster
 6 – Limes for Building
 9 – Plaster Mixes
15 – Sands for Plasters
21 – Plastering Building Boards
47 – Dampness in Buildings
61 – Condensation

Historic Buildings and Monuments Commission Technical Notes
No. 4 – Gypsum Plasters

'Mortars Plasters and Renders in Conservation' – J. Ashurst.

2.7 Windows and Doors

2.7.1 *Historical Note*
Of all building elements, windows, doors, their fittings and embellishments can often tell more of the history of a building than any other.

(A) Windows: Glazed windows were certainly in use in Roman times but it was not until the 17th century that any but the very wealthy could afford them. The earlier forms were either fixed lights or side hung casements but by 1700 the vertically sliding box sash had become the most popular form.

Glazing patterns and associated joinery details developed and changed but this basic form remained in vogue into the beginning of the 20th century, when factory made metal and wooden casements became widely available at relatively low costs.

Side hung casements were used to a limited degree throughout the same period. Cottages built by the larger landowners were very often fitted with this type of window.

Leaded windows have also been in use since very early times. In the late 18th century some of the simpler forms of leaded window were copied in cast-iron, but again these forms are rare in comparison to the vertically-sliding timber sash.

Early sliding sashes were fitted from the outside so that the full depth of the box frame is exposed. This method of fitting continued throughout the popularity of this window type but it became gradually more usual to fit the box behind the masonry or brick reveal. Early windows, and in later years small windows, were not hung, i.e. had no weights or cords or sometimes had only one sash of the pair hung. Early glazing patterns are for small panes of glass; this was simply dictated by manufacturing limitations. Blown glass was replaced in the 18th century by glass spun on a cylinder. Both these types have very attractive irregularities that set up characteristic reflection patterns. In the 19th century new techniques developed sheet and plate glass. These methods of manufacture provide much larger and more regular pieces and therefore much more freedom in glazing patterns. By the end of

231

the 19th century a sash could be glazed with one single sheet of glass. This put more stress onto fewer joints, and to counteract this weakness, horns were formed on the vertical members. The second half of the 19th century also saw the end of window tax (which had operated from 1696–1851) and the production of cheap stained glass. Both factors added to the growing variety and size of domestic windows.

By the time the sliding sash had developed, home grown timber was in very short supply and most of these units were made from imported soft woods from Northern Europe; later examples make use of timber from the forests of the Empire, mainly North America. The expertise needed in selecting and working these timbers developed through the 18th century to produce incredibly slender and beautifully moulded components, not only for the windows themselves but for beautifully panelled and shuttered encasements which became important parts of the designs for room interiors as well as the appearance of the building from the outside. Because of the timbers used and the methods of construction, these sliding windows were always painted in this country. There are rare examples of oak being used unpainted.

Most box sash windows are single rectangular units with the vertical dimension greater than the horizontal. However, fashion brought variations to more prestigious buildings. Some examples are:

(i) the grouping of three units together and known as Venetian windows, the centre unit having a semi-circular head; these began to appear about 1730;

(ii) one semi-circular opening containing three units, known as the Diocletian windows; pointed or ogee-headed openings with interlacing glazing bars known as Gothick; both made their appearance in about 1765;

(iii) a rectangular opening containing three rectangular units became fashionable from 1790 onwards;

(iv) a pair of similar sized sashes within a single rectangular opening was the last significant development of about 1860;

(v) horizontally sliding sashes do exist but are very rare indeed, they have the same appearance as the true paired vertically opening unit, but are usually much older.

The changing forms of panelling and mouldings that form encasements are also good guides to dating alterations if not the original construction of the building. If during repairs these features are not recognised and retained much of the historic interest of the building will be lost to future generations.

(B) Doors: The development of doors closely follows that of windows. The joinery details, mouldings, etc., are all related. In most cases the timbers used were the same, although imported hardwoods are used for internal panelled doors in some of the more important buildings. Such doors were not painted. Most old doors belong to one of two basic types – the boarded or sheeted door and the panelled door.

Early boarded doors were made from very wide planks simply jointed and held together by broad horizontal rails on the inner face. As time went on the boards became narrower and the jointing more involved. To the ledges were added diagonal braces and latterly a complete jointed frame. Most early hinges are simple forged straps fixed with wrought nails; in the 19th century the 'T' hinge fixed with screws takes its place. Early fastenings are timber draw bars or lifting latches which in the 19th century are replaced by iron thumb latches and later still by mass produced steel latches of a similar pattern.

Panelled doors in the 17th and early 18th century come in a wide variety of panel formations; architraves are broad and often heavily moulded. By the end of the 18th century the 6-panelled door was the most popular form with a careful gradation of size, proportion and detail. Separately applied bolection mouldings had been replaced in time by carefully worked mouldings on the arrises of the frame rails and muntins while scholarly copies of classical details are assembled to form the encasements, often linked with a decorative fanlight and side lights. Porches are rare until well into the 19th century when these features were often added to older buildings not always with the sympathy that such an important feature deserves. As the 19th century proceeded 4-panelled doors became a more popular pattern, bolection mouldings came again into use and the pattern of architraves and encasements were courser and no longer followed recorded antique forms.

Fittings developed from face fitted 'H' or 'L' shaped hinges to the forged, and later to cast leaf hinges concealed in the interface between door and frame. Early locks are all rim fittings mostly operated by iron or brass drop ring handles; lock facings and finger plates are sometimes highly decorative. For external doors, locks with a double throw action were often used, backed up by simple but sturdy draw bars.

By 1800, knob furniture was more common, often made of porcelain and highly decorative. Later mortice locks replaced the rim patterns and lever or simple undecorated knob furniture was used. Generally external doors did not have handles as part of the lock or latch, but were drawn to by means of a heavy knob centrally placed or a ring that may also serve as a knocker.

Like windows, external doors were painted until in the late 19th century imported hardwoods became cheap enough for some people to use them for entrance doors as well as internal doors to the principal rooms.

2.7.2 Faults and Repair

The timber used for joinery in the 18th and 19th century was generally carefully selected and the joints were tightly formed, the tenon being drawn by a peg into the mortice against the shoulders of wedges. As an added precaution the joint was fitted before assembly with hot animal glue or white lead thus making it waterproof. Consequently, provided the unit has not been forced or otherwise abused while repainting, and glazing putty, etc., has been regularly attended to, faults should be few.

However, the sad fact is that many of these carefully constructed units have not been cared for as they deserve. Sheer neglect coupled with misuse are the major destroyers of historic joinery. Windows commonly suffer from broken cords, siezed pulleys, and distorted catches. During reglazing instead of cleaning out the reveals, successive levels of perished putty have often been built up one upon another; condensation has entered the timber through the perished putty so that finally there is nothing to hold the glass in place. These units become drafty and are no longer weatherproof; they are then condemned wholesale without serious regard for possible repair.

Doors similarly suffer from the neglect of painting, and the severe wear of hinges and thresholds. Often these faults are not analysed and the decision is made to replace the entire unit with a needless loss of historical material.

Structural movement, the failure of lintels or other local failures such as the rusting and consequent swelling of iron cramps in adjacent stonework are all serious threats to the joinery itself. Distortion of the opening leads

the masonry and joinery to part company, water enters the gap and decay follows. More movement may strain open (wrack) the joinery joints followed again by entry of rain or condensation and consequently the decay of the timber around the joint.

Insect attack is rare unless beetle has infected the timber before it was converted for joinery.

Regular checks for all windows and doors should be made in advance of each programme for redecoration and the necessary repairs completed before redecoration is implemented.

NOTE – with higher heating standards and increased heating bills, owners are becoming more aware of heat loss around windows and doors. Properly fitting units will go a long way towards reducing heat loss. The setting of ironmongery, stops beads, etc., will greatly improve performance, and further increased efficiency can be obtained by fitting draft proofing strips. Most of the better draftproofing strips are best fitted when the units are dismantled. This modification can be made without any change in the appearance of the units themselves.

Double glazing is another means of heat conservation. Many older buildings have relatively small glazed areas in comparison with the overall area of wall and the savings to be obtained may well not be an economic proposition. However, if a calculation is made and it is found that there is a useful saving to be had then the type of unit must be carefully chosen so that the historic character of the old windows is not lost. There is no complete standard double-glazed window on the market at this time which can be considered to retain historic detailing so that the choice will be in the range of units having a separate second frame applied inside the old.

2.7.3 Notes on the Preparation of Contract Specifications

- Identify units for repair and replacement.
- Describe the necessary repairs for each unit and the design – mouldings, panels, shape of glazing bars, etc., to be used for replacement.
- Describe the materials to be used – type of timber, type of glass, ironmongery, etc.
- Give instructions for dismantling, stripping off old paint and putty, storage and care of material for reuse.
- Name any preservative treatment of timber and the priming for all surfaces before assembly or glazing.

2.7.4   *Technical References*

British Standards

Windows
B.S. 644   – Timber Windows
B.S. 5642 – Masonry Sills and Copings
B.S.C.P. 153 – Durability and Maintenance
B.S. 6262 – Glazing in Buildings
B.S. 6375 – Resistance to Weather

Doors
B.S.C.P. 151 – Doors, Frames and Linings
B.S. 4951 ⎫
B.S. 1227 ⎭ – Ironmongery

General
B.S. 1186 – Joinery Quality of Timber
B.S. 6150 – Painting of Buildings

Building Research Establishment Digests
 72 – Home Grown Softwoods for Buildings
 73 – Preventing Decay in External Joinery
106 – Painting Woodwork
182 – Natural Finishes for External Timber
201 – Wood Preservatives – Application Methods

D.O.E. Advisory Leaflet
 29 – Care in use of Timber

Building Design 'Easibrief'
28 Aug. 1982 – Glazing
5 Nov. 1982 – A Guide to Softwoods

Advisory Organisations
British Wood Preserving Association – Premier House,
  150 Southampton Row, London WC1 B5AL
British Woodworking Federation – 82 New Cavendish
  Street, London W1M 8AD.
Timber Research & Development Association – Stocking
  Lane, Hughenden Valley, High Wycombe, Buckingham-
  shire HP14
Timber Trade Federation, Clareville House, Whitcomb
  Street, London WC2H 7DL.

2.8   Ferrous Metals (excluding 2.3)

2.8.1   *Historical Note*

Iron has been available for building construction from
very early times, but until the Industrial Revolution smelting from the ore was a tedious business carried out on a
small scale. All the resulting products, down to the smal-

lest of nails had to be hand-wrought. In consequence the
material was used sparingly.

However, as supplies of good quality timber ran short
improved methods of smelting developed and iron in the
form of straps, coach screws and the like, gradually
replaced the fine timber joinery of earlier constructions.

Unfortunately for us today it was sometimes used
instead of more stable metals like bronze to make cramps
and ties for masonry work, with consequent failures that
have proved very costly to correct.

Casting iron has also been a technique known for
many hundreds of years. In building, castings were not in
common use until the Industrial Revolution of the late
18th century. Methods had been developed mainly in the
production of military ordnance but by the 1770s a wide
variety of standard castings were available to builders
including, firegrates, chimney pots, railings, windows,
sash weights, locks, latches and hinges, and many others.

The structural use of iron was developed at the same
time both as wrought and cast work. Such was the

demand for structural ironwork that in the 1840s rolling mills were built to produce standard profiled sections, thus eliminating the time consuming cutting and rivetting that had previously been necessary to build up structural sections. The expansion of the railway system and the building of iron ships resulted in enormous expansion of the industry. Complete iron buildings were constructed – the great train sheds, and conservatories everywhere with of course, the most famous of all being The Crystal Palace (1850). The prime example in the Province is the Palm House in the Botanic Gardens, Belfast. Standard buildings were shipped all over the world and every town of any size could boast its public lavatory, bandstand and its decorative street lamps.

Techniques of blending in other minerals to give increased strength and durability were perfected and in 1866 the first standard rolled steel joists were available.

In recent years welding has taken the place of rivetting.

2.8.2 *Faults and Repair*

Corrosion:
Old wrought iron is very pure and when exposed to the weather forms a skin of black oxide which protects it against further decay.

However, when it is kept continously damp, for example in the core of a wall where it has been built in as a cramp or lintel, then it forms red oxide which eats deeply into the body of the iron causing lamination and expansion. The forces released during this expansion are enormous and will burst stones and erupt the surrounding masonry. Once this corrosion has begun it may be aggrevated by electrolysis set up as an interaction with run lead which was originally poured to exclude water. As cracks in the masonry open more and more water can enter so that the process gradually accelerates.

Modern steel corrodes in the same way but very much faster and must always be given a protective coating.

Mild corrosion can be arrested; all oxide and scaling must first be cleaned off. Shotblasting in a workshop is the most effective way otherwise a portable blasting unit must be used. Alternatively the surface must be pecked and wire-brushed by hand. The surface can then be pickled using phosphoric acid, followed by paint priming, galvanizing or other durable protective coating.

If corrosion is really bad then replacement in whole or in part is the only course of repair. When repairing old iron work try to use old iron scrap, possibly salvaged from one of the mass of old farm gates that sadly litter the hedgerows.

Fracture:
Wrought iron fractures only if it is continually subjected to changing stresses, but cast-iron fractures very easily. Provided the object is non-structural it may well be possible to glue it back together using epoxy resins.

If the component is structural it may be possible to carry the load in some other way and then effect a repair using epoxy resins. If this is impossible then a new casting is the only remedy. Quite a variety of 18th and 19th century casting designs are still available as standard items. Fractured steel can usually be repaired by welding.

All external ferrous metal surfaces should be inspected regularly every three years. If local defects are attended to at this frequency serious decay is unlikely. If not attended to, a very expensive scheme of repair is likely to follow.

2.8.3 *Notes on the Preparation of Contract Specifications*

Identify the items for replacement, repair and cleaning. Specify what work is to be executed 'in situ' and what is 'shop work' requiring dismantling and transportation.

Specify protection and storage.

Describe the methods to be used in replacement, repair and cleaning and any special protective treatments which will not be covered in the section concerned with painting. If any of the work is to be carried out by specialists make this clear.

Name the standards of workmanship and finish that is required and state if any items are to be approved in the workshop before they are brought to site.

2.8.4 *Technical References*

British Standards
B.S. 217 – Red Lead
B.S. 460 – Cast-iron Rainwater Goods
B.S. 729 – Hot-dip Galvanizing
B.S. 4921 – Sheradizing
B.S. 6180 – Metal Balustrades and Railings
B.S. 5493 – Protection of Iron and Steel against corrosion
B.S.C.P. 3012 – Cleaning Metal Surfaces

Building Research Establishment Digest
No. 70 – Painting: Iron and Steel

Advisory Organisations
Stainless Steel Fabricators Association of Great Britain –
14 Knoll Road, Dorking, Surrey
Steel Lintel Manufacturers Assocation – PO Box 10, Newport, Gwent, NPTOXN
Zinc Development Association and Galvanizers Association – 34 Berkeley Square, London W1X 6AJ.

2.9 Paint

2.9.1 *Historical Note*

All paints consist of three basic ingredients – pigment, binder and solvent.

Before the 17th century all but the simplest most basic paintwork had been reserved for decorative interior work. External painting generally made use of earth pigments such as lime, umber and ochres and durability was not a prime factor. These materials were all used in water solutions. A basic change took place when native timber supplies were exhausted and European red and white pine became the common materials for windows and doors. Paint now had to be used for protection and had to be durable. Oil took the place of water and since the paint was to last longer, more care had to be taken in the selection and preparation of the pigments. These early oil paints were 'flat' (matt), but were sometimes given a gloss finish by applying varnish over the paint. Painters ground their own pigments and mixed their own paint, with the result, because of the toxicity of so many of the materials used, a painter's life was notoriously short.

The use of water based paints for walls remained universal until the advent of oil based stucco and Roman Cement renders. Even these were at first either self coloured or painted with water based paints but increasing pollution of the atmosphere caused practice to change so that from early in the 19th century buildings have been painted mainly with oil based paints.

Since the Second World War a fundamental change has taken place in the formulae and manufacture of paints. The one common characteristic is an increased impermeability which can be a severe problem when choosing suitable materials to decorate buildings with solid walls which have no damp-proof courses.

2.9.2 *Faults and Repair*

A great deal of original paintwork survives very often covered by a failing application in more modern times.
Paint failures fall into two basic groups:

(i) failures apparent soon after application which are usually due to one of the following reasons:

(a) in the case of redecorating old surfaces poor preparation can leave old flaking paint, dirt, grease, damp or mould growth. Failure can also be due to the new paint having a totally different physical characteristic to the paint onto which it is applied; a common example of this follows the application of dense resin vinyl or latex based paint onto a weak water soluble paint surface;

(b) in the case of decorating new work the most common faults are caused by insufficient time being left for the underlying surface to dry out; the fluid may be water or the solvent in a wood preservative treatment. This condition is aggravated when heat is introduced after decoration, especially if the fuel used by the heater produces moisture during combustion (e.g. paraffin or gas).

(c) faulty priming, sealing of knots, etc.

(ii) failures after the paint has had time to mature. All paints have a limited life span. This period of time varies widely depending on paint type, care in preparation and application and climatic conditions.

Most old paints are lime or lead based and as they age, the surface dusts. On external surfaces this gives them a fresh appearance because the dust is washed off by the weather continually revealing a new surface. This process will continue until damp can penetrate the skin when cracking and flaking will begin.

Harsh climatic conditions will accelerate this process as well as the more obvious effects of wind and rain; sunlight will bleach colours and sometimes cause blistering and cracking. Blistering in sunlight is usually due to substances melting in the heat behind the paint surface, for example, resin in timber knots or old varnish disguised by later paint. Sunlight will also be destructive where overpainting has left a series of absorbant and reflective colours overlaying each other causing local heat to build up due to relatively different expansions within the paint film itself. It is very common to find an 18th century

236

reflective lead based paint, over painted with a dark 19th century layer and finally a reflective modern application; such a combination does not stand much change in direct sunlight conditions.

When assessing paint failure always check that the backing of timber, metal or plaster is sound. Failure on the surface is often a symptom of failure below and until the root cause is corrected, every future coat of paint will have a very limited chance of survival.

Where a paint film has failed, there is no alternative to stripping back to a firm surface. This process offers a unique chance to record the history of decoration in an old building. Whatever is found should influence the choice for redecoration.

The stripping process itself must be carefully executed. Modern warm air strippers are good, they keep dust to a minimum and do not damage the underlying features, mouldings, etc. Chemical strippers can be used for oil based paints but beware of the caustic varieties. Caustic salts can build up in the surface of timber and plaster resulting in later damage to the newly applied paint. Remember that lead dust is highly toxic so that the rubbing-down of the old lead paint must be done using wet abrasive papers or wet sugar soap – remember too when decorating that lead based paints are only toxic if they get into the mouth.

There are no toxic fumes from new paint.

If the failure in the paint is due to defects in the material on to which it is applied, i.e. damp, rot efflorescence, weeping knots, rusting, etc., then these must all be attended to first.

There are a wide variety of modern preparatory dressings – epoxy binders, anti-suction primers, alkali resistant primers, fungacidal washes, rust arresting preparations, etc.

When considering the use of any of these preparations it is a wise precaution to consult the technical advisory section of the manufacturer of the paint which it is intended to use in subsequent applications. One rule always applies – never seal damp into a wall – or simply paint over defects. If you do, your problems will gradually get worse. When you have to decorate onto walls which do reach relatively high saturation levels use only porous paints. For external use paints with this quality are lime based, cement based or silicate based. Be wary of builders who give low prices for decoration. You are likely to be given poor preparation and/or low quality paint. Either or both will result in a much shorter life than would otherwise be the case.

For regular preventive maintenance external paintwork should be inspected every three years and certainly no less than every five, and the necessary redecoration put in hand.

Internal paintwork will have a life varying with the style of use or abuse to which it is subjected. It is not performing a protective function and therefore is not critical except in terms of appearance.

When chosing decorative schemes be selective not only over the clinical composition of the paint but also texture and finish. Textured paints are all recent innovations and alter the appearance of older buildings. So called 'natural finishes' are also innovations. They are generally only suitable for hardwoods, the use of which for external joinery is practically unknown during the 18th century and most of the 19th century; they also have a relatively short life and therefore are more costly to maintain than opaque paint.

2.9.3 *Notes on the Preparation of Contract Specifications*

Describe which surfaces are to be treated:

(a) surfaces for redecoration;
(b) new surfaces receiving their first decoration.

Describe protection for adjacent surfaces, and methods of preparation to be used. No application of paint should be made until the owner or his consultant has inspected the prepared surfaces.

If older decorative schemes are to be investigated by scrapes, etc., this should be stated.

If sample areas are to be provided before a final choice is made for the final decoration, describe what is to be done and where.

Describe any required surface treatments or repairs in advance of painting.

Describe the types, manufacturers and colours of the paints to be used, the number of coats and the preparation between coats. Finally describe the protective measures to be taken.

NOTE – if there is any technical advice necessary from paint manufacturers or advisory bodies it should be obtained by the owner or the professional consultant, not left to the painter. Any such information received must be made freely available to the painters themselves while they are working. It will do no good lying in an office miles from the job in hand.

2.9.4 Technical References

British Standards
B.S. 217 – Red Lead
B.S. 729 – Galvanizing
B.S. 890 – Lime
B.S. 1615 – Anodizing
B.S. 3919 – Tallow
B.S. 3987 – Anodizing
B.S. 5493 – Protective Coatings against Corrosion
B.S. 6150 – Painting of Buildings
B.S.C.P. 3012 – Cleaning Metal Surfaces.

Building Research Establishment Digests
Digest 70   – 'Painting Iron and Steel'
Digest 106 – 'Painting Woodwork'
Digest 113 – Cleaning the External Surfaces of Buildings'
Digest 149 – 'The Co-ordination of Building Colours'
Digest 182 – 'Natural Finishes for Exterior Timber'
Digest 197 – 'Painting Walls: Pt. 1 Choice of Paint'
Digest 198 – 'Painting Walls: Pt. 2 Failures and Remedies.

D.O.E. Advisory Leaflets
 1 – Painting New Plaster and Cement
11 – Painting Metalwork
25 – Painting Woodwork
37 – Emulsion Paints
57 – Newer Types of Paint and their Uses

Historic Buildings and Monuments Commission Technical Notes
1
2 } – Control of Organic Growths
7 – Limewash

Building Design 'Easibrief'
25 June 1982 – Paint

Other Publications
Lead Paint Regulations 1927 (H.M.S.O.) [officially superceded but very practical as a guide]
Painting and Decorating – by H. E. Hurst and G. H. Goodier (9th Edition 1980)
Your House – the Outside View – by John Prizeman 1975
Mortars, Plasters and Renders in Conservation – by John Ashurst – 1983.

Advisory Organisations
Paint Research Association – 6 Waldegrave Road, Teddington TW11 8LD.

NOTE – all the major manufacturers maintain a Technical Advisory Service. If in doubt of an address to contact refer to either the Paint Research Association or one of The Building Centre listed in section 1.2.

2.10 Fire Protection and Thermal Insulation

Recent developments in the standards which people will accept both voluntarily and through legislation have created additional problems in the proper repair and maintenance of older buildings. It is hoped that these brief notes will help to prevent the needless loss of historic detail in attaining increased standards and be a guide to good practice.

2.10.1 Fire Protection
The present requirements are administered through the

Building Regulations (N.I.) Pt. E and Pt. EE but some classes of buildings open to the general public and assemblies of people must obtain a certificate from the Fire Authority. Precautions fall into two main categories:

(A) Compartmentation

Fire protected compartments may be required horizontally, affecting floors and ceilings or vertically affecting doorways, stairs, screens and partition walls.

Floors and ceilings – the simplest way to achieve increased fire protection is to apply a fire-proof lining to the underside but this may destroy decorative plasterwork and other historically important detail.

In the case of exposed joists there must be enough surplus material (i.e. structural oversizing) to allow a structural strength giving deflection no greater than 1/30th of the span after exposure to fire during the specified period for fire resistance. The addition of protective fillings between the joists or the addition of a protective lining to the floor above will usually allow decorative ceilings to remain undisturbed.

Doors – the simplest means to achieve increased fire protection for a panelled door is to face the door with a sheet material having the approved fire rating and, if necessary, to increase the rebate on the frame.

In most instances the increased rebate on the frame, if carefully detailed, can be achieved without serious disruption of the architectural detailing. An alternative can be to fit an intumescent strip.

The door itself will have a framework (i.e. jambs, rails and muntins) which will normally meet all but the most severe fire protection requirements; however, the panels may not. If there is a door of the same construction which can be sacrificed it may be tested to the British Standard. Otherwise the options are either to dismantle the door and refit panels using a material having the required fire resistance (where architectural detail is important the old panels can be split to make veneers) but in many cases intumescent paint and strips will suffice.

(B) Escape: as well as the required standards for doors discussed above, the enclosing wall, floor and ceiling surfaces must meet requirements in respect of spread of flame. These standards can usually be attained without detriment to design detail. Additional fire protecting screens may be required; it is usually possible with care to design these in such a way that architectural detail, for example, plaster cornice mouldings, are not damaged.

Alternatively, imitative detailing can be introduced to panel out the ceiling in a way that includes the new screen into the overall modified design.

As well as protection of existing stairways, it may be necessary to provide a new means of escape. Very careful consideration must be given to the location and design of any new structure. So that proper thought is given to the matter, the fire protection requirements must be researched at an early stage; last minute hurried decisions can be catastrophic to the long-term appearance of a building.

Some new uses will require the installation of heat or smoke detectors. All too often the details of this type of installation are left to the operatives doing the installation without any proper forethought. This lack of consideration can lead to serious architectural damage in high quality historic interiors. The type of system, location of the detectors and routing of the wiring should all be planned in detail to cause as little visual disruption as possible.

2.10.2 *Technical References*

Building Regulations (N.I.) Part E and Part EE
B.S.C.P. 3 – Precautions against Fire
B.S.C.P. 153 – Fire Hazards associated with Glazing
B.S. 6180 – Metal Railings and Balustrades
B.S. 476 Pt. 7 – Fire Tests on Building Materials and Structures
B.S. 5395 – Stairways
B.S.C.P. 326 – Protection of Structures against Lightning.

Building Research Establishment
'Results of Surface Spread of Flame Tests on Building Products' – H.M.S.O. 1976
Digest 208 and 220
'Fire Prognostication Tests on Building Products' – H.M.S.O. 1976
'The Architect' Oct. 1977

National Building Agency 'Easiguide'
Fire Protection in Housing
Stairs and Means of Escape in Housing.

2.10.3 *Thermal Insulation*

Most older buildings of traditional construction required a

certain degree of ventilation to prevent decay. However, the levels of heat loss from such buildings can be dramatically reduced while maintaining a safe minimum level of air movement if due consideration is given to the methods by which it is to be achieved.

(A) Flues
All older buildings have flues, many of them are no longer used and undoubtedly they contribute to general heat loss. However, the ventilation they provide is essential to buildings having solid masonry construction and no effective damp-proofing. The flow of air in disused flues can safely be reduced to a practical minimum by providing a small register or grill to do the job of the fireplace, but to block it entirely can lead to very serious problems of accumulated moisture and subsequent decay.

(B) Roofs
Thatch, of course, provides first class thermal insulation but other types of traditional roof construction are very poor in this respect and enormous quantities of heat escape in this direction. When designing roof insulation do not prevent air movement around the timbers of the roof space. If ventilation is prevented, and heat with moisture builds up, serious problems of decay will follow.

(C) Walls
Most older buildings in the Province have rubble stone or mud walls 500 mm or more in thickness. These constructions provide relatively high levels of thermal insulation. The ratio of solid wall to window and door openings is likely to be high and this factor too will contribute to low heat losses. In an old brick building the walls may however be considerably thinner, possibly only 225 mm thick, in which case additional insulation will certainly pay dividends even if window and door openings are few and small. In choosing the best insulation method the relative importance of architectural design both inside and out will often make the choice.

(D) Windows and External Doors
The advertising media have focused on the heat loss from these elements. In most old buildings openings are relatively small compared to more recent buildings which have vast areas of glass.

Usually the primary cause of heat loss is ill-fitting joinery. The proper overhaul of windows and doors, adjusting the moving elements so that they once again fit snugly into their frames, at the same time resetting beads and ironmongery, will make a great improvement in the thermal performance of these elements. Further improvement can be achieved by making window shutters work again – these fittings are a feature of most of Ulster's 18th and 19th century buildings but often they have not worked for many years. If doors are taken off their hinges and windows dismantled, well designed modern 'weather-strips' can be effectively fitted before reassembly.

Only after all these measures have been taken will there be any noticeable benefit from the fitting of double glazing. If it is to be installed the architectural implications must be very carefully considered before a choice is made.

(E) Floors
Traditional floor construction contains practically no insulation qualities. Therefore if it becomes necessary to replace a ground floor either completely or in part, it will be well worthwhile to incorporate insulation into the new construction.

2.10.4 *Technical References*

Building Regulations (N.I.) Pt. F
B.S. 874 – Methods of Determining Thermal Insulation properties with definitions of Thermal Insulation terms
B.S. 5422 – Specification for the use of Thermal Insulation Materials

D.O.E. Advisory Leaflet
No. 34 – Thermal Insulation

Building Research Establishment Digests
No. 108 – Standardised U-Values
No. 110 – Condensation
No. 140 – Double Glazing and Double Windows
No. 145 – Heat Losses Through Ground Floors
No. 180 – Condensation in Roofs
No. 190 – Heat Losses from Dwellings
No. 210 – Principles of Natural Ventilation
No. 233 – Fire Hazard from Insulation Materials

National Building Agency 'Easiguide'
Thermal Insulation

C.I.B.S. Guide A3 – Thermal Properties of Building Structures

2.11 Cleaning Masonry Buildings (Brick, Stone and External Renders)

2.11.1 Introduction

In most instances the possibilities of cleaning a building are first considered for aesthetic reasons. If after a proper appraisal of the situation there is any doubt as to the usefulness of cleaning then the decision should be to leave the building alone.

Before embarking on a contract for cleaning there are a number of questions to be answered:

(i) does the surface or the pointing need repair?

Most cleaning methods involve water. If excessive amounts are allowed to enter through fractures or decayed joints it may later be the cause of outbreaks of fungal decay in embedded timbers and/or the corrosion and expansion of iron cramps and lintels. These faults must be attended to before any cleaning is attempted;

(ii) what is the nature of the material which is to be removed?

It may be organic in the form of algae, lichens or mosses or it may be chemical discolouration and the build up of chemical deposits.

Organic growth is the most common cause of surface discolouration met with in Northern Ireland. It can be removed by the application of biocides to kill the growth which is then brushed off dry, followed by the application of a chemical dressing to inhibit recolonization.

Organic growths are not normally damaging to the masonry itself but they do excrete acids which attack metal work (flashings and lower metal clad roofs) and the matrix of asbestos cement products.

Weather staining and surface salt deposits may be the symptom of faults elsewhere allowing long term saturation of the masonry. These must be found and corrected. Deposits of this nature are not usually harmful except in appearance, however, deposits from atmospheric pollution can be a very real and great danger. Thankfully they are rare in Northern Ireland, but where they do exist they must be removed.

2.11.2 Cleaning Methods

The methods available for cleaning chemical deposits are:

(A) Water Washing – first the deposits are soaked and softened, then loosened by brushing. Do not use steel wire brushes because the detached wires will be left behind and corrode causing stains. Finally the surface is washed down.

The amount of water used must be kept to a practical minimum. Local areas of dirt may be persistent, in which case a pressure water lance or a different cleaning method may be used to complete the work. Do not simply continue to saturate the fabric until the dirt moves.

(B) Abrasive – these methods are noisy and create dust or slurry, and may be considered too great a nuisance. Care is required on the part of the operatives not to over clean destroying the surface and detailing. Properly handled, these methods are fast and effective. Wet abrasive techniques clean with the least damage to the surface. They use less water than pure washing with water and so reduce the dangers of fungal and other later decay, but they are more difficult to operate than dry methods and so are not generally popular with contractors.

(C) Chemical – alkaline or caustic strippers are only designed to be used on limestones or ceramics. Their disadvantage is the danger of depositing salts in solution which later discolour the surface. The advantage is that they do not attack polished and glazed surfaces. Of the acid cleaners, hydrofluoric acid either in straight dilution or in combination with other chemicals (as in Neolith 625 ss – Agrément certified) is the only material not to deposit salts in solution. It does however, attack polishes and glazes and these must be masked.

If there is any doubt as to the suitability of a particular chemical for cleaning then an analysis of the masonry should be obtained be it stone, brick or render.

(D) Mechanical – this method includes the use of power tools, scrapers, etc. It is generally labour intensive and is most suitable for plain flat surfaces rather than detail.

Steam cleaning has been used but it has no shown advantages over other methods unless it is necessary to remove a film of paint or similar material.

2.11.3 *Post-Cleaning Treatment*

After cleaning is complete the drains and gulleys must all be checked and left clean and in working order.

Now that the building is clean the application of a water repellent may be considered. The decision must be carefully made since the wrong use of these materials can accelerate decay. Treatment of this type will be most beneficial in coastal locations when it can prevent saturation with salt laden spray. Vulnerable copings and sills can also be protected. Care must always be taken not to entirely encapsulate the wall, one masonry surface must be allowed to breathe freely otherwise salt deposits are likely to build up behind the protected surface resulting in the complete face becoming detached. Remember that the life of these products is limited and certainly cannot be expected to give more than ten years service before re-application.

2.11.4 *Technical References*

B.S. 3826 – Silicone based water repellents
Class A – for Sandstone, Fireclay, Cement based material
Class B – for Limestone, Calcium Silicate brick, cast stone
Class C – as B but excluding calcium silicate brick
B.S. 6270 Pt. 1 – Stone and Brickwork – Cleaning and Repair.

Building Research Establishment Digests
113 – Cleaning external surfaces of buildings
125 – Colourless Treatment for masonry
139 – Control of Lichens, Moulds and similar growths.

Historic Buildings & Monuments Commission Technical Note 1 – 'Control of Organic Growth'.

S.P.A.B. Technical Pamphlet
4 – 'Cleaning Stone and Brick'
5 – 'Pointing'.

Building Design 'Easibrief'
15 Oct. 82 – Cleaning Masonry Surfaces.

'Period Home'
Vol. 2, No. 4, p. 53
Vol. 5, No. 4, p. 60.

Stone Cleaners Section: The Stone Federation, 82 New Cavendish Street, London W1.

An analysis of stone, brick and plasterwork can be obtained from:
The Queen's University, Joint Conservation Laboratory, 13 University Square, Belfast 7.

Index